Intelligent Optimization Modelling in Energy Forecasting

Intelligent Optimization Modelling in Energy Forecasting

Special Issue Editor

Wei-Chiang Hong

MDPI • Basel • Beijing • Wuhan • Barcelona • Belgrade • Manchester • Tokyo • Cluj • Tianjin

Special Issue Editor
Wei-Chiang Hong
School of Computer Science and Technology
Jiangsu Normal University
Xuzhou
China

Editorial Office
MDPI
St. Alban-Anlage 66
4052 Basel, Switzerland

This is a reprint of articles from the Special Issue published online in the open access journal *Energies* (ISSN 1996-1073) (available at: https://www.mdpi.com/si/energies/IOM_Energy_Forecasting).

For citation purposes, cite each article independently as indicated on the article page online and as indicated below:

LastName, A.A.; LastName, B.B.; LastName, C.C. Article Title. *Journal Name* **Year**, *Article Number*, Page Range.

ISBN 978-3-03928-364-4 (Pbk)
ISBN 978-3-03928-365-1 (PDF)

© 2020 by the authors. Articles in this book are Open Access and distributed under the Creative Commons Attribution (CC BY) license, which allows users to download, copy and build upon published articles, as long as the author and publisher are properly credited, which ensures maximum dissemination and a wider impact of our publications.

The book as a whole is distributed by MDPI under the terms and conditions of the Creative Commons license CC BY-NC-ND.

Contents

About the Special Issue Editor . . . . **vii**

Wei-Chiang Hong and Guo-Feng Fan
Hybrid Empirical Mode Decomposition with Support Vector Regression Model for Short Term Load Forecasting
Reprinted from: *Energies* 2019, *12*, 1093, doi:10.3390/en12061093 . . . . **1**

Guo-Feng Fan, Yan-Hui Guo, Jia-Mei Zheng and Wei-Chiang Hong
Application of the Weighted K-Nearest Neighbor Algorithm for Short-Term Load Forecasting
Reprinted from: *Energies* 2019, *12*, 916, doi:10.3390/en12050916 . . . . **17**

Jiang Wu, Yu Chen, Tengfei Zhou and Taiyong Li
An Adaptive Hybrid Learning Paradigm Integrating CEEMD, ARIMA and SBL for Crude Oil Price Forecasting
Reprinted from: *Energies* 2019, *12*, 1239, doi:10.3390/en12071239 . . . . **37**

Yuansheng Huang, Lei Yang, Shijian Liu and Guangli Wang
Multi-Step Wind Speed Forecasting Based On Ensemble Empirical Mode Decomposition, Long Short Term Memory Network and Error Correction Strategy
Reprinted from: *Energies* 2019, *12*, 1822, doi:10.3390/en12101822 . . . . **61**

Hongwei Wang, Yuansheng Huang, Chong Gao and Yuqing Jiang
Cost Forecasting Model of Transformer Substation Projects Based on Data Inconsistency Rate and Modified Deep Convolutional Neural Network
Reprinted from: *Energies* 2019, *12*, 3043, doi:10.3390/en12163043 . . . . **83**

Danxiang Wei, Jianzhou Wang, Kailai Ni and Guangyu Tang
Research and Application of a Novel Hybrid Model Based on a Deep Neural Network Combined with Fuzzy Time Series for Energy Forecasting
Reprinted from: *Energies* 2019, *12*, 3588, doi:10.3390/en12183588 . . . . **105**

Taiyong Li, Yingrui Zhou, Xinsheng Li, Jiang Wu, Ting He
Forecasting Daily Crude Oil Prices Using Improved CEEMDAN and Ridge Regression-Based Predictors
Reprinted from: *Energies* 2019, *12*, 3603, doi:10.3390/en12193603 . . . . **143**

Yuansheng Huang, Lei Yang, Chong Gao, Yuqing Jiang and Yulin Dong
A Novel Prediction Approach for Short-Term Renewable Energy Consumption in China Based on Improved Gaussian Process Regression
Reprinted from: *Energies* 2019, *12*, 4181, doi:10.3390/en12214181 . . . . **169**

Oscar V. De la Torre-Torres, Evaristo Galeana-Figueroa and José Álvarez-García
A Test of Using Markov-Switching GARCH Models in Oil and Natural Gas Trading
Reprinted from: *Energies* 2020, *13*, 129, doi:10.3390/en13010129 . . . . **187**

Jesús Ferrero Bermejo, Juan Francisco Gómez Fernández, Rafael Pino, Adolfo Crespo Márquez and Antonio Jesús Guillén López
Review and Comparison of Intelligent Optimization Modelling Techniques for Energy Forecasting and Condition-Based Maintenance in PV Plants
Reprinted from: *Energies* 2019, *12*, 4163, doi:10.3390/en12214163 . . . . **211**

Cheng Yan, Jianfeng Zhu, Xiuli Shen, Jun Fan, Dong Mi and Zhengming Qian
Ensemble of Regression-Type and Interpolation-Type Metamodels
Reprinted from: *Energies* **2020**, *13*, 654, doi:10.3390/en13030654 . . . . **229**

About the Special Issue Editor

Wei-Chiang Hong, Jiangsu Distinguished Professor, School of Computer Science and Technology, Jiangsu Normal University, China. His research interests mainly include computational intelligence (neural networks, evolutionary computation) and application of forecasting technology (ARIMA, support-vector regression, and chaos theory). In May 2012, his paper had been evaluated as "Top Cited Article 2007–2011" by Applied Mathematical Modeling, Elsevier Publisher. In August 2014, he was awarded the "Outstanding Professor Award", by Far Eastern Y. Z. Hsu Science and Technology Memorial Foundation (Taiwan). In Nov. 2014, he was nominated as "Taiwan Inaugural Scopus Young Researcher Award—Computer Science", by Elsevier Publisher, in the Presidents' Forum of Southeast and South Asia and Taiwan Universities. In June 2015, he was named as one of the "Top 10 Best Reviewers" of Applied Energy in 2014. In August 2017, he was named as one "Best Reviewers" of Applied Energy in 2016. In September 2019, he was named the "Top Peer Reviewer (Computer Science; Engineering; Cross-Field)" by Publons.

Preface to "Intelligent Optimization Modelling in Energy Forecasting"

Accurate energy forecasting is important to facilitate the decision-making process to achieve higher efficiency and reliability in power system operation and security, economic energy usages, contingency scheduling, planning, and maintenance of energy supply systems, and so on. In recent decades, many energy forecasting models have been continuously proposed to improve the forecasting accuracy, including traditional statistical models (such as ARIMA, SARIMA, ARMAX, multi-variate regression, exponential smoothing models, Kalman filtering, Bayesian estimation models, and so on) and artificial intelligent models (such as artificial neural networks (ANNs), knowledge-based expert systems, evolutionary computation models, support-vector regression, and so on). Particularly, in the Big Data era, forecasting models are always based on a complex function combination, and energy data are always complicated, such as seasonality, cyclicity, fluctuation, dynamic nonlinearity, and so on. Comprehensively addressing this issue not only involves concentrating on hybridizing evolutionary algorithms with each other, or hybridizing chaotic mapping mechanism, quantum computing mechanism, recurrent mechanism, seasonal mechanism, and fuzzy inference theory with evolutionary algorithms to determine suitable parameters for an existed model, but also on hybridizing or combining two or above existed models. These novel hybrid advanced techniques can provide better energy forecasting performances.

Recently, due to the great development of optimization modeling methods (quadratic programming method, differential empirical mode method, evolutionary algorithms, meta-heuristic algorithms, and so on) and intelligent computing mechanisms (e.g., quantum computing mechanism, chaotic mapping mechanism, cloud mapping mechanism, seasonal mechanism, and so on), many novel hybrid or combined with the mentioned intelligent-optimization-based models are also proposed to achieve satisfactory forecasting accuracy. It is deserved to explore the tendency and development of intelligent-optimization-based modeling methodology and to enrich the practical performances, particularly for marine renewable energy forecasting.

This book contains articles from the Special Issue "Intelligent Optimization Modeling in Energy Forecasting", which published articles from researchers with an interest in the research areas described. As Zhang and Hong [1] indicate that the research direction of energy forecasting in the recent years is concentrated on proposing hybrid or combined models: (1) hybridizing or combining these artificial intelligent models with each other; (2) hybridizing or combining with traditional statistical tools; and (3) hybridizing or combining with those superior evolutionary algorithms. Therefore, the Special Issue contains contributions that address recent developments, i.e., hybridizing or combining any advanced techniques in energy forecasting. The hybrid forecasting models should have superior capabilities over the traditional forecasting approaches, and are able to overcome some embedded drawbacks, and, eventually, to significantly improve forecasting accuracy.

The 11 articles in this compendium all display a broad range of cutting-edge topics in the hybrid advanced technologies. The preface author believes that the applications of hybrid technologies will play a more important role in energy forecasting accuracy improvements, such as hybrid different evolutionary algorithms/models to overcome some critical shortcomings of a single evolutionary algorithm/model or directly improve the shortcoming by theoretical innovative arrangements.

Based on these collected articles, an interesting (future research tendency) issue is how to guide researchers to employ proper hybrid technology for different data sets. This is because, in any analysis models (including classification model, forecasting model, and so on), the most important problem is how to catch the data pattern, and applied the learned patterns or rules to achieve satisfactory performance, i.e., the key to success is how to suitably look for data patterns. However, each model has an excellent ability to catch a specific data pattern. For example, exponential smoothing and ARIMA models focus on strict increasing (or decreasing) time-series data, i.e., linear pattern, even they have seasonal modification mechanism to analyze seasonal (cyclic) change; due to artificial learning function to adjust the suitable training rules, the ANN model excels only if historical data pattern has been learned, it lacks the systematic explanation of how the accurate forecasting results are obtained; the support-vector regression (SVR) model can acquire superior performance only if the proper parameters determination search algorithms. Therefore, it is essential to construct an inference system to collect the characteristic rules to determine the data pattern category.

Secondly, it should assign appropriate approach to implement forecasting: for (1) ARIMA or exponential smoothing approaches, the only work is to adjust their differential or seasonal parameters; (2) ANN or SVR models, the forthcoming problem is how to determine the best parameters combination (e.g., numbers of hidden layer, units of each layer, learning rate; or hyper-parameters) to acquire superior forecasting performance. Particularly, for the focus of this discussion, in order to determine the most proper parameter combination, a series of evolutionary algorithms should be employed to test which data pattern the model is familiar with. Based on experimental findings, those evolutionary algorithms themselves also have merits and drawbacks, for example, GA and IA could handle excellently in a regular trend data pattern (real number) [2–5], SA excelled in fluctuation, or noise data pattern (real number) [6], and ACO is well done in integer number searching [7].

It is possible to build an intelligent support system to improve the efficiency of hybrid evolutionary algorithms/models or improving by theoretical innovative arrangements (chaotization and cloud theory) in all forecasting/prediction/classification applications. Firstly, filter the original data by the database with a well-defined characteristic rule set of data patterns, such as linear, logarithmic, inverse, quadratic, cubic, compound, power, growth, exponential, etc., to recognize the appropriate data pattern (fluctuation, regular, or noise). The recognition decision rules should include two principles: (1) the change rate of two continuous data; and (2) the decreasing or increasing trend of the change rate, i.e., the behavior of the approached curve. Secondly, adequate improvement tools (hybrid evolutionary algorithms, hybrid seasonal mechanism, chaotization of decision variables, cloud theory, and any combination of all tolls) should be selected to avoid getting trapped in local optimum, improvement tools could be employed in these optimization problems to obtain an improved, satisfactory solution.

This discussion of the work by the author of this preface highlights work in an emerging area of hybrid advanced techniques that have come to the forefront over the past decade. The collected articles in this text span a great deal more cutting edge areas that are truly interdisciplinary in nature.

Wei-Chiang Hong
Guest Editors

References

1. Zhang, Z.-C.; Hong, W.-C. Electric load forecasting by complete ensemble empirical model decomposition adaptive noise and support vector regression with quantum-based dragonfly algorithm. *Nonlinear Dyn.* **2019**, *98*, 1107–1136.
2. Fan, G.F.; Peng, L.L.; Hong, W.C. Short term load forecasting based on phase space reconstruction algorithm and bi-square kernel regression model. *Appl. Energy* **2018**, *224*, 13–33.
3. Hong, W.-C.; Fan, G.-F. Hybrid empirical mode decomposition with support vector regression model for short term load forecasting. *Energies* **2019**, *12*, 1093.
4. Hong, W.-C.; Li, M.-W.; Geng, J.; Zhang, Y. Novel chaotic bat algorithm for forecasting complex motion of floating platforms. *Appl. Math. Model.* **2019**, *72*, 425–443.
5. Li, M.-W.; Geng, J.; Hong, W.-C.; Zhang, L.-D. Periodogram estimation based on LSSVR-CCPSO compensation for forecasting ship motion. *Nonlinear Dyn.* **2019**, *97*, 2579–2594.
6. Geng, J.; Huang, M.L.; Li, M.W.; Hong, W.C. Hybridization of seasonal chaotic cloud simulated annealing algorithm in a SVR-based load forecasting model. *Neurocomputing* **2015**, *151*, 1362–1373.
7. Hong, W.C.; Dong, Y.; Zheng, F.; Lai, C.Y. Forecasting urban traffic flow by SVR with continuous ACO. *Appl. Math. Model.* **2011**, *35*, 1282–1291.

Article

Hybrid Empirical Mode Decomposition with Support Vector Regression Model for Short Term Load Forecasting

Wei-Chiang Hong [1],* and Guo-Feng Fan [2],*

1. School of Computer Science and Technology, Jiangsu Normal University, Xuzhou 221116, Jiangsu, China
2. School of Mathematics and Statistics, Ping Ding Shan University, Ping Ding Shan 467000, Henan, China
* Correspondence: hongwc@jsnu.edu.cn (W.-C.H.); guofengtongzhi@pdsu.edu.cn (G.-F.F.); Tel.: +86-516-8350-0307 (W.-C.H.)

Received: 3 March 2019; Accepted: 15 March 2019; Published: 21 March 2019

Abstract: For operational management of power plants, it is desirable to possess more precise short-term load forecasting results to guarantee the power supply and load dispatch. The empirical mode decomposition (EMD) method and the particle swarm optimization (PSO) algorithm have been successfully hybridized with the support vector regression (SVR) to produce satisfactory forecasting performance in previous studies. Decomposed intrinsic mode functions (IMFs), could be further defined as three items: item A contains the random term and the middle term; item B contains the middle term and the trend (residual) term, and item C contains the middle terms only, where the random term represents the high-frequency part of the electric load data, the middle term represents the multiple-frequency part, and the trend term represents the low-frequency part. These three items would be modeled separately by the SVR-PSO model, and the final forecasting results could be calculated as A+B-C (the defined item D). Consequently, this paper proposes a novel electric load forecasting model, namely H-EMD-SVR-PSO model, by hybridizing these three defined items to improve the forecasting accuracy. Based on electric load data from the Australian electricity market, the experimental results demonstrate that the proposed H-EMD-SVR-PSO model receives more satisfied forecasting performance than other compared models.

Keywords: empirical mode decomposition (EMD); particle swarm optimization (PSO) algorithm; intrinsic mode function (IMF); support vector regression (SVR); short term load forecasting

1. Introduction

Due to the characteristic of being not easy to reserve, electricity suppliers need precise short term load forecasting results to guarantee the power supply and load dispatch of power plants and security strategies. On the user side, accurate short term load forecasting guides the user to efficiently consume (saving electricity usage expenditures) the electricity between peak and valley periods. As mentioned in a recent paper [1], a 1% improvement in forecasting accuracy would have an annual operational benefit.

There are abundant studies proposing ways to improve electric load forecasting accuracy in the literature, which are classified into two categories: statistical models and intelligent models. Statistical models, including the ARIMA model [2–4], regression model [5–7], exponential smoothing model [8–10], Kalman filtering model [11,12], and Bayesian estimation models [13,14], etc., are well known. These statistical models are superior choices to deal with simple linear electric load patterns, such as their increasing tendency. For example, Scarpa and Bianco [12] applied a Kalman filter to validate the natural gas consumption forecasting results by a standard regression technique in the Italian residential sector. Their forecasting results for 2030 indicate that there is only a difference of about 0.05% with these two models, and even when the forecasting window is extended out to 2040, the obtained forecasts demonstrate slow divergence. However, as mentioned above, these models are theoretically based on the assumption of linear electric loads, so they can hardly deal well with more complicated relationships among electric loads. Recently, Bianco et al. [15] proposed a very different analysis on the inequality of the consumption of electricity in the period 2008–2016 within the European Union. They used the Theil index as a synthetic measure of the inequality of the electricity consumption to analyze in detail the sources of inequality according to the level of GDP per capita. They concluded that as GDP is considered as the weighting variable with an increasing trend, energy consumption is not equally distributed among the countries according to their GDP; on the contrary, energy consumption tends to be distributed like the population when population is weighted with the decreasing trend.

Since the 1980s, intelligent models are also well researched, including artificial neural networks (ANNs) [16–19], expert system models [20,21], and fuzzy system models [22–24]. These models could obtain some level of improvement in load forecasting accuracy. However, these models almost all have inherent drawbacks which limit the scope and breadth of these models' applications. Recently, these intelligent models have been hybridized or combined with other superior intelligent techniques to effectively overcome the inherent shortcomings, and these hybridized or combined methods have received higher attention [25–30]. As indicated in Fan et al. [31] these hybrid or combined models have three classic types: (1) hybridizing or combining these intelligent models with each other [25,26]; (2) hybridizing or combining them with statistical models [27,28]; and (3) hybridizing or combining them with evolutionary algorithms [29,30]. It is feasible to apply one of these three types to achieve more accurate forecasting results. However, these hybrid or combined models also have several inherent shortcomings within these hybridized or combined theoretical mechanisms, such as time consuming searching, and getting trapped into local optima, i.e., prematurity problems [32].

Due to its superior learning capacity for non-linear modelling, the support vector regression (SVR) model has been successfully used to deal with electric load forecasting [32–37]. In the meanwhile, to overcome the premature convergence problem during the non-linear optimization process while its three parameters are determined. Recently, a series of evolutionary algorithms hybridized with an SVR model have been proposed by Hong and his colleagues [32–39]. Among those employed algorithms, the particle swarm optimization (PSO) algorithm is not only easily implemented, but also it is more appropriate to solve real problems. In addition, to allow equal comparison conditions between this study and Fan et al. [35], this paper also uses the PSO algorithm to determine the three parameters of each SVR-based model. Recently, the empirical mode decomposition (EMD) method [40] was employed to effectively extract the basic components from non-linear (or non-stationary) time series into a series of single and apparent components [41]. The EMD technique has also been used in many application fields [40–43]; in addition, it is also applied to extract several detailed components from electric load data sets with several associate intrinsic mode functions (IMFs). Then, for each IMF, load can be forecast by an SVR model with only one suitable kernel function, hence successfully improving the forecasting performance, as demonstrated in Fan et al. [35]. However, these IMFs contain random IMF and residual IMF, respectively. Due to different compositions, these two kind of IMFs should be modeled by the SVR model separately to effectively improve the forecasting performance.

In this paper, based on the theoretical knowledge of the EMD, the PSO algorithm, and the SVR-based model, the authors propose a new combined model, namely the hybrid EMD-SVR-PSO model (H-EMD-SVR-PSO), to achieve a satisfactory improved forecasting performance. The principal idea is illustrated as follows: Firstly, we apply the EMD to decompose the electric load data into nine IMFs. Secondly, these IMFs are further divided into three categories, the random term, the middle term, and the trend (residual) term, respectively; the first term represents the high-frequency part of the electric load data, the middle term represents the multiple-frequency part, and the trend term represents the low-frequency part. Thirdly, we define the following items: "A" contains the random term plus the middle term, "B" contains the middle term plus the trend (residual) term, "C" only contains the middle term, and "D" contains all decomposed IMFs. Fourthly, items A, B, C, and D are modeled separately by the SVR-PSO model proposed in [35]. For item A, the middle term contains multiple frequencies, so it can effectively neutralize the volatility of the random item, thus, it would have a good effect by using the SVR-PSO model. For item B, the trend term could be fine-tuned under the non-linear action of the middle term, it is also very effective by using the SVR-PSO model. For item C, it is suitably modeled by the SVR-PSO model. Finally, for item D, the electric load forecasting results with complete decomposed effects are calculated by the forecasting values of A + B − C, i.e., D = A + B − C. The proposed H-EMD-SVR-PSO model has the following capabilities: (1) the capability of smoothing and reducing the noise (inherited from EMD); (2) the capability of filtering datasets and improving microcosmic forecasting performance (inherited from the SVR-PSO model); and (3) the capability of effectively forecasting the macroscopic outline and future tendencies (inherited from the SVR-PSO model). The forecasting outputs obtained by using the hybrid method will be described in the following sections.

In addition, to demonstrate the superiority of the proposed model, the employed electric load data, collected from New South Wales (Australia) in two different sample sizes with 0.5-h type (i.e., 48 data points a day), are used to compare the forecasting performance among the proposed model and other compared models, namely, the original SVR model and the SVR-PSO model (hybridizing the PSO algorithm with the SVR model). The experimental results indicate that the proposed H-EMD-SVR-PSO model has the following advantages: (1) it simultaneously satisfies the need for high accuracy forecasting results and interpretability; (2) the proposed model can tolerate more redundant information than the original SVR model, thus, it has better generalization ability.

This paper is organized as follows: a brief introduction of the proposed H-EMD-SVR-PSO model is illustrated in Section 2. Section 3 presents the experimental results among other compared models proposed in the existing papers. Section 4 concludes this paper.

2. The Proposed H-EMD-SVR-PSO Model

2.1. The Empirical Mode Decomposition (EMD) Technique

The EMD assumes that the original data set is derived from its inherent characteristics, and it can be decomposed into several intrinsic mode functions (IMFs) [40]. Each decomposed IMF, it should satisfy these two conditions: (1) each IMF has only one extreme value among continuous zero-crossings; (2) the mean value of the envelope (see below) of the local maxima and local minima should be zero. Thus, the EMD can effectively avoid premature convergent problem. For the original data set, $x(t)$, the detailed decomposition processes of the EMD are briefly described as follows:

Step 1: Recognize. Recognize all maxima and minima of the data set, $x(t)$.

Step 2: Mean Envelope. Use two cubic spline functions to connect all maxima and minima of the data set, $x(t)$, to fit out the upper envelope and lower envelope, respectively. Then, calculate the mean envelope, m_1, by taking the average value of the upper envelope and the lower envelope.

Step 3: Decomposing. Produce the first IMF candidate, c_1, by taking that the data set $x(t)$ subtract m_1, as illustrated in Equation (1):

$$c_1 = x(t) - m_1 \qquad (1)$$

If c_1 does not meet the two conditions of IMF, then, it could be viewed as the original data set, and m_1 would be zero. Repeat the above evolution k times, the k-th component, c_{1k}, is illustrated by Equation (2):

$$c_{1k} = c_{1(k-1)} - m_{1k} \qquad (2)$$

where c_{1k} and $c_{1(k-1)}$ are the data set after k times and $k - 1$ times evolutions, respectively.

Step 4: IMF Identify. If c_{1k} satisfies the condition of the standard deviation (SD) for the k-th component, as shown in Equation (3), then, c_{1k} can be identified as the first IMF component, IMF_1:

$$SD = \sum_{t=1}^{T} \frac{\left|c_{1(k-1)}(t) - c_{1k}(t)\right|^2}{c_{1k}^2(t)} \in (0.2, 0.3) \qquad (3)$$

where T is the total number of the data set.

After IMF_1 is identified, a new series, d_1, by subtracting IMF_1 (as shown in Equation (4)), would continue the decomposition procedure:

$$Sd_1 = x(t) - IMF_1 \tag{4}$$

Step 5: IMF Composition. Repeat above Steps 1 to 4, until there are no new IMFs can be decomposed from d_n. The decomposition details of these n IMFs are illustrated in Equation (5). Obviously, as shown in Equation (6), the series, d_n, is the remainder of $x(t)$, i.e., it is also the residual of $x(t)$:

$$\begin{aligned} d_1 &= x(t) - IMF_1 \\ d_2 &= d_1 - IMF_2 \\ d_n &= d_{n-1} - IMF_n \end{aligned} \tag{5}$$

$$x(t) = \sum_{i=1}^{n} IMF_i + d_n \tag{6}$$

2.2. The Hybrid Support Vector Regression with Particle Swarm Optimization (SVR-PSO) Model

The brief modeling processes of the hybrid SVR-PSO model are as follows: the given non-linear electric load data set, $\{x_i, y_i\}_{i=1}^{N}$ (where $x_i \in \Re^n$ and represents the actual electric load data), is mapped to a high dimensional feature space ($\Re^{n_h}$) where theoretically exists a linear function, $f(x)$, the so-called SVR function (as shown in Equation (7)), to formulate the nonlinear relationship among the electric load data set:

$$f(\mathbf{x}) = \mathbf{w}^T \varphi(\mathbf{x}) + b \tag{7}$$

where $\varphi(\mathbf{x}) : \Re^n \to \Re^{n_h}$ is the mapping function. The $\mathbf{w}$ and b are adjustable coefficients; they could be determined during the SVR optimization modeling process. Based on the SVR theory, it aims to solve the quadratic optimization problem with inequality constraints as shown in Equation (8):

$$\min_{\mathbf{w},b,\xi,\xi^*} R(\mathbf{w},\xi,\xi^*) = \frac{1}{2}\mathbf{w}^T\mathbf{w} + c\sum_{i=1}^{N}(\xi_i + \xi_i^*) \tag{8}$$

with the constraints:

$$\begin{aligned} y_i - \mathbf{w}^T\varphi(\mathbf{x}_i) - b &\leq \varepsilon + \xi_i^* \\ -y_i + \mathbf{w}^T\varphi(\mathbf{x}_i) + b &\leq \varepsilon + \xi_i \\ \xi_i, \xi_i^* &\geq 0 \quad i = 1, 2 \ldots, N \end{aligned}$$

where $\frac{1}{2}\mathbf{w}^T\mathbf{w}$ is used to maximize the distance of two separated training data; C is used to measure the flatness of the SVR function; ε is the width of the so-called ε-insensitive loss function, which defines the loss is zero only if the forecasting value is within the range of ε; two positive slack variables, ξ and ξ^*, are used to demonstrate the training statuses, training error above ε, denotes as ξ^*, training error below $-\varepsilon$, denotes as ξ. After solving the quadratic problem, Equation (8), the solution of the weight, $\mathbf{w}$, in Equation (7) is computed by Equation (9):

$$\mathbf{w} = \sum_{i=1}^{N}(\alpha_i - \alpha_i^*)\varphi(x) \tag{9}$$

where α_i and α_i^* are the Lagrangian multipliers.

Eventually, the SVR function is estimated as Equation (10):

$$f(\mathbf{x}) = \sum_{i=1}^{N}(\alpha_i - \alpha_i^*)K(\mathbf{x}, \mathbf{x}_i) + b \tag{10}$$

where $K(\mathbf{x}, \mathbf{x}_i)$ is a kernel function, which is computed as $K(\mathbf{x}, \mathbf{x}_i) = \varphi(\mathbf{x}) \circ \varphi(\mathbf{x}_i)$, the operator, "$\circ$", means the inner product of two vectors, $\mathbf{x}$ and $\mathbf{x}_i$. Any functions that meet Mercer's condition [44] can play the role of the kernel function. Because of simply implementation, the Gaussian function, $K(\mathbf{x}, \mathbf{x}_i) = \exp(-||\mathbf{x} - \mathbf{x}_i||^2/2\sigma^2)$, is also employed in this study. Therefore, there are totally three parameters, ε, σ and C, in the Gaussian kernel-based SVR model, excellent determination of these three parameters would play the critical role in improving the forecasting accuracy of the SVR model. Authors have conducted a series of researches using different algorithms to determine these three parameters. For comparison with Fan et al. [35], this study also uses the PSO algorithm to look for suitable parameters of the SVR model.

Based on the simple design: each particle flies in the feature space to search for a better position, by simultaneously adjusting the direction from its local search and the global search of the swarm at each generation, particle swarm optimization (PSO) algorithm has been widely applied in optimization modeling process. The modeling processes of the SVR-PSO model are briefly summarized below:

Step 1: Initialization. Randomly initialize the population, the positions, and the velocities of the three particles (σ, ε, C) in the n-dimensional feature space.

Step 2: Initial fitness. Calculate the fitness using the three initialized particles. The initial local fitness, $f_{(lo\text{-}best)i}$, is based on the own best position of the three particles. The initial global fitness, $f_{(glo\text{-}best)i}$, is based on the global best position of the three particles.

Step 3: Position update. Update the velocities and the positions of the three particles by Equations (11) and (12), the associate fitness is also renewed.

$$V_i^{(k)} = l_i^{(k)} * V_{i-1}^{(k)} + q_1 * rand(\cdot) * \left(p_{(lo-best)i-1}^{(k)} - X_{i-1}^{(k)}\right) + q_2 * Rand(\cdot) * \left(P_{(glo-best)i-1}^{(k)} - X_{i-1}^{(k)}\right) \quad (11)$$

where q_1 and q_2 are positive constants; $rand(\cdot)$ and $Rand(\cdot)$ are independently uniformly distributed random variables with range [0, 1]; $p_{(lo-best)i}^{(k)}$ is the own best position of the kth particle; $P_{(glo-best)i}^{(k)}$ is the global best position of the kth particle; $X_i^{(k)}$ is the position of the kth particle; $k = \sigma$, ε, C; $i = 1, 2, \ldots, N$.

$$X_i^{(k)} = X_{i-1}^{(k)} + V_{i-1}^{(k)} \quad (12)$$

The inertia weight is also applied the linear decreasing function [35], as shown in Equation (13).

$$l_i^{(k)} = \alpha * l_{i-1}^{(k)} \quad (13)$$

where α is a constant, it is less than 1 and is approximate to 1.

Step 4: Fitness Value Update. Use the updated positions of the three particles to calculate the current fitness value, and compare with $f_{(lo\text{-}best)i}$. If the current fitness value is superior, then, update the new fitness value. In this study, the fitness value (forecasting error) is computed by the mean absolute percentage error (MAPE) and the root mean square error (RMSE), as shown in Equations (14) and (15), respectively:

$$\text{MAPE} = \frac{1}{N} \sum_{i=1}^{N} \left|\frac{y_i - f_i}{y_i}\right| \times 100\% \quad (14)$$

$$\text{RMSE} = \sqrt{\frac{\sum_{i=1}^{N}(y_i - f_i)^2}{N}} \quad (15)$$

where N is the total number of electric load data; y_i is the actual load at comparing point i; f_i is the forecasted load at comparing point i.

Step 5: Recognize the Best Solution. If the current fitness value is also superior to $f_{(glo\text{-}best)i}$, then, the best solution is recognized in the current iteration.

Step 6: Stopping Criteria. The forecasting error indexes (MAPE and RMSE) can be served as the stopping criteria, if the values of these two indexes are reached the required standards, then, the latest $f_{(glo\text{-}best)i}$ can be recognized as the final solution; otherwise go back to *Step 3*.

2.3. The Full Procedure of the Proposed H-EMD-PSO-SVR Model

The full procedure of the proposed H-EMD-PSO-SVR model is demonstrated in Figure 1 and is briefly described as follows:

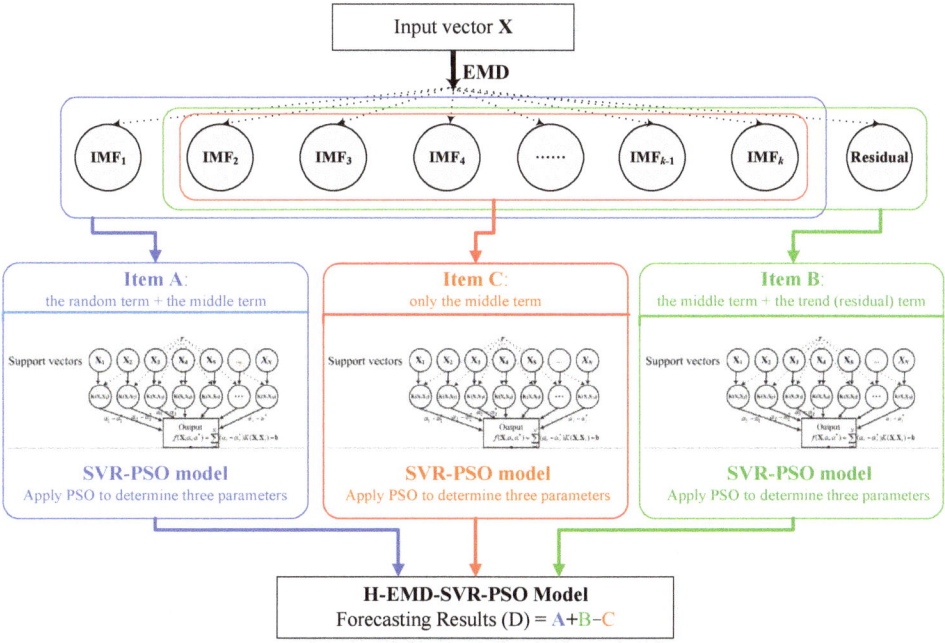

Figure 1. The full flowchart of the proposed H-EMD-SVR-PSO model.

Step 1: Decomposed the input data by EMD. Each electric load data set (i.e., the input data) is decomposed into a number of IMFs. As mentioned above, these IMFs are further divided into three categories, the random term, the middle term, and the trend (residual) term, respectively. The first term represents high-frequency part of the electric load data, the middle term represents multiple-frequency part, and the trend term represents the low-frequency part.

Furthermore, we define the following items: (1) "A", which contains the random term plus the middle term; (2) "B", which contains the middle term plus the trend (residual) term; (3) "C", which only contains the middle term; and (4) "D", which contains all decomposed IMFs.

Step 2: SVR-PSO modeling. The SVR-PSO model is used to forecast the three items (A, B, C and D) separately, as shown in Figure 1. For the relevant settings of the SVR-PSO model in the modeling processes, such as different sizes of fed-in/fed-out subsets, the initial population, the positions, and the velocities for three particles (parameters) readers may refer to Section 2.2 to receive more details of the SVR-PSO model.

Step 3: Forecasting by the H-EMD-SVR-PSO model. The forecasting values of the three items (A, B and C) are received separately from their associated SVR-PSO models. Then, the final electric load forecasting results (with complete decomposed effects, i.e., the item (D) can be eventually calculated by the forecasting values of A + B − C.

3. Experimental Examples

3.1. Data Sets of Experimental Examples

The electric load data set is collected from New South Wales (NSW) market in Australia. It is used to illustrate the superiority and generality of the proposed H-EMD-SVR-PSO model. In addition, to present the overtraining effect for different data sizes, this paper also divides the data set into two different data sizes, the small sample and the large sample, respectively.

For the small sample, the proposed model is trained by the collected electric load from 2 to 7 May 2007 (in total 288 load data points), and the testing data is on 8 May 2007 (in total 48 load data points). As mentioned the load data is based on 0.5 h basis, there are 48 data a day. On the other hand, for the large sample, there are totally 768 load data from 2 to 17 May 2007 as the training data, the testing load data is from 18 to 24 May 2007 (in total 336 load data).

3.2. Parameter Settings of the SVR-PSO Model

To be based on the same comparison condition, the controlled parameters in the PSO algorithm are set as the same in Fan et al. [35] as follows: for the small sample, the maximum iteration number (itmax) is 50, number of particles is 20, length of particle is 3, weight q_1 and q_2 are set as 2; for the large sample, the maximum iteration number (itmax) is 20, number of particles is 5, length of particle is 3, weight q_1 and q_2 are also set as 2; for original sample, the maximum iteration number (itmax) is 300, number of particles is 30, length of particle is 3, weight q_1 and q_2 are set as 2. The search ranges of C and σ in the SVR-PSO model, for all sample sizes, are all set as $[C_{min}, C_{max}] = [0, 200]$ and $[\sigma_{min}, \sigma_{max}] = [0, 200]$, respectively.

3.3. Forecasting Accuracy Indexes

This study uses four forecasting accuracy indexes to evaluate the forecasting performances of the proposed model against other compared models. These four indexes are: (1) the mean absolute percentage error (MAPE), the root mean square error (RMSE), the mean absolute error (MAE), and the correlation coefficient (R). The definitions are shown in Equations (14) to (17), respectively:

$$\text{MAE} = \frac{\sum_{i=1}^{N} |y_i - f_i|}{N} \qquad (16)$$

$$R = \frac{\sum_{i=1}^{N}(y_i - \overline{y})(f_i - \overline{f})}{\sqrt{\sum_{i=1}^{N}(y_i - \overline{y})}\sqrt{\sum_{i=1}^{N}(f_i - \overline{f})}} \qquad (17)$$

where N is the total number of electric load data; y_i is the actual load at comparing point i; $\overline{y}$ is the average actual load; f_i is the forecasted load at comparing point i; $\overline{f}$ is the average forecasted load.

3.4. Decomposition Results after EMD

After decomposition by the EMD technique, it is obvious that the large sample data can be classified in nine terms. These nine decomposed terms are demonstrated in Figure 2a–i, in which the first term, Figure 2a, is the random term, the last term, Figure 2i, is the trend (residual) term. It is similar to the decomposed results for the small sample data, the detailed results of which can be seen in Fan et al. [35].

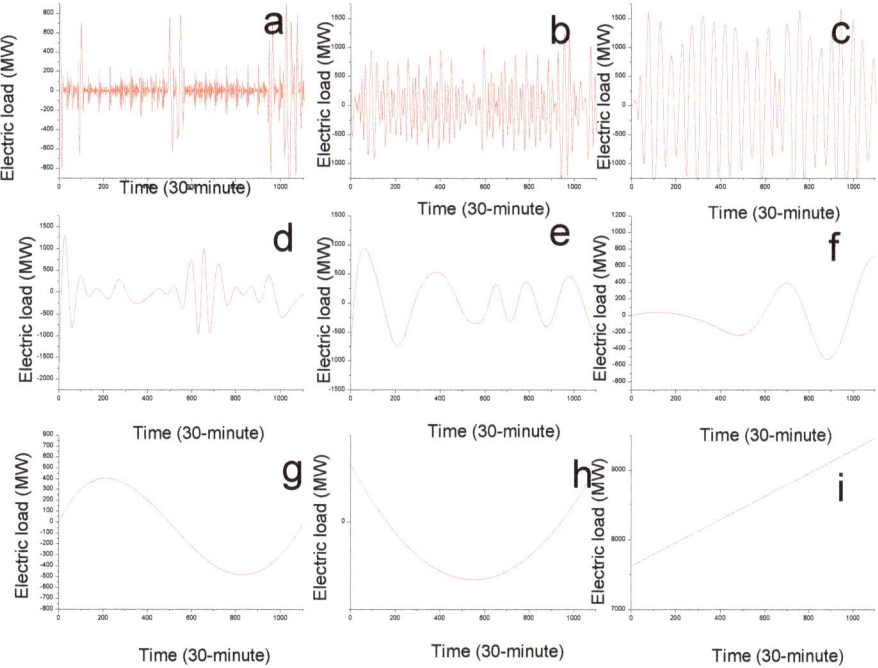

Figure 2. The decomposed items for the large sample data. (**a**) IMF1 (the random term); (**b**) IMF2 (the middle term 1); (**c**) IMF3 (the middle term 2); (**d**) IMF4 (the middle term 3); (**e**) IMF5 (the middle term 4); (**f**) IMF6 (the middle term 5); (**g**) IMF7 (the middle term 6); (**h**) IMF8 (the middle term 7); and (**i**) IMF9 (the trend (residuals) term).

3.5. Forecasting Results by the SVR-PSO Model for Three Defined Items

Figure 3 is the raw data of the large sample. It demonstrates the fluctuation characteristics, such as non-linearity and multiple peaks and valleys. The trend (residual) term is difficult to capture. The non-stationarity characteristics of data implies the dynamics between various time periods in the data sequence, which may change the correlation between the past time period and the future period. Thus, the dynamic changing process is unable to be dealt well only by a single time series analysis model. However, it is useful to apply the EMD technique to reduce the non-stationarity. In addition, the noisy level fluctuation also varies in different time periods in the time series data, particularly for the random term, which demonstrates the disturbing details of the continuous changes. A single time series model could encounter local under-fitting or over-fitting problems extracting features from different time periods with various noisy levels.

The SVR model is very adaptive to solve such continuous changing details of time series forecasting problems. To reduce the performance volatility with different parameters of the SVR model, the PSO algorithm is appropriate to optimize the combination of the parameters. Particularly, the rolling-based procedure [34], is employed in the training stage to assist the PSO algorithm to find the most appropriate parameters combination of an SVR model. Firstly, as mentioned above, the decomposed IMFs are defined to form the following items, A, B, C and D. These four items are simultaneously modeled by the SVR-PSO model, and the suitable parameter combination for the four items in the small and the large samples are illustrated in Table 1.

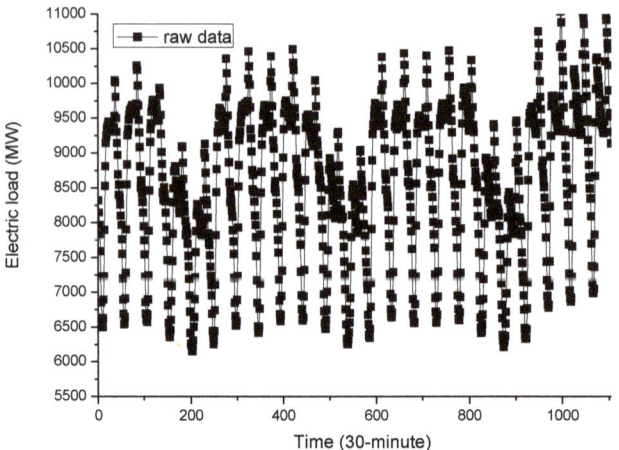

Figure 3. The raw data of the large sample data.

Table 1. The optimized parameters of the SVR-PSO model for different items in both samples.

Sample Size/Defined Items	The Parameters of an SVR Model		
	σ	C	ε
The small sample data			
Item A: the random term + the middle term	0.14	89	0.0022
Item B: the middle term + the trend (residual) term	0.14	88	0.0020
Item C: the middle term	0.15	91	0.0025
Item D: A + B − C (all IMFs, i.e., complete decomposed effects)	0.15	92	0.0025
The large sample data			
Item A: the random term + the middle term	0.18	95	0.0011
Item B: the middle term + the trend (residual) term	0.18	96	0.0011
Item C: the middle term	0.20	98	0.0013
Item D: A + B − C (all IMFs, i.e., complete decomposed effects)	0.20	98	0.0012

The performances for different defined items in the training and testing (forecasting) sets for the small and the large samples are demonstrated in Figures 4 and 5, respectively.

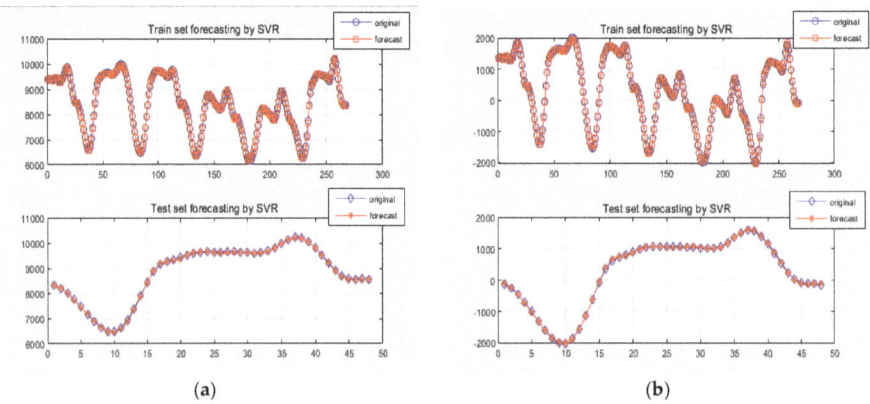

Figure 4. *Cont.*

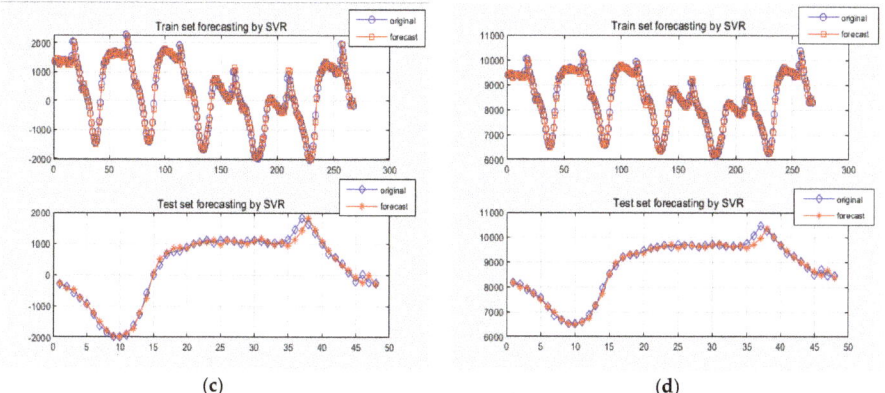

Figure 4. Comparison the forecasting results for different defined items by the SVR-PSO model (the small sample; one-day ahead forecasting on 8 May 2007). (**a**) Item A: the random term + the middle term; (**b**) Item B: the middle term + the trend (residual) term; (**c**) Item C: the middle term; (**d**) Item D: A + B − C (all IMFs, i.e., complete decomposed effects).

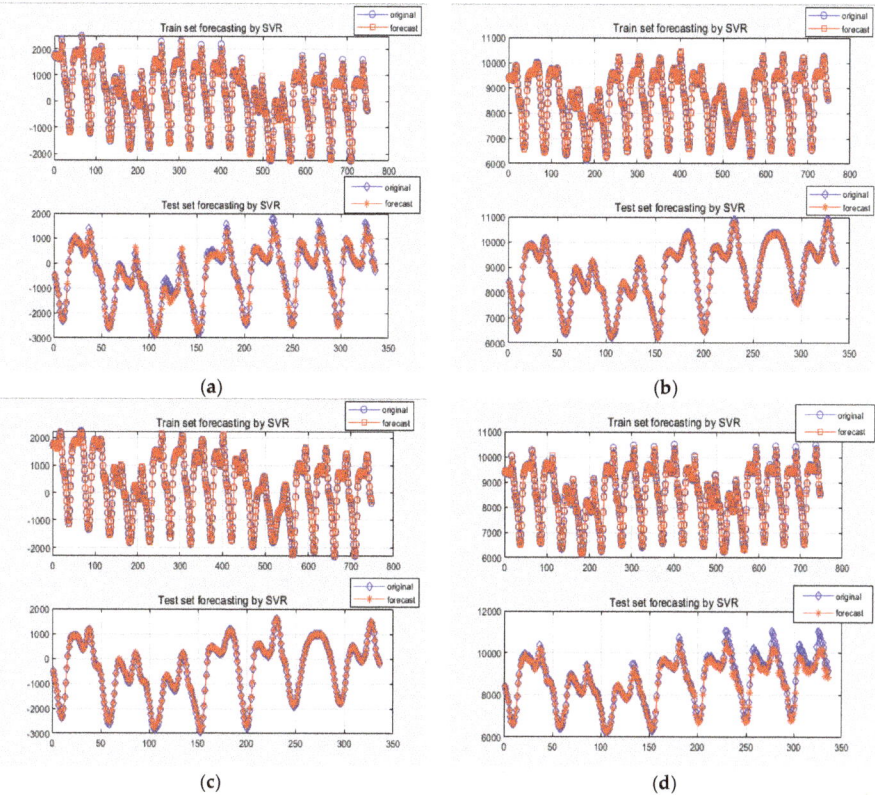

Figure 5. Comparison the forecasting results for different defined items by the SVR-PSO model (the large sample; one-week ahead forecasting on 18 to 24 May 2007). (**a**) Item A: the random term + the middle term; (**b**) Item B: the middle term + the trend (residual) term; (**c**) Item C: the middle term; (**d**) Item D: A + B − C (all IMFs, i.e., complete decomposed effects).

The values of different forecasting indexes for different defined items in the training and testing stages for the small and the large samples are illustrated in Table 2. It is obviously that the forecasting performance of all items are outstanding, particularly for items A and B, whose forecasting accuracies are almost zero in terms of the square of RMSE. The results imply that the decomposition effects of the EMD technique are useful to increase the forecasting performance from the data composition side. In addition, the forecasting accuracy of the item D by the SVR-PSO model is also superior to the one achieved by the original SVR model. It also indicates that the optimization effects from the PSO algorithm are helpful to improve the forecasting accuracy from the parameter selection side.

Table 2. Summary of the forecasting results for each defined items.

Forecasting Accuracy Indexes	The Defined Items				
	Item A (by SVR-PSO)	Item B (by SVR-PSO)	Item C (by SVR-PSO)	Item D (by SVR-PSO)	Item D (by SVR)
	The Small Sample				
RMSE^2 (training stage)	0.0001936	0.0001635	0.0029	0.0009	0.0021
RMSE^2 (testing stage)	0.0001806	0.0001641	0.0033	0.0011	0.0026
R (training stage)	0.9993	0.9995	0.9888	0.9884	0.9871
R (testing stage)	0.9994	0.9995	0.9867	0.9881	0.9890
	The Large Sample				
RMSE^2 (training stage)	0.0001280	0.0001090	0.0007	0.0007	0.0012
RMSE^2 (testing stage)	0.0002281	0.0002814	0.0033	0.0096	0.0099
R (training stage)	0.9994	0.9994	0.9962	0.9965	0.9916
R (testing stage)	0.9992	0.9991	0.9982	0.9756	0.9912

3.6. Analyses of Forecasting Accuracy and the Relevant Applications

For the small sample, the forecasting results of the original SVR model, the SVR-PSO model, and the proposed H-EMD-SVR-PSO model are demonstrated in Figure 6a. It indicates that the forecasting curve of the proposed H-EMD-SVR-PSO model fits closer than other compared models. For the large sample, Figure 6b illustrates the forecasting results obtained from the proposed H-EMD-SVR-PSO model fits better than other compared models, particularly for those peak load values. In addition, from the local enlarged figure (Figure 7), the peak points of the small and the large samples demonstrate that the proposed H-EMD-SVR-PSO model can capture the mutative changes of the electric loads and can provide effective forecasting the reduced situation of electricity demand, thus, successfully reducing the losses of the power company.

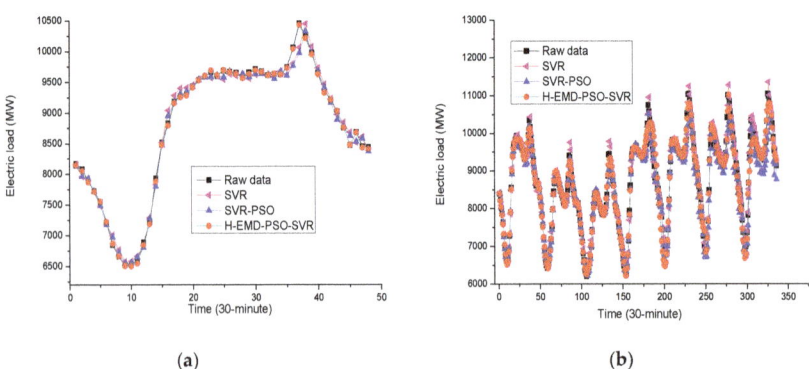

Figure 6. Comparison of the forecasting results among the H-EMD-SVR-PSO model and other models. (**a**) The small sample; (**b**) The large sample.

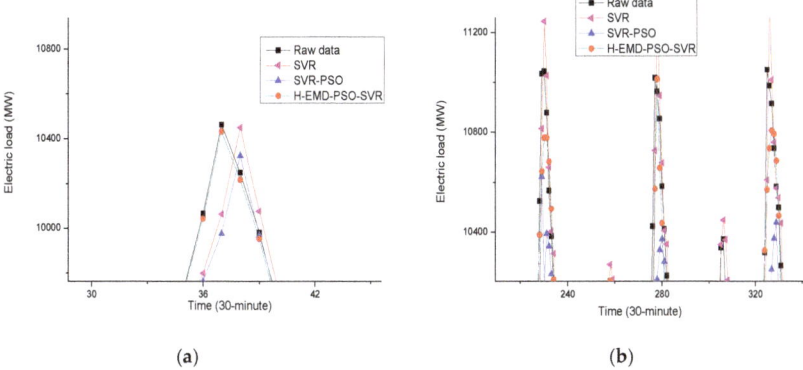

Figure 7. The local enlargement (peak) comparison of the H-EMD-SVR-PSO model and other models. (**a**) The small sample; (**b**) The large sample.

Furthermore, the proposed H-EMD-SVR-PSO model has better generalization ability than other compared models. The comparison results are summarized in Table 3.

Table 3. Summary of results of the forecasting models.

Compared Models	MAPE	RMSE	MAE	Running Time (s)
The Small Sample				
Original SVR [32]	11.70	145.87	10.92	180.4
SVR-PSO [32]	11.41	145.69	10.67	165.2
PSO–BP [32]	10.91	142.26	10.14	159.9
SVR-GA [35]	13.52	150.38	11.88	171.3
EMD-SVR-AR [32]	9.86	117.16	9.10	**80.7**
EMD-PSO-GA-SVR [35]	**9.09**	**123.38**	9.19	135.7
H-EMD-SVR-PSO	10.01	125.38	9.75	120.5
The Large Sample				
Original SVR [32]	12.88	181.62	12.05	**116.8**
SVR-PSO [32]	13.50	271.43	13.07	192.7
PSO–BP [32]	12.24	175.24	11.36	163.1
SVR-GA [35]	14.31	183.57	15.31	195.7
EMD-SVR-AR [32]	5.10	134.20	9.82	162.0
EMD-PSO-GA-SVR [35]	**3.92**	142.41	**9.04**	179.1
H-EMD-SVR-PSO	5.83	**130.17**	9.56	167.4

The proposed model is also compared with other alternative models proposed in references [32] and [35]. Firstly, the general observation in both samples is that the proposed model tends to fit closer to the actual electric load values with a smaller forecasting error. In addition, it is also found that proposed model outperforms the compared models (except EMD-SVR-AR and EMD-PSO-GA-SVR models) in terms of all the used forecasting accuracy indexes and the running times.

For the small sample, the proposed H-EMD-SVR-PSO model outperforms the original SVR model, SVR-PSO model [32], PSO-BP model [32], and SVR-GA model [35]. A slight forecasting accuracy index value behind the EMD-SVR-AR model [32] and EMD-PSO-GA-SVR model [35], i.e., the advantages of this kind of EMD-SVR-based models are superior to other SVR-based models, however, they are not much different in forecasting performance due to their use of the same hybridization structure. In the running time comparison, these kinds of EMD-SVR-based models often have high running speed, however, the running time would increase when the number of hybridizing techniques is large or the hybridized technique is very complicate in computing terms, such as the EMD-PSO-GA-SVR model which is the most time consuming among these three EMD-SVR-based models; on the contrary, when the number of hybridizing techniques is small or the hybridized technique is easy to model, such as the EMD-SVR-AR model is the most time saving among these EMD-SVR-based models.

On the other hand, from Table 3, the forecasting accuracy of the SVR-PSO model [32] is not outstanding when it is applied directly. This results from the interactive effects of the random term and the trend (residual) term, the so-called inherent non-linearity of the electric load data. After hybridizing with the EMD technique, the proposed H-EMD-SVR-PSO model is capable of capturing the inherent non-linearity by separately modeling these decomposed IMFs and these defined items (A, B, C and D). The forecasting performance of items A and B are significantly improved, which indicates that the inherent non-linearity of the electric load data can be effectively explained by the proposed model. In the other words, the proposed H-EMD-SVR-PSO model provides a very powerful tool to easily implement the electric load forecasting work.

The significance of the forecasting performance from the proposed H-EMD-SVR-PSO model should be further verified. The recommended statistical test by Derrac et al. [45] and Fan et al. [31], namely Wilcoxon signed-rank test is used to conduct the forecasting performance comparison among the proposed H-EMD-SVR-PSO model and the alternative models. The test is based on one-tail-test and is under two significance levels, $\alpha = 0.025$ and $\alpha = 0.05$. The test results are shown in Table 4. Clearly, the proposed H-EMD-SVR-PSO model significantly outperforms other compared models. In other words, the hybrid model leads to better accuracy and statistical interpretation.

Table 4. Wilcoxon signed-rank test.

Compared Models	Wilcoxon Signed-Rank Test	
	$\alpha = 0.025; W = 4$	$\alpha = 0.05; W = 6$
The Small Sample		
H-EMD-SVR-PSO vs. Original SVR	3 *	3 *
H-EMD-SVR-PSO vs. SVR-PSO	2 *	2 *
H-EMD-SVR-PSO vs. PSO–BP	2 *	3 *
H-EMD-SVR-PSO vs. SVR-GA	2 *	3 *
H-EMD-SVR-PSO vs. EMD-SVR-AR	6	4 *
H-EMD-SVR-PSO vs. EMD-PSO-GA-SVR	6	8
The Large Sample		
H-EMD-SVR-PSO vs. Original SVR	3 *	2 *
H-EMD-SVR-PSO vs. SVR-PSO	3 *	2 *
H-EMD-SVR-PSO vs. PSO–BP	3 *	2 *
H-EMD-SVR-PSO vs. SVR-GA	3 *	2 *
H-EMD-SVR-PSO vs. EMD-SVR-AR	6	2 *
H-EMD-SVR-PSO vs. EMD-PSO-GA-SVR	6	4 *

Note: * denotes that the H-EMD-SVR-PSO model significantly outperforms other alternative models.

Finally, some real life applications of the proposed methodology could be as followings. Via the EMD operation, (1) the random (stochastic) volatility term can be obviously revealed, which could be viewed as the microeconomic behavior; (2) the trend (residual) term is the inertial behavior, i.e., the general tendency of the economy, which could be viewed as the macroeconomic behavior; and (3) the middle term could be expressed from the unique economic behavior or production and living characteristics of each industry. Thus, the reason that the item A (the random term plus the middle term) could be well simulated during the modeling processes of the SVR-PSO model is that the characteristics of economic behaviors in each industry and their interactive influences (i.e., the random fluctuations) are in line with the modeling rules of the PSO algorithm (i.e., from random solution to adaptability). On the other hand, while the item B (the middle term plus the trend (residual) term) is characterizing, the SVR-based model (with the generalized linear capability in the feature space) can reveal the characteristics of economic behaviors along with the optimization processes of the PSO algorithm.

Based on the observation from the above two items (items A and B), the proposed H-EMD-SVR-PSO model is obviously to have superior forecasting results, as shown in Table 2. In addition, the proposed model can be furtherly applied not only in electricity load forecasting, but also for the disclosure of other energy consumption behaviors or similar rules.

4. Conclusions

This paper proposes a novel H-EMD-SVR-PSO electric load forecasting model, by classifying the IMFs decomposed by the EMD technique into four different defined items (A, B, C and D). It is effective at overcoming the interactive effects of the random term and the trend (residual) term, and the inherent non-linearity of the electric load data. In addition, by hybridizing the PSO algorithm to optimize the parameter combination of the SVR model for these four items, respectively, it can effectively guarantee the better forecasting performance of each item by using the SVR-PSO model. Via two experiments with different sample sizes from the Australian market data, the proposed model has obtained significant forecasting results than other alternative models in the existed papers, such as original SVR, SVR-PSO, PSO-BP, SVR-GA, EMD-SVR-AR and EMD-PSO-GA-SVR models.

The results also verify the feasibility and the generalization capability of the EMD-SVR-based model to deal with the complicate interactions inherent in the electric load data. Various data characteristics of electric load are decomposed and identified by the employed EMD technique, which can guide researchers to select more suitable SVR-based forecasting models. For future research, the EMD-SVR-based model can be hybridized with other advanced classification tools to further improve the electric load forecasting accuracy.

Author Contributions: G.-F.F. and W.-C.H. conceived and designed the experiments; G.-F.F. performed the experiments and analyzed the data; W.-C.H. wrote the paper.

Funding: This paper is sponsored by the Academic and Technical Leader of Pingdingshan University, Program for Young Scholar of Pingdingshan University, and the support from Jiangsu Normal University (no. 9213618401), China.

Conflicts of Interest: The authors declare no conflict of interest.

References

1. Xiao, L.; Shao, W.; Liang, T.; Wang, C. A combined model based on multiple seasonal patterns and modified firefly algorithm for electrical load forecasting. *Appl. Energy* **2016**, *167*, 135–153. [CrossRef]
2. Hussain, A.; Rahman, M.; Memon, J.A. Forecasting electricity consumption in Pakistan: The way forward. *Energy Policy* **2016**, *90*, 73–80. [CrossRef]
3. Tarsitano, A.; Amerise, I.L. Short-term load forecasting using a two-stage sarimax model. *Energy* **2017**, *133*, 108–114. [CrossRef]
4. Boroojeni, K.G.; Amini, M.H.; Bahrami, S.; Iyengar, S.S.; Sarwat, A.I.; Karabasoglu, O. A novel multi-time-scale modeling for electric power demand forecasting: From short-term to medium-term horizon. *Electr. Power Syst. Res.* **2017**, *142*, 58–73. [CrossRef]
5. Dudek, G. Pattern based local linear regression models for short term load forecasting. *Electr. Power Syst. Res.* **2016**, *130*, 139–147. [CrossRef]
6. Vu, D.H.; Muttaqi, K.M.; Agalgaonkar, A.P. A variance inflation factor and backward elimination based robust regression model for forecasting monthly electricity demand using climatic variables. *Appl. Energy* **2015**, *140*, 385–394. [CrossRef]
7. Wu, J.; Wang, J.; Lu, H.; Dong, Y.; Lu, X. Short term load forecasting technique based on the seasonal exponential adjustment method and the regression model. *Energy Convers. Manag.* **2013**, *70*, 1–9. [CrossRef]
8. Maçaira, P.M.; Souza, R.C.; Oliveira, F.L.C. Modelling and forecasting the residential electricity consumption in Brazil with pegels exponential smoothing techniques. *Procedia Comput. Sci.* **2015**, *55*, 328–335. [CrossRef]
9. Dong, Z.; Yang, D.; Reindl, T.; Walsh, W.M. Short-term solar irradiance forecasting using exponential smoothing state space model. *Energy* **2013**, *55*, 1104–1113. [CrossRef]

10. De Oliveira, E.M.; Oliveira, F.L.C. Forecasting mid-long term electric energy consumption through bagging ARIMA and exponential smoothing methods. *Energy* **2018**, *144*, 776–788. [CrossRef]
11. Takeda, H.; Tamura, Y.; Sato, S. Using the ensemble Kalman filter for electricity load forecasting and analysis. *Energy* **2016**, *104*, 184–198. [CrossRef]
12. Scarpa, F.; Bianco, V. Assessing the quality of natural gas consumption forecasting: An application to the Italian residential sector. *Energies* **2017**, *10*, 1879. [CrossRef]
13. Niu, D.X.; Shi, H.F.; Wu, D.D. Short-term load forecasting using Bayesian neural networks learned by hybrid Monte Carlo algorithm. *Appl. Soft Comput.* **2012**, *12*, 1822–1827. [CrossRef]
14. Hippert, H.S.; Taylor, J.W. An evaluation of Bayesian techniques for controlling model complexity and selecting inputs in a neural network for short-term load forecasting. *Neural Netw.* **2010**, *23*, 386–395. [CrossRef] [PubMed]
15. Bianco, V.; Cascetta, F.; Marino, A.; Nardini, S. Understanding energy consumption and carbon emissions in Europe: A focus on inequality issues. *Energy* **2019**, *170*, 120–130. [CrossRef]
16. Kelo, S.; Dudul, S. A wavelet Elman neural network for short term electrical load prediction under the influence of temperature. *Int. J. Electr. Power Energy Syst.* **2012**, *43*, 1063–1071. [CrossRef]
17. Ghofrani, M.; Ghayekhloo, M.; Arabali, A.; Ghayekhloo, A. A hybrid short-term load forecasting with a new input selection framework. *Energy* **2015**, *81*, 777–786. [CrossRef]
18. Singh, P.; Dwivedi, P. Integration of new evolutionary approach with artificial neural network for solving short term load forecast problem. *Appl Energy* **2018**, *217*, 537–549. [CrossRef]
19. Khwaja, A.S.; Zhang, X.; Anpalagan, A.; Venkatesh, B. Boosted neural networks for improved short-term electric load forecasting. *Electr. Power Syst. Res.* **2017**, *143*, 431–437. [CrossRef]
20. Duan, Q.; Liu, J.; Zhao, D. Short term electric load forecasting using an automated system of model choice. *Int. J. Electr. Power Energy Syst.* **2017**, *91*, 92–100. [CrossRef]
21. Karimi, M.; Karami, H.; Gholami, M.; Khatibzadehazad, H.; Moslemi, N. Priority index considering temperature and date proximity for selection of similar days in knowledge-based short term load forecasting method. *Energy* **2018**, *144*, 928–940. [CrossRef]
22. Chaturvedi, D.K.; Sinha, A.P.; Malik, O.P. Short term load forecast using fuzzy logic and wavelet transform integrated generalized neural network. *Int. J. Electr. Power Energy Syst.* **2015**, *67*, 230–237. [CrossRef]
23. Sadaei, H.J.; Guimarães, F.G.; da Silva, C.J.; Lee, M.H.; Eslami, T. Short-term load forecasting method based on fuzzy time series, seasonality and long memory process. *Int. J. Approx. Reason.* **2017**, *83*, 196–217. [CrossRef]
24. Efendi, R.; Ismail, Z.; Deris, M.M. A new linguistic out-sample approach of fuzzy time series for daily forecasting of Malaysian electricity load demand. *Appl. Soft Comput.* **2015**, *28*, 422–430. [CrossRef]
25. Hooshmand, R.A.; Amooshahi, H.; Parastegari, M. A hybrid intelligent algorithm based short-term load forecasting approach. *Int. J. Electr. Power Energy Syst.* **2013**, *45*, 313–324. [CrossRef]
26. Lou, C.W.; Dong, M.C. A novel random fuzzy neural networks for tackling uncertainties of electric load forecasting. *Int. J. Electr. Power Energy Syst.* **2015**, *73*, 34–44. [CrossRef]
27. Niu, M.; Sun, S.; Wu, J.; Yu, L.; Wang, J. An innovative integrated model using the singular spectrum analysis and nonlinear multi-layer perceptron network optimized by hybrid intelligent algorithm for short-term load forecasting. *Appl. Math. Model.* **2016**, *40*, 4079–4093. [CrossRef]
28. Zhao, J.; Liu, X. A hybrid method of dynamic cooling and heating load forecasting for office buildings based on artificial intelligence and regression analysis. *Energy Buildings* **2018**, *174*, 293–308. [CrossRef]
29. Yu, F.; Xu, X. A short-term load forecasting model of natural gas based on optimized genetic algorithm and improved BP neural network. *Appl. Energy* **2014**, *134*, 102–113. [CrossRef]
30. Liu, N.; Tang, Q.; Zhang, J.; Fan, W.; Liu, J. A hybrid forecasting model with parameter optimization for short-term load forecasting of micro-grids. *Appl. Energy* **2014**, *129*, 336–345. [CrossRef]
31. Fan, G.-F.; Peng, L.-L.; Hong, W.-C. Short term load forecasting based on phase space reconstruction algorithm and bi-square kernel regression model. *Appl. Energy* **2018**, *224*, 13–33. [CrossRef]
32. Fan, G.; Wang, H.; Qing, S.; Hong, W.-C.; Li, H.-J. Support vector regression model based on empirical mode decomposition and auto regression for electric load forecasting. *Energies* **2013**, *6*, 1887–1901. [CrossRef]
33. Geng, J.; Huang, M.L.; Li, M.W.; Hong, W.C. Hybridization of seasonal chaotic cloud simulated annealing algorithm in a SVR-based load forecasting model. *Neurocomputing* **2015**, *151*, 1362–1373. [CrossRef]

34. Hong, W.-C.; Dong, Y.; Lai, C.-Y.; Chen, L.-Y.; Wei, S.-Y. SVR with hybrid chaotic immune algorithm for seasonal load demand forecasting. *Energies* **2011**, *4*, 960–977. [CrossRef]
35. Fan, G.-F.; Peng, L.-L.; Zhao, X.; Hong, W.-C. Applications of hybrid EMD with PSO and GA for an SVR-based load forecasting model. *Energies* **2017**, *10*, 1713. [CrossRef]
36. Hong, W.-C.; Dong, Y.; Zhang, W.; Chen, L.-Y.; Panigrahi, B.K. Cyclic electric load forecasting by seasonal SVR with chaotic genetic algorithm. *Int. J. Electr. Power Energy Syst.* **2013**, *44*, 604–614. [CrossRef]
37. Ju, F.-Y.; Hong, W.-C. Application of seasonal SVR with chaotic gravitational search algorithm in electricity forecasting. *Appl. Math. Model.* **2013**, *37*, 9643–9651. [CrossRef]
38. Li, M.; Hong, W.-C.; Kang, H. Urban traffic flow forecasting using Gauss-SVR with cat mapping, cloud model and PSO hybrid algorithm. *Neurocomputing* **2013**, *99*, 230–240. [CrossRef]
39. Chen, R.; Liang, C.; Hong, W.-C.; Gu, D. Forecasting holiday daily tourist flow based on seasonal support vector regression with adaptive genetic algorithm. *Appl. Soft Comput.* **2015**, *26*, 435–443. [CrossRef]
40. Huang, B.; Kunoth, A. An optimization based empirical mode decomposition scheme. *J. Comput. Appl. Math.* **2013**, *240*, 174–183. [CrossRef]
41. An, X.; Jiang, D.; Zhao, M.; Liu, C. Short-term prediction of wind power using EMD and chaotic theory. *Commun. Nonlinear Sci. Numer. Simul.* **2012**, *17*, 1036–1042. [CrossRef]
42. Fan, G.; Qing, S.; Wang, S.Z.; Hong, W.C.; Dai, L. Study on apparent kinetic prediction model of the smelting reduction based on the time series. *Math. Probl. Eng.* **2012**, 720849. [CrossRef]
43. Premanode, B.; Toumazou, C. Improving prediction of exchange rates using Differential EMD. *Expert Syst. Appl.* **2013**, *40*, 377–384. [CrossRef]
44. Dong, Y.; Zhang, Z.; Hong, W.-C. A hybrid seasonal mechanism with a chaotic cuckoo search algorithm with a support vector regression model for electric load forecasting. *Energies* **2018**, *11*, 1009. [CrossRef]
45. Derrac, J.; García, S.; Molina, D.; Herrera, F. A practical tutorial on the use of nonparametric statistical tests as a methodology for comparing evolutionary and swarm intelligence algorithms. *Swarm Evol. Comput.* **2011**, *1*, 3–18. [CrossRef]

© 2019 by the authors. Licensee MDPI, Basel, Switzerland. This article is an open access article distributed under the terms and conditions of the Creative Commons Attribution (CC BY) license (http://creativecommons.org/licenses/by/4.0/).

Article

Application of the Weighted K-Nearest Neighbor Algorithm for Short-Term Load Forecasting

Guo-Feng Fan [1], Yan-Hui Guo [1], Jia-Mei Zheng [1] and Wei-Chiang Hong [2,*]

1. School of Mathematics and Statistics Science, Ping Ding Shan University, Ping Ding Shan 467000, China; guofengtongzhi@pdsu.edu.cn (G.-F.F.); guoyanhui2016@pdsu.edu.cn (Y.-H.G.); zhengjiamei2016@pdsu.edu.cn (J.-M.Z.)
2. Department of Information Management, Oriental Institute of Technology/No. 58, Sec. 2, Sichuan Rd., Panchiao, New Taipei 226, Taiwan
* Correspondence: fi013@mail.oit.edu.tw

Received: 11 January 2019; Accepted: 6 March 2019; Published: 9 March 2019

Abstract: In this paper, the historical power load data from the National Electricity Market (Australia) is used to analyze the characteristics and regulations of electricity (the average value of every eight hours). Then, considering the inverse of Euclidean distance as the weight, this paper proposes a novel short-term load forecasting model based on the weighted k-nearest neighbor algorithm to receive higher satisfied accuracy. In addition, the forecasting errors are compared with the back-propagation neural network model and the autoregressive moving average model. The comparison results demonstrate that the proposed forecasting model could reflect variation trend and has good fitting ability in short-term load forecasting.

Keywords: short-term load forecasting; weighted k-nearest neighbor (W-K-NN) algorithm; comparative analysis

1. Introduction

Short-term load forecasting is used to forecast the power loads in the coming months, weeks, or even shorter, with greater accuracy than long-term load forecasting. In the competitive power market, the forecasting accuracy directly affects the economic cost of operators, so it occupies an important position in modern power demand management [1]. According to the data of short-term load forecasting, it not only can optimize the combination of generator sets, economic dispatching, and the power flow calculation for power generation, but also can guarantee the economical safe operations of the power system [2].

Classical deterministic theories are mainly applied to conduct the traditional short-term load forecasting. Such as time series method [3], back-propagation neural network (BPNN) model [4], gray model [5,6], and support vector regression [7–9], etc. Although these methods are widely adopted, there are still some outstanding problems, for example, (1) it is difficult to simulate the relationships between the variables affecting the electricity loads and the loads themselves by accurate mathematical model; (2) the forecasting accuracy requires improvements; (3) the forecasting effect is not satisfied; and (4) the real situation of the electricity load cannot be reflected in real time. Therefore, it is of great practical significance to study and establish a more accurate and intuitive short-term load forecasting model.

Recently, Martínez-Álvarez et al. [10] indicate the importance of pattern sequence similarity, and introduce the pattern sequence-based forecasting (PSF) algorithm, which contains clustering (selection of the optimum number of clusters) and prediction (like optimum window size selection for specific patterns and prediction of future values). Later, Bokde et al. [11] published the R code for modeling. Due to the similar theoretical designing of PSF, the k-nearest neighbor (K-NN) algorithm [12] is a mature theoretical tool and is easily implemented. It is often used to solve nonlinear problems, such as credit ratings and bank customer rankings, in which the collected data do not always follow the theoretical linear assumption, thus it should be one of the first choices when there is little or no prior knowledge about the distribution data. In addition, it can successfully reduce the influences of the variables on the experimental processes [13]. It has higher forecasting accuracy and has no assumptions for the collected data, and particularly, it is not sensitive to the outliers. It has been widely applied in real-world problems, such as analyzing the structure of the stock market [14], fault detection and diagnosis for photovoltaic systems [15], and social images recognition in social networks [16]. In addition, several improved K-NN algorithms have also been explored, for example, Zhang et al. [17] propose an improved K-NN algorithm by reconstructing a sparse coefficient matrix between test samples and training data to keep the local structures of data for achieving the efficiency. Their proposed improved K-NN algorithm is applied to classification, regression, and missing data imputation with superior results. Bhattacharya et al. [13] employs the weights obtained from the analytic hierarchy process (AHP) for different features to propose a weighted distance function for the K-NN algorithm. Their results demonstrate that the performance of the proposed K-NN classifier can receive improved results in terms of pairwise comparison of features.

The original W-K-NN forecasting algorithm was developed and introduced by Troncoso et al. in 2007 [18]. Thereafter, several researchers have considered empowering weight for each nearest neighbor [19], for instance, Chen and Hao [20] proposed a support vector machine (SVM)-based weighted K-NN algorithm to effectively predict stock market indices by using support vector machines to obtain the associated weight for each feature. Their forecasting results are better than other models. Biswas et al. [21] propose the parameter independent fuzzy class-specific feature weighted K-NN (PIFW-K-NN) classifier, in which, the class dependent optimum weight is based on the distances from the query point using a fuzzy membership function. Their classification results demonstrate the improved accuracy of the proposed PIFW-K-NN than other state-of-the-art classifiers. Su [22] proposes the weighted K-NN (W-K-NN) by hybridizing the genetic algorithm with K-NN (k-nearest neighbor) to detect large-scale attacks. The weight for each nearest neighbor is weighted by Euclidean distance, then, the genetic algorithm (GA) is used to find an optimal weight vector for all nearest neighbors. Their results demonstrate that the detection accuracy is improved significantly. Lei and Zuo [23] also propose the weighted K-NN (W-K-NN) classification algorithm by using Euclidean distance evaluation technique (EDET) to select sensitive features and remove fault-unrelated features. The applied results of the proposed method demonstrate its effectiveness. Ren et al. [24] propose a weighted sparse neighbor algorithm based on Gaussian kernel function to resolve face recognition problems. In which, the weights are calculated distance-based on Gaussian kernel to measure the similarity between test sample and each training sample. Their results demonstrate that the proposed algorithm could reach a higher recognition rate than other existing alternative models. Recently, Mateos-García et al. [25] propose the simultaneous weighting of attributes and neighbors (SWAN) to improve the classification accuracy, by using an evolutionary computation technique to adjust the contribution of the neighbors and the significance of the features of the data. Their results demonstrate that the proposed SWAN is superior to other alternative weighted K-NN methods. Llames et al. [26] propose a new approach for big data forecasting based on the weight K-NN to conduct distributed computing under the Apache Spark framework, in which four different weight calculations are employed. A Spanish energy consumption big data time series (measured every 10 min for nine years) has been used to test the algorithm. The results also support the superiority of the proposed weight K-NN model.

Based on above relevant literature reviews, the inverse of Euclidean distance is employed as the weight, then, it is hybridized with the K-NN algorithm (namely W-K-NN algorithm) to improve the forecasting accuracy. Thus, this paper proposes a short-term load forecasting model based on the new parametrization of the W-K-NN algorithm so that it is adapted to China patterns: (1) According to a known sample set, forecast the electricity loads at a certain time; (2) calculate the Euclidean distance using its proximity data, the reciprocal of the calculated distance is used to determine the weight for each data point; (3) the closer the distance, the greater the weight, thus the data points can be better classified and the short-term load can be better forecasted. Comparing the model structure with the similar works proposed by Llames et al. [26], Rana et al. [27], and Troncoso et al. [28], which use 10-min electricity demand, hourly electricity load, and price, respectively, for one day ahead to calculate the weight by the distance of the neighbors. On the contrary, the proposed model in this paper can extract the inertia of the electricity consumption behaviors from larger historical load data (i.e., the normal production life cycle in China: three load data patterns for each eight hours in a day) to calculate the weights by the reciprocal of the distance, which also avoid being bounded in the characteristics of the short cycle. It can be emphasized that the proposed model is based on the state space and the production life cycle to determine the weights, which can capture the weight more accurately.

The rest of this paper is organized as follows. In Section 2, the details of the K-NN algorithm are introduced briefly. In Section 3, a short-term load forecasting model based on the W-K-NN algorithm is proposed and the main steps of the proposed model are also illustrated. In Section 4, the proposed model is simulated and compared with two common alternative models (i.e., the autoregressive-moving average (ARMA) and the BPNN models). In Section 5, a brief conclusion of this paper and the future research are provided.

2. The K-NN Algorithm

The K-NN algorithm is proposed to find out k training samples that are closest to the target object in the training set. Furthermore, determine the dominant category from the k training samples; then, assign this dominant category to the target object, where k is the number of training samples.

Therefore, the principal mechanism of the K-NN algorithm is that all samples have the same characteristics while they are classified in the same category in a feature space, which the category contains the k most neighboring samples. In determining the classification decision, the method determines the category to which the sample belongs only according to the category of the nearest one or several samples. In addition, the K-NN algorithm is only relevant to a very small number of adjacent samples in category decision making. Since the K-NN algorithm mainly relies on the surrounding limited adjacent samples, rather than relying on the method of discriminant domain method to determine the category, thus the K-NN algorithm is more suitable than other methods for the pending sample sets where the class domain crosses or overlaps more. The idea of the K-NN algorithm is demonstrated in Figure 1. In which, X_u belongs to the category (ω_1) because four neighboring samples belong to ω_1, only one neighboring sample belongs to ω_3.

The specified implementation process of the K-NN algorithm contains the following six steps,

(1) Select the k value;
(2) Calculate the distance between the point in the known category data set and the current point;
(3) Sort in increasing order of distance;
(4) Select k points with the smallest distance from the current point;
(5) Determine the frequency of occurrence of the category in which k points are located;
(6) Return to the category with the highest frequency of occurrence of the first k points as the predicted classification of the current point.

The K-NN algorithm needs to calculate the distance between the forecasted data point and the known data point, so as to the select the nearest k labeled data, $\{y_1, y_2, \ldots, y_k\}$, where y_1 represents the known data point closest to the forecasted point; y_2 represents the known data point that is the second closest to the forecasted point, and so on. Therefore, the short-term load forecasting can be conducted by the K-NN algorithm regression as Equation (1),

$$s_i = \frac{1}{k} \times \sum_{j=1}^{k} s_{y_j} \qquad (1)$$

where s_i represents the ith forecasted value, which is the average value of s_{y_j} $(j = 1, 2, \ldots, k)$; s_{y_j} represents the forecasted value of the jth closest known data point (y_j).

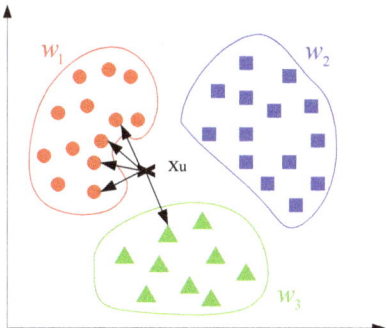

Figure 1. K-NN proximity algorithm map.

3. Short-Term Load Forecasting Model Based on W-K-NN

In order to establish the short-term load forecasting model based on the proposed W-K-NN algorithm, the specified implementation process contains the following three steps, and the associated flow chart is demonstrated in Figure 2.

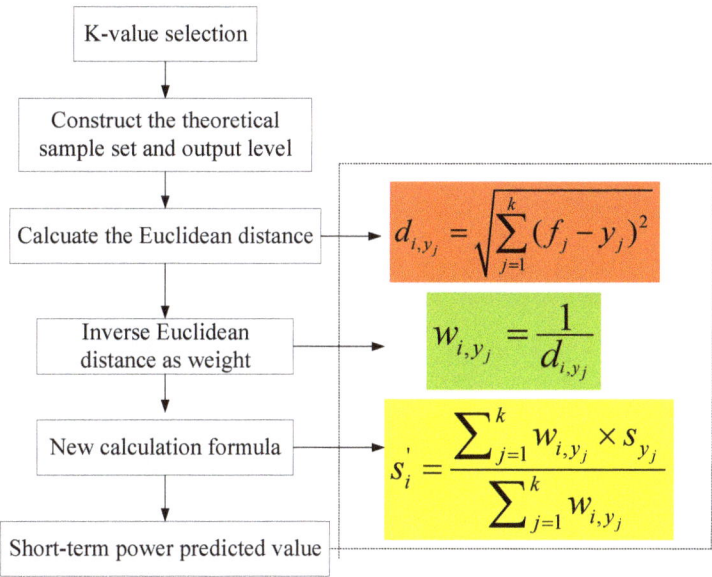

Figure 2. The flowchart of the proposed W-K-NN algorithm.

(1) Selection of the value of k. For a research sample (S) in its associated feature space, most of the K nearest adjacent samples belonged to a certain category, and the sample, S, also belonged to this category. Then, the appropriate nearest neighbor parameter, k, is selected based on the characteristics of the research samples in this category. In which the characteristics mean that similar historical electricity consumption behaviors will definitely form agglomeration in a certain space.

(2) Construct the theoretical sample set and output set. Based on the principle of random distribution (to ensure all historical electricity consumption behaviors are likely to be traversed not limited to the local optima), calculate the Euclidean distance between the forecasted data point and the known data point. Then, the reciprocal of the distance is used as the weight for each forecasted data point. Eventually, the forecasted value of each data point could be received (by Equation (6), refer Section 3.2).

(3) Forecasting accuracy evaluation. To verify the forecasting accuracy, the root mean square error (RMSE) and the normalized mean square error (NMSE) are employed as the principal evaluation indexes. They are calculated as Equations (2) and (3), respectively. The smaller the value for the forecasting errors, the more accurate the forecasting results. Thus, the forecasting results, computed by MATLAB software R2017a version, would be used to calculate the forecasting errors with the actual data values, the reliability and the forecasting accuracy of the proposed model would be further verified.

$$\text{RMSE} = \sqrt{\frac{\sum_{i=1}^{N}(a_i - s_i)^2}{N-1}} \quad (2)$$

$$\text{NMSE} = \frac{\sum_{i=1}^{N}(a_i - s_i)^2}{\sqrt{N}\sum_{i=1}^{N}(a_i - \bar{a})^2} \quad (3)$$

where s_i represents the ith forecasted electricity load value; a_i represents the ith actual electricity load value; $\bar{a}$ represents the mean value of N actual electricity load values; N represents the total number of forecasted electricity load.

To demonstrate the universal applicability of the proposed model, the data are divided into large sample and small sample, respectively. The large sample is divided by quarter (i.e., in each quarter, the data of the first two months are used as the theoretical modeling samples to forecast the electricity load values of the third month). The small sample is divided by month (i.e., in each month, the data of the first three weeks are used as the theoretical modeling samples to forecast the electricity load values of the fourth week).

The following two sub-sections would introduce the details of the first two steps.

3.1. Selection of the Value of k

Based on the K-NN algorithm, k is a user-defined neighbor parameter, which is used to classify samples to be classified according to the category label with the highest frequency of occurrence among the k training samples that are closest to the selected data point. If the value of k is too large or too small, it will increase the interference to the data and reduce the classification accuracy. In the case where the value of k is small, the complexity of the model is higher (i.e., it is easy to suffer from the over-fitting problem), and there is an increase of the estimation errors. Eventually, the forecasting results are very sensitive to the neighbor data points. On the contrary, in the case where the value of k is large, it would reduce the estimation errors; however, the approximation errors would be simultaneously increased, and the training data points farther from the input data point will also affect the forecasting results. Therefore, in general applications of the K-NN algorithm, the value of k is often set as a relatively small value, but must be an integer.

In this paper, the trial and error method was adopted to observe the experimental results and to determine the suitable value of k (i.e., the determined value of k were fixed during the forecasting processes). For example, the determined suitable values of k for small samples and large samples are illustrated in Tables 1 and 2, respectively. In which, the small samples were based on the electricity loads for three weeks; the large samples were based on two months.

Table 1. Comparison of the errors of different nearest neighbor numbers (the value of *k*) in small samples (unit: MW).

Forecasting Period	k = 1		k = 2		k = 3	
	RMSE	NMSE	RMSE	NMSE	RMSE	NMSE
Jan.	853.27	0.39	586.03	0.18	798.43	0.41
Feb.	367.07	0.08	342.87	0.07	413.52	0.12
Mar.	1081.62	0.95	636.97	0.33	903.17	0.76
Apr.	415.30	0.20	435.60	0.22	466.76	0.25
May.	347.23	0.12	415.28	0.17	423.52	0.17
Jun.	302.43	0.05	230.31	0.03	326.34	0.06
Jul.	571.71	0.32	585.92	0.34	631.41	0.39
Aug.	1146.88	1.24	825.47	0.64	780.13	0.57
Sep.	467.92	0.28	485.79	0.30	554.39	0.51
Oct.	1917.09	0.90	1885.15	0.87	1883.64	0.86
Nov.	343.61	0.10	320.80	0.08	229.73	0.04
Dec.	1324.44	0.89	1106.39	0.62	1111.05	0.63

Table 2. Comparison of the errors of different nearest neighbor numbers (the value of *k*) in large samples (unit: MW).

Forecasting Period	k = 1		k = 2		k = 3	
	RMSE	NMSE	RMSE	NMSE	RMSE	NMSE
Mar.	868.63	0.48	857.60	0.46	864.07	0.47
Jun.	1433.48	0.56	1369.56	0.45	1458.62	0.51
Sep.	497.69	0.15	553.51	0.18	656.58	0.25
Dec.	1148.63	0.99	814.08	0.50	744.02	0.42

Based on the comparison of the experimental results in Tables 1 and 2, it was found that when *k* was determined as 2, the experimental error was relatively small and the fitting effect was good.

3.2. Weights Calculation and New Forecasting Values

As mentioned in Section 3.1, if the nearest neighbor number, *k*, is determined as 2, then the Euclidean distance between the forecasted data point (s_j) and the known data point (y_j) was calculated by Equation (4).

$$d_{i,y_j} = \sqrt{\sum_{j=1}^{k} (s_j - y_j)^2} \quad (4)$$

The weight for each forecasted data point was calculated by the reciprocal of the distance, as shown in Equation (5).

$$w_{i,y_j} = \frac{1}{d_{i,y_j}} \quad (5)$$

Then, the final forecasted value (s'_i) of each data point was calculated by Equation (6).

$$s'_i = \frac{\sum_{j=1}^{k} w_{i,y_j} \times s_{y_j}}{\sum_{j=1}^{k} w_{i,y_j}} \quad (6)$$

Finally, the proposed W-K-NN model was used to forecast the electricity load values of the third month (for the large sample) and the electricity load values of the fourth week (for the small sample), respectively.

3.3. Forecasting Accuracy Evaluation Indexes

As mentioned above, RMSE (Equation (2)) and NMSE (Equation (3)) were used to evaluate the forecasting accurate level in this paper. In addition, for comparing with other models in existing paper, two other evaluation indexes were also employed: (1) the mean absolute error (MAE); and (2) the mean absolute percentage error (MAPE). They are calculated as Equations (7) and (8), respectively.

$$\text{MAE} = \frac{1}{N}\sum_{i=1}^{N}|a_i - s_i| \qquad (7)$$

$$\text{MAPE} = \frac{1}{N}\sum_{i=1}^{N}\left|\frac{a_i - s_i}{a_i}\right| \times 100\% \qquad (8)$$

where s_i represents the ith forecasted electricity load value; a_i represents the ith actual electricity load value; $\overline{a}$ represents the mean value of N actual electricity load values; N represents the total number of forecasted electricity load.

Via the accuracy evaluation indexes, such as the RMSE and the NMSE, the degree of variation and dispersion of the forecasting results could be further explained, and compared, so as to verify the reliability and accuracy of the model.

4. Results and Discussions

4.1. Forecasting Results and Analysis

The proposed W-K-NN model performed the forecasting processes and the associated results. The employed electricity load data were acquired from National Electricity Market (NEM, Australia), in total 1095 electricity load data, and data time period was from 8:00 on 1 January 2007 to 0:00 on 1 January 2008. In this paper, the collected data were based on an eight-hour scale (i.e., mean value of every eight hours), which often adopts the eight-hour work system (i.e., three shifts), as shown in Table 3. The electricity load forecasting values of the third month (for the large sample) or of the fourth week (for the small sample) were obtained by the proposed W-K-NN model, the associated forecasting results are demonstrated in Figure 3 (large sample) and Figure 4 (small sample), respectively.

Table 3. The eight-hour scale for three stages in a day.

Stages	Time Periods	Real Statuses	Measurements
Stage 1	0:00 to 8:00	The period is at night	Mean load value of these eight hours
Stage 2	8:00 to 16:00	The period is the first half of a day	
Stage 3	16:00 to 0:00	The period is the next half day	

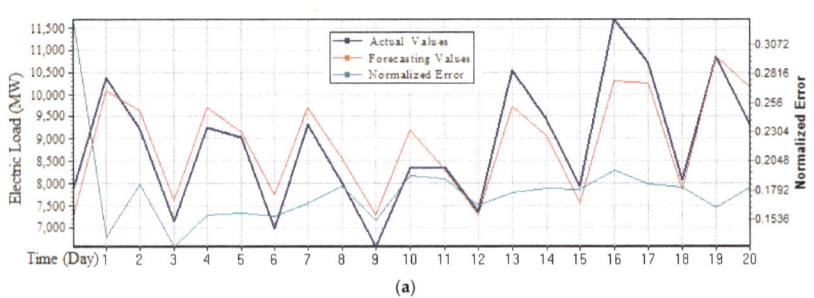

(a)

Figure 3. Cont.

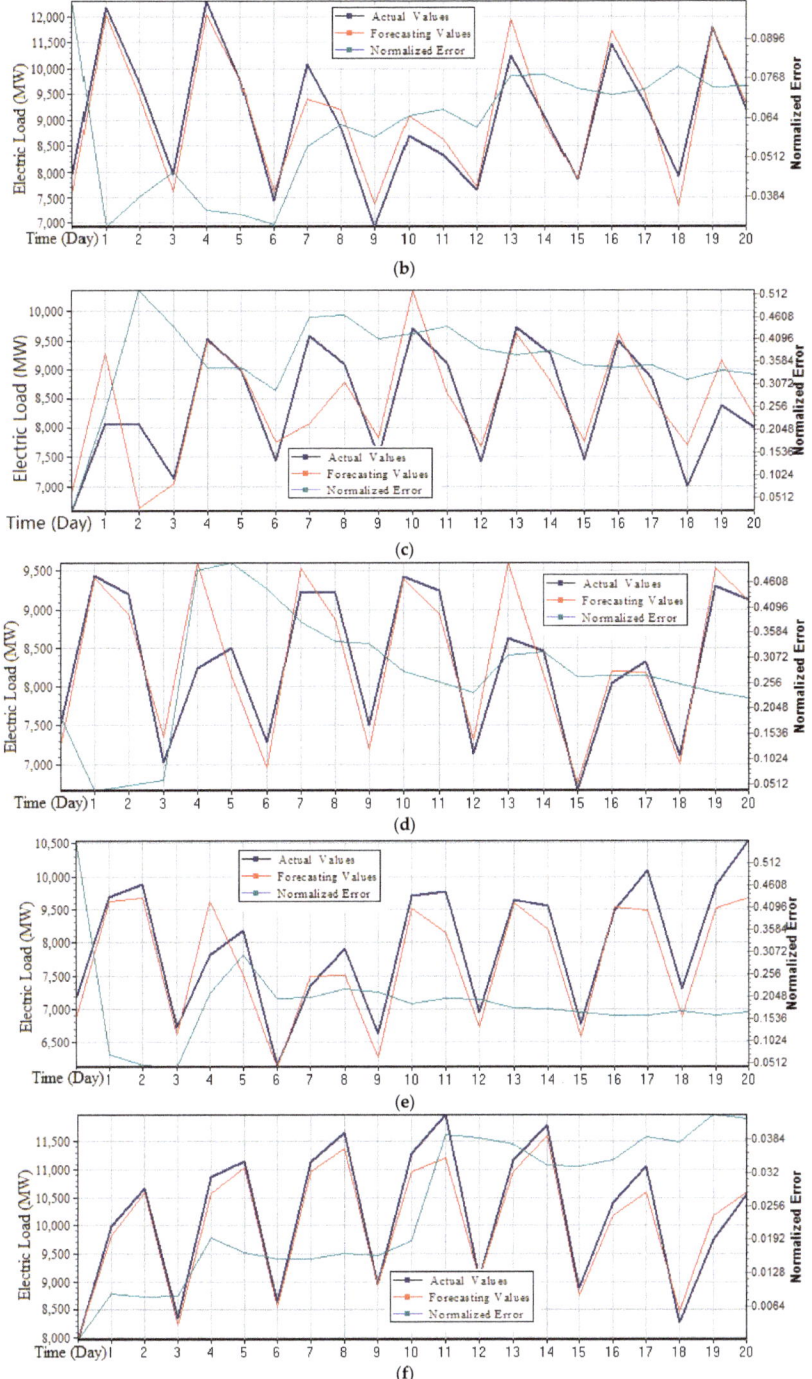

Figure 3. *Cont.*

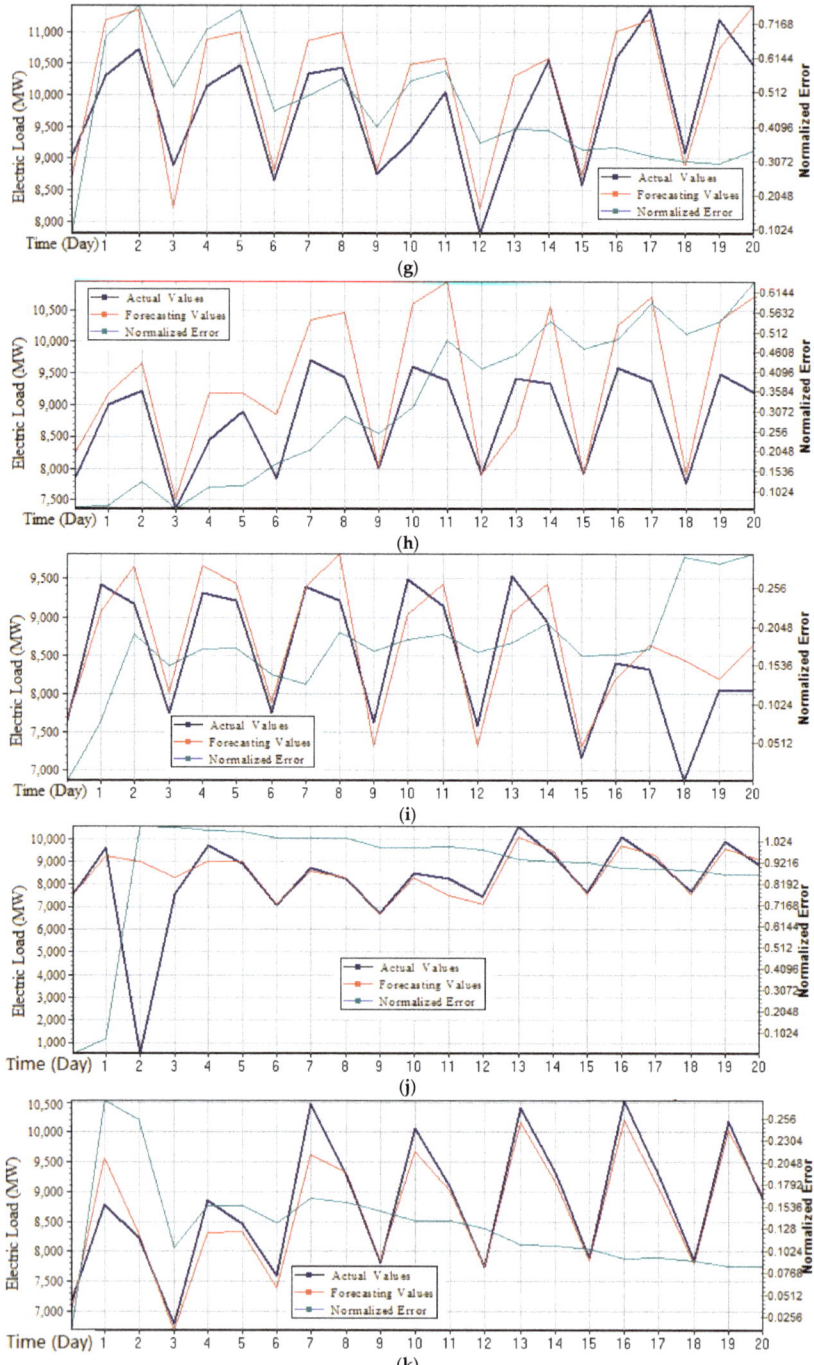

Figure 3. *Cont.*

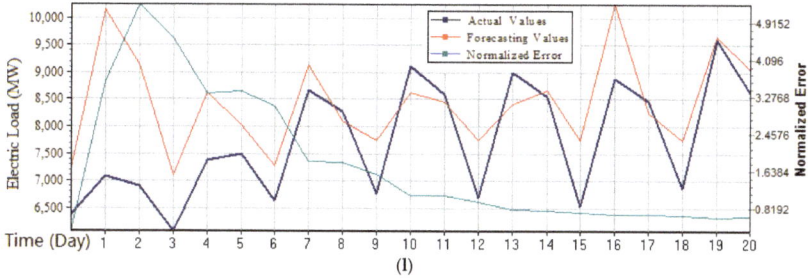

(l)

Figure 3. Forecasting results for small sample (from January to December). (**a**) January; (**b**) February; (**c**) March; (**d**) April; (**e**) May; (**f**) Jun; (**g**) July; (**h**) August; (**i**) September; (**j**) October; (**k**) November; (**l**) December.

It can be learned from Figure 3 that the forecasting curve changed periodically, due to the three-stage-division of the data in a day. The first stage was from 0:00 to 8:00 (i.e., the period is at night, also is the origin in the figures); the second stage was from 8:00 to 16:00 (i.e., that is the first half of a day, the first point in the figures); and, the third stage was from 16:00 to 0:00 (i.e., that is the next half of a day, the second point in the figures. The three stages form a cycle (i.e., one activity cycle); in addition, a work cycle contains a total of seven cycles. The specific characteristics of electricity used in a cycle could be illustrated as follows: (1) The night was from 0:00 to 8:00, the residents' daily electricity and educational electricity were at their lowest valley; the industrial electricity consumption was also small, so the lowest value of electricity consumption would occur during this period. (2) Start working at 8:00 in the morning, so the electricity consumption would gradually increase, until reaching the peak. (3) After 16:00, according to the production capacity demand plans, industrial production work load was generally reduced, so the electricity consumption would gradually decline.

Based on above observations, the trend of the curve variation in Figure 3 is in line with the actual electricity consumption. The third stage forecasting curve of each cycle in Figure 3a deviates from the actual curve, it may be caused from: (1) increased demand at this stage; or (2) a sudden increase in the workload of industrial production. Therefore, it can be learned from Figure 3 that the trend of the actual data and the forecasting data were generally consistent. Although there were certain errors, it was in line with the actual situation, and it indicates that the proposed W-K-NN model is suitable for short-term neighbor behavior detection, impact characterization, and could be weighted by the collected information, and, eventually, provide more effective and accurate forecasting results.

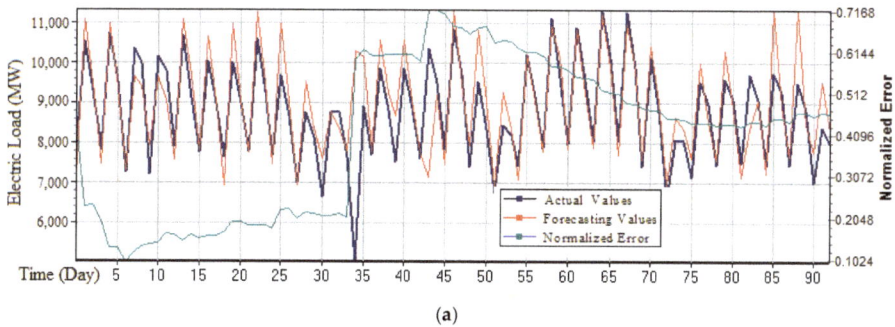

(a)

Figure 4. *Cont.*

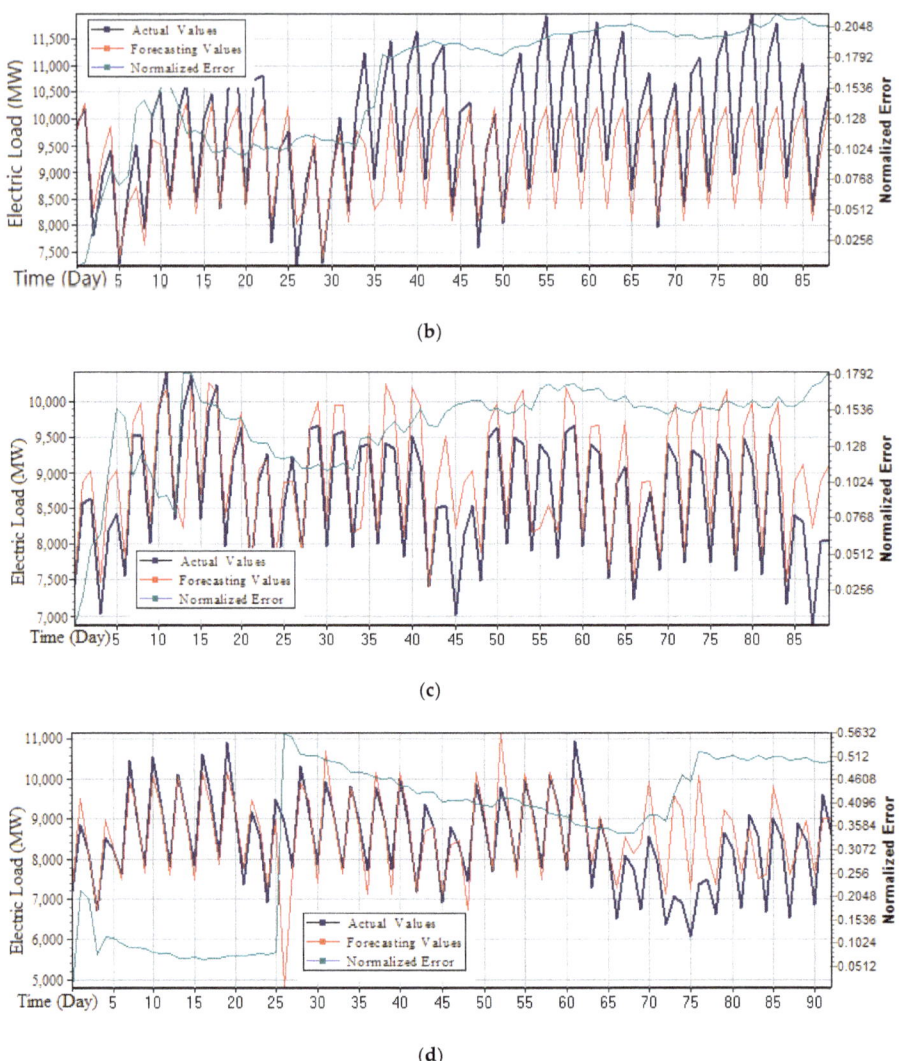

Figure 4. Forecasting results for large sample. (**a**) March, (**b**) June, (**c**) September, and (**d**) December.

It can be learned from Figure 4, that the forecasting data curve demonstrates a rising and downward trend of cyclical variation, and consists of the actual data change trend. Similar to the small sample, the day data was also divided into three stages: from 0:00 to 8:00 (the first stage), from 8:00 to 16:00 (the second stage); and from 16:00 to 0:00 (the third stage). According to the arrangement of one day's workload, it can reflect the cyclical variations, which indicates that this model can effectively reveal the rules of electricity consumption activities in each divided time period, particularly in the lowest points (i.e., the valley period). It demonstrates that this model can detect the information of the demand turning point (i.e., the demand is greater than the production capacity of the enterprise in this moment). Therefore, at this moment (valley period), for the power sector, it needs to organize production to simultaneously take into account market's needs and own resources, managers should use their relatively fixed production capacity to meet changing market needs, such as several units are used to complete the power generation task.

Based on above observations, it can be seen from the Figure 4a,d that their fitting effects were good, while in Figure 4b,c, the fitting process shows a certain deviation, especially when the demand was turning to decrease (i.e., the top point, or the peak point), the fitting performance was not good. It also demonstrates that this model found it difficult to detect the oversupply information from the market. It was also affected by uncertain factors such as vacation and work plan; however, the error was not large and was within the controllable range.

4.2. Forecasting Results Comparison

In order to demonstrate the superiority of the proposed model, the ARMA model and BPNN model were selected for comparison analysis. The comparison results for both small sample and large sample are shown in Tables 5 and 6, respectively.

The following brief the modeling processes for these two employed models.

ARMA model is one of the most common time series models, it is widely used in economic field forecasting. The ARMA model principle is to regard the data sequence formed by the forecasting index over time as a random sequence. The dependence of this random sequence reflects the continuity of the original data in time. On the one hand, the influencing factors are relatively fixed and are easily expressed and explained. On the other hand, it has its own regulations of change, and the inertia is easily described. Therefore, the ARMA model was used to compare with the proposed W-K-NN model. By using MATLAB software R2017a version, after multiple tests, the AR order was determined to be 3. The electricity load forecasting values of the third month (for the large sample) could be obtained by using the data of the first two months, or, of the fourth week (for the small sample) could be obtained by using the data of the first three weeks. Then, the forecasting accuracy indexes, the RMSE and the NMSE (Equations (2) and (3)), were employed to calculated the forecasting accuracy for each case.

In general, for the stationary time series, the forecasting model could be determined from the auto-correlation function (ACF) and the partial auto-correlation function (PACF), the judgment criteria of the ARMA model are shown in Table 4. The ACF and the PACF graphs for the small sample and the large sample are illustrated in Figures 5 and 6, respectively. It can be easily found that, in both samples, the ACF was trailing and the PACF was truncated, and there was a large attenuation after the third order (Figure 5 is outside the blue circle, while Figure 6 is outside the red circle). Thus, the AR (3) model was selected.

Table 4. Summary of ARMA model recognition graph judgment method.

Functions	AR (p)	MA (q)	ARMA (p,q)
ACF	tailing	trailing after q period	tailing
PACF	trailing after p period	tailing	tailing

Autocorrelation	Partial Correlation		AC	PAC	Q-Stat	Prob
		1	-0.480	-0.480	27.376	0.000
		2	-0.470	-0.909	53.877	0.000
		3	0.939	0.545	160.68	0.000
		4	-0.468	-0.049	187.43	0.000
		5	-0.455	-0.129	212.93	0.000
		6	0.895	-0.058	312.61	0.000
		7	-0.459	-0.171	339.07	0.000
		8	-0.433	-0.133	362.79	0.000
		9	0.870	0.008	459.70	0.000
		10	-0.440	0.041	484.71	0.000
		11	-0.415	-0.019	507.19	0.000
		12	0.849	0.051	602.03	0.000
		13	-0.437	-0.105	627.41	0.000
		14	-0.412	-0.212	650.22	0.000
		15	0.830	-0.124	743.49	0.000

Figure 5. The ACF and PACF of electricity load sequences for the small sample.

Autocorrelation	Partial Correlation		AC	PAC	Q-Stat	Prob
		1	-0.483	-0.483	17.248	0.000
		2	-0.466	-0.911	33.556	0.000
		3	0.934	0.494	100.03	0.000
		4	-0.463	0.041	116.63	0.000
		5	-0.447	-0.084	132.32	0.000
		6	0.870	-0.175	192.64	0.000
		7	-0.442	-0.207	208.49	0.000
		8	-0.411	-0.080	222.41	0.000
		9	0.825	0.036	279.28	0.000
		10	-0.415	0.086	293.89	0.000
		11	-0.389	-0.064	306.98	0.000
		12	0.787	-0.032	361.34	0.000
		13	-0.399	-0.103	375.55	0.000
		14	-0.371	-0.063	388.05	0.000
		15	0.746	-0.056	439.55	0.000

Figure 6. The ACF and PACF of electricity load sequences for the large sample.

In Figures 5 and 6, the ACF was defined as the correlation between time series y_t and y_{t-j}, as shown in Equation (9),

$$\rho_j = \frac{cov(y_t - y_{t-j})}{\sqrt{var(y_t)var(y_{t-j})}}, \quad j = 0, \pm 1, \pm 2, \ldots \ldots \tag{9}$$

The PACF was defined as the correlation between $y_{t-1}, y_{t-2}, \ldots$, and y_{t-k+1}. Q-statistics was defined as Equation (10),

$$Q = n \sum_{k=1}^{m} \hat{\rho}_k^2 \tag{10}$$

where n is the number of the forecasting points; m is the delay points.

Q-statistics would be approximated to Chi-square (χ^2) distribution with m-degree of freedom; therefore, the decision rule is "Q-statistics is larger than $\chi^2_{1-\alpha}(m)$" or "p-value is smaller than significant level (α)".

As mentioned above, the characteristics of the National Electricity Market (NEM, Australia) data set obviously reveal that a day can be regarded as a physiological cycle (the so-called micro-production cycle), and it can be divided into three stages: (1) the first stage, from 0:00 to 8:00; (2) the second stage, from 8:00 to 16:00; and (3) the third stage, from 16:00 to 0:00. The electricity load forecasting values in the third stage can be found by using the electricity load data from the first two stages, it also reflects the applicability and rationality of this model.

The BPNN model, also known as the back propagation neural network, which is, through the training of the sample data, to continuously revise the network weights and thresholds to reduce the forecasting errors along the negative gradient direction, and eventually approximate the expected output. BPNN model has been widely applied in function approximation, data compression, and time series forecasting. In order to reveal the self-adaptability and sensitivity of electricity demanding behavior, the BP neural training toolbox of the MATLAB software, R2017a version, was implemented to forecast electricity load values by using the data of the first two months (for the large sample), or using the data of the first three weeks (for the small sample). In the BPNN modeling process, network layers were chosen as three, and intermediate neurons were selected as 10. The functions for hidden layer and output layer function were chosen as follows: Tansig (Tangent S type transfer function) and Logsig (Logarithmic sigmoid transfer function) were used as the implicit layer node transfer function, and Trainglx function was selected as the output layer node transfer function. Then, the forecasting accuracy indexes for each sample were calculated for comparison.

The proposed W-K-NN model not only has several theoretical advantages, such as less training parameters and good timeliness, but also had higher forecasting accuracy than ARMA and BPNN models, for both the small sample and large sample, as shown in Tables 5 and 6, respectively. Thus, it is more suitable for solving the nonlinear problem with time-varying uncertainties in short-term load forecasting. The error values of RMSE and NMSE, obtained by the proposed W-K-NN model, in the small and large samples were both relatively small, and from Figures 3 and 4, the stability of the proposed W-K-NN model had certain volatility. However, with the better performances of these two evaluation indexes, the proposed W-K-NN model could provide more accurate forecasting results. For ARMA model, its accuracy may be affected by different parameters, due to the assumptions of the ARMA model that even if all the errors are completely objective, the forecasting process will still be affected by some uncertainties. Thus, the forecasting errors were unable to be reduced. However, the stability of the forecasting errors of the ARMA model was better, which indicates that it has its own robustness and inherent regularity. For the BPNN model, not only were the forecasting errors large, but also the stability of the forecasting errors fluctuated largely. This may be caused by the lack of training set of the BPNN model. After the case comparison and empirical investigation, the specific reasons for the above situation were found as follows: (1) The summer vacation of Australian schools is often from the middle of November to the end of February; therefore, the electricity consumption demonstrates great differences and instabilities from December to January; (2) From the view point of the annual plan of industrial production, a large amount of industrial production is generally carried out at the beginning of the year. Principal marketing activities are carried out in the middle of the year, namely clearance of stock. Additionally, some output may be increased at the end of the year. Therefore, the differences of the electricity consumption are relatively large between the beginning and the end of a year, but the middle of the year is relatively stable.

Finally, verification of the significance of the accuracy improvement of the proposed W-K-NN model was also an important issue. The forecasting accuracy comparisons in both samples among ARMA, BPNN, and W-K-NN models were implemented by the Wilcoxon signed-rank test under 0.025 and 0.05 significant levels (one-tail), respectively [29,30]. The Wilcoxon signed-rank test is a famous statistical test tool. It is suitable for pair comparison to evaluate whether their performance is different. It often uses Student's t-test as the statistics, particularly for those cases that the associate population could not be guaranteed to satisfy the normally distributed [31]. The Wilcoxon signed-rank test results for small and large samples are demonstrated in Tables 7 and 8, respectively. Obviously, the proposed models all received significant forecasting results, compared with other alternative models, under two significant levels.

Table 5. Comparison of four forecasting models for the small sample (RMSE, NMSE, MAE and MAPE). Unit: MW.

Forecasting Period	W-K-NN				K-NN				ARMA				BPNN			
	RMSE	NMSE	MAE	MAPE (%)	RMSE	NMSE	MAE	MAPE (%)	RMSE	NMSE	MAE	MAPE (%)	RMSE	NMSE	MAE	MAPE (%)
Jan.	586.03	0.34	1.04	3.87	853.27	0.39	1.17	5.93	1007.1	0.38	1.31	15.21	2263.2	0.41	1.72	20.29
Feb.	342.29	0.64	1.22	3.50	367.07	0.08	1.66	5.71	977.34	0.55	1.23	13.95	2113.39	0.58	1.71	19.28
Mar.	636.97	0.30	0.98	3.58	1081.62	0.95	1.09	5.38	782.04	0.35	1.10	13.2	1712.83	0.57	1.34	16.88
Apr.	435.60	0.87	0.97	3.96	415.30	0.20	1.08	7.94	729.12	0.34	1.02	12.8	2429.68	0.46	1.85	23.09
May.	415.28	0.08	0.95	3.77	347.23	0.12	1.03	5.70	737.64	0.39	1.06	12.1	1260.25	0.95	1.11	12.88
Jun.	271.31	0.62	1.12	4.12	302.43	0.05	1.25	6.18	1026.18	0.48	1.47	14.86	3972.30	0.49	3.03	30.45
Jul.	585.92	0.34	0.92	3.93	571.71	0.32	1.03	5.99	752.94	0.47	1.07	11.13	1350.94	0.41	1.01	11.01
Aug.	825.47	0.64	0.88	3.74	1146.88	1.24	0.93	6.61	833.6	0.41	0.91	10.61	1411.80	0.58	1.17	13.45
Sep.	485.79	0.30	0.85	3.55	467.92	0.28	0.95	5.33	654.54	0.36	0.91	11.22	1395.50	0.57	1.15	13.89
Oct.	1,885.15	0.87	1.33	4.39	1917.09	0.90	1.48	6.96	1560	0.35	1.67	90.09	2972.63	0.46	2.04	78.82
Nov.	320.80	0.08	1.10	4.01	343.61	0.10	1.23	8.27	864.72	0.29	1.13	12.87	2355.56	0.95	1.59	17.58
Dec.	1106.39	0.62	1.01	3.68	1324.44	0.89	1.04	5.52	1240.3	0.33	1.08	14.01	1489.43	0.49	1.13	16.15

Table 6. Comparison of four forecasting models for the large sample (RMSE, NMSE, MAE and MAPE). Unit: MW.

Forecasting Period	W-K-NN				K-NN				ARMA				BPNN			
	RMSE	NMSE	MAE	MAPE (%)	RMSE	NMSE	MAE	MAPE (%)	RMSE	NMSE	MAE	MAPE (%)	RMSE	NMSE	MAE	MAPE (%)
Mar.	857.63	0.46	1.03	4.37	868.63	0.48	1.42	8.02	1300.8	0.22	1.37	16.22	1793.77	0.22	1.44	16.67
Jun.	847.39	0.21	0.98	3.48	1433.48	0.56	1.45	7.33	1557.44	0.19	1.47	15.57	1199.19	0.09	1.00	10.58
Sep.	553.50	0.18	1.04	3.78	497.69	0.15	1.10	5.54	909.6	0.18	1.03	12.15	4885.83	3.39	3.84	43.06
Dec.	814.08	0.50	1.14	4.89	1148.63	0.99	1.15	9.57	1128.56	0.23	1.19	14.34	1708.64	0.23	1.41	16.21

Table 7. Wilcoxon signed-rank test for the small sample.

Compared Models	Wilcoxon Signed-Rank Test	
	$\alpha = 0.025; W = 4$	$\alpha = 0.05; W = 6$
W-K-NN vs. K-NN	2 [a]	3 [a]
W-K-NN vs. ARMA	3 [a]	2 [a]
W-K-NN vs. BPNN	3 [a]	3 [a]

[a] denotes that the W-K-NN model significantly outperforms other alternative models.

Table 8. Wilcoxon signed-rank test for the large sample.

Compared Models	Wilcoxon Signed-Rank Test	
	$\alpha = 0.025; W = 4$	$\alpha = 0.05; W = 6$
W-K-NN vs. K-NN	3 [a]	3 [a]
W-K-NN vs. ARMA	3 [a]	2 [a]
W-K-NN vs. BPNN	2 [a]	2 [a]

[a] denotes that the W-K-NN model significantly outperforms other alternative models.

In order to compare the advantages of the proposed model, a similar model (namely recency effect model) from a published paper [32] in GEFCom2012, was employed. The recency effect model was also used to extract similar features in time, the more prominent forecasting effect was reflected in summer and winter. According to [32], in summer, the electricity load data from June 1 to June 17, 2007 (17 days in total) were employed as the training set to forecast the electricity load from June 18 to June 24 (total 7 days); in winter, the electricity load data from October 21 to November 13, 2007 (24 days in total) to forecast the electricity load from November 14 to November 21, 2007 (total eight days).

The forecasting results of the proposed model are demonstrated in Figure 7. In which, it was found that the forecasting accuracy was superior at both the peak point and the valley period, particularly for the valley, its forecasting performances were very prominent. Table 9 shows the forecasting errors in terms of RMSE, NMSE, MAE, and MAPE. It can be seen that it had the same advantages and effects as the recency effect model. It was more prominent in summer, which indicates that it was superior in capturing the laws of summer economic activities.

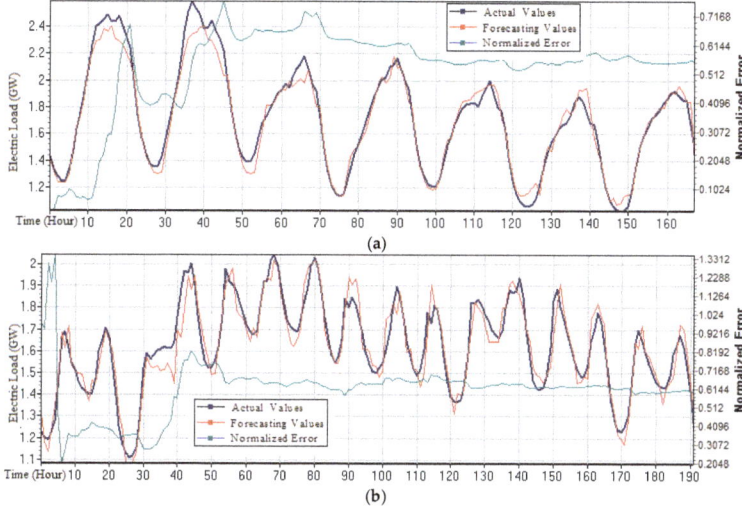

Figure 7. Forecasting results for (**a**) a week in summer and (**b**) a week in winter.

Table 9. The forecasting errors of the proposed model.

Seasons	RMSE	NMSE	MAE	MAPE *
Summer	0.0759	0.555	5.50	3.74 (3.86)
Winter	0.0636	0.595	6.71	3.90 (3.86)

*: The MAPE is based on the hourly average error values; and the value inside of () is the average error value from the recency effect model.

5. Conclusions

In this paper, the nearest neighbor distance algorithm was adopted to give the appropriate weights for each data point to construct a new short-term load forecasting model (the so-called W-K-NN model), and this proposed model was then applied to the actual short-term load forecasting job. Some important conclusions were as follows:

(1) Through the different samples verification and forecasting error analysis, it is found that the proposed W-K-NN model has higher forecasting accuracy and effectiveness. Additionally, it can be widely applied in short-term load production decision making, for example, power users can make efficient energy-saving renovation plans based on the evaluation results, and eventually improve the electricity efficiency.

(2) Compared with the ARMA model and the BPNN model, the fitting ability of the proposed W-K-NN model is more superior to these other two models. It can not only objectively and comprehensively reflect the actual energy efficiency level of power users, but also better meet the development needs of modern smart grid and intelligent control systems.

(3) In the future, authors will combine the short-term forecasting approach with the medium-short-term forecasting approach, to detect the market demand shrinking information problem, particularly for the upper-point point (peak) of the electric behavior regulations. Meanwhile, authors will also look for an optimized approach to optimize the weight, in order to improve the forecasting accuracy, for example, for the complete, the same, or very closed commodities, their weights would be set as huge or even infinite; therefore, when calculating the reciprocal distance, some constant can be added to revise the distance.

Author Contributions: G.-F.F. conceived and analyzed the experiments; Y.-H.G. and J.-M.Z. collected the data and performed the experiments; W.-C.H. conceived, designed the experiments, and wrote the paper.

Funding: Guo-Feng Fan thanks the support from the project grants: Science and Technology of Henan Province of China (No. 182400410419), the Startup Foundation for Doctors (no. PXY-BSQD-2014001), and The Foundation for Fostering the National Foundation of Pingdingshan University (No. PXY-PYJJ-2016006); Wei-Chiang Hong thanks the support from the Ministry of Science and Technology, Taiwan (MOST 106-2221-E-161-005-MY2).

Conflicts of Interest: The authors declare no conflicts of interest.

Nomenclature

X_u	an arbitrary data point
ω_1	sample category 1
ω_2	sample category 2
ω_3	sample category 3
k	the training samples that are closest to the target object
$\{y_1, y_2, \ldots, y_k\}$	the nearest k labeled data
s_i	the ith forecasted value
s_{y_j}	the forecasted value of the jth closest known data point (y_j)
S	the research sample

d_{i,y_j}	the Euclidean distance between s_j and y_j
w_{i,y_j}	the weight for each forecasted data point
s'_i	the final forecasted value of each data point
a_i	the ith actual electricity load value
$\bar{a}$	the mean value of N actual electricity load values
N	the total number of forecasted electricity load
BPNN	the back-propagation neural network
K-NN	the k-nearest neighbor
RMSE	the root mean square error
NMSE	the normalized mean square error
MAE	the mean absolute error
MAPE	the mean absolute percentage error
NEM	National Electricity Market (Australia)
ACF	the auto-correlation function
PACF	the partial auto-correlation function
ρ_j	the correlation between time series y_t and y_{t-j}
Q	the Q-statistics

References

1. Moreno, B.; Díaz, G. The impact of virtual power plant technology composition on wholesale electricity prices: A comparative study of some European Union electricity markets. *Renew. Sustain. Energy Rev.* **2019**, *99*, 100–108. [CrossRef]
2. Andini, C.; Cabral, R.; Santos, J.E. The macroeconomic impact of renewable electricity power generation projects. *Renew. Energy* **2019**, *131*, 1047–1059. [CrossRef]
3. Pickering, E.M.; Hossain, M.A.; French, R.H.; Abramson, A.R. Building electricity consumption: Data analytics of building operations with classical time series decomposition and case based subsetting. *Energy Build.* **2018**, *177*, 184–196. [CrossRef]
4. He, Y.; Qin, Y.; Wang, S.; Wang, X.; Wang, C. Electricity consumption probability density forecasting method based on LASSO-Quantile regression neural network. *Appl. Energy* **2019**, *233–234*, 565–575. [CrossRef]
5. Wu, L.; Gao, X.; Xiao, Y.; Yang, Y.; Chen, X. Using a novel multi-variable grey model to forecast the electricity consumption of Shandong Province in China. *Energy* **2018**, *157*, 327–335. [CrossRef]
6. Ding, S.; Hipel, K.W.; Dang, Y. Forecasting China's electricity consumption using a new grey prediction model. *Energy* **2018**, *149*, 314–328. [CrossRef]
7. Sujjaviriyasup, T. A new class of MODWT-SVM-DE hybrid model emphasizing on simplification structure in data pre-processing: A case study of annual electricity consumptions. *Appl. Soft Comput.* **2017**, *54*, 150–163. [CrossRef]
8. Li, M.-W.; Geng, J.; Hong, W.-C.; Zhang, Y. Hybridizing chaotic and quantum mechanisms and fruit fly optimization algorithm with least squares support vector regression model in electric load forecasting. *Energies* **2018**, *11*, 2226. [CrossRef]
9. Dong, Y.; Zhang, Z.; Hong, W.-C. A hybrid seasonal mechanism with a chaotic cuckoo search algorithm with a support vector regression model for electric load forecasting. *Energies* **2018**, *11*, 1009. [CrossRef]
10. Álvarez, F.M.; Alicia Troncoso, A.; Riquelme, J.C.; Ruiz, J.S.A. Energy time series forecasting based on pattern sequence similarity. *IEEE Trans. Knowl. Data Eng.* **2010**, *23*, 1230–1243. [CrossRef]
11. Bokde, N.; Cortés, G.A.; Álvarez, F.M.; Kulat, K. PSF: Introduction to R package for pattern sequence based forecasting algorithm. *R Journal* **2017**, *9*, 324–333. [CrossRef]
12. Altman, N.S. An introduction to kernel and nearest-neighbor nonparametric regression. *Am. Stat.* **1992**, *46*, 175–185.
13. Bhattacharya, G.; Ghosh, K.; Chowdhury, A.S. Granger causality driven AHP for feature weighted kNN. *Pattern Recognit.* **2017**, *66*, 425–436. [CrossRef]
14. Nie, C.-X.; Song, F.-T. Analyzing the stock market based on the structure of kNN network. *Chaos Solitons Fractals* **2018**, *113*, 148–159. [CrossRef]

15. Madeti, S.R.; Singh, S.N. Modeling of PV system based on experimental data for fault detection using kNN method. *Sol. Energy* **2018**, *173*, 139–151. [CrossRef]
16. Wazarkar, S.; Keshavamurthy, B.N.; Hussain, A. Region-based segmentation of social images using soft KNN algorithm. *Procedia Comput. Sci.* **2018**, *125*, 93–98. [CrossRef]
17. Zhang, S.; Cheng, D.; Deng, Z.; Zong, M.; Deng, X. A novel kNN algorithm with data-driven k parameter computation. *Pattern Recognit. Lett.* **2018**, *109*, 44–54. [CrossRef]
18. Troncoso, A.; Santos, J.M.R.; Expósito, A.G. Electricity market price forecasting based on weighted nearest neighbors techniques. *IEEE Trans. Power Syst.* **2007**, *22*, 1294–1301.
19. Martín H, J.A.; de Lope, J.; Maravall, D. Robust high performance reinforcement learning through weighted k-nearest neighbors. *Neurocomputing* **2011**, *74*, 1251–1259. [CrossRef]
20. Chen, Y.; Hao, Y. A feature weighted support vector machine and K-nearest neighbor algorithm for stock market indices prediction. *Expert Syst. Appl.* **2017**, *80*, 340–355. [CrossRef]
21. Biswas, N.; Chakraborty, S.; Mullick, S.S.; Das, S. A parameter independent fuzzy weighted k-nearest neighbor classifier. *Pattern Recognit. Lett.* **2018**, *101*, 80–87. [CrossRef]
22. Su, M.-Y. Real-time anomaly detection systems for Denial-of-Service attacks by weighted k-nearest-neighbor classifiers. *Expert Syst. Appl.* **2011**, *38*, 3492–3498. [CrossRef]
23. Lei, Y.; Zuo, M.J. Gear crack level identification based on weighted K nearest neighbor classification algorithm. *Mech. Syst. Signal Process.* **2009**, *23*, 1535–1547. [CrossRef]
24. Ren, D.; Hui, M.; Hu, N.; Zhan, T. A weighted sparse neighbor representation based on Gaussian kernel function to face recognition. *Optik* **2018**, *167*, 7–14. [CrossRef]
25. Mateos-García, D.; García-Gutiérrez, J.; Riquelme-Santos, J.C. On the evolutionary weighting of neighbours and features in the k-nearest neighbour rule. *Neurocomputing* **2019**, *326–327*, 54–60. [CrossRef]
26. Llames, R.T.; Chacón, R.P.; Troncoso, A.A.; Álvarez, F.M. Big data time series forecasting based on nearest neighbours distributed computing with Spark. *Knowl.-Based Syst.* **2018**, *161*, 12–25. [CrossRef]
27. Rana, M.; Koprinska, I.; Troncoso, A.; Agelidis, V.G. Extended weighted nearest neighbor for electricity load forecasting. *Lect. Notes Comput. Sci.* **2016**, *9887*, 299–307.
28. Troncoso, A.; Riquelme, J.C.; Santos, J.M.R.; Martinez-Ramos, J.L.; Gomez-Exposito, A. Electricity market price forecasting: Neural networks versus weighted-distance k nearest neighbours. *Lect. Notes Comput. Sci.* **2002**, *2453*, 321–330.
29. Derrac, J.; García, S.; Molina, D.; Herrera, F. A practical tutorial on the use of nonparametric statistical tests as a methodology for comparing evolutionary and swarm intelligence algorithms. *Swarm Evol. Comput.* **2011**, *1*, 3–18. [CrossRef]
30. Fan, G.F.; Peng, L.L.; Hong, W.C. Short term load forecasting based on phase space reconstruction algorithm and bi-square kernel regression model. *Appl. Energy* **2018**, *224*, 13–33. [CrossRef]
31. Lowry, R. *Concepts & Applications of Inferential Statistics*; Vassar College: New York, NY, USA, 2011.
32. Wang, P.; Liu, B.; Hong, T. Electric load forecasting with recency effect: A big data approach. *Int. J. Forecast.* **2016**, *32*, 585–597. [CrossRef]

© 2019 by the authors. Licensee MDPI, Basel, Switzerland. This article is an open access article distributed under the terms and conditions of the Creative Commons Attribution (CC BY) license (http://creativecommons.org/licenses/by/4.0/).

Article

An Adaptive Hybrid Learning Paradigm Integrating CEEMD, ARIMA and SBL for Crude Oil Price Forecasting

Jiang Wu [1,2], Yu Chen [1], Tengfei Zhou [1] and Taiyong Li [1,2,*]

[1] School of Economic Information Engineering, Southwestern University of Finance and Economics, Chengdu 611130, China; wuj_t@swufe.edu.cn (J.W.); aa5959562@163.com (Y.C.); ztf10708@163.com (T.Z.)
[2] Institute of Chinese Payment System, Southwestern University of Finance and Economics, 55 Guanghuacun Street, Chengdu 610074, China
* Correspondence: litaiyong@gmail.com; Tel.: +86-28-8709-2220

Received: 26 February 2019; Accepted: 25 March 2019; Published: 1 April 2019

Abstract: Crude oil is one of the main energy sources and its prices have gained increasing attention due to its important role in the world economy. Accurate prediction of crude oil prices is an important issue not only for ordinary investors, but also for the whole society. To achieve the accurate prediction of nonstationary and nonlinear crude oil price time series, an adaptive hybrid ensemble learning paradigm integrating complementary ensemble empirical mode decomposition (CEEMD), autoregressive integrated moving average (ARIMA) and sparse Bayesian learning (SBL), namely CEEMD-ARIMA&SBL-SBL (CEEMD-A&S-SBL), is developed in this study. Firstly, the decomposition method CEEMD, which can reduce the end effects and mode mixing, was employed to decompose the original crude oil price time series into intrinsic mode functions (*IMF*s) and one residue. Then, ARIMA and SBL with combined kernels were applied to predict target values for the residue and each single *IMF* independently. Finally, the predicted values of the above two models for each component were adaptively selected based on the training precision, and then aggregated as the final forecasting results using SBL without kernel-tricks. Experiments were conducted on the crude oil spot prices of the West Texas Intermediate (WTI) and Brent crude oil to evaluate the performance of the proposed CEEMD-A&S-SBL. The experimental results demonstrated that, compared with some state-of-the-art prediction models, CEEMD-A&S-SBL can significantly improve the prediction accuracy of crude oil prices in terms of the root mean squared error (RMSE), the mean absolute percent error (MAPE), and the directional statistic (Dstat).

Keywords: crude oil price forecasting; time series forecasting; hybrid model; complementary ensemble empirical mode decomposition (CEEMD); sparse Bayesian learning (SBL)

1. Introduction

With the increase of global energy consumption, energy demand will continue to grow, according to the recent British Petroleum (BP) energy outlook 2018 [1]. Crude oil, as one of the fundamental energies, plays a key role in global economic growth and social development. The tendency of crude oil price has been paid world-wide attention with the increase of importance of petroleum in the international political and economic environment. Therefore, the accurate prediction of crude oil prices would have great economic impacts and practical significance. However, crude oil prices are influenced by a variety of factors, such as climate change, stock levels, technology development, supply and demand, market speculation, substitution with other energy forms, geopolitical conflicts and wars, etc., which cause the high nonstationary and nonlinear characteristics of the price series [2–5]. Therefore, it is a great challenge for the accurate forecast of crude oil prices.

In the past decades, a variety of models have been proposed for forecasting crude oil prices. These prediction models can be generally classified into two main categories: (1) statistical /econometric models and (2) artificial intelligence (AI) models [5,6]. Statistical/econometric models used in crude oil forecasting include vector autoregressive (VAR) models [7,8], error correction models (ECM) [9], random walk model (RWM) [10], autoregressive integrated moving average (ARIMA) model [11,12], generalized autoregressive conditional heteroskedasticity (GARCH) model [13,14], etc. For instance, Baumeister and Kilian indicated that VAR models were capable of achieving lower mean squared prediction error (MSPE) at short horizons than autoregressive (AR) and autoregressive moving average (ARMA) models [7,8]. Lanza et al. investigated crude oil and predicted crude oil prices from January 2002 to June 2002 using ECM [9]. The ARIMA model was selected to forecast and analyze the macroeconomic impact of oil price fluctuations in Ghana using annual data from 2000 to 2011 [12]. Morana applied GARCH to crude oil price forecasting and the experimental results suggested that the forecasting method could gain a performance measure for the forward price [13]. Furthermore, there are a vast number of studies that assess the volatility of crude oil market via comparing the statistical/econometric models. For example, Hou and Suardi showed the nonparametric GARCH model outperformed the commonly used parametric GARCH model in forecasting accuracy of oil price return volatility [14]. Mohammadi and Su investigated the forecasting accuracies of four models—GARCH, exponential GRACH (EGARCH), asymmetric power autoregressive conditional heteroskedasticity model (APARCH) and fractionally integrated GARCH (FIGARCH) and the forecasting results demonstrated that the APARCH model outperformed the others in most cases [15]. Wei et al. used linear and nonlinear GARCH-class models and found that the nonlinear GARCH-class models exhibited better forecasting performance than the linear ones [16]. Generally, the above statistical/econometric models achieve good forecasting accuracies when the original time series is linear or near linear. However, as we all know, crude oil prices have highly complex characteristics of nonlinearity and nonstationarity, which makes it hard to employ these statistical/econometric models to achieve satisfactory forecasting performance.

Due to the drawbacks of the statistical/econometric models, a variety of AI models, including genetic algorithm (GA), support vector regression (SVR), artificial neural networks (ANN) and sparse Bayesian learning (SBL), have been increasingly used in crude oil price forecasting. Kulkarni and Haidar used a multilayer feed forward neural network to forecast the direction of crude oil price at short horizons [17]. Mirmirani and Li applied VAR and GA-based ANN to forecast the U.S. oil price movements and the forecasting results suggested that the GA-based ANN model noticeably outperformed the VAR model [18]. Haidar et al. employed a three-layer feed forward neural network to predict crude oil prices in the short-term and results showed that feed forward neural networks were capable of forecasting crude oil prices with high accuracy [19]. Mostafa and El-Masry used ANN and gene expression programming (GEP) to forecast crude oil prices from January 2, 1986 to June 12, 2012 and the results revealed that the GEP technique outperformed the ANN and ARIMA models [20]. Xie et al. compared the forecasting accuracy of support vector machine (SVM) with those of ARIMA and back propagation neural network (BPNN) for the crude oil price prediction and the experiment results showed that SVM outperformed the other two methods [21]. Li and Ge employed SVR with a dynamic correction factor to predict crude oil prices [22]. Mustaffa et al. presented least squares support vector machine (LSSVM) with enhanced artificial bee colony (eABC-LSSVM) to predict crude oil prices and the proposed eABC-LSSVM showed higher prediction accuracy compared with LSSVM, ABC-LSSVM and GA-LSSVM [23]. Khashman and Nwulu compared the forecasting performance of SVM with that of neural networks for the crude oil price prediction and the experiment results showed that the neural networks outperformed SVM with minimal computational expense [24]. Furthermore, time series forecasting can be seen as a typical problem of regression. Therefore, Li et al. proposed that any regression approach in the signal recovery and AI could be applied to forecast time series [2]. SBL without kernel-tricks and SBL with kernel-tricks were utilized to predict crude oil spot prices and the experiment results demonstrated that SBL was promising for predicting crude oil prices compared with traditional econometric models and AI models [2,6].

However, the above AI models also have their own limitations. SVR, GP and ANN are sensitive to parameter optimization, while the ANN model easily traps into over-fitting and local minima [3]. To address the limitations, some hybrid forecasting models have been proposed to forecast crude oil prices and achieve promising performance recently. Wang et al. proposed a novel hybrid AI system framework for crude oil price forecasting by means of ANN and rule based expert system (RES) [25]. Amin-Naseri and Gharacheh incorporated feed-forward neural networks, k-means clustering and genetic algorithm, and developed a hybrid AI model for monthly crude oil price forecasting [26]. Tehrani and Khodayar proposed a novel hybrid optimum model based on GA and feed forward neural network (FNN) for crude oil spot price forecasting [27]. The advantages of the above hybrid models are capable of overcoming the weakness of individual models and achieving better forecasting performance.

Due to the complexity of signal, the scholars in the field of signal processing usually use signal decomposition approaches to decompose the original signal into several components for better performance of classification and regression [28–30]. This idea can be used for reference in crude oil price forecasting because of the nonlinearity and nonstationarity of crude oil price series. By decomposing an original time series into a group of relatively simple sub-modes with stationary fluctuation, multiscale ensemble prediction was capable of enhancing the forecasting performance [31]. A kind of "divide-and-conquer" framework of "decomposition and ensemble" was introduced to effectively improve prediction accuracy, especially for the series data with nonlinearity and nonstationarity [32]. The main idea of the "decomposition and ensemble" framework is to decompose the original complex prediction task into several relatively simple subtasks, then, each subtask is predicted by a single forecasting method, and finally, these forecasting results are aggregated as the final forecasting results [3,33,34]. Therefore, the framework of "decomposition and ensemble" can effectively simplify the modeling complexity. Furthermore, it has been reported that this framework can achieve higher prediction accuracy, better directional predictions and higher robustness, showing that it is promising for forecasting complex time series [35–39]. The main data decomposition techniques include Wavelet Decomposition (WD), empirical mode decomposition (EMD), ensemble EMD (EEMD), and complete ensemble EMD (CEEMD), independent component analysis (ICA), etc. For example, Jammazi and Aloui used WD to decompose the crude oil prices into sub-modes, forecasted the sub-mode prices using neural network model, and assembled the final forecasting results [35]. Zheng et al. built a hybrid prediction model for short-term load forecasting by means of EMD, similar days selection and long short-term memory (LSTM) neural networks [36]. Although these decomposed sub-modes have their own data characteristics, most of the existing "decomposition and ensemble" models predicted all the sub-modes employing a uniform model rather than choosing an appropriate one for each sub-mode. Therefore, some studies improved the prediction steps [31,37–39]. The obtained sub-modes are identified as the differentiated components according to their own characteristics, and then, an appropriate prediction model is chosen to predict these sub-modes. For instance, Zhu et al. employed LSSVM to predict the low-frequency components and ARIMA or GARCH to forecast the high-frequency components of energy prices [31,37]. Fan et al. applied SVR model to forecast the high-frequency components and AR model to forecast the residuals of electric load series [38]. Zhang et al. presented a particle swarm optimization-based least square support vector machine (LSSVM–PSO) for nonlinear component forecasting and GARCH model for time-varying component forecasting respectively [39]. Although the above models achieve better forecasting performance compared with single prediction models, differentiated components need to be distinguished before choosing appropriate prediction models. Therefore, model selection for each component is of utmost importance for the forecasting performance. There are two major drawbacks in existing studies. First, there is no general rule about how to recognize differentiated components. The main methods are based on the frequency or linearity of sub-modes. Second, there is no general method to choose appropriate forecasting models. For example, Zhu et al. selected ARIMA or GARCH to predict the high-frequency components and LSSVM to forecast the low-frequency ones [31,37]; while Fan et al. employed SVR for high-frequency component prediction and AR model for low-frequency component prediction [38].

To address the existing drawbacks and improve the forecasting performance, this research proposes an adaptive hybrid ensemble leaning model incorporating CEEMD, ARIMA and SBL with kernel-tricks, and SBL without kernel-tricks, namely CEEMD-ARIMA&SBL-SBL (CEEMD-A&S-SBL), to improve the forecasting accuracy of nonstationary and nonlinear crude oil prices. The raw series of crude oil prices is firstly decomposed into several components using CEEMD, which can effectively reduce the end effects and mode mixing. Then, without considering the data characteristics of each component, ARIMA and SBL with combined kernel-tricks are applied to forecast each component independently. Finally, the two groups of predicted values of each component are selected based on the training precision, and then aggregated as the final forecasting results using SBL without kernel-tricks, so as to further improve the prediction accuracy of crude oil prices. Empirically, the proposed CEEMD-A&S-SBL has been tested with the data of the West Texas Intermediate (WTI) and Brent spot crude oil prices. Compared with traditional prediction models, the experimental results show that the proposed model can cope well with the nonlinearity and nonstationarity of crude oil prices and achieve promising performance. The main contributions of this research lie in three aspects: (1) a novel adaptive hybrid forecasting model for crude oil prices that integrates CEEMD, ARIMA and SBL was proposed. The proposed prediction model CEEMD-A&S-SBL adaptively selects an appropriate prediction model for forecasting each decomposed component without identifying its characteristic in advance. To our knowledge, it is the first time that adaptive hybrid model selection for the forecasting of components (*IMFs* and residue) is developed in crude oil price forecasting. (2) Experiments were conducted on the WTI and Brent spot crude oil prices, and the experimental results demonstrated that the proposed prediction model outperformed several state-of-the-art models for forecasting crude oil prices. (3) We further analyzed some characteristics of the proposed model for forecasting crude oil prices, including CEEMD parameter settings, individual component prediction model and selection and the weights of components in aggregation.

The rest of this paper is organized as follows. Section 2 briefly introduces CEEMD and SBL. Section 3 gives the description of the proposed CEEMD-A&S-SBL method in detail, including CEEMD, SBL with combined kernel-tricks and the ensemble method based on SBL without kernel-tricks. Section 4 reports experimental results and evaluates the proposed model using several metrics, followed by conclusions in Section 5.

2. Preliminaries

2.1. The Framework of Decomposition and Ensemble

In view of the highly complex characteristics of nonlinearity and nonstationarity, it is hard to achieve satisfactory predictive performance on the original time series. Therefore, the framework of decomposition and ensemble has been presented for forecasting time series [32]. This framework takes the idea of divide and conquer, and includes three stages: (1) dividing the original complex prediction task into several relatively simple subtasks using a data decomposition technique; (2) predicting each subtask by a single forecasting method individually; and (3) aggregating individual forecasting results as the final forecasting results.

2.2. Complete Ensemble Empirical Mode Decomposition

Complete ensemble empirical mode decomposition (CEEMD) [40] is proposed from the decomposition techniques of ensemble empirical mode decomposition (EEMD) [41] and empirical mode decomposition (EMD) [42]. EMD is a kind of adaptive time-frequency data analysis method developed for nonlinear and nonstationary signal or time series analysis and has been widely used for engineering, sciences, financial data analysis, etc. However, there is a drawback of mode-mixing in EMD, where widely disparate scales could appear in one intrinsic mode function (*IMF*) component. In order to cope with the mode mixing problem, the noise added method of ensemble EMD (EEMD) has been proposed. Although EEMD has effectively resolved the mode mixing problem, the residue noise in the signal reconstruction has been raised. Hence, CEEMD was developed, where a different noise realization is added at each phase of the decomposition process and a unique residue is calculated to generate each mode. The decomposition result of CEEMD is complete, with a negligible error [40]. Let us define the operator $E_j(\cdot)$, which generates the *j*-th mode obtained by EMD when a signal is given. Let w^i be white noise with $N(0, 1)$, and allow the ε_i coefficients to select the Signal-Noise Ratio (SNR) at each stage. If $x[n]$ is the original signal, the decomposition procedure of CEEMD method can be described as follows:

Step 1: repeat the decomposition *I* times using different noise realizations and calculate the ensemble average as the first mode of the signal:

$$IMF_1[n] = \frac{1}{I} \sum_{i=1}^{I} E_1\left(x[n] + \varepsilon_0 w^i[n]\right) \qquad (1)$$

Step 2: at the first stage ($k = 1$), compute the first signal residue $r_1[n]$:

$$r_1[n] = x[n] - IMF_1[n] \qquad (2)$$

Step 3: decompose realizations $r_1[n] + \varepsilon_1 E_1(w^i[n])$, $i = 1, \ldots, I$, until they satisfy their first *IMF* conditions. Define the ensemble average as the second mode:

$$IMF_2[n] = \frac{1}{I} \sum_{i=1}^{I} E_1\left(r_1[n] + \varepsilon_1 E_1\left(w^i[n]\right)\right) \qquad (3)$$

Step 4: For $k = 2, \ldots, K$, calculate the *k*-th residue:

$$r_k[n] = r_{(k-1)}[n] - IMF_k[n] \qquad (4)$$

Step 5: decompose realizations $r_k[n] + \varepsilon_k E_k(w^i[n])$, $i = 1, \ldots, I$, and calculate their ensemble average:

$$IMF_{(k+1)}[n] = \frac{1}{I} \sum_{i=1}^{I} E_1\left(r_k[n] + \varepsilon_k E_k\left(w^i[n]\right)\right) \qquad (5)$$

Step 6: The sifting process continues until the residue does not have more than two extrema. The final residue satisfies:

$$R[n] = x[n] - \sum_{k=1}^{K} IMF_k \qquad (6)$$

Thus, the original signal can be expressed as:

$$x[n] = \sum_{k=1}^{K} IMF_k + R[n] \qquad (7)$$

In summary, the original signal $x[n]$ can be expressed as the sum of K IMF_j ($j = 1, 2, \ldots, K$) and one residue R. Generally, these decomposed components, including K IMFs and one residue, are simpler than the original complex crude oil price series. Thus the hard forecasting task of crude oil prices is divided into forecasting relatively simple components.

2.3. Sparse Bayesian Learning

Sparse Bayesian learning (SBL) [43], a Bayesian competitor of the traditional SVM, was first developed as a machine learning method with kernel-tricks, which is also known as the relevance vector machine (RVM). Owing to its good performance in regression and classification, SBL has been applied in various fields, such as streamflow simulation [44], face recognition [45], fault diagnosis [46], object localization [47], signal recovery [48], energy price prediction [2,6], etc. Compared with SVM, SBL not only achieves comparable classification or prediction accuracy, but also performs better in sparse property, computational cost and generalization ability [49].

Given a set of samples $\{x_i, y_i\}_{i=1}^{N}$, where $x_i \in R^d$ represent d-dimensional input vectors and $y_i \in R$ indicate real target values, and assuming that $t_i = f(x_i; w) + \epsilon_i$ with $\epsilon_i \sim N(0, \sigma^2)$, the SBL model for regression can be formulated as:

$$y = f(x; w) = \sum_{i=1}^{N} w_i K(x, x_i) + w_0 \tag{8}$$

where $K(x, x_i)$ represents a kernel function, and w_i denotes the weight of the kernel. The learning process of SBL is to seek the parameters of the function $f(x; w)$. SBL model usually has the sparsity of kernel function, because it inducts a priori distribution of the weights.

Assuming the samples $\{x_i, y_i\}_{i=1}^{N}$ are independently generated, the probability of y is expressed as follows:

$$p(y|w, \sigma^2) = (2\pi\sigma^2)^{-\frac{N}{2}} \exp\left(-\frac{\|t - \Phi w\|^2}{2\sigma^2}\right) \tag{9}$$

where $y = (y_1, y_2, \ldots, y_N)^T$, $w = (w_1, w_2, \ldots, w_N)^T$, and the Φ is a design matrix having the size $N \times (N+1)$:

$$\Phi = [\phi(x_1), \phi(x_2), \ldots, \phi(x_N)]^T \tag{10}$$

$$\phi(x_n) = [1, K(x_n, x_1), K(x_n, x_2), \ldots, K(x_n, x_N)]^T \tag{11}$$

With as many parameters as the training samples, simple making the probability w and σ^2 maximum will lead to over-fitting. To deal with this, Tipping imposed a prior probability distribution over the weight $w_i \sim N(0, \alpha_i^{-1})$, where α is an $N + 1$ vector named hyperparameters [43]. Assuming the hyperparameter is Gamma distributed, the associated weights will be concentrated at zero due to the posteriori distribution of hyperparameters, which will lead to the "irrelevance" of most input vectors.

Like SVM, the kernel function in SBL plays a key role, which greatly influences the prediction performance of SBL. Li et al. have indicated that SBL with combined kernels outperformed that with a single fixed kernel in forecasting crude oil prices [6]. Therefore, SBL with combined kernel-tricks was adopted to forecast the sub-modes in this study.

In addition, SBL without kernel-tricks has also been proved effective in sparse signal recovery and time series prediction [2,50]. SBL without kernel-tricks can be formulated by Equation (12):

$$y = Dw + \epsilon \tag{12}$$

where $D \in R^{N \times M}$ is a matrix with N samples and M attributes; $y = [y_1, y_2, \ldots, y_N]^T$ is a vector of targets, $w = [w_1, w_2, \ldots, w_M]^T$ is the weight vector to represent the weights of each column in D. The training goal of SBL is to seek an optimal vector of weights w [50].

In order to obtain sparse solutions, SBL estimates a parameterized prior over weights, which is expressed as follows:

$$p(w; \gamma) = \prod_{i=1}^{M} (2\pi\gamma_i)^{-\frac{1}{2}} \exp\left(-\frac{w_i^2}{2\gamma_i}\right) \tag{13}$$

where $\gamma = [\gamma_1, \gamma_2, \ldots, \gamma_M]^T$ is a vector of M hyperparameters.

Compared with kernel version, SBL without kernel-tricks has a faster training speed. Furthermore, the weights found by SBL can reflect the importance of each component for forecasting crude oil prices, which make the aggregation method better interpretability. Therefore, we chose SBL without the kernel-trick to aggregate the prediction values of individual components to obtain the final prediction results of crude oil prices in this study.

3. The Proposed CEEMD-A&S-SBL Model

Inspired by the framework of "decomposition and ensemble", this study proposes an adaptive hybrid ensemble model that integrates CEEMD, ARIMA and SBL with combined kernel-tricks, and SBL without kernel-tricks, termed as CEEMD-A&S-SBL, to forecast crude oil prices. The proposed model is shown in Figure 1, which includes three stages:

Stage 1: Decomposition. CEEMD is used to decompose the original series of crude oil prices $x(n)$ into two parts: (1) K IMF components IMF_j ($j = 1, 2, \ldots, K$); (2) one residue component R.

Stage 2: Individual forecasting. The data samples in each decomposed component are respectively divided into a training set and a test set. The prediction models of ARIMA and SBL with combined kernel-tricks are built on the training set independently, and then, these two prediction models are applied to the test set separately.

Stage 3: Ensemble forecasting. These two groups of prediction results of all components are adaptively selected based on the training precision, and then are aggregated by SBL without kernel-tricks as the final forecasting results.

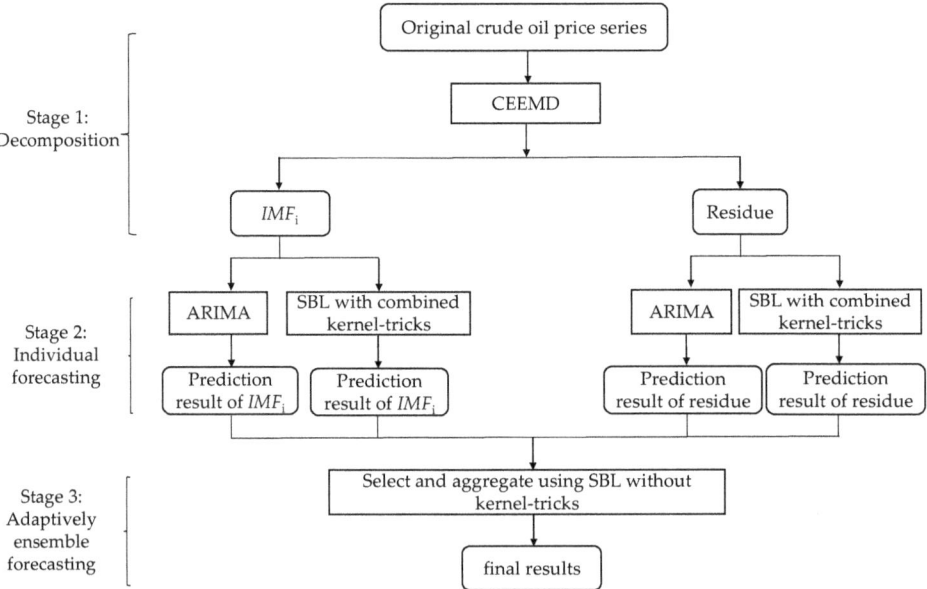

Figure 1. The flowchart for the CEEMD-A&S-SBL. CEEMD: complete ensemble empirical mode decomposition; A&S: autoregressive integrated moving average (ARIMA) and sparse Bayesian learning (SBL); SBL: sparse Bayesian learning.

The proposed CEEMD-A&S-SBL employs the strategy of "divide and conquer". The complex task of crude oil price forecasting is divided into a group of relatively simple sub-tasks of forecasting components independently. The CEEMD-A&S-SBL firstly applies CEEMD to decompose the original series of crude oil price into several components (IMFs and one residue), and each component contains some specific characteristics of crude oil prices. Generally, the first several IMFs imply high-frequency parts, while the last ones and the residue involve the low-frequency parts of crude oil prices. Secondly, the ARIMA and SBL with a combined kernel are independently applied to each component without distinguishing between high- and low-frequency in the prediction stage. We selected these two models because each belongs to one of the two typical types of differential prediction models (i.e., statistical method and AI method). ARIMA is one of the most representative statistical methods and SBL with a combined kernel, as a type of AI method, has been proven promising for crude oil price forecasting [6]. Finally, the predicted values of the above two models for each component are adaptively selected based on the training precision, and then are aggregated as the final forecasting results of crude oil prices using SBL without kernel-tricks. This framework of "decomposition and ensemble" makes it possible for the CEEMD-A&S-SBL to improve the performance of crude oil price forecasting.

Significantly, some recent studies applied differential models to forecast the high-frequency and low-frequency components separately. These studies obviously differed from the current research with respect to individual component forecasting and ensemble in that (1) they distinguished the decomposed crude oil prices into two parts: high-frequency and low-frequency components, and employed appropriate models to forecast the two parts; (2) they aggregated the prediction results of all components as the final forecasting results using simple addition or learning methods. In contrast, the current study uses two kinds of differential prediction models (i.e., ARIMA and SBL with combined kernel-tricks) to forecast each single component independently without identifying high-frequency and low-frequency, and then adaptively selects and aggregates the predicted values of two models as the final forecasting results of crude oil prices.

4. Experimental Results

4.1. Data Description

In order to better evaluate the performance of the proposed CEEMD-A&S-SBL, this study collected WTI and Brent crude oil spot prices in view of their representative significance in global crude oil markets. The daily closing price data set is divided into two subsets: the first 80% of sample data for training and the last 20% for testing. The training set is used to train models and optimize parameters, and the testing data set is applied to evaluate the performance of established prediction models. The divided samples of crude oil prices are shown in Table 1.

Table 1. Samples of crude oil prices.

Market		Size	Date
West Texas Intermediate (WTI)	Sample set	8312	2 January 1986~17 December 2018
	Training set	6649	2 January 1986~9 May 2012
	Testing set	1663	10 May 2012~17 December 2018
Brent	Sample set	8018	20 May 1987~17 December 2018
	Training set	6414	20 May 1987~28 August 2012
	Testing set	1604	29 August 2012~17 December 2018

The original crude oil price series and corresponding components (i.e., *IMF*s and residue) decomposed by CEEMD of WTI and Brent are demonstrated in Figures 2 and 3, respectively.

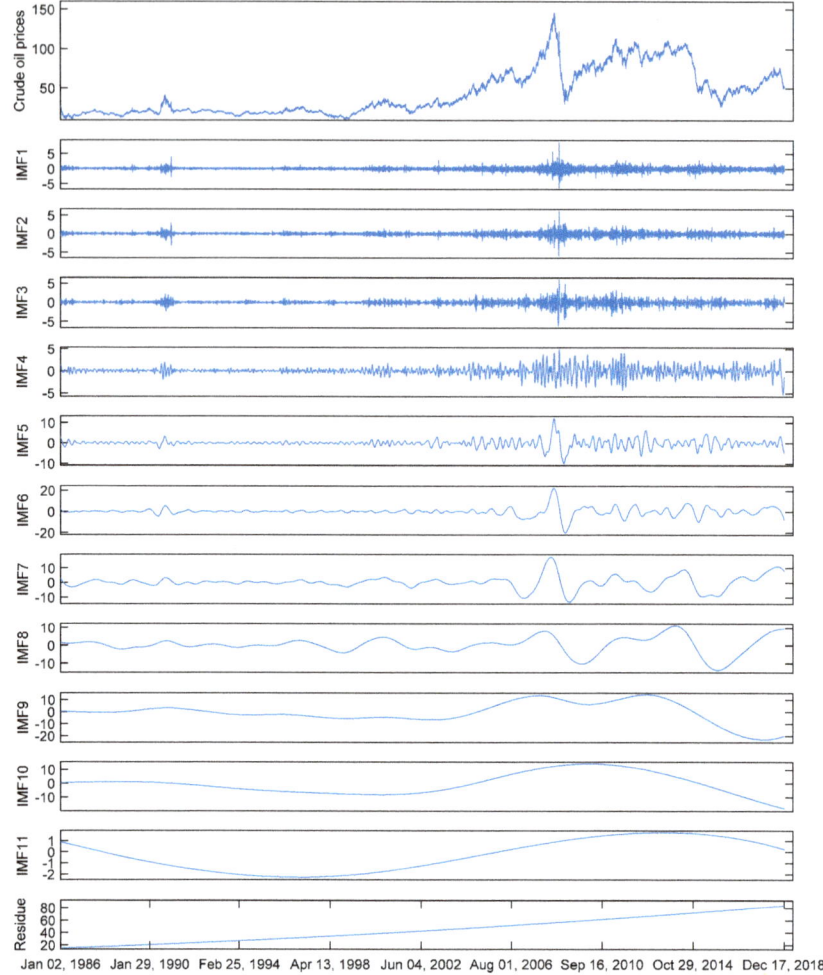

Figure 2. The original series and corresponding components decomposed by complete ensemble empirical mode decomposition (CEEMD) of WTI crude oil prices.

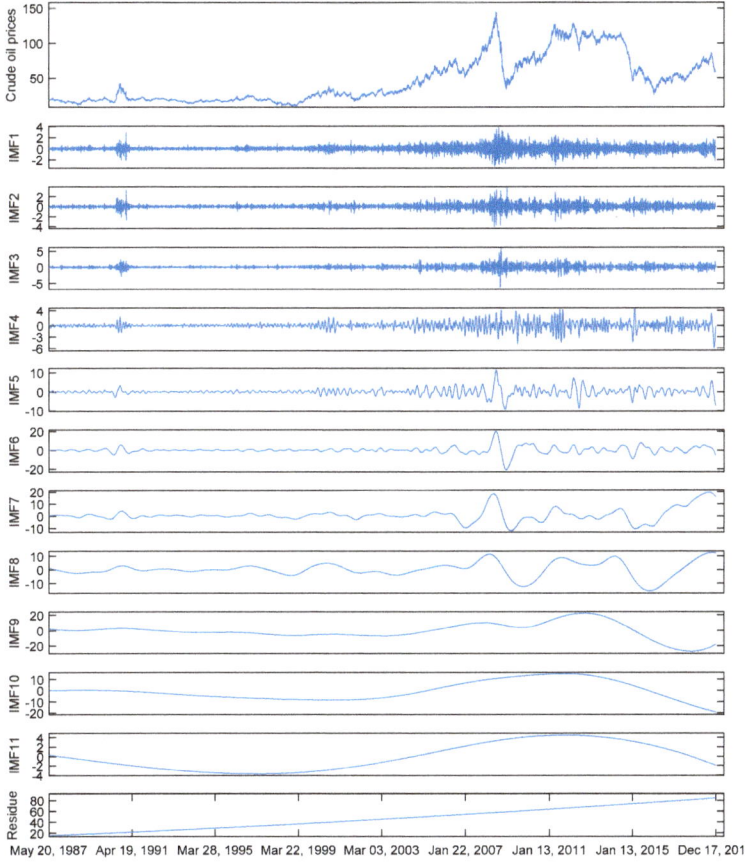

Figure 3. The original series and corresponding components decomposed by CEEMD of Brent crude oil prices.

4.2. Evaluation Measures

In order to evaluate the model from multiple aspects, we employed four frequently used evaluation metrics, including two error indexes: the mean absolute percent error (MAPE) and the root mean squared error (RMSE), one direction index: the directional statistic (Dstat) and one statistic index: the Diebold–Mariano (DM) statistic. Firstly, MAPE and RMSE were selected to evaluate the prediction accuracy, as defined by Equations (14) and (15), respectively:

$$\text{MAPE} = \frac{1}{n} \sum_{t=1}^{n} \left| \frac{y_t - \hat{y}_t}{y_t} \right| \tag{14}$$

$$\text{RMSE} = \frac{1}{n} \sqrt{\sum_{t=1}^{n} (y_t - \hat{y}_t)^2} \tag{15}$$

where $\hat{y}_t$ is the predicted value and y_t is the actual value at time t and n is the total number of data in a testing data set.

The Dstat was used to evaluate the ability of direction prediction, which is defined as follow:

$$D_{stat} = \frac{1}{n} \sum_{t=1}^{n} \alpha_t \times 100\% \qquad (16)$$

where $\alpha_t = \begin{cases} 1, & (y_t - y_{t-1}) \times (\hat{y}_t - y_{t-1}) \geq 0; \\ 0, & otherwise. \end{cases}$

Generally, the smaller the MAPE and RMSE, the greater the Dstat, which represents a higher prediction accuracy and a better performance of direction prediction.

In order to better evaluate whether the prediction accuracy of the proposed prediction model is significantly better than those of previous models or not, the Diebold–Mariano (DM) statistic was introduced in this study, as defined by Equation (17):

$$S = \frac{\bar{d}}{\sqrt{Var(\bar{d})}} \qquad (17)$$

where $\bar{d} = \frac{1}{n}\sum_{t=1}^{n} d_t$, $d_t = (y_t - \hat{y}_{1t})^2 - (y_t - \hat{y}_{2t})^2$, $Var(\bar{d}) = \frac{1}{n}(\gamma_0 + 2\sum_{k=1}^{n-1}\gamma_k)$ and $\gamma_k = cov(d_t - d_{t-k})$. $\hat{y}_{1t}$ are the predicted values of the first prediction model, and $\hat{y}_{2t}$ are those of the second prediction model at time t. When the DM statistic is negative, the first prediction model statistically outperforms the second one.

4.3. Experimental Settings

In this study, the development and evaluation of prediction model included three aspects:

First, previous research has demonstrated that ensemble models outperformed single models in crude oil price forecasting [6]. Therefore, the overall performance of CEEMD-A&S-SBL was only compared with that of some state-of-the-art ensemble prediction models in terms of the above evaluation metrics in this study. Thus, on the basis of the same crude oil price data, we evaluated whether our proposed CEEMD-A&S-SBL was effective for improving prediction precision. The compared models included one classical statistical method (ARIMA), three popular AI models (LSSVR, ANN, CK-SBL) and a hybrid model that forecasts high-frequency, low-frequency and trend components individually (HLT) [31]. In addition, since SBL with a combined kernel has shown better prediction performance compared with that with a single kernel, SBL with a combined kernel was selected as the predict model. Therefore, we had five individual prediction methods (ARIMA, LSSVR, ANN, CK-SBL and HLT) for each component to compare forecasting with A&S. All prediction methods are shown in Table 2.

Table 2. Descriptions of all the prediction methods in the experiments.

Method	Description
ARIMA	Autoregressive integrated moving average
LSSVR	Least squares support vector regression
ANN	Back propagation neural network
CK-SBL	SBL with a combined kernel
HLT	ARIMA for high-frequency components and combined kernel LSSVR for low-frequency and trend components
A&S	All component are predicted by ARIMA and CK-SBL independently and then are aggregated adaptively

Following the previous work [6], an adaptive PSO (APSO) method was used to optimize the parameters in CK-SBL, which adaptively adjusted the inertia weight of each particle based on the distance between the global best particle and the current one. In addition, the Akaike information criterion (AIC) [51] was used to determine the ARIMA parameters (p-d-q). RBF kernel was applied in

LSSVR and grid search was used to seek the optimal parameters. For ANN, a back propagation neural network was employed, the number of hidden nodes was set to 10, and the iteration time was set to 10,000. For HLT, the PSO was used for adaptive parameter selection for LSSVR.

Second, we evaluated the three different decomposition methods (EMD, EEMD, CEEMD) for the proposed model in this study. In this phase, on the basis of same aggregation method (SBL) and prediction method (A&S), we evaluated the performance of different decomposition methods.

Third, we compared the two different ensemble methods (simple addition and SBL) for the proposed model in this study. In this phase, on the basis of same decomposition method (CEEMD) and prediction method (A&S), we evaluated the performance of the SBL ensemble method.

In addition, data normalization is an important work for computational efficiency and fair comparison of AI-based time series forecasting [6]. In this study, we applied the Min-Max normalization, a frequently-used normalization method, for AI-based predictors. It is worth pointing out that inverse normalization needs to be executed after the normalized predicted values are obtained. We conducted three-step-ahead predictions with horizon h = 1, 2, 3 and lag order lo = 6 in this study.

Especially, in CEEMD-A&S-SBL, the predicted values of the two differential models for each component were adaptively selected based on the training precision. Therefore, how to accurately evaluate the training precision is utmost important for adaptive selection of models. RMSE and MAPE are frequently used evaluation indexes. In this study, we selected RMSE mainly because there existed some actual zero values after CEEMD, thus RMSE was more effective for reflecting the training precision than MAPE.

All the experiments were performed by MATLAB R2017a on a 64-bit Microsoft Windows 10 with an i5-7820X CPU @1.8 GHz and 8 GB RAM.

4.4. Results and Analysis

4.4.1. Experimental Results of Overall Predictive Models

On the basis of same decomposition (i.e., CEEMD), we firstly compared the overall performance of the five extant prediction models (i.e., CEEMD-ARIMA-ADD, CEEMD-LSSVR-ADD, CEEMD-ANN-ADD, CEEMD-CK-SBL-ADD, CEEMD-HLT-ADD) with our proposed adaptively prediction model (CEEMD-A&S-SBL) in terms of MAPE, RMSE, and Dstat. We adopted these five models because they were the most frequently used and effective prediction methods [2,6,11,12,21–24,31]. Among all these models, ARIMA is one classical statistical method; LSSVR, ANN and CK-SBL are three popular AI models; HLT is one recent hybrid prediction model. The experimental results are reported in Tables 3–5, respectively.

Table 3. The mean absolute percent error (MAPE) values of different prediction models on WTI and Brent crude oil prices.

Market	Horizon	CEEMD-ARIMA-ADD	CEEMD-LSSVR-ADD	CEEMD-ANN-ADD	CEEMD-CK-SBL-ADD	CEEMD-HLT-ADD	CEEMD-A&S-SBL
WTI	One	0.0169	0.0063	0.0120	0.0058	0.0049	**0.0048**
	Two	0.0302	0.0080	0.0184	0.0079	0.0075	**0.0074**
	Three	0.0371	0.0111	0.0279	0.0099	0.0082	**0.0081**
Brent	One	0.0408	0.0057	0.0146	0.0053	0.0044	**0.0043**
	Two	0.0824	0.0080	0.0423	0.0071	0.0066	**0.0065**
	Three	0.1158	0.0106	0.0254	0.0092	0.0075	**0.0074**

CEEMD: complete ensemble empirical mode decomposition; ARIMA: autoregressive integrated moving average; LSSVR: least squares support vector regression; ANN: back propagation neural network; SBL: sparse Bayesian learning; CK-SBL: SBL with a combined kernel; HLT: a hybrid model that forecasts high-frequency, low-frequency and trend components individually; ADD: addition.

Among all these models, CEEMD-A&S-SBL model achieved the lowest (the best) MAPE values in all cases on both markets. Although the previous hybrid model CEEMD-HLT-ADD achieved the lowest MAPE values compared with the single prediction models, the proposed hybrid model CEEMD-A&S-SBL outperformed the CEEMD-HLT-ADD model in all cases. For each prediction model, the MAPE values increased with the horizon.

Table 4 reported the RMSE values of all prediction models on WTI and Brent crude oil prices. It can be seen that CEEMD-A&S-SBL outperformed the hybrid model CEEMD-HLT-ADD and all single prediction models in all cases. Of all single models, the statistical model ARIMA obtained the worst RMSE values in all six cases. For the AI models, LSSVR, ANN and CK-SBL achieved close RMSE values, and the model CK-SBL was slightly better than others. As to the hybrid models, CEEMD-A&S-SBL achieved the lower RMSE values than CEEMD-HTL-ADD model, showing that the former was more powerful for crude oil price forecasting.

Table 4. The root mean squared error (RMSE) values of different prediction models on WTI and Brent crude oil prices.

Market	Horizon	CEEMD-ARIMA-ADD	CEEMD-LSSVR-ADD	CEEMD-ANN-ADD	CEEMD-CK-SBL-ADD	CEEMD-HLT-ADD	CEEMD-A&S-SBL
WTI	One	1.0983	0.5317	0.9536	0.4766	0.3963	**0.3878**
	Two	1.9390	0.6468	1.3625	0.6425	0.6113	**0.5977**
	Three	2.3850	0.9331	2.2405	0.7883	0.6578	**0.6474**
Brent	One	3.0815	0.4494	1.1034	0.4410	0.3697	**0.3590**
	Two	6.2689	0.6611	3.6149	0.5902	0.5560	**0.5424**
	Three	8.8840	0.8237	2.0899	0.7536	0.6251	**0.6111**

As to the directional statistics, it can be seen from Table 5 that CEEMD-A&S-SBL model achieved the highest values in five out of six cases, indicating that the CEEMD-A&S-SBL model had better performance in the direction forecasting of crude oil prices. For each model, the corresponding Dstat values decreased with the increase of the horizon. Amongst the single prediction models, ANN, LSSVR and CK-SBL obtained the higher Dstat values than ARIMA, showing that the AI models were capable of achieving better directional predictions compared with the statistical model ARIMA. Moreover, the hybrid models greatly outperformed the single prediction models.

Table 5. The directional statistic (Dstat) values of different prediction models on WTI and Brent crude oil prices.

Market	Horizon	CEEMD-ARIMA-ADD	CEEMD-LSSVR-ADD	CEEMD-ANN-ADD	CEEMD-CK-SBL-ADD	CEEMD-HLT-ADD	CEEMD-A&S-SBL
WTI	One	0.6949	0.8598	0.8147	0.8712	0.8995	**0.9007**
	Two	0.5716	0.8303	0.7244	0.8388	0.8394	**0.8418**
	Three	0.5626	0.7521	0.7118	0.7593	0.8135	**0.8147**
Brent	One	0.6301	0.8528	0.7511	0.8740	0.8734	**0.8784**
	Two	0.5727	0.7972	0.6925	**0.8447**	0.8390	0.8422
	Three	0.5527	0.7480	0.6881	0.7698	0.8091	**0.8185**

From the overall results above, it can be seen that the hybrid prediction models consistently outperformed the single prediction models in all cases in terms of MAPE, RMSE, and Dstat. Between the two hybrid models, our proposed CEEMD-A&S-SBL achieved better prediction performance compared with CEEMD-HLT-ADD.

In order to better evaluate whether the prediction accuracy of CEEMD-A&S-SBL is significantly better than those of other models or not, the Diebold–Mariano (DM) test [52] was used in this study. The statistics and *p*-values (in brackets) are reported in Tables 6 and 7.

DM test results on the prediction of WTI and Brent crude oil prices demonstrated that the CEEMD-A&S-SBL model significantly outperformed CEEMD-ARIMA-ADD, CEEMD-ANN-ADD, CEEMD-LSSVR-ADD, CEEMD-CK-SBL-ADD and CEEMD-HLT-ADD, and the corresponding *p*-values were much less than 0.05 in all cases.

Table 6. The Diebold–Mariano (DM) test results on WTI crude oil prices.

Horizon	Tested Model	Benchmark Model				
		CEEMD-ARIMA-ADD	CEEMD-ANN-ADD	CEEMD-LSSVR-ADD	CEEMD-CK-SBL-ADD	CEEMD-HLT-ADD
One	CEEMD-ANN-ADD	−6.401 (0.000)				
	CEEMD-LSSVR-ADD	−37.579 (0.000)	−22.376 (0.000)			
	CEEMD-CK-SBL-ADD	−34.935 (0.000)	−20.175 (0.000)	−4.014 (0.000)		
	CEEMD-HLT-ADD	−39.696 (0.000)	−23.213 (0.000)	−10.167 (0.000)	−9.846 (0.000)	
	CEEMD-A&S-SBL	−39.822 (0.000)	−23.262 (0.000)	−10.865 (0.000)	−9.971 (0.000)	−3.682 (0.000)
Two	CEEMD-ANN-ADD	−17.100 (0.000)				
	CEEMD-LSSVR-ADD	−41.834 (0.000)	−21.798 (0.000)			
	CEEMD-CK-SBL-ADD	−41.245 (0.000)	−22.272 (0.000)	−0.406 (0.685)		
	CEEMD-HLT-ADD	−42.080 (0.000)	−23.126 (0.000)	−4.288 (0.000)	−4.984 (0.000)	
	CEEMD-A&S-SBL	−42.329 (0.000)	−23.339 (0.000)	−5.489 (0.000)	−5.710 (0.000)	−3.887 (0.000)
Three	CEEMD-ANN-ADD	−2.722 (0.007)				
	CEEMD-LSSVR-ADD	−43.031 (0.000)	−24.609 (0.000)			
	CEEMD-CK-SBL-ADD	−41.550 (0.000)	−24.130 (0.000)	−6.002 (0.000)		
	CEEMD-HLT-ADD	−43.561 (0.000)	−25.395 (0.000)	−11.064 (0.000)	−12.549 (0.000)	
	CEEMD-A&S-SBL	−43.684 (0.000)	−25.423 (0.000)	−1.290 (0.000)	−11.200 (0.000)	−2.792 (0.005)

Table 7. The Diebold–Mariano (DM) test results on Brent crude oil prices.

Horizon	Tested Model	Benchmark Model				
		CEEMD-ARIMA-ADD	CEEMD-ANN-ADD	CEEMD-LSSVR-ADD	CEEMD-CK-SBL-ADD	CEEMD-HLT-ADD
One	CEEMD-ANN-ADD	−24.977 (0.000)				
	CEEMD-LSSVR-ADD	−25.324 (0.000)	−19.530 (0.000)			
	CEEMD-CK-SBL-ADD	−25.333 (0.000)	−19.737 (0.000)	−0.934 (0.350)		
	CEEMD-HLT-ADD	−25.500 (0.000)	−21.137 (0.000)	−9.783 (0.000)	−9.724 (0.000)	
	CEEMD-A&S-SBL	−25.521 (0.000)	−21.339 (0.000)	−10.420 (0.000)	−10.095 (0.000)	−4.202 (0.000)
Two	CEEMD-ANN-ADD	−16.241 (0.000)				
	CEEMD-LSSVR-ADD	−25.250 (0.000)	−26.451 (0.000)			
	CEEMD-CK-SBL-ADD	−25.273 (0.000)	−26.728 (0.000)	−6.775 (0.000)		
	CEEMD-HLT-ADD	−25.299 (0.000)	−26.814 (0.000)	−10.215 (0.000)	−6.072 (0.000)	
	CEEMD-A&S-SBL	−25.311 (0.000)	−26.847 (0.000)	−10.869 (0.000)	−6.949 (0.000)	−4.261 (0.000)
Three	CEEMD-ANN-ADD	−23.494 (0.000)				
	CEEMD-LSSVR-ADD	−24.832 (0.000)	−22.274 (0.000)			
	CEEMD-CK-SBL-ADD	−24.841 (0.000)	−23.071 (0.000)	−4.521 (0.000)		
	CEEMD-HLT-ADD	−24.898 (0.000)	−24.284 (0.000)	−13.058 (0.000)	−12.715 (0.000)	
	CEEMD-A&S-SBL	−24.9040 (0.000)	−24.394 (0.000)	−12.995 (0.000)	−11.982 (0.000)	−4.135 (0.000)

On one hand, when we chose the single prediction models, including CEEMD-ARIMA-ADD, CEEMD-ANN-ADD, CEEMD-LSSVR-ADD, CEEMD-CK-SBL-ADD, as the benchmark models, CEEMD-A&S-SBL was statistically superior to these single prediction models, indicating that the former was more powerful for nonlinear and nonstationary crude oil price forecasting. On the other hand, when we chose the hybrid model CEEMD-HLT-ADD as the benchmark model, the prediction results of CEEMD-A&S-SBL were also significantly better. In summary, the hybrid model CEEMD-A&S-SBL achieved the best prediction accuracy in all models. The DM test results further statistically confirmed the conclusion.

4.4.2. Experimental Results of Decomposition Methods

On the basis of same prediction (A&S) and ensemble (SBL) methods, we evaluated the performance of the various decomposition methods. Tables 8–10 report the corresponding prediction results in terms of MAPE, RMSE and Dstat, respectively. It can be found that the CEEMD method was the best decomposition method that achieved the lowest MAPE and RMSE values and the highest Dstat values at each horizon.

Table 8. The MAPE values of different decomposition methods on WTI and Brent crude oil prices.

Market	Horizon	EMD	EEMD	CEEMD
WTI	One	0.0083	0.0079	**0.0048**
	Two	0.0100	0.0095	**0.0074**
	Three	0.0117	0.0097	**0.0081**
Brent	One	0.0078	0.0079	**0.0043**
	Two	0.0091	0.0089	**0.0065**
	Three	0.0112	0.0091	**0.0074**

Table 9. The RMSE values of different decomposition methods on WTI and Brent crude oil prices.

Market	Horizon	EMD	EEMD	CEEMD
WTI	One	0.6661	0.6225	**0.3878**
	Two	0.8185	0.7511	**0.5977**
	Three	0.9497	0.7758	**0.6474**
Brent	One	0.6750	0.6447	**0.3590**
	Two	0.7713	0.7274	**0.5424**
	Three	0.9296	0.7456	**0.6111**

Table 10. The Dstat values of decomposition methods on WTI and Brent crude oil prices.

Market	Horizon	EMD	EEMD	CEEMD
WTI	One	0.8189	0.8189	**0.9007**
	Two	0.7966	0.7768	**0.8418**
	Three	0.7341	0.7714	**0.8147**
Brent	One	0.8341	0.7998	**0.8784**
	Two	0.8035	0.7711	**0.8422**
	Three	0.7299	0.7623	**0.8185**

In order to better evaluate whether the decomposition method CEEMD is significantly better than other decomposition methods or not, the DM test was used. The statistics and p-values (in brackets) are reported in Table 11. DM test results on the prediction of WTI and Brent crude oil prices demonstrated that the CEEMD decomposition method significantly outperformed EEMD and EMD in all cases, and the corresponding p-values were much less than 0.05 in all cases.

Table 11. The Diebold–Mariano (DM) test results on WTI and Brent crude oil prices.

Market	Horizon	Tested Model	Benchmark Model	
			EMD	EEMD
WTI	One	EEMD	−2.373 (0.018)	
		CEEMD	−14.79 (0.000)	−15.93 (0.000)
	Two	EEMD	−3.168 (0.002)	
		CEEMD	−11.63 (0.000)	−11.12 (0.000)
	Three	EEMD	−8.208 (0.000)	
		CEEMD	−14.04 (0.000)	−9.944 (0.000)
Brent	One	EEMD	−1.143 (0.253)	
		CEEMD	−9.993 (0.000)	−18.632 (0.000)
	Two	EEMD	−2.172 (0.030)	
		CEEMD	−11.296 (0.000)	−13.513 (0.000)
	Three	EEMD	−9.024 (0.000)	
		CEEMD	−14.566 (0.000)	−10.694 (0.000)

4.4.3. Experimental Results of Ensemble Methods

Traditional ensemble method uses addition operation. All *IMF*s and residue are simply added as the final forecasting results. In order to potentially enhance the prediction precision, SBL without kernel-tricks was chosen as the ensemble method in our proposed model. We chose SBL without kernel-tricks mainly because it is a kind of fast and efficient ensemble method. Tables 12–14 show the corresponding prediction results using addition or SBL ensemble method for A&S model in terms of MAPE, RMSE and Dstat, respectively. It can be easily seen that the SBL ensemble method outperformed the simple addition, achieving the lower MAPE and RMSE values, and the highest Dstat values at each horizon.

Table 12. The MAPE values of different prediction models on WTI and Brent crude oil prices.

Market	Horizon	CEEMD-A&S-ADD	CEEMD-A&S-SBL
WTI	One	0.0049	**0.0048**
	Two	0.0075	**0.0074**
	Three	0.0082	**0.0081**
Brent	One	0.0044	**0.0043**
	Two	0.0066	**0.0065**
	Three	0.0075	**0.0074**

Table 13. The RMSE values of different prediction models on WTI and Brent crude oil prices.

Market	Horizon	CEEMD-A&S-ADD	CEEMD-A&S-SBL
WTI	One	0.3955	**0.3878**
	Two	0.6106	**0.5977**
	Three	0.6562	**0.6474**
Brent	One	0.3659	**0.3590**
	Two	0.5555	**0.5424**
	Three	0.6247	**0.6111**

Table 14. The Dstat values of different prediction models on WTI and Brent crude oil prices.

Market	Horizon	CEEMD-A&S-ADD	CEEMD-A&S-SBL
WTI	One	0.9001	**0.9007**
	Two	0.8388	**0.8418**
	Three	0.8123	**0.8147**
Brent	One	0.8727	**0.8784**
	Two	0.8421	**0.8422**
	Three	0.8110	**0.8185**

In order to better evaluate whether the SBL ensemble method is significantly better than the addition ensemble method, the DM test was used. The statistics and *p*-values (in brackets) are reported in Table 15. DM test results on the prediction of WTI and Brent crude oil prices showed that the SBL ensemble method significantly outperformed the simple addition method in all cases, and the corresponding *p*-values were much less than 0.05 in all cases.

Table 15. The Diebold–Mariano (DM) test results on WTI and Brent crude oil prices.

Market	Horizon	Tested Model	Benchmark Model
			Addition
WTI	One	SBL	−3.402 (0.001)
	Two	SBL	−3.764 (0.000)
	Three	SBL	−2.333 (0.020)
Brent	One	SBL	−2.952 (0.003)
	Two	SBL	−4.336 (0.000)
	Three	SBL	−4.146 (0.000)

4.5. Discussions

In order to better analyze the proposed CEEMD-A&S-SBL, we will further discuss some characteristics of the proposed model for forecasting crude oil prices, including CEEMD parameter settings, the impact of the lag order, individual component prediction model and selection and the weights of components in aggregation.

4.5.1. CEEMD Parameter Settings

In the decomposition of the original series, a particular white noise was added at each stage of CEEMD. Let the parameter St be the white noise strength and I be the number of realizations in CEEMD. In order to investigate the impact of these parameters for crude oil price forecasting, we conducted the experiments on WTI crude oil prices with one-step-ahead forecasting. First, we fixed $I = 100$ and ran CEEMD-A&S-SBL with a variable St in the range of {0.01, 0.02, 0.03, 0.05, 0.1, 0.2, 0.3, 0.5}. The results are shown in Figure 4. Second, we fixed $St = 0.2$ and repeated the experiments with a variable I in the range of {20, 40, 60, 80, 100, 200, 500, 1000, 2000, 5000}; the results are shown in Figure 5.

As shown in Figure 4, the values of RMSE, MAPE and Dstat simultaneously achieve the best values when the noise strength in CEEMD equals to 0.1. When the noise strength is greater or less than 0.1, the prediction performance becomes worse and worse. This indicates that too much or too little added noise decreases the forecasting precision. The experimental results show that the noise strength has a significant impact on forecasting accuracy, and an ideal value of added noise strength is about 0.1.

On the other hand, with the increase of the number of realizations in CEEMD, the values of both RMSE and MAPE decrease and Dstat increases when the number of realizations is less than 1000, showing that the forecasting performance continuously improves as shown in Figure 5. However, when the number of realizations is greater than 1000, RMSE, MAPE and Dstat tend to be roughly stable. Therefore, if time cost is considered, 1000 is an appropriate value for the number of realizations in CEEMD in terms of RMSE, MAPE and Dstat.

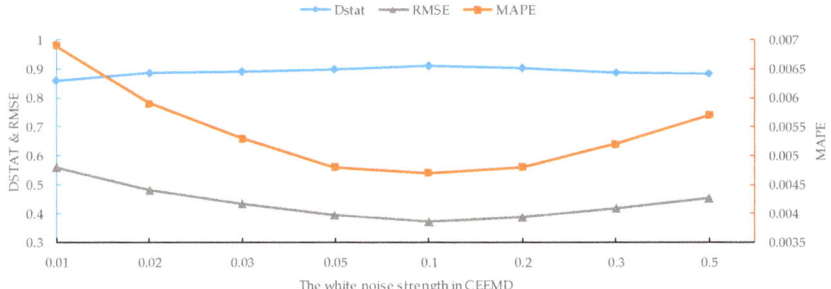

Figure 4. The impact of the noise strength of CEEMD on WTI crude oil prices with one-step-ahead forecasting.

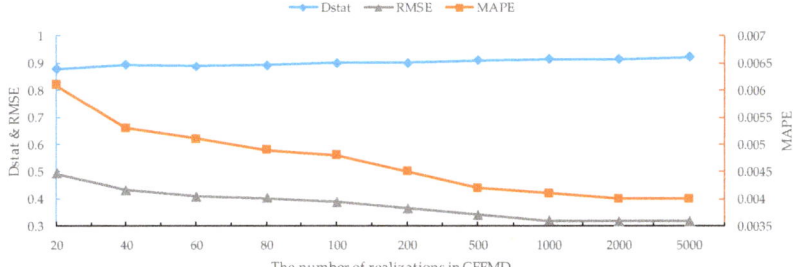

Figure 5. The impact of the number of realizations of CEEMD on WTI crude oil prices with one-step-ahead forecasting.

4.5.2. The Impact of the Lag Order

In order to further investigate the impact of the lag order on our proposed CEEMD-A&S-SBL model, we conducted the one-step-ahead forecasting experiment on WTI crude oil prices with the number of lag orders from 1 to 10. The results are shown in Figure 6. It can be seen that the forecasting performance significantly improves with the increase of the lag order from 1 to 4. Then, RMSE slightly decreases with the increase of lag order from 5 to 6, while MAPE and Dstat remain unchanged. When the lag order is greater than 6, all three metrics tend to be stable. The experimental results demonstrate that the lag order has a significant impact on forecasting accuracy, and an ideal value of lag order is about 6.

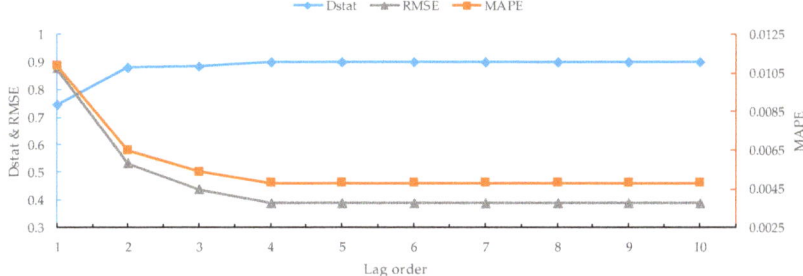

Figure 6. The impact of lag order on WTI crude oil prices with one-step-ahead forecasting.

4.5.3. Individual Component Prediction Model and Selection

In the proposed CEEMD-A&S-SBL model, the prediction models of ARIMA and SBL with combined kernel-tricks are built on the training set independently for each component, and then these two prediction models are applied to the test set separately. These two groups of prediction results of all individual components are adaptively selected based on the training precision. Table 16 shows the prediction model selection results for each component in terms of RMSE.

Table 16. Prediction model selection for each component on WTI and Brent crude oil prices.

Market	IMF_1	IMF_2	IMF_3	IMF_4	IMF_5	IMF_6	IMF_7	IMF_8	IMF_9	IMF_{10}	IMF_{11}	Residue
WTI	ARIMA	ARIMA	ARIMA	ARIMA	ARIMA	ARIMA	ARIMA	CK-SBL	CK-SBL	ARIMA	ARIMA	CK-SBL
Brent	ARIMA	ARIMA	ARIMA	ARIMA	ARIMA	CK-SBL	CK-SBL	CK-SBL	ARIMA	ARIMA	ARIMA	ARIMA

From the above table, we can find that ARIMA and CK-SBL were adaptively selected for forecasting different components. For WTI crude oil data, CK-SBL was chosen for forecasting the IMF_8, IMF_9 and residue, while ARIMA was chosen for forecasting the rest of the components. Regarding Brent crude oil data, CK-SBL was chosen for forecasting the IMF_6, IMF_7 and IMF_8, while ARIMA was chosen for forecasting the rest of the components. In the previous HTL model, the first $IMFs$ were identified as low-frequency components and the rest as high-frequency ones, and then the appropriate models were employed to forecast the two parts respectively. Our proposed CEEMD-A&S-SBL model is capable to adaptively select appropriate prediction models based on the training precision without identifying the characteristic of each component. Therefore, the proposed CEEMD-A&S-SBL model is more flexible and can better adapt to differential components, showing higher forecasting performance on crude oil prices.

4.5.4. The Weights of Components in Aggregation

Most previous models aggregate the prediction results of all components as the final forecasting results using simple addition. The proposed CEEMD-A&S-SBL model uses SBL without kernel-tricks to aggregate the prediction values of individual components to obtain the final prediction results of crude oil prices. Table 17 shows the weights of components in aggregation using SBL for WTI and Brent oil price forecasting.

Table 17. Weights of components in aggregation using SBL.

Market	IMF_1	IMF_2	IMF_3	IMF_4	IMF_5	IMF_6	IMF_7	IMF_8	IMF_9	IMF_{10}	IMF_{11}	Residue
WTI	0.9296	1.1345	0.9983	1.0038	0.9925	1.0032	0.9969	0.9982	1.0050	0.9938	1.0140	1.0001
Brent	0.9256	1.1440	1.0241	1.0146	1.0004	1.0013	0.9988	1.0001	1.0009	0.9979	1.0035	1.0000

In the ensemble of addition, each component has an equal weight. It can be seen from Table 17 that each component has a differential aggregation weight when using the SBL ensemble. Especially, IMF_1 has a relatively small weight mainly because IMF_1 fluctuates dramatically, making it hard to accurately forecast. Figures 7 and 8 show the prediction result of each component in one-step-ahead forecasting on WTI and Brent crude oil prices. It can be seen that all components can be accurately predicted except IMF_1. Therefore, each component should have a differential weight in the aggregation stage. Due to the relatively larger prediction error, the IMF_1 should have a relatively smaller weight in the aggregation stage. Compared with addition and other ensemble methods, ensemble using SBL has some advantages as follows: (1) good interpretability, (2) better prediction accuracy.

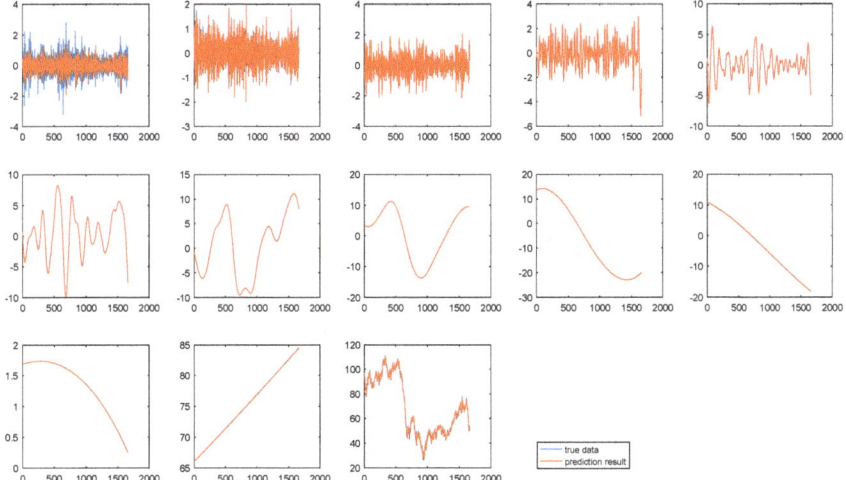

Figure 7. Prediction result of each component in one-step-ahead forecasting on WTI crude oil prices.

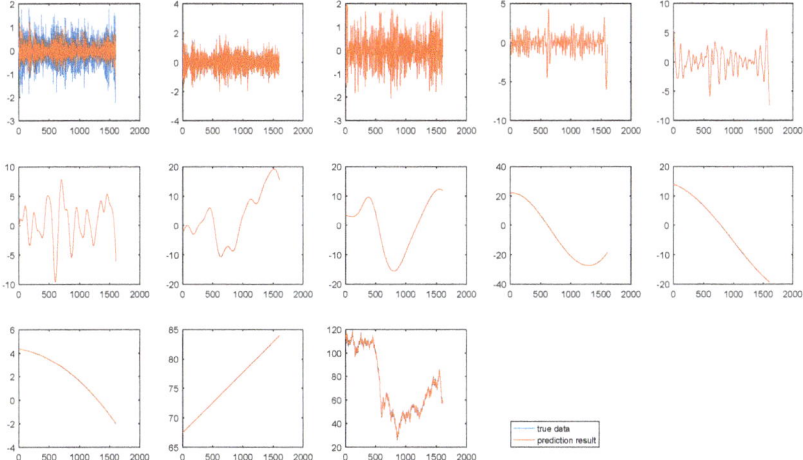

Figure 8. Prediction result of each component in one-step-ahead forecasting on Brent crude oil prices.

4.6. Summary

From the above results and analysis, some findings can be summarized as follows:

(1) The AI models outperform the traditional statistical/econometric models in terms of MAPE, RMSE and Dstat, indicating that AI models are much better at forecasting nonlinear and nonstationary crude oil price series.
(2) The hybrid ensemble models, including CEEMD-HLT-ADD and CEEMD-A&S-SBL, can further improve the prediction performance.
(3) Our proposed prediction model CEEMD-A&S-SBL adaptively selects an appropriate prediction model for forecasting each component without identifying high-frequency and low-frequency in advance, and the adaptive hybrid model significantly outperforms the other compared hybrid model.
(4) The CEEMD method achieves better prediction results than the counterpart EEMD and EMD methods, indicating that CEEMD is more suitable for decomposing original crude oil price series.

(5) The SBL ensemble method outperforms the traditional addition method in terms of MAPE, RMSE and Dstat, showing that SBL is more suitable for aggregating individual prediction components.

5. Conclusions

It is a great challenge for the accurate forecast of crude oil prices because of its nonlinearity and nonstationarity. To better forecast the crude oil price time series, this paper proposed a novel adaptive hybrid ensemble learning paradigm (CEEMD-A&S-SBL) incorporating CEEMD, ARIMA and SBL. Firstly, the decomposition method CEEMD was employed to decompose the original time series of crude oil prices into several IMFs and one residue. In the individual forecasting phase, ARIMA and SBL with combined kernel-tricks were used to predict target values for the residue and each single IMF independently. Finally, the prediction results of the above two models for each component were adaptively selected based on the training precision, and then aggregated as the final forecasting results using SBL without kernel-tricks. To our knowledge, this is the first time that the adaptive model selection for individual component forecasting has been developed to forecast crude oil prices. The experimental results show that: (1) compared with five state-of-the-art prediction models, the proposed model can significantly improve the prediction accuracy of crude oil prices; (2) CEEMD is superior to EEMD and EMD for decomposing the original time series of crude oil prices; and (3) SBL outperforms addition method in aggregating the individual forecasting results of components.

Future work could be extended in four aspects: (1) selecting more appropriate prediction approaches to build the hybrid ensemble model for forecasting crude oil prices; (2) developing more metrics for evaluating the training precision instead of RMSE only; (3) applying the CEEMD-A&S-SBL to forecast other time series of energy, such as carbon price, wind speed and electricity load; and (4) assessing the scaling ability of CEEMD-A&S-SBL to other time series with various volume of data, such as hourly price series and weekly price series.

Author Contributions: Formal analysis, J.W.; Investigation, Y.C. and T.Z.; Methodology, J.W.; Software, J.W. and T.L.; Supervision, T.L.; Writing—Original draft, J.W.; Writing—Review & editing, J.W. and T.L.

Funding: This research was funded by the Fundamental Research Funds for the Central Universities, grant number JBK1902029, the Ministry of Education of Humanities and Social Science Project, grant number 19YJAZH047, and the Scientific Research Fund of Sichuan Provincial Education Department, grant number 17ZB0433.

Conflicts of Interest: The authors declare no conflict of interest.

References

1. British Petroleum. BP Energy Outlook 2018. Available online: https://www.bp.com/en/global/corporate/energy-economics/energy-outlook.html (accessed on 29 January 2019).
2. Li, T.; Hu, Z.; Jia, Y.; Wu, J.; Zhou, Y. Forecasting crude oil prices using ensemble empirical mode decomposition and sparse Bayesian learning. *Energies* **2018**, *11*, 1182. [CrossRef]
3. Yu, L.; Wang, S.; Lai, K.K. Forecasting crude oil price with an EMD-based neural network ensemble learning paradigm. *Energy Econ.* **2008**, *30*, 2623–2635. [CrossRef]
4. Yu, L.; Dai, W.; Tang, L.; Wu, J. A hybrid grid-GA-based LSSVR learning paradigm for crude oil price forecasting. *Neural Comput. Appl.* **2016**, *27*, 2193–2215. [CrossRef]
5. He, K.; Yu, L.; Lai, K.K. Crude oil price analysis and forecasting using wavelet decomposed ensemble model. *Energy* **2012**, *46*, 564–574. [CrossRef]
6. Li, T.; Zhou, M.; Guo, C.; Luo, M.; Wu, J.; Pan, F.; Tao, Q.; He, T. Forecasting crude oil price using EEMD and RVM with adaptive PSO-based kernels. *Energies* **2016**, *9*, 1014. [CrossRef]
7. Baumeister, C.; Kilian, L. Real-time forecasts of the real price of oil. *J. Bus. Econ. Stat.* **2012**, *30*, 326–336. [CrossRef]
8. Baumeister, C.; Kilian, L. What central bankers need to know about forecasting oil prices. *Int. Econ. Rev.* **2014**, *55*, 869–889. [CrossRef]
9. Lanza, A.; Manera, M.; Giovannini, M. Modeling and forecasting cointegrated relationships among heavy oil and product prices. *Energy Econ.* **2005**, *27*, 831–848. [CrossRef]

10. Murat, A.; Tokat, E. Forecasting oil price movements with crack spread futures. *Energy Econ.* **2009**, *31*, 85–90. [CrossRef]
11. Koutroumanidis, T.; Ioannou, K.; Arabatzis, G. Predicting fuelwood prices in Greece with the use of ARIMA models, artificial neural networks and a hybrid ARIMA-ANN model. *Energy Policy* **2009**, *37*, 3627–3634. [CrossRef]
12. Abledu, G.K.; Agbodah, K. Stochastic forecasting and modeling of volatility of oil prices in Ghana using ARIMA time series model. *Eur. J. Bus. Manag.* **2012**, *4*, 122–131.
13. Morana, C. A semiparametric approach to short-term oil price forecasting. *Energy Econ.* **2001**, *23*, 325–338. [CrossRef]
14. Hou, A.; Suardi, S. A nonparametric GARCH model of crude oil price return volatility. *Energy Econ.* **2012**, *34*, 618–626. [CrossRef]
15. Mohammadi, H.; Su, L. International evidence on crude oil price dynamics: Applications of ARIMA-GARCH models. *Energy Econ.* **2010**, *32*, 1001–1008. [CrossRef]
16. Wei, Y.; Wang, Y.; Huang, D. Forecasting crude oil market volatility: Further evidence using GARCH-class models. *Energy Econ.* **2010**, *32*, 1477–1484. [CrossRef]
17. Kulkarni, S.; Haidar, I. Forecasting model for crude oil price using artificial neural networks and commodity futures prices. *Int. J. Comput. Sci. Inf. Secur.* **2009**, *2*, 81–88.
18. Mirmirani, S.; Li, H.C. A comparison of VAR and Neural Networks with Genetic Algorithm in Forecasting Price of Oil. In *Applications of Artificial Intelligence in Finance and Economics 2004*; Emerald Group Publishing Limited: Bingley, UK, 2004; pp. 203–223.
19. Haidar, I.; Kulkarni, S.; Pan, H. Forecasting Model for Crude Oil Prices Based on Artificial Neural Networks. In Proceedings of the Intelligent Sensors, Sensor Networks and Information Processing (ISSNIP 2008), Sydney, Australia, 15–18 December 2008; pp. 103–108.
20. Mostafa, M.M.; El-Masry, A.A. Oil price forecasting using gene expression programming and artificial neural networks. *Econ. Model.* **2016**, *54*, 40–53. [CrossRef]
21. Xie, W.; Yu, L.; Xu, S.; Wang, S. A new method for crude oil price forecasting based on support vector machines. In *Computational Science—ICCS 2006*; Springer: Berlin/Heidelberg, Germany, 2006; pp. 444–451.
22. Li, S.; Ge, Y. Crude oil price prediction based on a dynamic correcting support vector regression machine. *Abstr. Appl. Anal.* **2013**, *2013*, 528678.
23. Mustaffa, Z.; Yusof, Y.; Kamaruddin, S. Enhanced ABC-LSSVM for Energy fuel price prediction. *J. Inf. Commun. Technol.* **2013**, *12*, 73–101.
24. Khashman, A.; Nwulu, N.I. Support Vector Machines Versus Back Propagation Algorithm for Oil Price Prediction. In Proceedings of the 8th International Symposium on Neural Networks (ISNN2011), Guilin, China, 29 May–1 June 2011; pp. 530–538.
25. Wang, S.; Yu, L.; Lai, K.K. A Novel Hybrid AI System Framework for Crude Oil Price Forecasting. In *Data Mining and Knowledge Management, Proceedings of the Chinese Academy of Sciences Symposium on Data Mining and Knowledge Management 2005, Beijing, China, 12–14 July 2004*; Springer: Berlin/Heidelberg, Germany, 2005; pp. 233–242.
26. Amin-Naseri, M.R.; Gharacheh, E.A. A Hybrid Artificial Intelligence Approach to Monthly Forecasting of Crude Oil Price Time Series. In Proceedings of the 10th International Conference on Engineering Applications of Neural Networks, Thessaloniki, Hellas, Greece, 29–31 August 2007; pp. 160–167.
27. Tehrani, R.; Khodayar, F. A hybrid optimized artificial intelligent model to forecast crude oil using genetic algorithm. *Afr. J. Bus. Manag.* **2011**, *5*, 13130–13135. [CrossRef]
28. Li, T.; Zhou, M. ECG classification using wavelet packet entropy and random forests. *Entropy* **2016**, *18*, 285. [CrossRef]
29. Deng, W.; Zhang, S.; Zhao, H.; Yang, X. A novel fault diagnosis method based on integrating empirical wavelet transform and fuzzy entropy for motor bearing. *IEEE Access* **2018**, *6*, 35042–35056. [CrossRef]
30. Zhao, H.; Meng, S.; Deng, W.; Yang, X. A new feature extraction method based on EEMD and multi-scale fuzzy entropy for motor bearing. *Entropy* **2017**, *19*, 14. [CrossRef]
31. Zhu, B.; Shi, X.; Chevallier, J.; Wang, P.; Wei, Y.M. An adaptive multiscale ensemble learning paradigm for nonstationary and nonlinear energy price time series forecasting. *J. Forecast.* **2016**, *35*, 633–651. [CrossRef]
32. Tang, L.; Dai, W.; Yu, L.; Wang, S. A novel CEEMD-based EELM ensemble learning paradigm for crude oil price forecasting. *Int. J. Inf. Technol. Decis. Mak.* **2015**, *14*, 141–169. [CrossRef]

33. Huan, J.; Cao, W.; Qin, Y. Prediction of dissolved oxygen in aquaculture based on EEMD and LSSVM optimized by the Bayesian evidence framework. *Comput. Electron. Agric.* **2018**, *150*, 257–265. [CrossRef]
34. Zhou, Y.; Li, T.; Shi, J.; Qian, Z. A CEEMDAN and XGBOOST-based approach to forecast crude oil prices. *Complexity* **2019**, *2019*. [CrossRef]
35. Jammazi, R.; Aloui, C. Crude oil price forecasting: Experimental evidence from wavelet decomposition and neural network modeling. *Energy Econ.* **2012**, *34*, 828–841. [CrossRef]
36. Zheng, H.; Yuan, J.; Chen, L. Short-term load forecasting using EMD-LSTM neural networks with a xgboost algorithm for feature importance evaluation. *Energies* **2017**, *10*, 1168. [CrossRef]
37. Zhu, B.; Ye, S.; Wang, P.; He, K.; Zhang, T.; Wei, Y.M. A novel multiscale nonlinear ensemble leaning paradigm for carbon price forecasting. *Energy Econ.* **2018**, *70*, 143–157. [CrossRef]
38. Fan, G.F.; Peng, L.L.; Hong, W.C.; Sun, F. Electric load forecasting by the SVR model with differential empirical mode decomposition and auto regression. *Neurocomputing* **2016**, *173*, 958–970. [CrossRef]
39. Zhang, J.L.; Zhang, Y.J.; Zhang, L. A novel hybrid method for crude oil price forecasting. *Energy Econ.* **2015**, *49*, 649–659. [CrossRef]
40. Torres, M.E.; Colominas, M.A.; Schlotthauer, G.; Flandrin, P. A Complete Ensemble Empirical Mode Decomposition with Adaptive Noise. In Proceedings of the IEEE International Conference on Acoustics, Speech and Signal Processing (ICASSP 2011), Prague, Czech Republic, 22–27 May 2011; pp. 4144–4147.
41. Wu, Z.; Huang, N.E. Ensemble empirical mode decomposition: A noise-assisted data analysis method. *Adv. Adapt. Data Anal.* **2009**, *1*, 1–41. [CrossRef]
42. Huang, N.E.; Shen, Z.; Long, S.R.; Wu, M.C.; Shih, H.H.; Zheng, Q.; Yen, N.C.; Tung, C.C.; Liu, H.H. The Empirical Mode Decomposition and the Hilbert Spectrum for Nonlinear and Non-Stationary Time Series Analysis. In *Proceedings of the Royal Society of London A: Mathematical, Physical and Engineering Sciences 1998*; The Royal Society: London, UK, 1998; pp. 903–995.
43. Tipping, M.E. Sparse Bayesian learning and the relevance vector machine. *J. Mach. Learn. Res.* **2001**, *1*, 211–244.
44. Ghosh, S.; Mujumdar, P.P. Statistical downscaling of GCM simulations to streamflow using relevance vector machine. *Adv. Water Resour.* **2008**, *31*, 132–146. [CrossRef]
45. Li, T.; Zhang, Z. Robust face recognition via block sparse Bayesian learning. *Math. Problems Eng.* **2013**, *2013*. [CrossRef]
46. Widodo, A.; Kim, E.Y.; Son, J.D.; Yang, B.S.; Tan, A.C.; Gu, D.S.; Choi, B.K.; Mathew, J. Fault diagnosis of low speed bearing based on relevance vector machine and support vector machine. *Expert Syst. Appl.* **2009**, *36*, 7252–7261. [CrossRef]
47. Williams, O.; Blake, A.; Cipolla, R. Sparse bayesian learning for efficient visual tracking. *IEEE Trans. Pattern Anal. Mach. Intell.* **2005**, *27*, 1292–1304. [CrossRef]
48. Zhang, Z.; Rao, B.D. Sparse signal recovery with temporally correlated source vectors using sparse Bayesian learning. *IEEE J. Sel. Top. Signal Process.* **2011**, *5*, 912–926. [CrossRef]
49. Xu, X.M.; Mao, Y.F.; Xiong, J.N.; Zhou, F.L. Classification Performance Comparison between RVM and SVM. In Proceedings of the International Workshop on Anti-Counterfeiting, Security, Identification, Xiamen, China, 16–18 April 2007; pp. 208–211.
50. Wipf, D.P.; Rao, B.D. Sparse Bayesian learning for basis selection. *IEEE Trans. Signal Process.* **2004**, *52*, 2153–2164. [CrossRef]
51. Liu, H.; Tian, H.Q.; Li, Y.F. Comparison of two new ARIMA-ANN and ARIMA-Kalman hybrid methods for wind speed prediction. *Appl. Energy* **2012**, *98*, 415–424. [CrossRef]
52. Diebold, F.X.; Mariano, R.S. Comparing predictive accuracy. *J. Bus. Econ. Stat.* **1995**, *13*, 253–263.

© 2019 by the authors. Licensee MDPI, Basel, Switzerland. This article is an open access article distributed under the terms and conditions of the Creative Commons Attribution (CC BY) license (http://creativecommons.org/licenses/by/4.0/).

Article

Multi-Step Wind Speed Forecasting Based On Ensemble Empirical Mode Decomposition, Long Short Term Memory Network and Error Correction Strategy

Yuansheng Huang [1], Lei Yang [1,*], Shijian Liu [1] and Guangli Wang [2]

1. School of Economics and Management, North China Electric Power University, Beijing 102206, China; hys2656@aliyun.com (Y.H.); liushijian1992@163.com (S.L.)
2. State Grid Jibei Electric Power Company Engineering Management Company, Beijing 100070, China; wangguangli@heesc.com
* Correspondence: 1162106026@ncepu.edu.cn; Tel.: +86-186-317-28689

Received: 26 March 2019; Accepted: 9 May 2019; Published: 14 May 2019

Abstract: It is of great significance for wind power plant to construct an accurate multi-step wind speed prediction model, especially considering its operations and grid integration. By integrating with a data pre-processing measure, a parameter optimization algorithm and error correction strategy, a novel forecasting method for multi-step wind speed in short period is put forward in this article. In the suggested measure, the EEMD (Ensemble Empirical Mode Decomposition) is applied to extract a series of IMFs (intrinsic mode functions) from the initial wind data sequence; the LSTM (Long Short Term Memory) measure is executed as the major forecasting method for each IMF; the GRNN (general regression neural network) is executed as the secondary forecasting method to forecast error sequences for each IMF; and the BSO (Brain Storm Optimization) is employed to optimize the parameter for GRNN during the training process. To verify the validity of the suggested EEMD-LSTM-GRNN-BSO model, eight models were applied on three different wind speed sequences. The calculation outcomes reveal that: (1) the EEMD is able to boost the wind speed prediction capacity and robustness of the LSTM approach effectively; (2) the BSO based parameter optimization method is effective in finding the optimal parameter for GRNN and improving the forecasting performance for the EEMD-LSTM-GRNN model; (3) the error correction method based on the optimized GRNN promotes the forecasting accuracy of the EEMD-LSTM model significantly; and (4) compared with all models involved, the proposed EEMD-LSTM-GRNN-BSO model is proved to have the best performance in predicting the short-term wind speed sequence.

Keywords: multi-step wind speed prediction; Ensemble Empirical Mode Decomposition; Long Short Term Memory; General Regression Neural Network; Brain Storm Optimization

1. Introduction

As the awareness of environmental protection increases, the application and promotion of renewable energy has attracted worldwide attention. As one type of promising renewable energy, wind power is experiencing a rapid development [1]. Nevertheless, owning to the instability and stochastic property of wind power generation, the instability of power system is caused easily when considering wind power [2]. Therefore, it is imperative to propose an accurate prediction method for wind speed to reduce the instability risk of the power system and the economic losses for wind power enterprises.

In recent years, many scholars have done extensive research on predicting the wind speed sequence. The traditional prediction measures are universally recognized as four kinds: (1) physical method; (2) statistical method; (3) intelligent approach; and (4) hybrid model [3]. The physical method commonly takes advantage of physical data, for example temperature, air density, topographic information and so on [4], which is mainly obtained through numerical weather prediction [5], to get the prediction results. However, the physical methods are not good at forecasting wind speed in short period and the methods also require plenty of time to compute and additional resources [6]. The statistical measures, such as the autoregressive integrated moving average (ARIMA) measure, are built with easy procedures of pattern recognition, parameter estimation and model checking [7]. However, this kind of methods cannot afford to deal with the non-linear problems [8]. Owning to the ability to recognize the non-linear characters, the intelligent approaches, for instance artificial neural networks (ANNs) [9–11], support vector machine (SVM) [12], the genetic algorithm [13] and the general regression neural network (GRNN) [14], have been utilized to forecast wind speed effectively. Due to the superior ability to recognize the non-linear structure, intelligent approach is better at forecasting the wind speed of short period than traditional time series based methods. Nevertheless, the single intelligent approaches also suffer form certain problems. For example, genetic algorithm measure has the problem of premature convergence, which limits its searching ability to obtain the optimal value. Furthermore, with the function to recognize deep characteristics in the data, the deep learning approaches, for example the deep convolutional neural network [15] and LSTM [16], have been investigated in the process of prediction for wind speed in recent studies.

However, due to the unstable property of wind speed, a single intelligent model may occasionally fall into local extremum and result in poor forecasting performance. Hence, to fix this problem, hybrid models to predict wind speed are put forward. There are four types of hybrid forecasting models [17].

(1) The hybrid methods involving weighting approaches give a weighing parameter to each single approach based on their forecasting performance and then add the weighted forecasting results together. For example, Shi et al. [18] put forward a weighting based hybrid approach involving grey relational analysis as well as the distribution characteristics of wind velocity, which integrates the LSSVM (least square support vector machine) and the RBFNN (Radial Basis Function Neural Networks). The weighting parameters in the approach can be calculated based on data sequences in each month. The results reveal that the suggested combination measure effectively promotes the performance in forecasting the wind speed in very short term. Xiao et al. [10] utilized the nonnegative constraint theory and hybrid smart approaches to obtain the wind speed prediction, in which the importance degrees of the latter combined approaches are decided utilizing the chaos particle optimization algorithm as well as the genetic algorithm. The afore-mentioned hybrid approaches take advantage of the strength of single forecasting methods, thus the forecasting accuracy is significantly improved.

(2) The signal pre-processing measure is executed to obtain a collection of sub-sequences, which are stationary and regular, from the initial non-linear time series. Different decomposition approaches have been utilized in latest hybrid prediction approaches extensively. For instance, in [19], the raw data series is preprocessed by wavelet transform (WT) before being brought into the forecasting procedure of SVM. The final outcomes indicate that the suggested approach consisting of WT and SVM is superior to the single SVM approach in prediction accuracy. Fan [20] used a combination measure integrating the empirical mode decomposition (EMD) and SVM, in which the initial wind speed data are processed with EMD for the purpose of fluctuation deduction. However, the EMD method cannot afford to dispose the problem of mode mixing. Therefore, to compensate for the disadvantage of EMD, the ensemble empirical mode decomposition (EEMD) measure is utilized in [21]. Cheng [22] utilized a hybrid model integrated with the EEMD approach to construct the forecasting process for wind speed, where the EEMD is applied for information extraction from the raw wind speed series. The final outcomes reveal that the suggested approach with EEMD shows a better prediction performance than the EMD or LSSVM method.

(3) Hybrid models integrating parameter optimization, which applies the optimization methods to find optimal setting for the prediction models in the training procedure, are investigated recently.

Chitsaz et al. [23] presented a novel prediction measure which has the structure of the Wavelet Neural Network (WNN) as well as multi-dimensional Morlet wavelet. The modified Clonal selection method is used for finding the optimal parameters in WNN with the training criterion of Maximum Correntropy Criterion. The final outcomes demonstrate the validity of the suggested method. In [24], a novel hybrid wind speed prediction measure in short period consisting of mutual information, wavelet transform, evolutionary particle swarm optimization (EPSO) and the adaptive neuro-fuzzy inference system (ANFIS) is developed, in which the EPSO is utilized to search the optimal parameter for ANFIS. The final results reveal that the suggested measure has advantages in forecasting accuracy over the other comparison models. Yuan et al. [25] presented the gravitational search algorithm (GSA) for searching the best parameter for LSSVM model. The experiment outcomes show that the suggested LSSVM-GSA combination measure have the highest forecasting accuracy, compared with other models. The Brain Storm Optimization (BSO) approach, which is enlightened from the process of brainstorming for people, is put forward in [26]. Modeling BSO algorithm requires simulating the form of gathering various experts together to propose potential solutions for the current problem [27]. Each individual is grouped into different teams for collaborative investigation. Various teams are able to locate different answer space areas to promote the possibility to find the best solution, which possesses an excellent global exploration ability [28]. The significance of BSO has been validated by numerous scholars [29,30].

(4) Unlike the aforementioned hybrid methods, the hybrid models based on the data post-processing technique emphasize using the error correction method to reduce the adverse effect brought by the forecasting error. For instance, Liang et al. [31] put forward a novel hybrid model, in which the forecasting step for the raw data sequence of wind power is conducted with the SVM, and then the prediction error for the SVM is forecasted utilizing the SVM together with the ELM. The numerical outcomes demonstrate that the proposed combination measure with error correction can promote the wind power prediction performance effectively. Jiang et al. [32] put forward a combined structure, in which the EEMD is executed to pre-process the wind speed sequences with mean zero, and the chosen sub-layers are forecasted using LSSVM. Then, the LSSVM and the Generalized Auto-Regressive Conditionally Heteroscedastic (GARCH) measure are applied for forecasting the error sequences. The outcomes demonstrate that the error correction method contributes to the forecasting accuracy improvement. Moreover, in [33], the prediction errors of the wind speed series in short period, which are acquired by the measure of grey forecasting, are forecasted utilizing the Markov method for wind speed forecasting error correction before it is turned into wind power forecasting, and the results show the superiorities of the proposed approach in forecasting accuracy improvement.

All four types of hybrid forecasting model mentioned above can contribute to the improvement of forecasting performance. In this paper, the signal pre-processing technique, the parameter optimization algorithm and the error correction method are considered. The suggested combination model involving the signal decomposition technique, the parameter optimization algorithm and the error correction method is built as follow: (1) The EEMD is applied to extract a collection of IMFs from the raw wind speed sequence. (2) The LSTM network is used to forecast each IMF. (3) The GRNN is conducted to predict the error sequence for each IMF (intrinsic mode function). (4) The BSO is executed to optimize the parameter for GRNN. (5) The ultimate prediction result is obtained through merging all the predictions of IMFs.

The major contribution in the article is proposing a novel multi-step wind speed prediction structure combining the data pre-processing technique, the parameter optimization algorithm and the error correction method to achieve a satisfactory forecasting performance, and to analyze the influences of every element of the proposed hybrid model in forecasting accuracy contribution. As far as we know, the potential performance of the suggested structure, which integrates three kinds of improvements in one hybrid model, has not been studied in the prediction for short-term wind speed. Thus, aiming at investigating the effectiveness of each component, the overall prediction performance and the generalization of the suggested combination measure, eight diverse approaches were applied to forecast two different 5-min wind speed sequences and one 30-min wind speed sequence. Finally, the prediction accuracy of all the approaches involved in this paper were estimated utilizing different evaluating indicators.

The structure for this article is described as below. Section 2 describes the application process of the suggested hybrid measure and the single models required. Section 3 introduces the evaluation criteria for prediction capacity. Section 4 presents two 5-min wind speed forecasting case studies to prove the forecasting capacity of the suggested hybrid measure. Section 5 presents an additional 30-min case to further validate the generalization of the suggested measure. Finally, the conclusions are drawn in Section 6.

2. Methodology

2.1. The Overall Structure of the Suggested Combination Measure

The structure of the suggested EEMD-LSTM-GRNN-BSO approach is shown in Figure 1. The specific processes are described below:

(1) The EEMD method is executed to extract a collection of IMFs from the wind speed observations. The ratio of the standard deviation of the added noise takes 0.01 and the ensemble number for the EEMD takes 100. Finally, 11 IMFs are obtained utilizing EEMD. The process of the EEMD measure are shown in Section 2.2.
(2) The IMFs are classified into two training sets. The input matrices and output matrices are formed with data in each set based on the procedures described in Figure 2 to train the forecasting models.
(3) The LSTM network is trained with the data in Training Set 1 to predict each IMF; the trained LSTM networks are tested with data in Training Set 2; the forecasting error series are obtained by finding the difference between the observations and predictions of Training Set 2. The procedures of the LSTM models are described in Section 2.3.
(4) The GRNN approach is trained with the error sequence of the Training Set 2 to model the prediction errors for the LSTM network. The BSO algorithm is executed to search the optimal smooth factor for further prediction accuracy improvement, in which the smooth factor is treated as the variable to be optimized and the mean absolute error (MAE) calculated with the predictions and observations is considered as the fitness function of BSO. Each value of smooth factor in the searching space is brought in to the GRNN to obtain the predictions and the corresponding fitness, until the optimal value is found. Sections 2.4 and 2.5 describe the details of GRNN and BSO, respectively.
(5) The LSTM network and the GRNN model optimized by BSO are combined to construct the proposed hybrid forecasting measure. The suggested combination measure is validated using the test set for getting each IMF predictions and the error predictions. The overall prediction for each IMF can be obtained with the equation below:

$$P_{IMF_i}^{corrected} = P_{IMF_i} + P_{ERR_i} \quad (1)$$

where i is the number of IMF determined by the EEMD method. $P_{IMF_i}^{corrected}$ stands for the corrected prediction for each IMF. P_{IMF_i} represents the original predictions for each IMF forecasted by BSO. P_{ERR_i} stands for the error prediction for each IMF forecasted by optimized GRNN. The final predicted wind speed sequences are gained by means of merging all the corrected predictions of IMF together.

(6) To test and verify the wind speed prediction performance of the suggested combination EEMD-LSTM-GRNN-BSO approach, seven other prediction methods were used as comparisons. The comparison models involved in this study are the ARIMA measure, the BP network, the GRNN measure, the LSTM measure, the LSTM-GRNN-BSO measure, the EEMD-LSTM measure, and the EEMD-LSTM-GRNN measure. Comparisons between models were also utilized to reveal the effectiveness of each component in forecasting accuracy improvement.

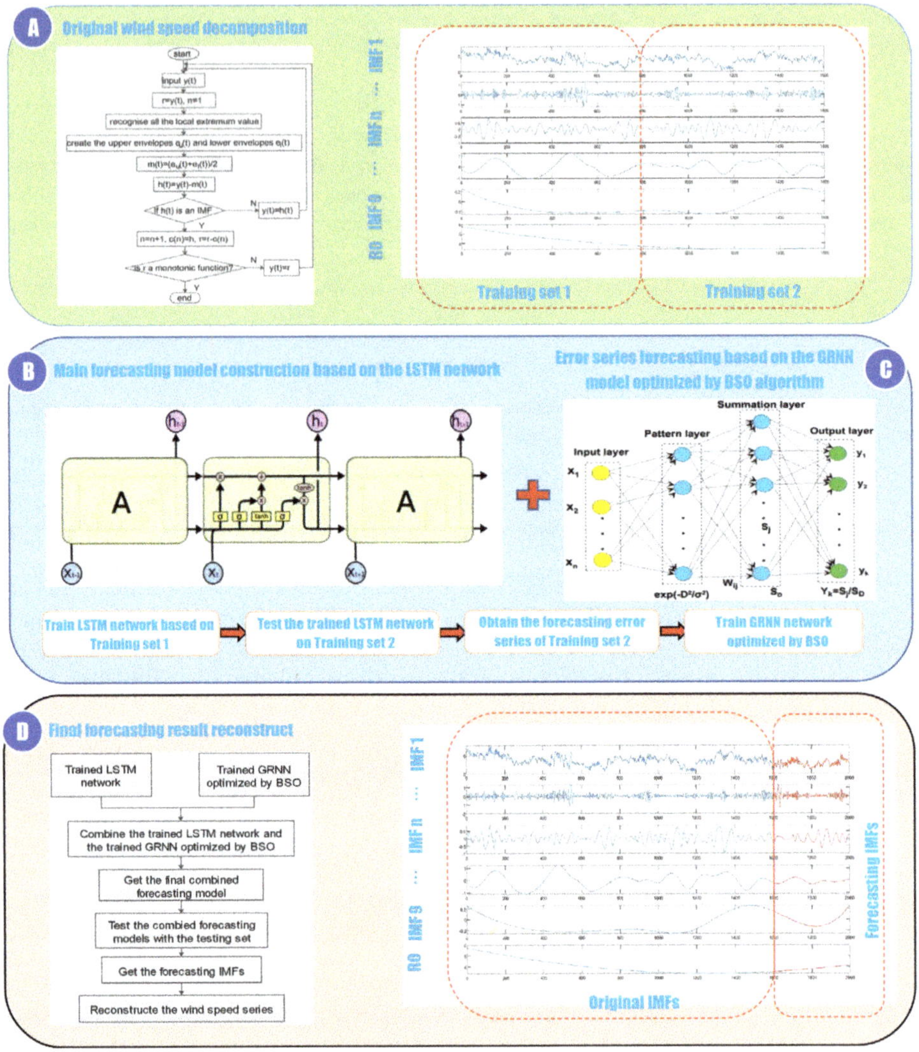

Figure 1. The whole process of the EEMD-LSTM-GRNN-BSO.

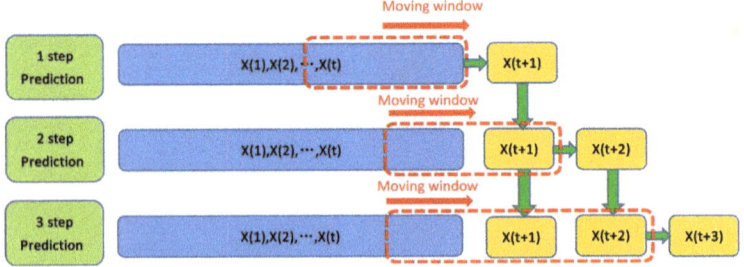

Figure 2. The structure of the multi-step forecasting strategy.

2.2. Ensemble Empirical Mode Decomposition

Being a valid data series disposing measure, empirical mode decomposition (EMD) can draw the feature information from the raw data series [34]. Utilizing the EMD approach, a collection of intrinsic mode functions (IMFs) are acquired. Following the EMD measure, the ensemble empirical mode decomposition (EEMD) was studied to handle the mode mixing issue, which cannot be solved by the EMD approach. The main process for the EEMD measure [22] is described as follows:

(1) Create a novel data series $y(t)$ by adding white noise into the raw data series $x(t)$.
(2) Recognize all the local extremum values for the data series $y(t)$.
(3) Construct the upper envelopes $e_u(t)$ and lower envelopes $e_l(t)$ for $y(t)$
(4) Generate the average value $m(t)$ with the upper envelope and the lower envelope.

$$m(t) = \frac{e_u(t) + e_l(t)}{2} \tag{2}$$

(5) Calculate the distinction between the raw data series $y(t)$ and $m(t)$ as the first part $h(t)$:

$$y(t) - m(t) = h(t) \tag{3}$$

(6) Iterated the sifting procedure several times. The iterative process continues for k times until $h(t)$ is an IMF. After that the first IMF part c_1 is shown as follow:

$$y(t) - c_1 = r_1 \tag{4}$$

(7) The residue r_1 is considered as a new series, and Steps (2)–(6) are repeated to get all r_j and a residue c_n. Finally, by adding up all the IMFs and the residue obtained, the following is acquired:

$$y(t) = \sum_{j=1}^{n} c_j + r_n \tag{5}$$

EEMD is regarded as an approach to help analyze data with noise by means of mixing white noise into the raw series, and it is useful to mitigate the problem caused by mode mixing.

2.3. Long Short Term Memory Measure

Improved from Recurrent Neural Network (RNN), the LSTM measure was put forward by Hochreiter and Schmidhuber [35] in 1997. The important parts of the LSTM network are its memory cells, which make it different from the traditional RNN. Graves and Schmidhuber [36] explained that three types of multiplicative units exist in the structure of LSTM model: the input gate, the output gate and the forget gate in the memory cells. These gates change the state of the memory cells following the steps below [37]: (a) by activating the input gate, as the latest data enters, the input message is able to be accumulated to the cell; (b) by activating the forget gate, the former cell states are to be abandoned during the procedure; and (3) the output gate is responsible for deciding if the latest cell output is propagated to the final state.

In terms of short wind speed forecasting, $x = (x_1, x_2, \cdots, x_T)$ is the historical wind speed series and $y = (y_1, y_2, \cdots, y_T)$ is the forecasting value. The prediction of the wind speed sequence is computed as below [38]:

$$i_t = \sigma(W_{ix}x_t + W_{im}m_{t-1} + W_{ic}c_{t-1} + b_i) \tag{6}$$

$$f_t = \sigma(W_{fx}x_t + W_{fm}m_{t-1} + W_{fc}c_{t-1} + b_f) \tag{7}$$

$$c_t = f_t \cdot c_{t-1} + i_t \cdot g(W_{cx}x_t + W_{cm}m_{t-1} + b_c) \tag{8}$$

$$o_t = \sigma(W_{ox}x_t + W_{om}m_{t-1} + W_{oc}c_t + b_o) \tag{9}$$

$$m_t = o_t \cdot h(c_t) \tag{10}$$

$$y_t = W_{ym}m_t + b_y \tag{11}$$

where i_t represents the input gate, f_t represents the forget gate, c_t represents the activation vector for every cell, o_t stands for the output gate, m_t stands for the activation vectors for every memory block, W represents the weigh matrices, b represents the bias vectors and the mathematical symbol "·" stands for the scalar product.

$\sigma(\cdot)$ stands for the standard logistic function:

$$\sigma(x) = \frac{1}{1+e^{-x}} \tag{12}$$

$g(\cdot)$ stands for the centered logistic function:

$$g(x) = \frac{4}{1+e^{-x}} - 2 x \in [-2,2] \tag{13}$$

$h(\cdot)$ stands for the centered logistic function:

$$h(x) = \frac{2}{1+e^{-x}} - 1 x \in [-1,1] \tag{14}$$

2.4. General Regression Neural Network

Specht put forward the GRNN method in 1991 [39]. The GRNN has many advantages such as strong non-linear mapping abilities, flexible network framework and satisfactory robustness, which makes it a perfect choice to deal with non-linear problems. Although the GRNN has a similar structure to the RBFNN, its approaching ability and learning speed is better. The structure of GRNN includes the input layer, the pattern layer, the summation layer and the output layer. The framework of GRNN is described in Figure 1C. The input for GRNN is $X = [X_1, X_2, \cdots, X_n]^T$ and the output is $Y = [Y_1, Y_2, \cdots, Y_k]^T$. The following descriptions explains the detailed process of GRNN:

(1) Input layer: The amount of neurons and the dimension of the input data of the training set should be kept consistent. Every neuron denotes an easy distribution unit that delivers the input information straightly to the pattern layer.
(2) Pattern layer: The number of neurons equals the number of training data. Every neuron denotes a diverse sample. The calculation for the neuron transfer function of the pattern layer p_i is shown below:

$$p_i = exp[-frac(X - X_i)^T(X - X_i)2\sigma^2], i = 1, 2, \cdots, n \tag{15}$$

where X stands for the input variables for the model and X_i stands for the training data of neuron i. The width parameter of the Gaussian function is controlled by smoothing factor σ.
(3) Summation layer: The procedure of summation is calculated with two kinds of neurons. One way is to merge the output of each neuron in pattern layer with the formula of $\sum_{i=1}^{n} exp[-frac(X - X_i)^T(X - X_i)2\sigma^2]$ to obtain the summation S_D for the summation layer. The combination weighting parameter connecting the pattern layer and each neuron is equal to one, and the transfer formula is shown below:

$$S_D = \sum_{i=1}^{n} p_i \tag{16}$$

The other way is to conduct the summation S_{Nj} of all the neurons in the pattern layer with different weights, whose formula is represented by $\sum_{i=1}^{n} Y_i exp[-frac(X - X_i)^T(X - X_i)2\sigma^2]$. The jth component of ith output sample Y_i defines the weighting parameter connecting the ith neuron in the pattern layer and the *j*th molecule in the summation layer. The corresponding transfer formula is as follow.

$$S_{Nj} = \sum_{i=1}^{n} y_{ij} p_i, j = 1, 2, \cdots, k \qquad (17)$$

(4) Output layer: The amount of neurons and the dimension of the output vector in the sample should be kept consistent. The output of neuron *j* is equal to the *j*th component of the calculated outcome $\hat{Y}(X)$, which is calculated as:

$$y_j = \frac{S_{Nj}}{S_D}, j = 1, 2, \cdots, k \qquad (18)$$

As the parameter σ takes a great value, $\hat{Y}(X)$ is closer to the average value of all the sample based variables. Conversely, as the value of parameter σ is closer to zero, $\hat{Y}(X)$ is similar to the training set. Under the situation that the predicted point are part of the training set, the prediction for the dependent variable is rather similar to the corresponding dependent variable of the training set. When this happens, the corresponding sample cannot be considered, which may lead to unsatisfactory forecasting performance and generalization. When the smooth factor σ takes a proper value, the calculation of $\hat{Y}(X)$ includes the dependent variable of all training data, and the distance between the dependent variable and the corresponding forecasting point is assigned with a larger weight. Thus, based on the significant influence of smooth factor σ on the forecasting performance of GRNN, the BSO is utilized to search the optima value for GRNN during the training process.

2.5. Brain Storm Optimization

The BSO [40,41] is an algorithm based on population aiming at mimicking brainstorming meetings conducted by people. In the process of BSO, each population can be considered as a set of ideas. Each idea stands for a solution for the issue. In every iteration, a population of ideas (solutions) is renewed. At first, ideas are allocated to search space randomly. Every single idea *idea^i* is renewed by the following steps.

- Firstly, k-means clustering can be utilized to identify similar solutions and the optimal idea of each cluster is marked as the cluster center.
- Secondly, BSO creates a novel idea *nidea^i* by making it equal to one of options mentioned below.

    - A probabilistically chosen cluster center
    - A randomly chosen idea from a probabilistically selected cluster
    - The stochastic integration of two probabilistically chosen cluster centers
    - The stochastic integration of two randomly chosen ideas from two probabilistically chosen clusters

    One of the options is randomly chosen according to several parameters, $p_{one-cluster}$, $p_{one-center}$, and $p_{two-centers}$. Besides, a cluster is probabilistically chosen based on its scale, which reflects the amount of ideas in the cluster.
- Thirdly, the created *nidea^i* is perturbed utilizing a step-size parameter ξ and Gaussian distribution.
- Finally, *nidea^i* substitutes the current *idea^i* if its fitness is better. If not, it is abandoned.

The main steps of BSO algorithm [42] is described in Figure 3, where *n* represents the population scale, *m* represents the amount of clusters, and $N(0,1)$ stands for a normal distribution in which the average value is 0 and the standard deviation is 1. ξ represents a dynamically updated step-size and *k* is for altering the slope of the *logsig* function. As the special evolution of BSO, making diverse groups to explore wide solution space area helps BSO to avoid local extremum trap and increase the probability to find the optimal value, thus making BSO a good choice to optimize the smooth factor for GRNN.

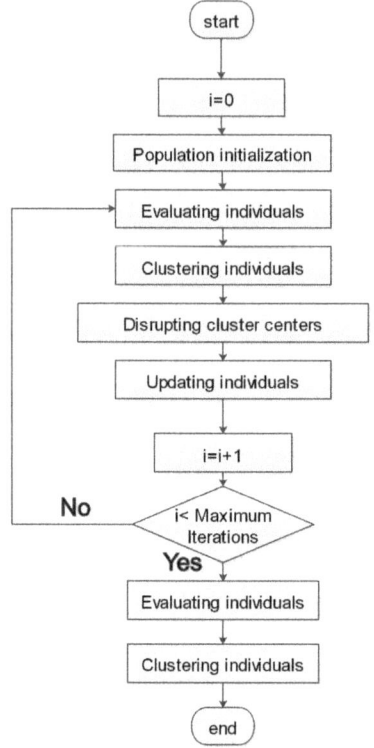

Figure 3. The main procedure of BSO.

3. Evaluation Criteria for Prediction Capacity

Aiming to investigate the forecasting capacity of the suggested combination forecasting model, three widely used evaluation indexes were applied to compare the prediction capacity: mean absolute error (MAE), root mean square error (RMSE), and mean absolute percent error (MAPE). The indicators are described as below:

$$MAE = \frac{1}{T}\sum_{t=1}^{T} |p_t^{ture} - p^{forecast}| \quad (19)$$

$$MAPE = \frac{1}{T}\sum_{t=1}^{T} |\frac{p^{ture}(t) - p^{forecast}(t)}{p^{ture}(t)}| \times 100\% \quad (20)$$

$$RMSE = \sqrt{\frac{1}{T}\sum_{t=1}^{T} |p^{ture}(t) - p^{forecast}(t)|^2} \quad (21)$$

where $p^{ture}(t)$ represents the actual observation data of the moment t and $p^{forecast}(t)$ represents the value of prediction for the corresponding moment. T is the number of predicted points. Moreover, aiming at analyzing the forecasting capacity increase of the suggested measure, the percentage improvements of MAE, MAPE and RMSE, which are represented by P_{MAE}, P_{MAPE}, P_{RMSE}, respectively, were also used in this study. These evaluation indexes can be defined as follows:

$$P_{MAE} = \frac{|MAE_1 - MAE_2|}{MAE_1} \times 100\% \quad (22)$$

$$P_{MAPE} = \frac{|MAPE_1 - MAPE_2|}{MAPE_1} \times 100\% \tag{23}$$

$$P_{RMSE} = \frac{|RMSE_1 - RMSE_2|}{RMSE_1} \times 100\% \tag{24}$$

4. Case Study

4.1. Datasets

Figures 4 and 5 demonstrate two different datasets with a time interval of 5 min collected from 1 January 2018 to 7 January 2018 and from 1 May 2018 to 7 May 2018 at different wind power plants in Zhang Jiakou, Hebei, China. Training Set 1, including samples from 1 to 800 of each sequence, were applied to train the LSTM network; and Training Set 2, including samples from 801 to 1600 of each sequence, were applied to create the error series and train the GRNN model, which was optimized by BSO. Samples 1601–2000 of each sequence were executed to test and estimate the prediction capacity of the models mentioned in this study.

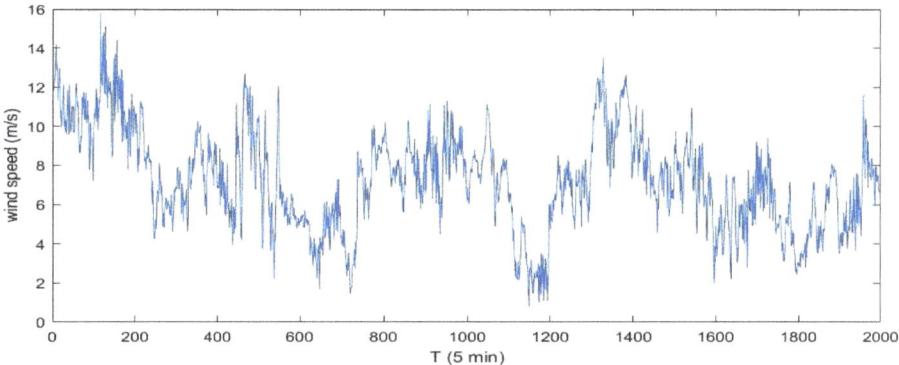

Figure 4. The observations for Wind Speed Sequence I.

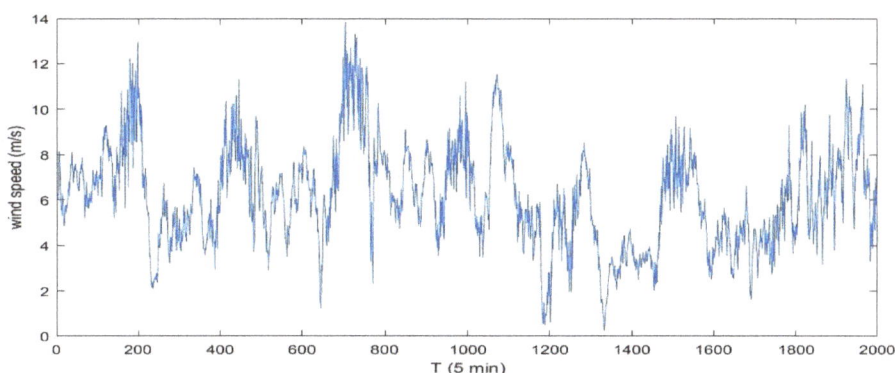

Figure 5. The observations for Wind Speed Sequence II.

4.2. Experiments

Aiming at validating the prediction capacity of the EEMD-LSTM-GRNN-BSO method, the suggested combination approach together with seven comparison methods were conducted on the two different datasets of wind speed. The comparison approaches were the ARIMA method, the BP method, the GRNN method, the LSTM method, the LSTM-GRNN-BSO measure, the EEMD-LSTM measure, and the EEMD-LSTM-GRNN measure. The actual wind speed sequence and the forecasting values of all involved approaches are presented in Figures 6 and 7. The calculation outcomes of evaluation indicators for the involved wind speed forecasting approaches are demonstrated in Tables 1 and 2.

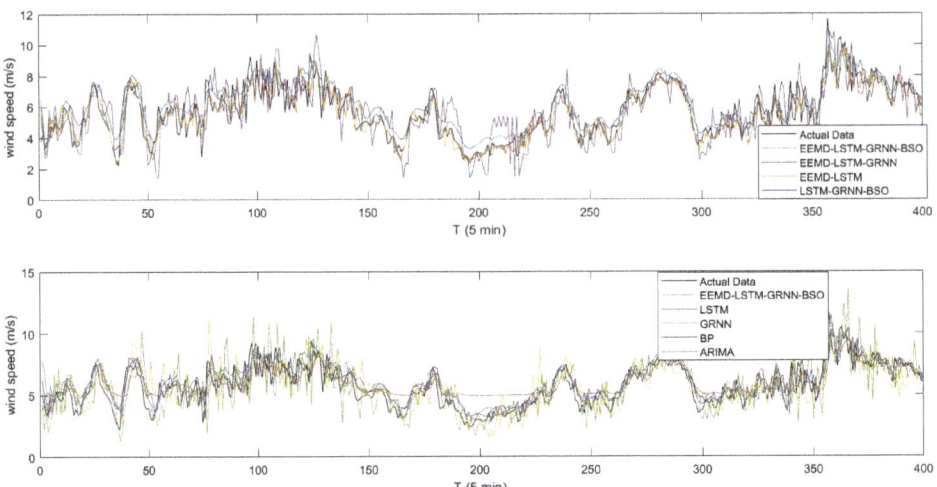

Figure 6. The comparisons between the observations and the predictions for Wind Speed Sequence I.

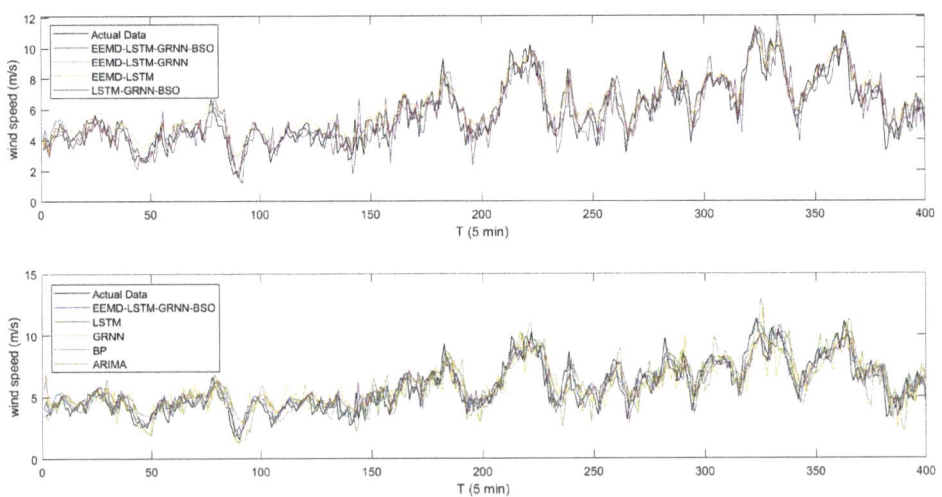

Figure 7. The comparisons between the observations and the predictions for Wind Speed Sequence II.

Table 1. The multi-step calculation results for evaluation indicators of involved approaches on Wind Speed Sequence I.

Prediction Approaches	Step	MAE (m/s)	MAPE (%)	RMSE (m/s)
EEMD-LSTM-GRNN-BSO	1	0.6052	0.0927	0.8025
	2	0.6649	0.1193	0.9286
	3	0.6644	0.1209	0.8991
	4	0.7838	0.1461	1.0246
	5	0.9113	0.1745	1.2160
EEMD-LSTM-GRNN	1	0.6195	0.1107	0.8293
	2	0.7038	0.1274	0.9598
	3	1.7694	0.3085	2.2488
	4	1.2821	0.2455	1.7051
	5	2.4081	0.4735	2.9840
EEMD-LSTM	1	0.6948	0.1055	0.8405
	2	0.7188	0.1429	0.9868
	3	1.5129	0.2657	1.9925
	4	1.5783	0.3143	2.0888
	5	2.6381	0.5188	3.2775
LSTM-GRNN-BSO	1	1.0445	0.2028	1.3149
	2	1.0845	0.2091	1.3628
	3	1.0855	0.2087	1.3749
	4	1.0747	0.2121	1.3699
	5	1.0210	0.2049	1.2979
LSTM	1	0.9138	0.1949	1.1499
	2	0.9910	0.2100	1.2299
	3	0.9637	0.1907	1.2330
	4	1.1164	0.2387	1.3970
	5	1.1484	0.2427	1.4212
GRNN	1	1.0490	0.1994	1.3159
	2	1.2893	0.2452	1.6017
	3	1.4521	0.2771	1.8032
	4	1.7666	0.3723	2.2328
	5	1.8136	0.3886	2.2956
BP	1	0.8109	0.1596	1.0438
	2	0.9709	0.1906	1.2429
	3	1.0365	0.2044	1.3238
	4	1.6595	0.3727	2.0423
	5	1.5991	0.3590	1.9573
ARIMA	1	1.1181	0.1997	1.5232
	2	1.7480	0.3160	2.3384
	3	2.2404	0.4093	2.9810
	4	2.8068	0.5142	3.6921
	5	3.3562	0.6153	4.4892

Table 2. The multi-step calculation results for evaluation indicators of involved approaches on Wind Speed Sequence II.

Prediction Approaches	Step	MAE (m/s)	MAPE (%)	RMSE (m/s)
EEMD-LSTM-GRNN-BSO	1	0.5749	0.1011	0.7241
	2	0.6818	0.1310	0.8750
	3	0.9345	0.1742	1.2028
	4	0.7572	0.1464	0.9812
	5	0.9239	0.1180	1.2261
EEMD-LSTM-GRNN	1	0.6004	0.1155	0.7539
	2	0.6953	0.1439	0.8909
	3	1.4508	0.2752	1.8090
	4	1.9493	0.3799	2.5754
	5	2.1149	0.4187	2.9147
EEMD-LSTM	1	0.7179	0.1530	0.8745
	2	0.9628	0.2039	1.1752
	3	2.0698	0.3929	2.5547
	4	2.3148	0.4569	2.8876
	5	3.7747	0.7488	4.7338
LSTM-GRNN-BSO	1	0.8960	0.1681	1.1275
	2	0.9132	0.1760	1.1789
	3	0.9542	0.1976	1.3128
	4	0.9043	0.1727	1.2007
	5	0.9848	0.1881	1.4490
LSTM	1	0.8545	0.1730	1.0871
	2	1.3254	0.2937	1.5884
	3	1.1863	0.2523	1.4632
	4	1.2628	0.2694	1.5758
	5	1.2905	0.2700	1.6110
GRNN	1	0.9569	0.1796	1.2244
	2	1.1424	0.2154	1.4702
	3	1.2899	0.2415	1.6464
	4	1.5085	0.3018	1.9219
	5	1.6906	0.3359	2.1260
BP	1	0.7674	0.1444	0.9793
	2	0.9225	0.1767	1.1698
	3	1.1302	0.2176	1.4051
	4	1.2835	0.2488	1.5905
	5	1.4013	0.2729	1.7293
ARIMA	1	1.0206	0.1884	1.3139
	2	1.3918	0.2624	1.7979
	3	1.7594	0.3355	2.2971
	4	2.1526	0.4130	2.7701
	5	2.5383	0.4864	3.2606

4.3. Comparison and Analysis

As shown in the above two tables, the calculation outcomes for evaluation indicators of the two wind speed sequences forecasting cases demonstrate the same trend. Tables 3 and 4 provide the percentage improvements for the three evaluation indicators of the suggested combination EEMD-LSTM-GRNN-BSO approach on the two different datasets in comparison with the other measures mentioned.

Table 3. The multi-step percentage improvements of the suggested EEMD-LSTM-GRNN-BSO approach in comparison with the other measures on Wind Speed Sequence I.

Prediction Approaches	Step	P_{MAE} (%)	P_{MAPE} (%)	P_{RMSE} (%)
EEMD-LSTM-GRNN	1	2.31	16.19	3.22
	2	5.52	6.32	3.25
	3	62.45	60.79	60.02
	4	38.86	40.51	39.91
	5	62.16	63.15	59.25
EEMD-LSTM	1	12.89	12.09	4.52
	2	7.50	16.51	5.89
	3	56.08	54.48	54.88
	4	50.34	53.52	50.95
	5	65.46	66.37	62.90
LSTM-GRNN-BSO	1	42.05	54.26	38.97
	2	38.69	42.93	31.86
	3	38.80	42.04	34.61
	4	27.07	31.14	25.20
	5	10.75	14.86	6.31
LSTM	1	33.77	52.42	30.21
	2	32.90	43.18	24.50
	3	31.06	36.59	27.08
	4	29.79	38.81	26.66
	5	20.65	28.11	14.44
GRNN	1	42.30	53.49	39.01
	2	48.43	51.33	42.02
	3	54.24	56.36	50.14
	4	55.63	60.77	54.11
	5	49.75	55.10	47.03
BP	1	25.37	41.89	23.12
	2	31.51	37.41	25.29
	3	35.90	40.83	32.08
	4	52.77	60.80	49.83
	5	43.01	51.41	37.87
ARIMA	1	45.87	53.56	47.31
	2	61.96	62.24	60.29
	3	70.35	70.45	69.84
	4	72.07	71.59	72.25
	5	72.85	71.65	72.91

Table 4. The multi-step percentage improvements of the suggested EEMD-LSTM-GRNN-BSO approach in comparison with the other measures on Wind Speed Sequence II.

Prediction Approaches	Step	P_{MAE} (%)	P_{MAPE} (%)	P_{RMSE} (%)
EEMD-LSTM-GRNN	1	4.25	12.50	3.96
	2	1.93	8.99	1.78
	3	35.59	36.72	33.51
	4	61.15	61.45	61.90
	5	56.31	47.93	57.93
EEMD-LSTM	1	19.93	33.94	17.20
	2	29.18	35.75	25.54
	3	54.85	55.67	52.92
	4	67.29	67.95	66.02
	5	75.52	70.88	74.10
LSTM-GRNN-BSO	1	35.84	39.87	35.78
	2	25.34	25.58	25.78
	3	2.07	11.87	8.37
	4	16.26	15.19	18.27
	5	6.18	37.25	15.38

Table 4. Cont.

Prediction Approaches	Step	P_{MAE} (%)	P_{MAPE} (%)	P_{RMSE} (%)
LSTM	1	32.73	41.58	33.39
	2	48.56	55.40	44.91
	3	21.23	30.98	17.79
	4	40.04	45.64	37.73
	5	28.41	19.26	23.89
GRNN	1	39.93	43.73	40.86
	2	40.32	39.20	40.48
	3	27.55	27.88	26.94
	4	49.80	51.48	48.94
	5	45.35	35.09	42.33
BP	1	25.09	30.00	26.06
	2	26.09	25.87	25.20
	3	17.32	19.98	14.39
	4	41.00	41.14	38.31
	5	34.07	20.12	29.10
ARIMA	1	43.68	46.36	44.89
	2	51.01	50.07	51.33
	3	46.89	48.09	47.64
	4	64.82	64.54	64.58
	5	63.60	55.18	62.40

From the results in Tables 1–4 and Figures 6 and 7, some analyses could be obtained. Take Wind Speed Sequence I as an example.

(a) The forecasting capacity of the EEMD-LSTM-GRNN-BSO approach was obviously superior to that of the ARIMA method. For example, in Case 1, the percentage improvement of MAE for the EEMD-LSTM-GRNN-BSO model, compared with the ARIMA approach, in 1–5-step predictions were 45.87%, 61.96%, 70.35%, 72.07% and 72.85%, respectively; the percentage improvement of MAPE for the EEMD-LSTM-GRNN-BSO model, compared with the ARIMA approach, in 1–5-step predictions were 53.56%, 62.24%, 70.45%, 71.59% and 71.65%, respectively; and the percentage improvement of RMSE for the EEMD-LSTM-GRNN-BSO model, compared with the ARIMA approach, in 1–5-step predictions were 47.31%, 60.29%, 69.84%, 72.25% and 72.91%, respectively.

(b) The forecasting capacity of the EEMD-LSTM-GRNN-BSO approach was obviously superior to that of the BP method. For example, in Case 1, the percentage improvement of MAE for the EEMD-LSTM-GRNN-BSO model, compared with the BP approach, in 1–5-step predictions were 25.37%, 31.51%, 35.90%, 52.77% and 43.01%, respectively; the percentage improvement of MAPE for the EEMD-LSTM-GRNN-BSO model, compared with the BP approach, in 1–5-step predictions were 41.89%, 37.41%, 40.83%, 60.80% and 51.41%, respectively; and the percentage improvement of RMSE for the EEMD-LSTM-GRNN-BSO model, compared with the BP approach, in 1–5-step predictions were 23.12%, 25.29%, 32.08%, 49.83%, and 37.87%, respectively.

(c) The forecasting capacity of the EEMD-LSTM-GRNN-BSO approach was obviously superior to that of the GRNN method. For example, in Case 1, the percentage improvement of MAE for the EEMD-LSTM-GRNN-BSO model, compared with the GRNN approach, in 1–5-step predictions were 42.30%, 48.43%, 54.24%, 55.63% and 49.75%, respectively; the percentage improvement of MAPE for the EEMD-LSTM-GRNN-BSO model, compared with the GRNN approach, in 1–5-step predictions were 53.49%, 51.33%, 56.36%, 60.77% and 55.10%, respectively; and the percentage improvement of RMSE for the EEMD-LSTM-GRNN-BSO model, compared with the GRNN approach, in 1–5-step predictions were 39.01%, 42.02%, 50.14%, 54.11% and 47.03%, respectively.

(d) The forecasting capacity of the EEMD-LSTM-GRNN-BSO approach was obviously superior to that of the LSTM method. For example, in Case 1, the percentage improvement of MAE for the EEMD-LSTM-GRNN-BSO model, compared with the LSTM approach, in 1–5-step predictions were 33.77%, 32.90%, 31.06%, 29.79% and 20.65%, respectively; the percentage improvement of

MAPE for the EEMD-LSTM-GRNN-BSO model, compared with the LSTM approach, in 1–5-step predictions were 52.42%, 43.18%, 36.59%, 38.81% and 28.11%, respectively; and the percentage improvement of RMSE for the EEMD-LSTM-GRNN-BSO model, compared with the LSTM approach, in 1–5-step predictions were 30.21%, 24.50%, 27.08%, 26.66% and 14.44%, respectively.

(e) The forecasting capacity of the EEMD-LSTM-GRNN-BSO approach was obviously superior to that of the LSTM-GRNN-BSO method. For example, in Case 1, the percentage improvement of MAE for the EEMD-LSTM-GRNN-BSO model, compared with the LSTM-GRNN-BSO approach, in 1–5-step predictions were 42.05%, 38.69%, 38.80%, 27.07% and 10.75%, respectively; the percentage improvement of MAPE for the EEMD-LSTM-GRNN-BSO model, compared with the LSTM-GRNN-BSO approach, in 1–5-step predictions were 54.26%, 42.93%, 42.04%, 31.14% and 14.86%, respectively; and the percentage improvement of RMSE for the EEMD-LSTM-GRNN-BSO model, compared with the LSTM-GRNN-BSO approach, in 1–5-step predictions were 38.97%, 31.86%, 34.61%, 25.20% and 6.31%, respectively.

(f) The forecasting capacity of the EEMD-LSTM-GRNN-BSO approach was obviously superior to that of the EEMD-LSTM method. For example, in Case 1, the percentage improvement of MAE for the EEMD-LSTM-GRNN-BSO model, compared with the EEMD-LSTM approach, in 1–3-step predictions were 32.44%, 21.44% and 20.60%, respectively; the percentage improvement of MAPE for the EEMD-LSTM-GRNN-BSO model, compared with the EEMD-LSTM approach, in 1–3-step predictions were 33.08%, 22.92% and 21.97%, respectively; and the percentage improvement of RMSE for the EEMD-LSTM-GRNN-BSO model, compared with the EEMD-LSTM approach, in 1–3-step predictions were 23.45%, 22.49% and 13.23%, respectively.

(g) The forecasting capacity of the EEMD-LSTM-GRNN-BSO approach was obviously superior to that of the EEMD-LSTM-GRNN method. For example, in Case 1, the percentage improvement of MAE for the EEMD-LSTM-GRNN-BSO model, compared with the EEMD-LSTM-GRNN approach, in 1–5-step predictions were 12.89%, 7.50%, 56.08%, 50.34% and 65.46%, respectively; the percentage improvement of MAPE for the EEMD-LSTM-GRNN-BSO model, compared with the EEMD-LSTM-GRNN approach, in 1–5-step predictions were 12.09%, 16.51%, 54.48%, 53.52% and 66.37%, respectively; and the percentage improvement of RMSE for the EEMD-LSTM-GRNN-BSO model, compared with the EEMD-LSTM-GRNN approach, in 1–5-step predictions were 4.52%, 5.89%, 54.88%, 50.95% and 62.90%, respectively.

(h) Among all the wind speed forecasting models involved in 1–5-step predictions, the proposed EEMD-LSTM-GRNN-BSO hybrid model showed the highest forecasting accuracy. For example, the error statistical estimation for one-step forecast of Wind Speed Sequence I are shown in Figure 8, which shows that most errors of the proposed method were less than 10%. The reasons for the satisfactory forecasting accuracy improvement were as follows: (1) In terms of the data pre-processing method, EEMD method could recognize the non-linear features of the dataset well and effectively decompose the original wind speed series effectively to provide abundant information to the forecasting model, which contributed to the forecasting accuracy improvements. (2) In terms of the parameter optimization algorithm, the BSO approach could effectively optimize the parameter of GRNN in the training process, which improved the performance of GRNN on error series forecasting. However, the forecasting performance might become worse if the parameter in GRNN were not set properly. (3) Combined with the error correction of the GRNN optimized by BSO, the forecasting accuracy of EEMD-LSTM was significantly improved. The accuracy improvements of data preprocess, error correction and parameter optimization in 1–5-step wind speed predictions for case one are shown in Table 5.

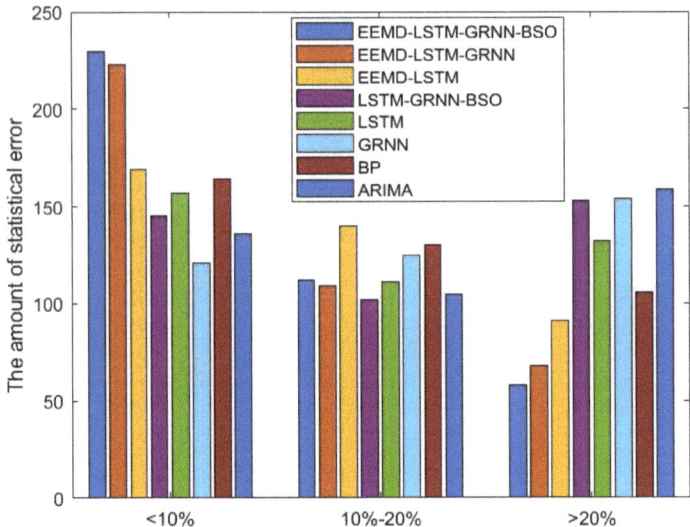

Figure 8. The error statistical estimation for one step forecast of Wind Speed Sequence I.

Table 5. The accuracy improvements of data preprocess, error correction and parameter optimization in 1–5-step prediction for Wind Speed Sequence I.

Prediction Approaches	Step	MAE (m/s)	MAPE (%)	RMSE (m/s)
data preprocessing	1	42.05	54.26	38.97
	2	38.69	42.93	31.86
	3	38.80	42.04	34.61
	4	27.07	31.14	25.20
	5	10.75	14.86	6.31
error correction	1	12.89	12.09	4.52
	2	7.50	16.51	5.89
	3	56.08	54.48	54.88
	4	50.34	53.52	50.95
	5	65.46	66.37	62.90
parameter optimization	1	2.31	16.19	3.22
	2	5.52	6.32	3.25
	3	62.45	60.79	60.02
	4	38.86	40.51	39.91
	5	62.16	63.15	59.25

5. Additional Prediction Case

Aiming at further studying the generalization capacity of the suggested hybrid measure, the proposed EEMD-LSTM-GRNN-BSO hybrid model was conducted on am additional case with 30-min interval: Wind Speed Sequence III. The actual data of Wind Speed Sequence III, taken from 1 October 2018 to 10 November 2018, are shown in Figure 9. The additional experiment was conducted with the same procedure of the aforementioned three experiments, and the forecasting results are shown in Figure 10. Table 6 demonstrates the multi-step calculation outcomes for evaluation indicators of all the models involved. Table 6 illustrates the multi-step percentage improvements of the three evaluation indices for the suggested EEMD-LSTM-GRNN-BSO approach compared with other comparison models on wind speed series III. It is observed in Tables 6 and 7 that the calculation outcomes of the evaluation indicators on the additional prediction case showed the same basic behavior as the the two aforementioned forecasting cases in Section 4. Again, the suggested combination

EEMD-LSTM-GRNN-BSO approach demonstrated the highest forecasting accuracy compared with all the other models mentioned. This additional case witnessed the generalization and validity of the suggested combination model on wind speed series with longer time interval.

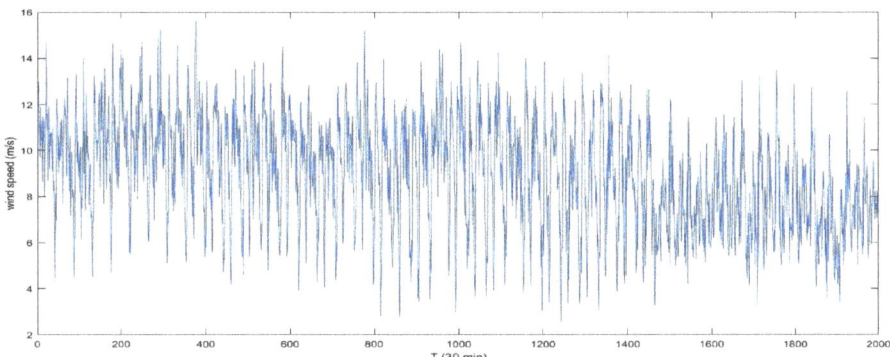

Figure 9. The observation values of Wind Speed Sequence III.

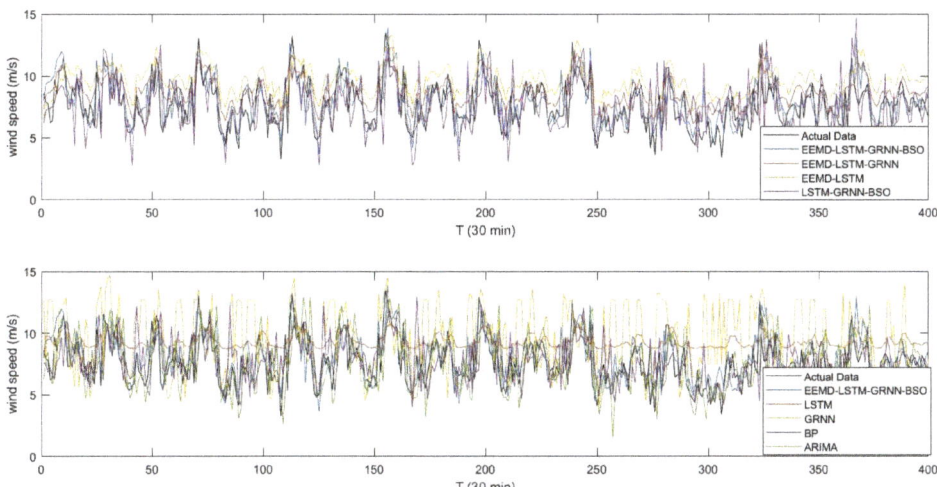

Figure 10. The comparisons between the observations and the predictions for Wind Speed Sequence III.

Table 6. The multi-step calculation results for evaluation indicators of involved approaches on Wind Speed Sequence II.

Prediction Approaches	Step	MAE (m/s)	MAPE (%)	RMSE (m/s)
EEMD-LSTM-GRNN-BSO	1	1.1553	0.1631	1.4812
	2	1.2928	0.1816	1.6554
	3	1.4338	0.2024	1.8314
	4	1.3277	0.1851	1.7075
	5	1.4870	0.2148	1.9070
EEMD-LSTM-GRNN	1	1.3137	0.2025	1.5879
	2	1.3249	0.1961	1.7026
	3	2.3211	0.3382	2.8471
	4	2.3920	0.3484	2.9433
	5	3.2694	0.4691	3.9644
EEMD-LSTM	1	2.1615	0.3299	2.4162
	2	2.2684	0.3437	2.5935
	3	2.4573	0.3723	3.0113
	4	3.2568	0.4846	3.8875
	5	4.0145	0.5730	4.8096
LSTM-GRNN-BSO	1	1.4949	0.2099	1.9741
	2	1.4677	0.2061	1.9411
	3	1.4970	0.2118	1.9690
	4	1.5179	0.2139	2.0147
	5	1.5380	0.2327	1.9915
LSTM	1	2.0185	0.3194	2.3705
	2	2.3486	0.3729	2.7340
	3	2.5871	0.4105	2.9903
	4	2.6391	0.4187	3.0463
	5	2.5679	0.4081	2.9729
GRNN	1	2.6329	0.3909	3.3579
	2	3.2111	0.4827	3.9924
	3	3.7123	0.5555	4.5100
	4	3.2417	0.4966	3.9374
	5	3.3656	0.5102	4.0175
BP	1	1.6059	0.2268	2.0372
	2	2.1095	0.3160	2.7228
	3	2.1614	0.3275	2.7456
	4	2.4640	0.3829	3.0138
	5	2.6728	0.4167	3.2329
ARIMA	1	1.4814	0.2022	1.9437
	2	2.2673	0.3117	2.9676
	3	3.0135	0.4298	3.8870
	4	3.7842	0.5379	4.9303
	5	4.4219	0.6265	5.8160

Table 7. The multi-step percentage improvements of the suggested EEMD-LSTM-GRNN-BSO approach in comparison with the other measures on Wind Speed Sequence III.

Prediction Approaches	Step	P_{MAE} (%)	P_{MAPE} (%)	P_{RMSE} (%)
EEMD-LSTM-GRNN	1	12.06	19.43	6.72
	2	2.42	7.43	2.78
	3	38.23	40.15	35.67
	4	44.49	46.88	41.99
	5	54.52	54.21	51.90
EEMD-LSTM	1	46.55	50.55	38.70
	2	43.01	47.18	36.17
	3	41.65	45.64	39.18
	4	59.23	61.81	56.08
	5	62.96	62.51	60.35

Table 7. Cont.

Prediction Approaches	Step	P_{MAE} (%)	P_{MAPE} (%)	P_{RMSE} (%)
LSTM-GRNN-BSO	1	22.72	22.28	24.97
	2	11.92	11.92	14.72
	3	4.22	4.45	6.99
	4	12.53	13.47	15.25
	5	3.31	7.67	4.24
LSTM	1	42.76	48.92	37.52
	2	44.96	51.31	39.45
	3	44.58	50.69	38.75
	4	49.69	55.80	43.95
	5	42.09	47.36	35.85
GRNN	1	56.12	58.27	55.89
	2	59.74	62.39	58.54
	3	61.38	63.56	59.39
	4	59.04	62.73	56.63
	5	55.82	57.89	52.53
BP	1	28.06	28.08	27.29
	2	38.72	42.54	39.21
	3	33.66	38.20	33.30
	4	46.12	51.67	43.34
	5	44.36	48.44	41.01
ARIMA	1	22.02	19.33	23.80
	2	42.98	41.75	44.22
	3	52.42	52.90	52.88
	4	64.92	65.59	65.37
	5	66.37	65.71	67.21

6. Conclusions

A new combination approach integrated with signal pre-processing, parameter optimization and the error correction strategy is proposed in this article. The combination approach consists of the EEMD measure, the LSTM algorithm, the GRNN measure and the BSO measure. The EEMD is executed to decomposed the original dataset into a collection of IMFs. The LSTM algorithm is applied as the major forecasting method of each IMF. The GRNN model is used as the secondary forecasting method to forecast error sequences for each IMF. The BSO algorithm is executed to optimize the parameter of GRNN during the training procedure. Aiming at validating the effectiveness and generalization of the suggested combination EEMD-LSTM-GRNN-BSO approach, seven other forecasting methods were conducted on three different datasets as comparisons: the ARIMA measure, the BP measure, the GRNN measure, the LSTM measure, the LSTM-GRNN-BSO measure, the EEMD-LSTM measure, and the EEMD-LSTM-GRNN measure. According to the calculation outcomes, the following conclusions are drawn: (1) the EEMD can contribute to the promotion of the wind speed prediction capacity and robustness of the LSTM approach effectively; (2) the BSO based parameter optimization method is effective in finding the optimal parameter for GRNN and improving the forecasting performance for the EEMD-LSTM-GRNN model; (3) the error correction based on the optimized GRNN promotes the prediction ability of the EEMD-LSTM method obviously; and (4) in comparison with all other measures involved, the suggested EEMD-LSTM-GRNN-BSO measure is certified to demonstrate the best prediction ability on wind speed forecasting in short period.

Author Contributions: L.Y. designed this study and wrote the original manuscript; S.L. offered review and editing advice; and Y.H. and G.W. offered modification suggestions.

Funding: This research received no external funding.

Conflicts of Interest: No conflict of interest are declared by the authors.

References

1. Ouyang, T.; Zha, X.; Liang, Q. A combined multivariate model for wind power prediction. *Energy Convers. Manag.* **2017**, *144*, 361–373. [CrossRef]
2. Jung, J.; Broadwater, R.P. Current status and future advances for wind speed and power forecasting. *Renew. Sustain. Energy Rev.* **2014**, *31*, 762–777. [CrossRef]
3. Li, H.; Wang, J.; Lu, H.; Guo, Z. Research and application of a combined model based on variable weight for short term wind speed forecasting. *Renew. Energy* **2018**, *116*, 669–684. [CrossRef]
4. Zhao, J.; Guo, Z.H.; Su, Z.Y.; Zhao, Z.Y.; Xiao, X.; Liu, F. An improved multi-step forecasting model based on WRF ensembles and creative fuzzy systems for wind speed. *Appl. Energy* **2016**, *162*, 808–826. [CrossRef]
5. Landberg, L.; Watson, S.J. Short-term prediction of local wind conditions. *J. Wind. Eng. Ind. Aerodyn.* **1994**, *89*, 235–245. [CrossRef]
6. Zhao, W.; Wei, Y.M.; Su, Z. One day ahead wind speed forecasting: A resampling-based approach. *Appl. Energy* **2016**, *178*, 886–901. [CrossRef]
7. Lei, M.; Luan, S.; Jiang, C.; Liu, H.; Yan, Z. A review on the forecasting of wind speed and generated power. *Renew. Sustain. Energy Rev.* **2009**, *13*, 915–920. [CrossRef]
8. Qin, M.; Li, Z.; Du, Z. Red tide time series forecasting by combining ARIMA and deep belief network. *Knowl.-Based Syst.* **2017**, *125*, 39–52. [CrossRef]
9. Zhang, Y.; Yang, J.; Wang, K.; Wang, Z. Wind Power Prediction Considering Nonlinear Atmospheric Disturbances. *Energies* **2015**, *8*, 475–489. [CrossRef]
10. Xiao, L.; Wang, J.; Dong, Y.; Wu, J. Combined forecasting models for wind energy forecasting: A case study in China. *Renew. Sustain. Energy Rev.* **2015**, *44*, 271–288. [CrossRef]
11. Yan, Y.; Li, J.; Gao, D.W. Condition Parameter Modeling for Anomaly Detection in Wind Turbines. *Energies* **2014**, *7*, 3104–3120. [CrossRef]
12. Hu, J.; Wang, J.; Zeng, G. A hybrid forecasting approach applied to wind speed time series. *Renew. Energy* **2013**, *60*, 185–194. [CrossRef]
13. Zhong, J.; Dong, G.; Sun, Y.; Zhang, Z.; Wu, Y. Application of the nonlinear time series prediction method of genetic algorithm for forecasting surface wind of point station in the South China Sea with scatterometer observations. *Chin. Phys. B* **2016**, *25*, 167–173. [CrossRef]
14. Da, L.; Wang, J.; Hui, W. Short-term wind speed forecasting based on spectral clustering and optimised echo state networks. *Renew. Energy* **2015**, *78*, 599–608.
15. Wang, H.Z.; Li, G.Q.; Wang, G.B.; Peng, J.C.; Hui, J.; Liu, Y.T. Deep learning based ensemble approach for probabilistic wind power forecasting. *Appl. Energy* **2017**, *188*, 56–70. [CrossRef]
16. Hui, L.; Mi, X.; Li, Y. Smart multi-step deep learning model for wind speed forecasting based on variational mode decomposition, singular spectrum analysis, LSTM network and ELM. *Energy Convers. Manag.* **2018**, *159*, 54–64.
17. Tascikaraoglu, A.; Uzunoglu, M. A review of combined approaches for prediction of short-term wind speed and power. *Renew. Sustain. Energy Rev.* **2014**, *34*, 243–254. [CrossRef]
18. Jie, S.; Ding, Z.; Lee, W.J.; Yang, Y.; Liu, Y.; Zhang, M. Hybrid Forecasting Model for Very-Short Term Wind Power Forecasting Based on Grey Relational Analysis and Wind Speed Distribution Features. *IEEE Trans. Smart Grid* **2014**, *5*, 521–526.
19. Liu, D.; Niu, D.; Wang, H.; Fan, L. Short-term wind speed forecasting using wavelet transform and support vector machines optimized by genetic algorithm. *Renew. Energy* **2014**, *62*, 592–597. [CrossRef]
20. Fan, G.F.; Peng, L.L.; Zhao, X.; Hong, W.C. Applications of hybrid EMD with PSO and GA for an SVR-based load forecasting model. *Energies* **2017**, *10*, 1713. [CrossRef]
21. Wu, Z.; Huang, N.E. Ensemble empirical mode decomposition: A noise-assisted data analysis method. *Adv. Adapt. Data Anal.* **2011**, *1*. [CrossRef]
22. Cheng, Q.; Chen, L.; Cheng, Y.; Zhang, Q.; Gao, J. Short-term wind power forecasting method based on EEMD and LS-SVM model. *Electr. Power Autom. Equip.* **2018**. [CrossRef]
23. Chitsaz, H.; Amjady, N.; Zareipour, H.; Chitsaz, H.; Amjady, N.; Zareipour, H. Wind power forecast using wavelet neural network trained by improved Clonal selection algorithm. *Energy Convers. Manag.* **2015**, *89*, 588–598. [CrossRef]

24. Osório, G.J.; Matias, J.C.O.; Catalão, J.P.S. Short-term wind power forecasting using adaptive neuro-fuzzy inference system combined with evolutionary particle swarm optimization, wavelet transform and mutual information. *Renew. Energy* **2015**, *75*, 301–307. [CrossRef]
25. Yuan, X.; Chen, C.; Yuan, Y.; Huang, Y.; Tan, Q. Short-term wind power prediction based on LSSVM–GSA model. *Energy Convers. Manag.* **2015**, *101*, 393–401. [CrossRef]
26. Cheng, S.; Qin, Q.; Chen, J.; Shi, Y. Brain storm optimization algorithm: A review. *Artif. Intell. Rev.* **2015**, *6728*, 1–14. [CrossRef]
27. Jordehi, A.R. Brainstorm optimisation algorithm (BSOA): An efficient algorithm for finding optimal location and setting of FACTS devices in electric power systems. *Int. J. Electr. Power Energy Syst.* **2015**, *69*, 48–57. [CrossRef]
28. El-Abd, M. Global-best brain storm optimization algorithm. *Swarm Evol. Comput.* **2017**, *37*, 27–44. [CrossRef]
29. Jadhav, H.; Sharma, U.; Patel, J.; Roy, R. Brain storm optimization algorithm based economic dispatch considering wind power. In Proceedings of the 2012 IEEE International Conference on Power and Energy (PECon), Kota Kinabalu, Malaysia, 2–5 December 2012; pp. 588–593.
30. Jia, Z.; Duan, H.; Shi, Y. Hybrid brain storm optimisation and simulated annealing algorithm for continuous optimisation problems. *Int. J. Bio-Inspired Comput.* **2016**, *8*, 109–121. [CrossRef]
31. Liang, Z.; Liang, J.; Wang, C.; Dong, X.; Miao, X. Short-term wind power combined forecasting based on error forecast correction. *Energy Convers. Manag.* **2016**, *119*, 215–226. [CrossRef]
32. Yan, J.; Huang, G. Short-term wind speed prediction: Hybrid of ensemble empirical mode decomposition, feature selection and error correction. *Energy Convers. Manag.* **2017**, *144*, 340–350.
33. Chen, S.; Lin, Y.; Zhang, G.; Zeng, C.; Dong, S.; Dai, C. Short-term wind power prediction based on combined grey-Markov model. In Proceedings of the International Conference on Advanced Power System Automation & Protection, Beijing, China, 16–20 Octorber 2011.
34. Lei, Y.; He, Z.; Zi, Y. Application of the EEMD method to rotor fault diagnosis of rotating machinery. *Mech. Syst. Signal Process.* **2009**, *23*, 1327–1338. [CrossRef]
35. Hochreiter, S.; Schmidhuber, J. Long short-term memory. *Neural Comput.* **1997**, *9*, 1735–1780. [CrossRef] [PubMed]
36. Graves, A.; Schmidhuber, J. Framewise phoneme classification with bidirectional LSTM and other neural network architectures. *Neural Netw.* **2005**, *18*, 602–610. [CrossRef]
37. Shi, X.; Chen, Z.; Hao, W.; Woo, W.C.; Woo, W.C.; Woo, W.C. Convolutional LSTM Network: A machine learning approach for precipitation nowcasting. In Proceedings of the International Conference on Neural Information Processing Systems, Montreal, QC, Canada, 7–12 December 2015.
38. Liu, H.; Tian, H.Q.; Liang, X.F.; Li, Y.F. Wind speed forecasting approach using secondary decomposition algorithm and Elman neural networks. *Appl. Energy* **2015**, *157*, 183–194. [CrossRef]
39. Specht, D.F. A general regression neural network. *IEEE Trans. Neural Netw.* **1991**, *2*, 568–76. [CrossRef] [PubMed]
40. Shi, Y. Brain Storm Optimization Algorithm. *IEEE Congr. Evol. Comput.* **2011**, *6728*, 1–14.
41. Shi, Y. An Optimization Algorithm Based on Brainstorming Process. In Proceedings of the International Symposium on Intelligence Computation & Applications, Budapest, Hungary, 21–22 November 2011; pp. 35–62.
42. Maa, X.; Jin, Y.; Dong, Q. *A Generalized Dynamic Fuzzy Neural Network Based on Singular Spectrum Analysis Optimized by Brain Storm Optimization for Short-Term Wind Speed Forecasting*; Elsevier Science Publishers B. V.: Amsterdam, The Netherlands, 2017; pp. 296–312.

© 2019 by the authors. Licensee MDPI, Basel, Switzerland. This article is an open access article distributed under the terms and conditions of the Creative Commons Attribution (CC BY) license (http://creativecommons.org/licenses/by/4.0/).

Article

Cost Forecasting Model of Transformer Substation Projects Based on Data Inconsistency Rate and Modified Deep Convolutional Neural Network

Hongwei Wang *, Yuansheng Huang, Chong Gao and Yuqing Jiang

School of Economics and Management, North China Electric Power University, Beijing 102206, China
* Correspondence: wanghongwei1980@126.com

Received: 17 July 2019; Accepted: 5 August 2019; Published: 7 August 2019

Abstract: Precise and steady substation project cost forecasting is of great significance to guarantee the economic construction and valid administration of electric power engineering. This paper develops a novel hybrid approach for cost forecasting based on a data inconsistency rate (DIR), a modified fruit fly optimization algorithm (MFOA) and a deep convolutional neural network (DCNN). Firstly, the DIR integrated with the MFOA is adopted for input feature selection. Simultaneously, the MFOA is utilized to realize parameter optimization in the DCNN. The effectiveness of the MFOA–DIR–DCNN has been validated by a case study that selects 128 substation projects in different regions for training and testing. The modeling results demonstrate that this established approach is better than the contrast methods with regard to forecasting accuracy and robustness. Thus, the developed technique is feasible for the cost prediction of substation projects in various voltage levels.

Keywords: substation project cost forecasting model; feature selection; data inconsistency rate; modified fruit fly optimization algorithm; deep convolutional neural network

1. Introduction

The inadequate management and supervision of substation projects tend to bring about high cost, which has critical effects on the economy and sustainability of power engineering. Thus, cost prediction is of great importance for expense saving [1]. However, the comparable projects are hard to collect due to limited engineering in the same period as well as various influential factors such as the overall plan of the power grid, total capacity, terrain features, design and construction level, and local economy [2]. Along with the less sample data, the difficulty of cost forecasting for substation projects has been increased. Therefore, it is of great significance for the sustainability of electric power engineering investment to study and construct the substation cost forecasting model and accurately forecast the substation cost.

Nowadays, many scholars have published their momentous work to handle the cost forecasting of engineering, but few studies have focused on substation projects. The approaches in regard to engineering cost prediction are primarily separated into two kinds—traditional prediction methods and intelligent algorithms. Traditional forecasting techniques primarily consist of time series [3], grey prediction [4], regression analysis [5] and so on. Reference [3] designed a time series prediction model for engineering cost based on bills of quantities and evaluation. The results indicated that this proposed model controlled the error range within 5%. Reference [4] put forward an improved grey forecasting method optimized by a time response function to predict main construction cost indicators in power projects, where the constant C was determined through the minimum Euclidean distance of an original series and constraints of simulation values. In reference [6], a forecasting technique grounded on multiple structure integral linear regression was established in line with the characteristics of engineering cost composition. Principal component analysis was introduced here to address the multicollinearity. In spite of their mature theories and simple calculations, the defects of these methods, including narrow application scope and unideal forecasting accuracy, cannot be ignored.

With the burgeoning development of artificial intelligence, the application of intelligent algorithms in the cost prediction of substation projects is of great significance. This kind of model is chiefly composed of artificial neural networks (ANNs) and a support vector machine (SVM) [6], wherein some ANNs are applicable to forecasting fields including a back propagation neural network (BPNN), an extreme learning machine (ELM), a radial basis function neural network (RBFNN), and a general regression neural network (GRNN) [7]. Reference [8] executed a three-layer BPNN to forecast the cost of a transmission line project where the related influential factors were taken as the input. The model was validated on the foundation of actual data. Reference [9] put up with an ELM-based approach for medium and long term electricity demand prediction with the target of a low carbon economy. Reference [10] evaluated the effectiveness of a BPNN and a RBFNN for engineering cost prediction. The case study indicated that the RBFNN had a better performance in terms of forecasting accuracy. In literature [11], a hybrid model which combined a GRNN with a fruit fly optimization algorithm (FOA) was utilized in wind speed prediction, and good prediction results were obtained. Nevertheless, the defects of slow convergence and getting stuck in local best in a BPNN brought about a decrease of forecasting accuracy. To this end, an SVM was applied to refrain from network structure selection and mitigate the premature convergence to local optimization in engineering cost prediction [12]. Reference [13] investigated an SVM integrated with adaptive particle swarm optimization (APSO) to forecast the cost of a practical substation project. In reference [14], a cuckoo search algorithm (CS) was introduced to optimize the parameters in an SVM. The results showed that the forecasting precision was obviously enhanced. Compared with a BPNN, the application of an SVM can achieve better performance in cost prediction, but the transformation that converts the solution into a quadratic programming problem by the use of a kernel function in an SVM resulted in the decrease of efficiency and precision [15]. The aforementioned approaches belong to shallow learning algorithms, whose ability to cope with complex function problems is limited. In addition, these models cannot fully reflect information features in virtue of prior knowledge. Hence, some scholars tried to develop a deep neural network (DNN) for prediction [16].

The real powerful computing capability of neural networks has been brought into play since the creation of a DNN with "multi-layer structure and learning ability layer by layer" by Professor Hinton, University of Toronto in Canada in 2006. The DNN has aroused great concern in both academia and industry and has become a hot tool for data analysis in the big data era [17]. Additionally, this technique has made breakthroughs in the fields of signal recognition, natural language processing, and so on; it has also kept updating all kinds of records with amazing speed in diverse application areas [18]. In 2012, Krizhevsky et al. [19] put forward the concept of depth into traditional a convolutional neural network (CNN) and proposed a deep convolutional neural network (DCNN). The DCNN, as the first approach that successfully trains multi-layer networks, has been widely used owing to self-study of data characteristics [20]. Thereinto, the CNN model realizes the optimization of a neural network structure by self-convolution for local features, weight sharing, subsampling and multiple perception layers. Additionally, the CNN technique not only reduces the number of neurons and weights but also uses pooling operation to make input features invariable in displacement, scaling and distortion, which contributes to the improvement of accuracy and robustness for network training [21]. The DCNN has been employed in the area of prediction [22–25]. For instance, an original hybrid model on the basis of the DCNN was built to forecast the deterministic photovoltaic power in reference [22], where the DCNN was applied to nonlinear feature and invariant structure extraction presented in every frequency. The computing results indicate that the novel models can improve forecasting precision with respect to seasons along with various prediction horizons in contrast with conventional forecasting approaches. In reference [24], the DCNN integrated with a concretely ordered feature came up for the intraday direction forecasting of Borsa Istanbul 100 stocks. The results displayed that this established classifier is superior to logistic regression and the CNN in use of randomly ordered features. Thus, for the purpose of training time and model complexity reduction, feature selection models can be employed.

Considering the influence of parameter selection on prediction performance of the DCNN, it is indispensable to select a proper intelligent algorithm to optimize parameters [26]. The fruit fly optimization algorithm (FOA), proposed by Dr. Pan Wenchao in June 2011, is a novel global optimization algorithm on the foundation of swarm intelligence [27]. This technique is derived from the simulation of foraging behaviors and is similar to the ant colony algorithm [28] and particle swarm optimization [29]. Due to its simple structure, few parameters, and easy realization, scholars at home and abroad have focused on this method and applied it to forecasting [30–35]. For example, reference [31] combined the improved FOA with a wavelet least square support vector machine. The case studies verified that the proposed method presents strong validity and feasibility in mid–long term power load prediction compared with other alternative approaches. Reference [33] studied monthly electricity consumption forecasting on the basis of a hybrid model that integrates the support vector regression method with an FOA with a seasonal index adjustment. The experimental results demonstrated this approach can be effectively utilized in the field of electricity consumption forecasting. A novel hybrid forecasting model was constructed in reference [35] for annual electric load prediction; here, an FOA was applied to automatically determine the appropriate parameter values in the proposed approach. In reference [36], the authors applied a modified firefly algorithm and a support vector machine to predict substation engineering cost. The case study of substation engineering in Guangdong Province proved that the proposed model has a higher forecasting accuracy and effectiveness. Remarkably, the potential weaknesses of premature convergence and easily trapping into local optimum make a certain restriction in the performance of an FOA. Thus, quantum behavior was utilized in this paper to modify the basic FOA. This improved approach, namely the MFOA, was exploited to select features with a data inconsistency rate (DIR) and optimize parameters for the DCNN model.

In view of the various influential factors of substation project cost, it is necessary to identify and select proper features as the input to avoid data redundancy and increase computation efficiency [37]. The filter method gives a score to each feature by statistical methods, sorts the features by score, and then selects the subset with the highest score. This method is only for each feature to be considered independently, without considering the feature, dependence or correlation. Compared with the filter method, the wrapper method takes the correlation between features into account by considering the effect of the combination of features on the performance of the model. It compares the differences between different combinations and selects the best combination of performance. The DIR model determines complete characteristic selection by dividing the feature set and calculating the minimum inconsistency of the subsets, as presented in reference [38]. The authors in reference [39] thought that the key sequential of features could be identified by selecting the minimum inconsistency rate, and the optimized feature subset could also be efficiently achieved based on the sequence forward search strategy. The experiments showed that the proposed data classification scheme obtains good performance. In reference [40], a discrete wavelet transform in combination with an inconsistency rate model was designed to achieve optimal feature selection. The experiment verified that this approach contributes to the reduction of redundancy in input vectors and outperforms other models in short-term power load prediction. It can be seen the DIR takes advantage of data inconsistency to eliminate redundant features. Furthermore, it allows for a correlation such that the selected optimal characteristics are able to cover all data information. As a result, the DIR method is introduced for feature selection in this paper.

Based on the aforementioned studies, this paper develops a novel hybrid approach for cost forecasting based on the DIR, the DCNN and the MFOA. Firstly, the DIR integrated with the MFOA is adopted for input feature selection. Simultaneously, the MFOA is utilized to realize parameter optimization in the DCNN. Thus, the proposed method can be applied to cost forecasting of substation projects on the foundation of the optimized input subset as well as the best parameters. The rest of the paper is organized as follows: Section 2 briefly introduces the established hybrid model including the MFOA, the DIR, the DCNN, and the concrete structure. Section 3 verifies the developed technique via a case study. Section 4 draws conclusions.

2. Methodology

2.1. Modified FOA

2.1.1. FOA

The FOA is a new optimization approach that simulates the foraging behaviors of a fruit fly swarm [27,41]. Their sensitive smell and sharp vision contribute to the discovery of food sources over 40 km and correct flight to the location [42,43]. The food searching procedure of a fruit fly swarm can be seen from Figure 1.

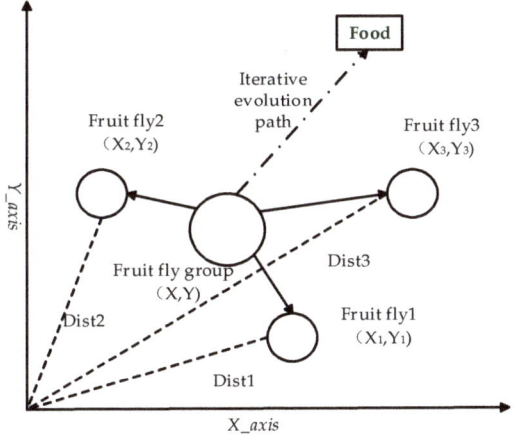

Figure 1. Food searching procedure of a fruit fly swarm.

According to the food searching features, the following is the specific description of the FOA:

(1) Initialize the location of the fruit fly swarm according to Equation (1).

$$InitX\_axis;\ InitY\_axis \quad (1)$$

(2) For an individual fruit fly, set the random direction and distance for food finding, as shown in Equations (2) and (3):

$$Xi = InitX\_axis + random() \quad (2)$$

$$Yi = InitY\_axis + random() \quad (3)$$

(3) Estimate the distance between the origin point and the smell concentration of each individual fruit fly S_i as follows:

$$Dist_i = \sqrt{X_i^2 + Y_i^2} \quad (4)$$

$$S_i = 1/Dist_i \quad (5)$$

(4) Take the value of smell concentration into its judgement function; then, in light of Equation (6), obtain the smell concentration $Smell_i$ at each location

$$Smell_i = Function(S_i) \quad (6)$$

(5) Find out the optimal smell concentration among the fruit fly swarm:

$$[bestSmell\ bestIndex] = \max[Smell_i] \tag{7}$$

(6) Keep a record of the optimal smell concentration as well as its x, y coordinates. Afterwards, the fruit flies can fly to the destination by the use of vision.

$$Smellbest = bestSmell,\ X\_axis = X(bestIndex),\ Y\_axis = Y(bestIndex) \tag{8}$$

(7) The iterative optimization is carried out by a repeat of Step (2) to Step (5). At each iteration, determine whether the smell concentration shows an advantage over the former one. If so, follow Step (6).

2.1.2. MFOA

(1) The development of quantum mechanics has greatly promoted the application of quantum computation in diverse fields. In quantum computation, a quantum bit is utilized to represent quantum state, and the 0 and 1 binary method is adopted to express quantum information. Here, the basic quantum state consists of the "0" and "1" states, and the state is able to achieve random linear superposition between "0" and "1." Therefore, these two states are allowed to exist simultaneously, which issues a large challenge to the classic bit expression approach in classical mechanics. The superposition of quantum state is described as Equation (9)

$$|\psi> = \alpha|0> + \beta|1>,\ |\alpha|^2 + |\beta|^2 = 1 \tag{9}$$

where $|0>$ and $|1>$ indicate two kinds of quantum states, α, and β is the probability amplitude. The possibility at quantum state of $|0>$ and $|1>$ are expressed by $|\alpha|^2$ and $|\beta|^2$, respectively.

The update can be achieved through quantum rotating gate in the MFOA, and the adjustment is expressed as Equation (10):

$$\begin{pmatrix} \alpha'_i \\ \beta'_i \end{pmatrix} = \begin{pmatrix} \cos(\theta) & -\sin(\theta) \\ \sin(\theta) & \cos(\theta) \end{pmatrix} \begin{pmatrix} \alpha_i \\ \beta_i \end{pmatrix} \tag{10}$$

Here, suppose $U = \begin{pmatrix} \cos(\theta) & -\sin(\theta) \\ \sin(\theta) & \cos(\theta) \end{pmatrix}$. From there, U and θ represent the quantum rotating gate and the angle, respectively. $\theta = \arctan(\alpha/\beta)$.

(2) Initialize the location of fruit fly. Additionally, take advantage of the probability amplitude of the quantum bit to code the current location of the individual fruit fly, as shown in Equation (11):

$$P_i = \begin{bmatrix} \cos(\theta_{i1}) & \cos(\theta_{i2}) & \cdots & \cos(\theta_{in}) \\ \sin(\theta_{i1}) & \sin(\theta_{i2}) & \cdots & \sin(\theta_{in}) \end{bmatrix} \tag{11}$$

where $\theta_{ij} = 2\pi rand()$; $rand()$ is equivalent to a random number between 0 and 1; $i = 1, 2, \cdots, m$; $j = 1, 2, \cdots, n$; m represents the number of fruit flies; and n is the quantity of space.

As a result, the homologous probability amplitudes of the quantum state $|0>$ and $|1>$ are presented in Equations (12) and (13).

$$P_{ic} = (\cos(\theta_{i1}), \cos(\theta_{i2}) \cdots \cos(\theta_{in})) \tag{12}$$

$$P_{is} = (\sin(\theta_{i1}), \sin(\theta_{i2}) \cdots \sin(\theta_{in})) \tag{13}$$

(3) In the MFOA, the search is implemented in the actual space $[a, b]$, while the position probability amplitude is set in $[0, 1]$. Thus, it is indispensable to decode the probability amplitude into $[a, b]$.

Suppose $\left[\alpha_i^j, \beta_i^j\right]^T$ represents the jth quantum bit of the individual fruit fly P_i; then, the related solution space is converted in accordance with Equation (14):

$$X_{ic}^j = \frac{1}{2}[b_i(1+\alpha_i^j) + a_i(1-\alpha_i^j)] \quad if\ rand() < P_{id} \tag{14}$$

$$X_{is}^j = \frac{1}{2}[b_i(1+\beta_i^j) + a_i(1-\beta_i^j)] \quad if\ rand() \geq P_{id} \tag{15}$$

where $rand()$ is the random value in the range of $[0,1]$, X_{ic}^j and X_{is}^j partly equal the actual value of the parameter in jth dimensional location when the quantum state of ith individual reaches $|0>$ or $|1>$. a_i and b_i represent the upper and lower limit, respectively.

Suppose the search of the MFOA is conducted in a two-dimensional space, namely $j = 1, 2$. $InitX\_axis$ and $InitY\_axis$ represent the initialization of the location. The solution space is described in Equations (16)–(19).

$if\ rand() < P_{id}$:

$$X_i = X\_axis + \frac{1}{2}[b_i(1+\alpha_i^1) + a_i(1-\alpha_i^1)] \tag{16}$$

$$Y_i = Y\_axis + \frac{1}{2}[b_i(1+\alpha_i^2) + a_i(1-\alpha_i^2)] \tag{17}$$

$if\ rand() \geq P_{id}$:

$$X_i = X\_axis + \frac{1}{2}[b_i(1+\beta_i^1) + a_i(1-\beta_i^1)] \tag{18}$$

$$Y_i = Y\_axis + \frac{1}{2}[b_i(1+\beta_i^2) + a_i(1-\beta_i^2)] \tag{19}$$

(4) The distance $Dist$ between the origin and location is estimated, and the judgement value of smell concentration $S(i)$, namely the reciprocal of distance, can be obtained—$Dist_i = \sqrt{X_i^2 + Y_i^2}$, $S_i = 1/Dist_i$.

(5) In accordance with Equation (20), the smell concentration $Smell_i$ of each fruit fly location is acquired:

$$[bestSmell\ bestindex] = \min(Smell_i) \tag{20}$$

(6) A quantum rotating gate is employed to update the individual location, as shown in Equation (21):

$$\begin{bmatrix} \alpha_{jd}^{k+1} \\ \beta_{jd}^{k+1} \end{bmatrix} = \begin{bmatrix} \cos\theta_{jd}^{k+1} & -\sin\theta_{jd}^{k+1} \\ \sin\theta_{jd}^{k+1} & \cos\theta_{jd}^{k+1} \end{bmatrix} \begin{bmatrix} \alpha_{jd}^k \\ \beta_{jd}^k \end{bmatrix} \tag{21}$$

where α_{jd}^{k+1} and β_{jd}^{k+1} represent the probability amplitude of jth fruit fly at $k+1$th iteration in d-dimensional space and θ_{jd}^{k+1} equals the rotating angle, as presented in Equation (22):

$$\theta_{jd}^{k+1} = s(\alpha_{jd}^k, \beta_{jd}^k)\Delta\theta_{jd}^{k+1} \tag{22}$$

where $s(\alpha_{jd}^k, \beta_{jd}^k)$ and $\Delta\theta_{jd}^{k+1}$ are equivalent to the direction and increment of the rotating angle, respectively.

Here, the updated α_{jd}^{k+1} and β_{jd}^{k+1} need to be converted to solution space to conform with the operation mechanism.

$$X_{jc}^d = \frac{1}{2}[b_j(1+\alpha_{jd}^{k+1}) + a_j(1-\alpha_{jd}^{k+1})] \quad if\ rand() < P_{id} \tag{23}$$

$$X_{js}^d = \frac{1}{2}[b_j(1+\beta_{jd}^{k+1}) + a_j(1-\beta_{jd}^{k+1})] \quad if\ rand() \geq P_{id} \tag{24}$$

if $rand() < P_{id}, d = 1$

$$X_j = X\_axis + \frac{1}{2}[b_j(1 + \alpha_{jd}^{k+1}) + a_j(1 - \alpha_{jd}^{k+1})] \qquad (25)$$

$$Y_j = Y\_axis + \frac{1}{2}[b_j(1 + \alpha_{jd}^{k+1}) + a_i(1 - \alpha_{jd}^{k+1})] \qquad (26)$$

if $rand() \geq P_{id}, d = 2$

$$X_j = X\_axis + \frac{1}{2}[b_j(1 + \beta_{jd}^{k+1}) + a_j(1 - \beta_{jd}^{k+1})] \qquad (27)$$

$$Y_j = Y\_axis + \frac{1}{2}[b_j(1 + \beta_{jd}^{k+1}) + a_j(1 - \beta_{jd}^{k+1})] \qquad (28)$$

(7) The loss of population diversity during searching leads to a premature convergence, together with an easy trapping into a local optimum. Thus, individual mutation is introduced in the MFOA to address this problem, as presented in Equation (29):

$$\begin{bmatrix} 01 \\ 10 \end{bmatrix} \begin{bmatrix} \cos(\theta_{ij}) \\ \sin(\theta_{ij}) \end{bmatrix} = \begin{bmatrix} \sin(\theta_{ij}) \\ \cos(\theta_{ij}) \end{bmatrix} = \begin{bmatrix} \cos(\frac{\pi}{2} - \theta_{ij}) \\ \sin(\frac{\pi}{2} - \theta_{ij}) \end{bmatrix} \qquad (29)$$

where P_m means the mutation probability and $rand()$ equals a random number in [0, 1]. If $rand() < P_m$, carry out mutation and make a change for the probability amplitude in the quantum bit. Thus, the mutated individual is successfully converted into the solution space.

(8) Keep a record of the individual with the optimal concentration value as well as the homologous coordinates.

$$X\_axis = X(bestindex); \ Y\_axis = Y(bestindex) \qquad (30)$$

$$Smellbest = bestSmell \qquad (31)$$

(9) Repeat Steps (4)–(7). If the smell concentration shows an advantage over the previous one, go to Step (8).

2.2. DIR

In the light of various characteristics of the substation project cost, it is of great necessity to select the most correlated features as the input to refrain from information redundancy and increase cost forecasting precision. The discrete features of input can be accurately displayed via data inconsistency [39]. Distinct features are divided into diverse patterns with corresponding frequency. The value of the DIR is able to discriminate the classification capability of data categories. The value of the DIR is positively correlated with the assortment ability of the feature vector.

Suppose there exist g features in substation project cost (e.g., main transformer capacity, area, price), expressed as $G_1, G_2, \ldots, G_g$. L represents the subset of the feature set Γ. According to the level of substation project cost, set the standard M with c classifications and N as data instances. z_{ji} and λ_i equal the values of feature and classification M, respectively. Data instances are represented by $[z_j, \lambda_i]$, $z_j = [z_{j1}, z_{j2}, z_{j3}, \cdots, z_{jg}]$. According to Equation (32), the DIR can be derived by

$$\tau = \frac{\sum\limits_{k=1}^{p}\left(\sum\limits_{l=1}^{c} f_{kl} - \max\limits_{l}\{f_{kl}\}\right)}{N} \qquad (32)$$

where f_{kl} equals the number of data instances that belongs to the feature subset of x_k and x_k implies that the number of feature division interval patterns existing in the data set equals p ($k = 1, 2, \ldots, p; p \leq N$).

The steps of feature selection by the DIR are shown as follows:

(1) Initialize the best subset as $\Gamma = \{\}$, namely an empty set.
(2) Estimate the DIR of $G_1, G_2, \ldots, G_g$ that are made up of Γ subset with each residual feature.
(3) Select the feature with minimum inconsistency rate G_i as the optimal one. Then, update it in the light of $\Gamma = \{\Gamma, G_i\}$.
(4) Make a list of the inconsistency rates of the feature subsets. After that, sort them in ascending order.
(5) Choose the feature subset L with fewer characteristics. If $\tau_L \approx \tau_{L\prime}$ or $\tau_{L\prime}/\tau_L$ is the minimum ratio of all the adjacent feature subsets, L is able to be screened as the optimal one, where $L\prime$ represents the adjacent previous subset.

Through the estimation of the inconsistency rate, the redundant features can be effectively eliminated. Meanwhile, correlation can be considered, which guarantees the selected features on behalf of all information.

2.3. DCNN

The DCNN is a kind of ANN with deep learning capability whose main characteristics are the local connection and weight sharing of neurons in the same layer [44]. Multiple feature extraction layers and the fully connected one are typically included in the network. Each feature extraction layer consists of two units, that is a convolutional layer and a subsampling one. The framework of the DCNN is shown in Figure 2. In the DCNN, the neural nodes between two layers are no longer fully connected. Instead, layer spatial correlation is adopted to link the neuron nodes of each layer merely to the ones in the adjacent upper layer. Hence, local connection is completed, and the parameter size of the network is greatly reduced.

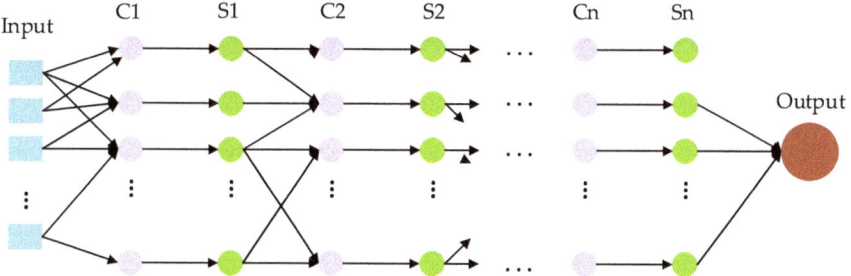

Figure 2. The typical structure of a deep convolutional neural network (DCNN).

The typical CNN is made up of four layers, namely the input layer, the convolutional layer, the subsampling layer and the full connection layer. In the convolutional layer, the convolutional kernel is used for feature extraction, and the corresponding output can be obtained by a weighted calculation through the activation function, as expressed in Equation (33)

$$x_j^l = f\left(\sum_{j=m}^{k} x_j^{l-1} w_j^l + \theta_j^l\right) \quad (j = 1, 2, \ldots, n; 0 < m \le k \le n) \tag{33}$$

where $f(I) = \frac{1}{1+e^{-I}}$, $I = \sum_{j=m}^{k} x_j^{l-1} w_j^l + b_j^l (j = 1, 2, \ldots, n; 0 < m \le k \le n)$, x_j^l and x_j^{l-1} equal the output in Layer 1 and the input in Layer $l-1$, respectively. j represents the local connection from the range of m to k; w_j^l and θ_j^l equal the weight and bias, respectively.

The subsampling process is implemented on the features of the convolutional layer for dimension-reduction. The characteristics are extracted from each $n \times n$ sampling pool by "pool average" or "pool maximum," as described in Equation (34):

$$x_j^l = g(x_j^{l-1}) + \theta_j^l \tag{34}$$

where $g(\sim)$ is the function that completes the selection of the average or maximum value. The operation of pooling is conducive to the complexity reduction of the convolutional layer and the avoidance of over fitting. In addition, it ameliorates the fault tolerance ability of feature vectors for data-characteristic micro deformation, and it enhances computational performance and robustness.

Finally, the attained data are linked to the fully connected layer, as expressed in Equation (35):

$$x^l = f(I^l), I^l = W^l x^{l-1} + \theta^l \tag{35}$$

where W_l equals the weight from Layer $l-1$ to Layer l and x^l is the output.

In the aforementioned computation, every convolutional kernel acts on all the input through slide. Multiple sets of output data are derived from the effects of diverse convolutional kernels in which the same kernel corresponds to the uniform weight. Conflate the output of diverse groups. Afterwards, transfer them to the subsampling layer. The range of values is further set, and the average or maximum value can be treated as the specific one in the scope through slide. In the end, the data are integrated to achieve dimension reduction, and the results are output through the full connection layer.

The application of the DCNN approach for cost prediction presents two merits: (i) The existence of deformed data is permitted, and (ii) the quantity of parameters decreases by local connection and weight sharing, so the efficiency and accuracy of cost prediction can be significantly improved. Nevertheless, in substation project cost prediction, the constancy of the forecasting results cannot be assured in virtue of the subjective determination of parameters. Thus, the MFOA is introduced here to optimize the parameters in the DCNN.

2.4. Approach of MFOA–DIR–DCNN

The framework of the established technique MFOA–DIR–DCNN for substation project cost prediction is displayed in Figure 3. The specific procedures of this novel method can be explained at length as follows:

(1) Determine the initial candidate features of substation project cost. In the DIR, initialize the optimal subset as an empty set $\Gamma = \{\}$.

(2) Complete parameter initialization in the MFOA. By trying a combination of multiple parameter settings, the best parameter initialization supposes that the maximum iteration number equals 200; the scope of the fruit fly position and random flight distance are set as [0, 10] and [−1, 1], respectively.

(3) Calculate inconsistency. Compute the inconsistency of $G_1, G_2, \ldots, G_g$ that is made up of Γ subsets with each residual feature. The feature with minimum inconsistency rate G_i is selected as the best one, and the updated optimal feature is set as $\Gamma = \{\Gamma, G_i\}$.

(4) Derive the optimal feature subset along with the best values of parameters in the DCNN. The feature subset at current iteration is brought into the DCNN, and both prediction accuracy $r(j)$ and fitness value $Fitness(j)$ can be calculated for this training process. Then, determine whether each iteration satisfies the termination requirements (reach the target error value or the maximum number of iterations). If not, reinitialize the feature subset and repeat the above steps until the conditions are met. It is noteworthy that the parameters in the DCNN also need to be optimized, and the initial values of weight w and threshold θ are randomly assigned. Therefore,

a fitness function based on both forecasting precision and feature selection quantity is set up, as shown in Equation (36):

$$Fitness(j) = -(a + r(j) + \frac{b}{Numfeature(j)}) \quad (36)$$

where $Numfeature(j)$ represents the quantity of selected best characteristics in each iteration, and a and b equal the constants in [0, 1].

(5) Forecast via the DCNN. When the iterative number reaches the maximum, the estimation stops. Here, the optimal feature subset, the best values of w, and θ are taken into the DCNN model for substation project cost forecasting.

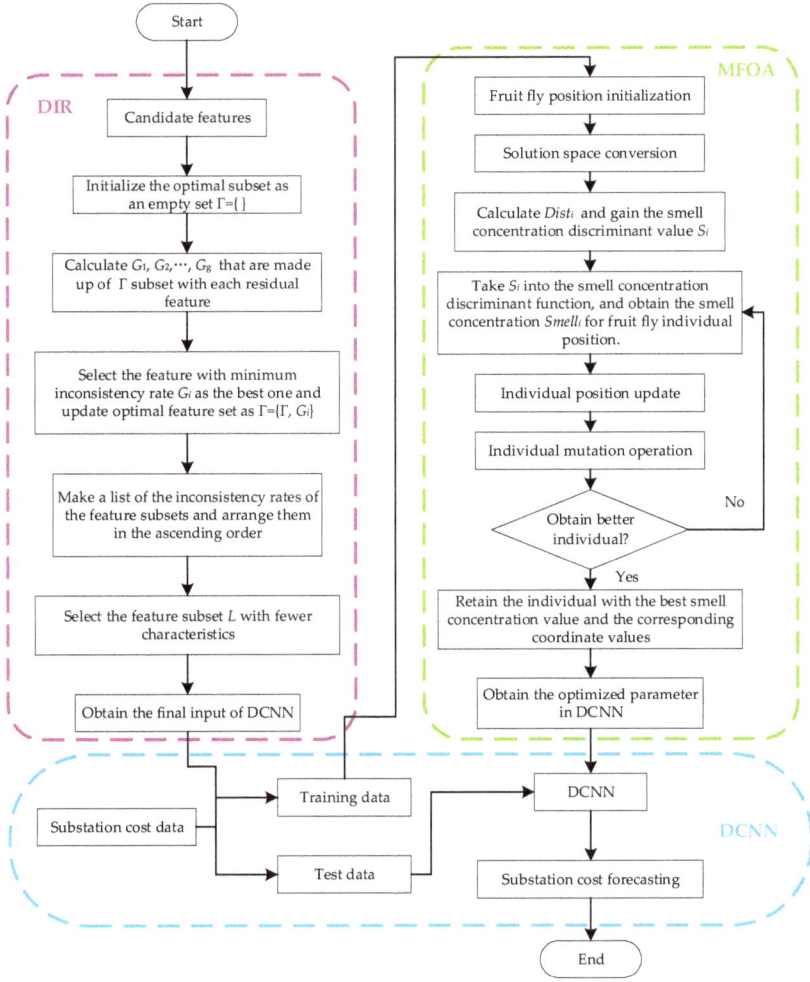

Figure 3. The flow chart of the modified fruit fly optimization algorithm– data inconsistency rate– deep convolutional neural network (MFOA–DIR–DCNN).

3. Case Study

3.1. Data Processing

This paper selected the cost data of 128 substation projects in various voltage levels and in different areas from 2015 to 2018, as shown in Table 1; the statistics of the substation features are shown in Table A1. In this paper, we selected the cost and corresponding influential factors of the first 66 projects as a training set. Correspondingly, the remaining data were employed as a testing set.

Table 1. Original cost data of projects (Unit: CNY/kV·A).

Serial Number	Cost	Serial Number	Cost	Serial Number	Cost	Serial Number	Cost
1	358.3	33	980.6	65	336.8	97	317.1
2	324.2	34	286.8	66	339.5	98	308.0
3	368.9	35	279.5	67	342.1	99	298.9
4	370.2	36	308.6	68	344.7	100	289.9
5	450.1	37	312.8	69	244.2	101	280.8
6	266.5	38	315.9	70	346.8	102	271.7
7	301.6	39	364.2	71	349.5	103	262.6
8	325.8	40	361.3	72	352.1	104	253.5
9	310.3	41	375.6	73	394.7	105	244.5
10	405.6	42	389.9	74	405.6	106	235.4
11	392.5	43	372.5	75	428.2	107	326.3
12	448.2	44	383.9	76	443.0	108	217.2
13	305.8	45	295.6	77	459.8	109	208.1
14	356.9	46	270.2	78	493.3	110	199.1
15	1058.6	47	260.8	79	289.4	111	390.0
16	501.2	48	240.7	80	293.7	112	280.9
17	337.1	49	223.3	81	297.9	113	285.1
18	304.5	50	239.3	82	402.2	114	476.5
19	291.8	51	381.7	83	491.5	115	449.3
20	279.2	52	406.9	84	491.3	116	470.4
21	299.3	53	315.6	85	212.6	117	491.8
22	285.6	54	285.5	86	452.6	118	306.4
23	305.5	55	252.5	87	353.7	119	310.7
24	208.6	56	214.5	88	254.8	120	274.9
25	356.2	57	325.8	89	155.9	121	319.2
26	401.5	58	328.4	90	375.9	122	283.4
27	378.6	59	311.1	91	375.9	123	369.5
28	369.5	60	333.7	92	397.0	124	373.8
29	253.8	61	336.3	93	418.1	125	398.6
30	300.5	62	309.0	94	344.3	126	244.8
31	272.7	63	341.6	95	335.3	127	256.9
32	423.4	64	334.2	96	326.2	128	472.9

Here, the construction types of substation projects can be divided into three categories: New substation, extended main transformer, and extended interval engineering are valued at 1, 2 and 3, respectively. The substation types were decomposed into three types where the indoor, the semi-indoor, and the outdoor were set as 1, 2 and 3, respectively. The landforms were parted into eight kinds, namely hillock, hillside field, flat, plain, paddy field, rainfed cropland, mountainous region and depression—these were valued at {1, 2, 3, 4, 5, 6, 7, 8}. In addition, the local GDP was employed to represent the economic development level of the construction area. The proportion of bachelor degree or above in the staff stood for the technical level of the designers. The difference between actual progress and the schedule stipulated in the contract was utilized on behalf of construction progress level. The data needed to be normalized with Equation (37).

$$Y = \{y_i\} = \frac{x_i - x_{\min}}{x_{\max} - x_{\min}} \quad i = 1, 2, 3, \ldots, n \tag{37}$$

where x_i and y_i represent the actual value and normalized value, respectively, while $x_{\min}$ and $x_{\max}$ equal the minimum and maximum of the sample data, respectively.

3.2. Model Performance Evaluation

Four commonly adopted error criteria are presented in this paper to measure the forecasting precision of substation project cost obtained by all involved approaches.

(1) Relative error (RE)

$$RE = \frac{x_i - \hat{x}_i}{x_i} \times 100\% \tag{38}$$

(2) Root mean square error (RMSE)

$$RMSE = \sqrt{\frac{1}{n}\sum_{i=1}^{n}(\frac{x_i - \hat{x}_i}{x_i})^2} \tag{39}$$

(3) Mean absolute percentage error (MAPE)

$$MAPE = \frac{1}{n}\sum_{i=1}^{n}|(x_i - \hat{x}_i)/x_i| \cdot 100\% \tag{40}$$

(4) Average absolute error (AAE)

$$AAE = \frac{1}{n}(\sum_{i=1}^{n}|x_i - \hat{x}_i|)/(\frac{1}{n}\sum_{i=1}^{n}x_i) \tag{41}$$

where n is the number of testing samples, while x and $\hat{x}$ represent the actual value and predictive value of substation project cost, respectively. The aforementioned indicators are negatively correlated with forecasting precision.

3.3. Feature Selection

The input of the forecasting techniques was determined on the basis of optimal feature subset selection by the DIR. In reference [45], the authors divided the substation project cost into two main types: Primary and secondary production cost and individual project costs associated with site, totaling more than 20 factors. In reference [46], authors selected more than 26 variables including the area and main transformer capacity as the influencing factors of substation cost. Based on the research of the above references, this paper screened 33 variables as the main influencing factors of substation cost, including area, construction type, voltage level of substation, main transformer capacity, transmission line circuits in the low and high voltage sides, topography, schedule, substation type, the number of transformers, the economic development level of the construction area, inflation rate, the price and number of the circuit breaker in the high voltage side, the quantity of low-voltage capacitors, the price of single main transformer, high-voltage fuse, current transformer, power capacitor, reactor, electric buses, arrester, measuring instrument, relay protection device, signal system, automatic device, the expense of site leveling and foundation treatment, the technical level of the designers, the number of accidents, engineering deviation rate, construction progress level, rainy days, and snowy days.

The program in this paper was run in MATLAB R2018b under Intel Core i5-6300U, 4 G and a Windows 10 system.

The iterative process of feature extraction is displayed in Figure 4, where the accuracy curve and the fitness curve show the forecasting precision of the DCNN and fitness values in different iterations, respectively, while option number indicates the quantity of best characteristics derived from the DIR model, and feature reduction refers to the number of characteristics eliminated by the MFOA.

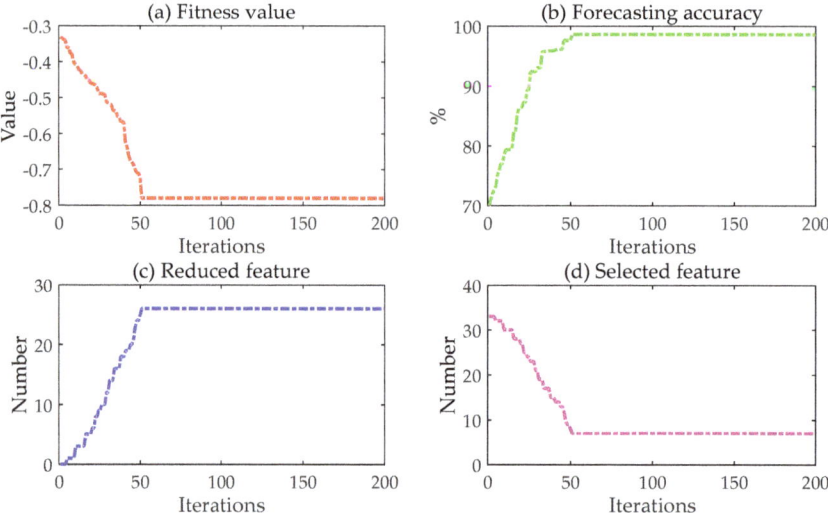

Figure 4. Convergence curves for feature selection. Note: (**a**) represents the fitness value, (**b**) represents the forecasting accuracy, (**c**) represents the reduced number of candidate feature, and (**d**) represents the selected number of optimization feature.

As we can see, the MFOA converged at the 39th iteration, and the homologous optimal fitness value and prediction accuracy equaled −0.91% and 98.9%, respectively, This indicates that the fitting ability of the DCNN can be enhanced, and the forecasting precision is able to reach the highest through learning and training. Furthermore, the quantity of chosen characteristics was inclined to be steady when the MFOA ran to the 51th time. Ultimately, the final selected characteristics embodied construction type, voltage level, main transformer capacity, substation type, the number of transformers, the price of single main transformer, and the area by eliminating 26 redundant features from 33 candidates. The importance of these seven features derived from the DIR was ordered as (from important to unimportant): The price of single main transformer, the number of transformers, main transformer capacity, construction type, area, substation type, and voltage level.

3.4. Results and Discussion

After the accomplishment of feature selection, the input vector was brought into the DCNN model for training and testing. Here, the wavelet kernel function [47], one of the most widely used kernel functions, was applied, and the parameters optimized by MFOA equaled: $\gamma = 43.0126$, $\sigma = 19.0382$.

For the purpose of verifying the performance of the established approach, four other methods incorporating the MFOA–DCNN, the DCNN, an SVM and the BPNN were used for comparison. In the BPNN, the topology was set as 9-7-1. Tansig and purelin were exploited as the transfer function in the hidden layer and the transfer function in the output layer, respectively. In this paper, we set the maximum number of convergence as 200, while the learning rate and the error equaled 0.1 and 0.0001, respectively. The initial values of weights and thresholds were decided by their own training. In the

SVM, the penalty parameter c and kernel parameter σ were valued at 10.276 and 0.0013, respectively, and ε in the loss function equaled 2.4375. In the DCNN, $\gamma = 15$, $\sigma = 5$. Table 2 lists the prediction results of the substation project cost achieved by five different models.

Table 2. Actual and predicted values of the testing sample (Unit: CNY/kV·A).

Serial Number	Actual Value	BPNN	SVM	DCNN	MFOA–DCNN	MFOA–DIR–DCNN
97	317.1	335.3	298.3	324.3	326.7	308.0
98	308.0	292.9	322.4	318.8	298.7	298.8
99	298.9	316.3	283.1	310.5	308.7	305.9
100	289.9	306.6	273.4	278.8	298.9	297.2
101	280.8	265.2	273.0	270.9	290.1	286.5
102	271.7	288.0	284.7	266.1	281.1	278.0
103	262.6	281.0	271.5	253.2	257.3	269.0
104	253.5	270.9	259.8	257.5	261.9	251.6
105	244.5	261.1	230.3	234.7	253.5	240.9
106	235.4	248.7	244.8	229.6	243.1	230.2
107	326.3	312.0	334.1	314.3	337.9	330.8
108	217.2	232.5	222.4	225.9	203.9	222.5
109	208.1	222.8	199.6	216.0	215.1	203.8
110	199.1	212.8	191.0	191.2	205.4	194.7
111	390.0	412.0	372.3	403.8	383.8	393.9
112	280.9	297.5	273.8	290.7	271.2	273.3
113	285.1	300.8	271.1	295.3	294.6	293.1
114	476.5	504.8	495.9	459.6	492.4	490.0
115	449.3	424.1	469.9	456.0	456.9	462.7
116	470.4	479.0	493.3	453.7	484.6	468.8
117	491.8	465.7	466.3	511.1	507.0	503.6
118	306.4	328.1	292.3	317.4	316.8	298.0
119	310.7	328.0	323.9	298.3	300.6	309.1
120	274.9	294.0	286.4	285.3	277.1	275.6
121	319.2	340.2	305.5	323.8	308.8	309.7
122	283.4	303.3	271.2	294.7	292.6	291.4
123	369.5	396.0	352.3	383.5	381.0	373.7
124	373.8	399.2	351.6	382.3	385.1	363.1
125	398.6	426.2	415.1	413.6	401.8	399.5
126	244.8	260.9	234.3	248.3	236.9	237.5
127	256.9	274.9	245.8	267.2	265.2	264.2
128	472.9	506.9	451.0	490.8	487.6	478.4

For a more intuitive analysis, Figure 5 presents the predictive values and Figure 6 exhibits the values of RE derived from the forecasting techniques. The forecasting error range of the MFOA–DIR–DCNN was within [−3%, 3%], while the number of error points of the MFOA–DCNN and the DCNN in this scope was 5 and 3 (that is, No.102, RE = −2.07%; No.121, RE = 1.44%; No.124, RE = 2.28%), respectively. Among them, the number of error points obtained from the MFOA–DIR–DCNN controlled in [−1%, 1%] equaled 5 (namely No.104, RE = −0.77%; No.116, RE = −0.35%; No.119, RE = −0.50%; No.120, RE = 0.23%; No.125, RE = 0.23%), while the corresponding number of the MFOA–DCNN and the DCNN was 2 (No.120, RE = 0.79%; No.125, RE = −0.82%) and 0, respectively. It can be seen the error points of the SVM mostly ranged in [−6%, −4%] and [4%, 6%], while there existed a large fluctuation in the errors of the BPNN, mainly in [−7%, −5%] and [5%, 7%]. In addition, the minimum absolute values of RE for the MFOA–DIR–DCNN, the MFOA–DCNN, the DCNN, the SVM and the BPNN were 0.23%, 0.79%, 1.44%, −2.52%, 2.83%, respectively, and the maximum absolute values of RE correspondingly equaled 2.99%, 6.12%, 6.51%, −6.94% and 7.17%, respectively. In this respect, these models can be sorted by the forecasting accuracy from the superior to the inferior: the MFOA–DIR–DCNN, the MFOA–DCNN, the DCNN, the SVM and the BPNN. This demonstrates that the application of the MFOA contributes to the enhancement of training and learning process as well as the improvement of global searching ability for the DCNN. Simultaneously, the input derived from the MFOA–DIR can obtain satisfactory prediction results. In contrast with the SVM and the BPNN, this indicates that the DCNN can achieve a better forecasting performance than shallow learning algorithms.

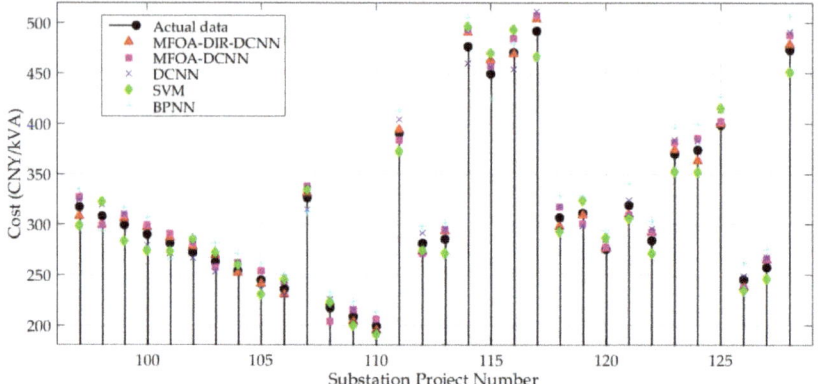

Figure 5. Forecasting results.

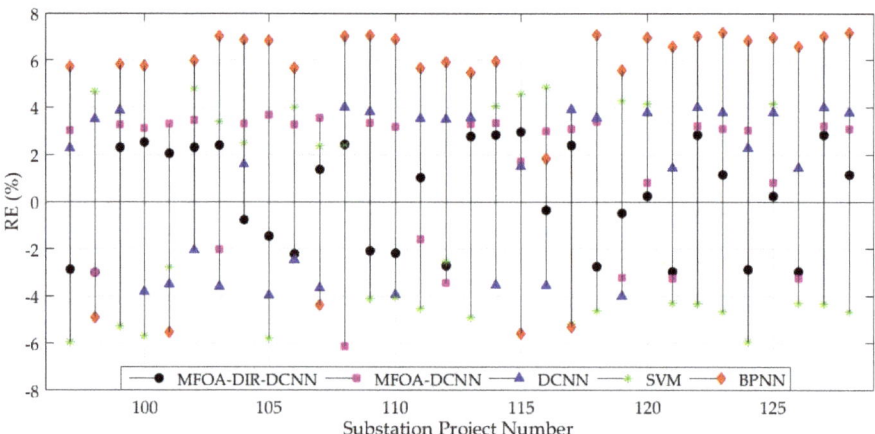

Figure 6. Relative error (RE) of prediction methods.

Figure 7 illustrates the comparative results gauged by the RMSE, the MAPE, and the AAE. THis proves that the established hybrid model is superior to the other four techniques from the perspective of the aforementioned error criteria. Concretely, the RMSE, the MAPE and the AAE of the MFOA–DIR–DCNN were 2.2345%, 2.1721% and 2.1700%, respectively. Additionally, the RMSEs of the MFOA–DCNN, the DCNN, the SVM and the BPNN were 3.1818%, 3.7103%, 4.5659%, and 6.2336%, respectively, while the MAPE of the corresponding methods equaled 3.2073%, 3.7148%, 4.4318% and 5.8772%, respectively. Accordingly, the AAE of the MFOA–DCNN, the DCNN, the SVM and the BPNN was equivalent to 3.1251%, 3.7253%, 4.4956% and 5.7347%, respectively. Owing to the fact that the DCNN has advantages over shallow learning algorithms, the MFOA was able to complete parameter optimization of the DCNN, and the DIR approach guarantees the completeness of the input information while reducing the redundant data, which ameliorates the prediction accuracy and robustness.

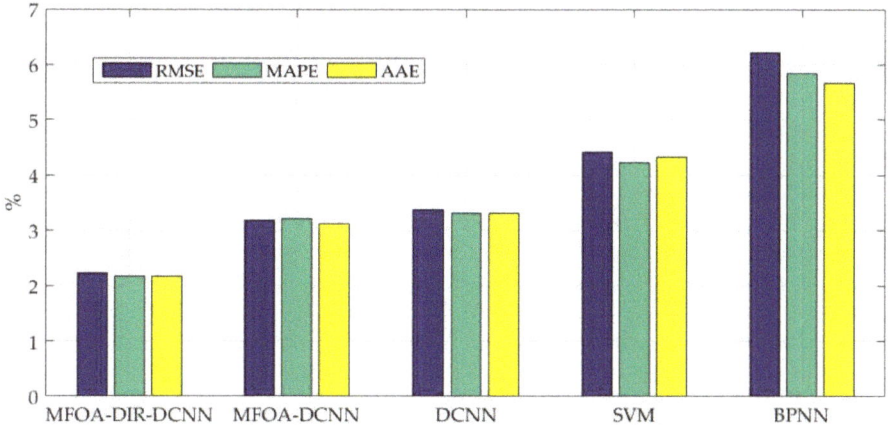

Figure 7. Root mean square error (RMSE), mean absolute percentage error (MAPE) and average absolute error (AAE) of the prediction techniques.

For further verification that the proposed method is better, the case was predicted by the methods proposed in Reference [8] (BP neural network), [14] (cuckoo search algorithm and support vector machine), and [36] (modified firefly algorithm and support vector machine). The input of these three models was 33—that is 33 candidate features—and the parameter settings were consistent with those mentioned in the text. Table 3 displays the comparative forecasting results.

Table 3. Comparison with the prediction results of the references' models.

Model	RMSE	MAPE	AAE
Proposed model	2.2345	2.1721	2.1700
Ref. [8]	6.2336	5.8772	5.7347
Ref. [14]	3.3641	3.4502	3.3122
Ref. [36]	3.2794	3.3471	3.2098

According to Table 3, it can be concluded that the forecasting precision of the established approach outperforms that of References [8,14,36]. The main reasons consist of three points. First, the feature selection process can remove the low correlation factors, thereby reducing the input of the model and reducing the training error of the model. Second, optimizing the parameters of the neural network or the support vector machine can provide the training accuracy of the model. For example, the prediction results of References [14] and [36] were superior to the prediction results of the SVM (mentioned in Figure 7). Third, the DCNN model not only reduces the number of neurons and weights, it also uses the pooling operation to make the input features have displacement, scaling and distortion invariance, thus improving the accuracy and robustness of network training, which is better than the SVM and the BPNN.

However, when training and testing the proposed model, it was found that the amount of sample data in the training set had a relatively large impact on the test results. The larger the sample size of the training set, the better the test results. Due to the limited number of new substation projects each year, when applying the proposed model, it is necessary to collect more data on the cost of the previous substation project cost to ensure that the DCNN can be fully trained.

4. Conclusions

This paper developed a novel hybrid approach for cost forecasting based on the DIR, the DCNN and the MFOA. Firstly, the DIR integrated with the MFOA was adopted for input feature selection. Simultaneously, the MFOA was utilized to realize parameter optimization in the DCNN. Thus, the proposed method could be applied to cost forecasting of substation projects on the foundation of the optimized input subset, as well as the best value of γ and σ. The proposed model outperformed the comparative approaches in terms of prediction precision. The case studies demonstrated that: (a) The use of the DIR is conducive to the elimination of unrelated noises and the improvement of prediction performance. (b) Improving the DCNN with the MFOA presents good performance mainly due to the fact that the MFOA enhances the global searching capability of the method. (c) The ideal prediction results were obtained by numerical examples of substation projects in different regions, different voltage levels, and different scales, which shows that the adaptability and stability of the proposed model are also strong. Therefore, this established approach for cost forecasting based on the MFOA–DIR–DCNN, considering its effectiveness and feasibility, provides an alternative for this field in the electric-power industry.

However, the feature selection methods have been researched more and more recently, and it is very important for substation project cost forecasting. Thus, the new feature selection method will be will be a research focus in the future.

Author Contributions: H.W. designed this study and wrote this paper; Y.H. provided professional guidance; C.G. and Y.J. revised this paper.

Funding: This work is supported by the Fundamental Research Funds for the Central Universities (Project No. 2017MS168).

Conflicts of Interest: The authors declare no conflict of interest.

Abbreviations

Abbreviation	Meaning
MFOA	modified fruit fly optimization algorithm
FOA	fruit fly optimization algorithm
DIR	data inconsistency rate
DCNN	deep convolutional neural network
ANNs	artificial neural networks
SVM	support vector machine
BPNN	back propagation neural network
ELM	extreme learning machine
RBFNN	radial basis function neural network
GRNN	general regression neural network
APSO	adaptive particle swarm optimization
CS	cuckoo search algorithm
DNN	deep neural network
CNN	convolutional neural network
RE	relative error
RMSE	root mean square error
MAPE	mean absolute percentage error
AAE	average absolute error

Appendix A

Table A1. The statistics of substation feature.

Candidate Features		Statistic Information		
Area	Type	<2000 m^2	>2000 m^2 and <4000 m^2	>4000 m^2
	Statistics	26	78	24
Construction type	Type	New substation	Extended main transformer	Extended interval engineering
	Statistics	56	48	24
Voltage level	Type	35 kV	110 kV	220 kV
	Statistics	27	82	19
Main transformer capacity	Type	<30 MVA	>30 MVA and <50 MVA	>50 MVA
	Statistics	32	78	18
High-voltage side outlet number	Type		<4	>4
	Statistics		64	64
Low-voltage side outlet number	Type		<4	>4
	Statistics		86	42
Topography	Type	Hillock, hillside field and flat	Plain, paddy field and rainfed cropland	mountainous region and depression
	Statistics	64	52	10
Schedule	Type	<90 days	>90 days and <180 days	>180 days
	Statistics	57	35	36
Substation type	Type	Indoor	Semi-indoor	Outdoor
	Statistics	82	20	26
Number of transformers	Type		1	2
	Statistics		27	101
Economic development level	Type	<200 billion CNY	>200 billion CNY and <400 billion CNY	>400 billion CNY
	Statistics	16	92	20
Inflation rate	Type	<2%	<2% and >4%	>4%
	Statistics	11	111	6
Main transformer price	Type		<100,000 CNY	>100,000 CNY
	Statistics		26	102
High-voltage side circuit breaker price	Type		<10,000 CNY	>10,000 CNY
	Statistics		45	83
Number of high-voltage side breakers	Type		<2	>2
	Statistics		68	60
Number of low voltage capacitors	Type		1	>1
	Statistics		56	72
High voltage fuse price	Type		<500 CNY	>500 CNY
	Statistics		59	69
Current transformer price	Type		<10,000 CNY	>10,000 CNY
	Statistics		23	105
Power capacitor price	Type		<100,000 CNY	>100,000 CNY
	Statistics		89	39
Reactor price	Type		<5000 CNY	>5000 CNY
	Statistics		57	71
Power bus price	Type		<2000 CNY/m	>2000 CNY/m
	Statistics		69	59
Arrester price	Type		<2000 CNY	>2000 CNY
	Statistics		76	52
Measuring instrument price	Type		<10,000 CNY	>10,000 CNY
	Statistics		39	89
Relay protection device price	Type		<10,000 CNY	>10,000 CNY
	Statistics		40	88
Signal system price	Type		<100,000 CNY	>100,000 CNY
	Statistics		44	84
Automatic device price	Type		<20,000 CNY	>20,000 CNY
	Statistics		90	38

Table A1. *Cont.*

Candidate Features		Statistic Information		
Site leveling cost	Type	<500,000 CNY		>500,000 CNY
	Statistics	65		63
Foundation treatment cost	Type	<1,000,000 CNY		>1,000,000 CNY
	Statistics	76		52
Technical level of the designers	Type	<50%	>50% and >80%	>80%
	Statistics	19	83	26
Number of accidents	Type	0		>0
	Statistics	122		6
Engineering deviatio rate	Type	<15%		>15%
	Statistics	107		21
Construction progress level	Type	0 day	>0 day and <15 days	>15 days
	Statistics	96	15	17
Rainy and snowy days	Type	<7 days	>7 days and <14 days	>14 days
	Statistics	48	67	13

References

1. Pal, A.; Vullikanti, A.K.S.; Ravi, S.S. A PMU Placement Scheme Considering Realistic Costs and Modern Trends in Relaying. *IEEE Trans. Power Syst.* **2017**, *32*, 552–561. [CrossRef]
2. Heydt, G.T. A Probabilistic Cost/Benefit Analysis of Transmission and Distribution Asset Expansion Projects. *IEEE Trans. Power Syst.* **2017**, *32*, 4151–4152. [CrossRef]
3. Hu, L.X. Research on Prediction of Architectural Engineering Cost based on the Time Series Method. *J. Taiyuan Univ. Technol.* **2012**, *43*, 706–709.
4. Wei, L.; Yuan, Y.-n.; Dong, W.-d.; Zhang, B. Study on engineering cost forecasting of electric power construction based on time response function optimization grey model. In Proceedings of the IEEE, International Conference on Communication Software and Networks, Xi'an, China, 27–29 May 2011; pp. 58–61.
5. Wei, L. A Model of Building Project Cost Estimation Based on Multiple Structur Integral Linear Regression. *Archit. Technol.* **2015**, *46*, 846–849.
6. Li, J.; Wang, R.; Wang, J.; Li, Y. Analysis and forecasting of the oil consumption in China based on combination models optimized by artificial intelligence algorithms. *Energy* **2018**, *144*, 243–264. [CrossRef]
7. Wang, M.; Zhao, L.; Du, R.; Wang, C.; Chen, L.; Tian, L.; Stanley, H.E. A novel hybrid method of forecasting crude oil prices using complex network science and artificial intelligence algorithms. *Appl. Energy* **2018**, *220*, 480–495. [CrossRef]
8. Ling, Y.P.; Yan, P.F.; Han, C.Z.; Yang, C.G. BP Neural Network Based Cost Prediction Model for Transmission Projects. *Electr. Power* **2012**, *45*, 95–99.
9. Liang, Y.; Niu, D.; Cao, Y.; Hong, W.C. Analysis and Modeling for China's Electricity Demand Forecasting Using a Hybrid Method Based on Multiple Regression and Extreme Learning Machine: A View from Carbon Emission. *Energies* **2016**, *9*, 941. [CrossRef]
10. Liu, J.; Qing, Y.E. Project Cost Prediction Model Based on BP and RBP Neural Networks in Xiamen City. *J. Huaqiao Univ.* **2013**, *34*, 576–580.
11. Niu, D.; Liang, Y.; Hong, W.C. Wind Speed Forecasting Based on EMD and GRNN Optimized by FOA. *Energies* **2017**, *10*, 2001. [CrossRef]
12. Nieto, P.G.; Lasheras, F.S.; García-Gonzalo, E.; de Cos Juez, F.J. PM 10, concentration forecasting in the metropolitan area of Oviedo (Northern Spain) using models based on SVM, MLP, VARMA and ARIMA: A case study. *Sci. Total Environ.* **2018**, *621*, 753–761. [CrossRef]
13. Peng, G.; Si, H.; Yu, J.; Yang, Y.; Li, S.; Tan, K. Modification and application of SVM algorithm. *Comput. Eng. Appl.* **2011**, *47*, 218–221.
14. Niu, D.; Zhao, W.; Li, S.; Chen, R. Cost Forecasting of Substation Projects Based on Cuckoo Search Algorithm and Support Vector Machines. *Sustainability* **2018**, *10*, 118. [CrossRef]
15. Zhu, X.; Xu, Q.; Tang, M.; Nie, W.; Ma, S.; Xu, Z. Comparison of two optimized machine learning models for predicting displacement of rainfall-induced landslide: A case study in Sichuan Province, China. *Eng. Geol.* **2017**, *218*, 213–222. [CrossRef]

16. Bai, Y.; Chen, Z.; Xie, J.; Li, C. Daily reservoir inflow forecasting using multiscale deep feature learning with hybrid models. *J. Hydrol.* **2016**, *532*, 193–206. [CrossRef]
17. Larson, D.B.; Chen, M.C.; Lungren, M.P.; Halabi, S.S.; Stence, N.V.; Langlotz, C.P. Performance of a Deep-Learning Neural Network Model in Assessing Skeletal Maturity on Pediatric Hand Radiographs. *Radiology* **2017**, *287*, 313–322. [CrossRef]
18. Siddiqui, S.A.; Salman, A.; Malik, M.I.; Shafait, F.; Mian, A.; Shortis, M.R.; Harvey, E.S. Automatic fish species classification in underwater videos: Exploiting pretrained deep neural network models to compensate for limited labelled data. *Ices J. Mar. Sci.* **2018**, *75*, 374–389. [CrossRef]
19. Yu, X.; Dong, H. PTL-CFS based deep convolutional neural network model for remote sensing classification. *Computing* **2018**, *100*, 773–785. [CrossRef]
20. Chen, Y.H.; Krishna, T.; Emer, J.S.; Sze, V. Eyeriss: An Energy-Efficient Reconfigurable Accelerator for Deep Convolutional Neural Networks. *IEEE J. Solid State Circuits* **2017**, *52*, 127–138. [CrossRef]
21. Rawat, W.; Wang, Z. Deep Convolutional Neural Networks for Image Classification: A Comprehensive Review. *Neural Comput.* **2017**, *29*, 2352–2449. [CrossRef]
22. Wang, H.; Yi, H.; Peng, J.; Wang, G.; Liu, Y.; Jiang, H.; Liu, W. Deterministic and probabilistic forecasting of photovoltaic power based on deep convolutional neural network. *Energy Convers. Manag.* **2017**, *153*, 409–422. [CrossRef]
23. Wang, H.Z.; Li, G.Q.; Wang, G.B.; Peng, J.C.; Jiang, H.; Liu, Y.T. Deep learning based ensemble approach for probabilistic wind power forecasting. *Appl. Energy* **2017**, *188*, 56–70. [CrossRef]
24. Liu, H.; Mi, X.; Li, Y. Smart deep learning based wind speed prediction model using wavelet packet decomposition, convolutional neural network and convolutional long short term memory network. *Energy Convers. Manag.* **2018**, *166*, 120–131. [CrossRef]
25. Gunduz, H.; Yaslan, Y.; Cataltepe, Z. Intraday prediction of Borsa Istanbul using convolutional neural networks and feature correlations. *Knowl. Based Syst.* **2017**, *137*, 138–148. [CrossRef]
26. Jin, K.H.; McCann, M.T.; Froustey, E.; Unser, M. Deep Convolutional Neural Network for Inverse Problems in Imaging. *IEEE Trans. Image Process.* **2017**, *26*, 4509–4522. [CrossRef]
27. Pan, W.T. A new Fruit Fly Optimization Algorithm: Taking the financial distress model as an example. *Knowl. Based Syst.* **2012**, *26*, 69–74. [CrossRef]
28. Yang, Q.; Chen, W.N.; Yu, Z.; Gu, T.; Li, Y.; Zhang, H.; Zhang, J. Adaptive Multimodal Continuous Ant Colony Optimization. *IEEE Trans. Evol. Comput.* **2017**, *21*, 191–205. [CrossRef]
29. Chen, Z.; Xiong, R.; Cao, J. Particle swarm optimization-based optimal power management of plug-in hybrid electric vehicles considering uncertain driving conditions. *Energy* **2016**, *96*, 197–208. [CrossRef]
30. Lin, J.; Sheng, G.; Yan, Y.; Dai, J.; Jiang, X. Prediction of Dissolved Gas Concentrations in Transformer Oil Based on the KPCA-FFOA-GRNN Model. *Energies* **2018**, *11*, 225. [CrossRef]
31. Niu, D.; Ma, T.; Liu, B. Power load forecasting by wavelet least squares support vector machine with improved fruit fly optimization algorithm. *J. Comb. Optim.* **2016**, *33*, 1122–1143.
32. Hu, R.; Wen, S.; Zeng, Z.; Huang, T. A short-term power load forecasting model based on the generalized regression neural network with decreasing step fruit fly optimization algorithm. *Neurocomputing* **2017**, *221*, 24–31. [CrossRef]
33. Cao, G.; Wu, L. Support vector regression with fruit fly optimization algorithm for seasonal electricity consumption forecasting. *Energy* **2016**, *115*, 734–745. [CrossRef]
34. Qu, Z.; Zhang, K.; Wang, J.; Zhang, W.; Leng, W. A Hybrid Model Based on Ensemble Empirical Mode Decomposition and Fruit Fly Optimization Algorithm for Wind Speed Forecasting. *Adv. Meteorol.* **2016**, *2016*, 3768242. [CrossRef]
35. Li, H.Z.; Guo, S.; Li, C.J.; Sun, J.Q. A hybrid annual power load forecasting model based on generalized regression neural network with fruit fly optimization algorithm. *Knowl. Based Syst.* **2013**, *37*, 378–387. [CrossRef]
36. Song, Z.; Niu, D.; Xiao, X.; Zhu, L. Substation Engineering Cost Forecasting Method Based on Modified Firefly Algorithm and Support Vector Machine. *Electr. Power* **2017**, *50*, 168–178.
37. Zhang, C.; Kumar, A.; Ré, C. Materialization Optimizations for Feature Selection Workloads. *ACM Trans. Database Syst.* **2016**, *41*, 2. [CrossRef]

38. Niu, D.; Wang, H.; Chen, H.; Liang, Y. The General Regression Neural Network Based on the Fruit Fly Optimization Algorithm and the Data Inconsistency Rate for Transmission Line Icing Prediction. *Energies* **2017**, *10*, 2066.
39. Chen, T.; Ma, J.; Huang, S.H.; Cai, A. Novel and efficient method on feature selection and data classification. *J. Comput. Res. Dev.* **2012**, *49*, 735–745.
40. Liu, J.P.; Li, C.L. The Short-Term Power Load Forecasting Based on Sperm Whale Algorithm and Wavelet Least Square Support Vector Machine with DWT-IR for Feature Selection. *Sustainability* **2017**, *9*, 1188. [CrossRef]
41. Li, C.; Li, S.; Liu, Y. A least squares support vector machine model optimized by moth-flame optimization algorithm for annual power load forecasting. *Appl. Intell.* **2016**, *45*, 1166–1178. [CrossRef]
42. Wu, L.; Cao, G. Seasonal SVR with FOA algorithm for single-step and multi-step ahead forecasting in monthly inbound tourist flow. *Knowl. Based Syst.* **2016**, *110*, 157–166.
43. Iscan, H.; Gunduz, M. A Survey on Fruit Fly Optimization Algorithm. In Proceedings of the International Conference on Signal-Image Technology & Internet-Based Systems. IEEE Computer Society, Bangkok, Thailand, 23–27 November 2015; pp. 520–527.
44. Zhang, F.; Cai, N.; Wu, J.; Cen, G.; Wang, H.; Chen, X. Image denoising method based on a deep convolution neural network. *IET Image Process.* **2018**, *12*, 485–493. [CrossRef]
45. Lu, Y.; Niu, D.; Qiu, J.; Liu, W. Prediction Technology of Power Transmission and Transformation Project Cost Based on the Decomposition-Integration. *Math. Probl. Eng.* **2015**, *2015*, 651878. [CrossRef]
46. Kang, J.X.; Ai, L.S.; Zhang, X.R.; LIU, S.M.; CAO, Y.; MA, L.; CHENG, Z.H. Analysis of Substation Project Cost Influence Factors. *J. Northeast Dianli Univ.* **2011**, *31*, 131–136. (In Chinese)
47. Zhang, L.; Zhou, W.; Jiao, L. Wavelet support vector machine. *IEEE Trans. Syst. Man Cybern. Soc.* **2004**, *34*, 34–39. [CrossRef]

© 2019 by the authors. Licensee MDPI, Basel, Switzerland. This article is an open access article distributed under the terms and conditions of the Creative Commons Attribution (CC BY) license (http://creativecommons.org/licenses/by/4.0/).

Article

Research and Application of a Novel Hybrid Model Based on a Deep Neural Network Combined with Fuzzy Time Series for Energy Forecasting

Danxiang Wei, Jianzhou Wang *, Kailai Ni and Guangyu Tang

School of Statistics, Dongbei University of Finance and Economics, Dalian 116025, China; danxiang130@gmail.com (D.W.); Kailai_Ni@126.com (K.N.); Tang_Guangyu@126.com (G.T.)
* Correspondence: wangjz@dufe.edu.cn; Tel.: +86-130-0948-0823

Received: 5 August 2019; Accepted: 6 September 2019; Published: 19 September 2019

Abstract: In recent years, although deep learning algorithms have been widely applied to various fields, ranging from translation to time series forecasting, researchers paid limited attention to modelling parameter optimization and the combination of the fuzzy time series. In this paper, a novel hybrid forecasting system, named CFML (complementary ensemble empirical mode decomposition (CEEMD)-fuzzy time series (FTS)-multi-objective grey wolf optimizer (MOGWO)-long short-term memory (LSTM)), is proposed and tested. This model is based on the LSTM model with parameters optimized by MOGWO, before which a fuzzy time series method involving the LEM2 (learning from examples module version two) algorithm is adopted to generate the final input data of the optimized LSTM model. In addition, the CEEMD algorithm is also used to de-noise and decompose the raw data. The CFML model successfully overcomes the nonstationary and irregular features of wind speed data and electrical power load series. Several experimental results covering four wind speed datasets and two electrical power load datasets indicate that our hybrid forecasting system achieves average improvements of 49% and 70% in wind speed and electrical power load, respectively, under the metric MAPE (mean absolute percentage error).

Keywords: multi-objective grey wolf optimizer; long short-term memory; fuzzy time series; LEM2; combination forecasting; wind speed; electrical power load

1. Introduction

Effective forecasting plays an essential role in various aspects, such as energy application, economic risk management, standardized management, policy making, and so on. Forecasting helps corporations, governments, and other organizations and institutions to evaluate the market and to make relative predictions to better understand potential relations among entities and to plan for the future, which is a useful way to make policies on both the private and the social levels. As a result, many forecasting methods have been proposed during the past decades. Among these, there are two different categories: time series forecasting and causal forecasting. Since causal forecasting has some inherent limitations, including the reliability and availability of independent variables, time series forecasting has been applied much more widely due to its convenience for data collection and its high accuracy as well as stability. Time series forecasting methods presume that history will repeat itself, which means that the forecasting of future values is based on present values and past observations. Nowadays, time series forecasting has achieved great success in many industries, especially in the energy industry.

With the rapid development of the energy industry and increasing demand for high-level management and application, its infrastructure has been upgraded by a great extent, as a result of which the prices, supply, as well as demand have oscillated to a greater extent and have become more unpredictable than ever before. This has posed a great challenge to the forecasting method in terms of accuracy and stability, since forecasting plays an essential role in qualifying those unfortune features by which people are able to gain more accurate forecasts that can be applied to risk management, energy planning, industry configuration, and so on. In previous years, electrical power load forecasting has been an important part of power system planning and the basis of the economic operation of power systems. Unfortunately, we have to confront several difficulties, such as meteorological factors, development speed, and some cases of unpredictable natural devastation, if we want to take good advantage of power load data. Researchers have focused on exploring nonsymmetrical faults [1], ground faults [2], microgrid distributions [3], etc. For instance, Qu et al. [4] explored and developed an intelligent damping controller which can reduce power fluctuations in hybrid power systems. Ye et al. [5] studied long-term load forecasting based on support vector regression (SVR) and explored nonlinear relationships between economic growth in terms of GDP and power load requirements. On the other hand, with the inadequate implementation of corresponding emission and environmental protection policies [6], wind power has attracted many scientists and researchers [7]. Currently, wind power accounts for roughly 10% of the total consumption of energy in Europe—15% more than that of Spain and Germany [8]. To utilize the wind more effectively and efficiently, we need to get accurate forecasts of the wind speed. Nevertheless, as for wind speed, it has an inherently volatile and irregular quality and is considered a fairly tricky weather element to predict accurately as a result of its randomness and nonlinearity [9]. Numerous researchers and scientists have made great contributions to the development of effective and robust wind speed forecasting models, which can also be used to forecast electrical power load data. According to time horizons, there are four different types of forecasting methods: long-range forecasting, medium-range forecasting, short-time-period forecasting, and very-short-term forecasting. Moreover, it can also be divided into the following four types: artificial intelligence methods, statistical methods, spatial correlation methods, and physical methods [10].

Physical models containing parameters ranging from temperature to topography to pressure are usually used on a massive scale for long-term wind speed prediction with multiple weather parameters [11]. On the contrary, statistical models, such as the autoregressive (AR) model, Auto-Regressive Average (ARMA) [12], Autoregressive Integrated Moving Average (ARIMA) [13], fractional ARIMA (FARIMA) [14], exponential smoothing (ES) [15], and grey prediction (GP) [16], are developed on the basis of the relationships among variables through mathematical statistics to illustrate the potential correlations within the historical data sampled from the observed wind speed data. Spatial correlation methods mainly take into account the other factors, such as the direction of the wind, the terrain roughness, and the height above the horizon. Sometimes, this kind of method achieves high accuracy [17].

With the rapid development of and increasing research on computer science, the performance of complex calculations in less time has become possible. Consequently, in the past few years, a large number of statistical learning models have been recorded, which eventually formed a mature theoretical system. The renowned ANN (artificial neurol network) is widely utilized for wind speed forecasting fields, which have the ability to carry on the parallel processing and to deliver nonlinear maps. This mainly includes back propagation (BP) [18], the radial basis function (RBF) [19], the Elman neural network (ENN) [20], the wavelet neural network (WNN) [21,22], and others. In addition, during the past twenty years, the neural network field has experienced some innovations which have resulted in well-known deep learning (DL) models [23]. Particularly, the large computational cost has been the largest drawback of conventional neural network algorithms. However, greedy layer-wise pretraining is able to train the so-called deep belief network (DBN) more efficiently [24,25]. Following pertinent progresses, scientists are now able to create and train neural networks with not only one hidden layer, which, in turn, has increased generalization capabilities and allowed better outcomes. This field has also been renamed "in-depth learning" to assess the depth of progress made [26]. The success of DL models can be seen in computer science applications, such as image recognition [27], speech recognition [28], and machine translation [29]. Moreover, the benefits have also spread to energy-related fields, such as wind power forecasting, which especially refers to wind speed forecasting. In the same field,

Wang et al. [30] proposed the convolutional neural networks (CNNs) to acquire precise probability prediction of wind power. However, there is still relatively less research about the DL-related models being applied in wind speed forecasting fields compared with the most active part of this technology. In Reference [31], a deep autoencoder (DAC) combined with extreme gradient boosting (XGB) was proposed to forecast the building cooling load; A deep neural network (DNN) was also applied to get the forecasting results; this method was more accurate than the other methods presented in the same paper. In Reference [32], the DL model was also shown to discern the islanding highly accurately. Therefore, regarding this point, we considered the application of these kinds of technologies in wind speed forecasting in an effort to get a higher accuracy. Furthermore, the authors of Reference [33] proposed a DL strategy applied to time series forecasting and demonstrated how it can be successfully used in electricity consumption forecasting, which correlates with the wind speed data to some extent. Except for ANNs, fuzzy logic methods [34] as well as support vector machine (SVM) [35]-related methods, such as least-squares support vector machines (LSSVMs) [36], Gaussian processes [37], and others, are also commonly applied in the forecasting of wind speed.

However, each method has different drawbacks and disadvantages as a result of its inherent nature. The drawbacks of the aforementioned models are summarized as follows:

(1) Because physical algorithms are very sensitive to market information, they need a long run time and a large amount of computing resources. In addition, these models have shortcomings in dealing with short-term forecasting problems and they do not have high accuracy and validity in short-term forecasting.

(2) Traditional statistical arithmetic methods fail to manage forecasting with fluctuations and high levels of noise, nonlinear and irregular trends, or other inherent characteristics of wind speed data that are primarily confined by the premise of a linear pattern along a time series. Moreover, oftentimes, these methods require a large amount of historical data on which they deeply depend in realistic cases. This means that once there is an abrupt and unexpected change in the original data as a result of social or environmental factors, prediction errors will proliferate all at once [38].

(3) Spatial correlation arithmetic methods based on vast quantities of information, for example, the wind speed information of many spatially correlated sites which is difficult to collect and analyze, makes it hard to perform perfect wind speed forecasting [39].

(4) Artificial intelligence arithmetic methods, different from other approaches, are able to deal with nonlinear features which are hidden among historical wind speed data. Although many studies have been carried out and the methods have been successfully applied to address complex data patterns, there are also some defects and drawbacks within artificial intelligence methods, such as showing a relatively low convergence rate and over-fitting, easily getting into a local optimum, etc.

(5) Individual forecasting models are good at forecasting to some extent, but they rarely focus on the importance and necessity of data preprocessing; therefore, these approaches cannot always get a good forecasting outcome.

Hence, with the objective of combining all the advantages and of avoiding the weaknesses, a number of combined forecasting methods have been proposed [40]. Bates and Granger proposed the combination prediction theory and showed promising outcomes in 1969 [41]. Since then, research on combinatorial forecasting theory has attracted extensive attention [42]. Xiao et al. developed two combined models for wind speed sequence prediction: the AI combination model [43–45] and NNCT (no negative constraint theory). The results indicate that more reliable and accurate forecasts are attained when the combined models are applied.

In addition, with the purpose of achieving highly accurate forecasting, some types of time series preprocessing techniques, such as wavelet packet decomposition (WPD) [46], fast ensemble empirical mode decomposition (FEEMD) [47], and singular spectrum analysis (SSA) [48] techniques, have been effectively applied in the data preprocessing stages of time series forecasting fields in an effort to decrease the random disturbance traits of the original windspeed data. Similarly, techniques have been widely used in such hybrid models to get a higher forecasting accuracy. Thus, the complementary ensemble empirical mode decomposition (CEEMD) that is modified from the ensemble empirical mode decomposition (EEMD) is applied in this paper.

Thus, in this study, the CEEMD-FTS (fuzzy time series)-MOGWO (multi-objective grey wolf optimizer)-long short-term memory (LSTM), a combined model with CEEMD as the preprocessing part, is based on LSTM, which belongs to the RNNs (recurrent neurol networks) within the DL field, but a modified version with less disadvantages and more powerful memorizing capability and the meritorious multi-objective optimization algorithm MOGWO is developed. Subsequently, to deal with the uncertain forecasting problems and to dig out more useful and constructive information hidden within the history data to get a better forecasting result, we also combine the aforementioned model with the fuzzy time series analyzing method based on rough set rule induction which contains the LEM2 (learning from examples module version two).

Generally, the innovations of this study can be summarized as follows:

(1). *This study proposes a hybrid forecasting model which can take advantage of deep learning networks as well as the fuzzy time analysis technique based on the LEM2 rule-generating algorithm, which increases the forecasting accuracy obviously.* To our knowledge, it has not been found that deep leaning neural networks are combined with the rough set induction theory. Hence, our study develops a hybrid model combining LSTM with the fuzzy time series analysis technique that uses rough sets to generate rules as a replacement for traditional rule-generating methods.

(2). *This study improves the forecasting stability and accuracy simultaneously with the deep learning neural network through the weight-determining method called MOGWO based on the leave-one-out strategy and swarm intelligence, which helps to find best weighting parameters for the LSTM neural network.* Most previous studies just paid attention to one aim (stability or accuracy). Therefore, to achieve high accuracy and stability, a multi-objective optimization algorithm, MOGWO, is successfully applied in this study.

(3). *This study provides a scientific and reasonable evaluation of the new hybrid forecasting model made to verify the forecasting performance of the combined forecasting model proposed in this paper.* Three experiments are carried out in this paper, including comparisons between different deep learning neutral networks, efficiency and effectiveness tests among various models in four different wind sites, and a contrast experiment in which the proposed hybrid forecasting system is applied to electrical load forecasting with two different electrical power load data series on Wednesday and Sunday. The outcome illustrates that this proposed system performs well.

(4). *This study delivers an insightful discussion about the developed forecasting system, illustrating the improvements brought about by different parts of the proposed forecasting model as well as the multistep forecasting ability.* Five discussion topics are presented in this paper, namely statistical significance, association strength, improvement percentage, multistep ahead forecasting, and sensitivity analysis. Through these discussions, the effectiveness of the hybrid forecasting framework is verified.

The remainder of this paper is organized as follows:

Section 2 gives the profile of principles of methods corresponding to the proposed hybrid models, namely the CFML model (CEEMD-FTS-MOGWO-LSTM). Relevant methodology is shown Also, in this section, including the data preprocessing method, the fuzzy time series technique with LEM2, the MOGWO, and the long short-term memory algorithm. Moreover, several evaluations and experiments that help to demonstrate the performance of the CFML model are presented in Section 3. Moreover, Section 4 gives a discussion about different comparison outcomes. Finally, Section 5 concludes this study.

2. Methodology

An innovative hybrid forecasting model is successfully developed and the corresponding components are introduced briefly in this section, including the data preprocessing technique named complementary ensemble empirical mode decomposition (CEEMD), the fuzzy analyzing part based on rough sets induction theory, the forecasting algorithm named LSTM, and the multi-objective optimization algorithm MOGWO.

2.1. Hybrid Forecasting Framework

Figures 1 and 2 shows combined the CFML forecasting model, from which the CFML system can be expounded as follows:

1. The original wind speed data is decomposed by applying the CEEMD method into several subseries named Intrinsic Mode Functions (IMFs).
2. The fuzzy analysis method is applied using the rough set induction LEM2 algorithm to generate the forecasting rules, and raw data are applied to these rules to generate preliminary forecasts. These forecasts obtained by fuzzy time series forecasting are not precise enough, but the difference between these forecasts and the actual values can demonstrate potential forecasting biases that are useful for modifying the learning process of the following neural network, namely the LSTM model optimized with MOGWO. As for the raw input data, we accept five dimensions for each forecast, including lag1, lag2, lag3, slope, and the present data, in order to forecast the following one for each subseries (Figure 2).
3. The output data generated from the previous steps is used as the input data for the LSTM forecasting module, which is optimized by the multi-objective optimization algorithm called MOGWO for each subseries. Specifically, real values of X_t, lag1, and lag2 and their differences, including D1, D2, and D3, are adopted as input data of the LSTM model modified by MOGWO (Table 1).
4. The forecasting outcomes of each subseries generated from the preprocessing part named CEEMD are aggregated to obtain the eventual forecasting results of CFML.

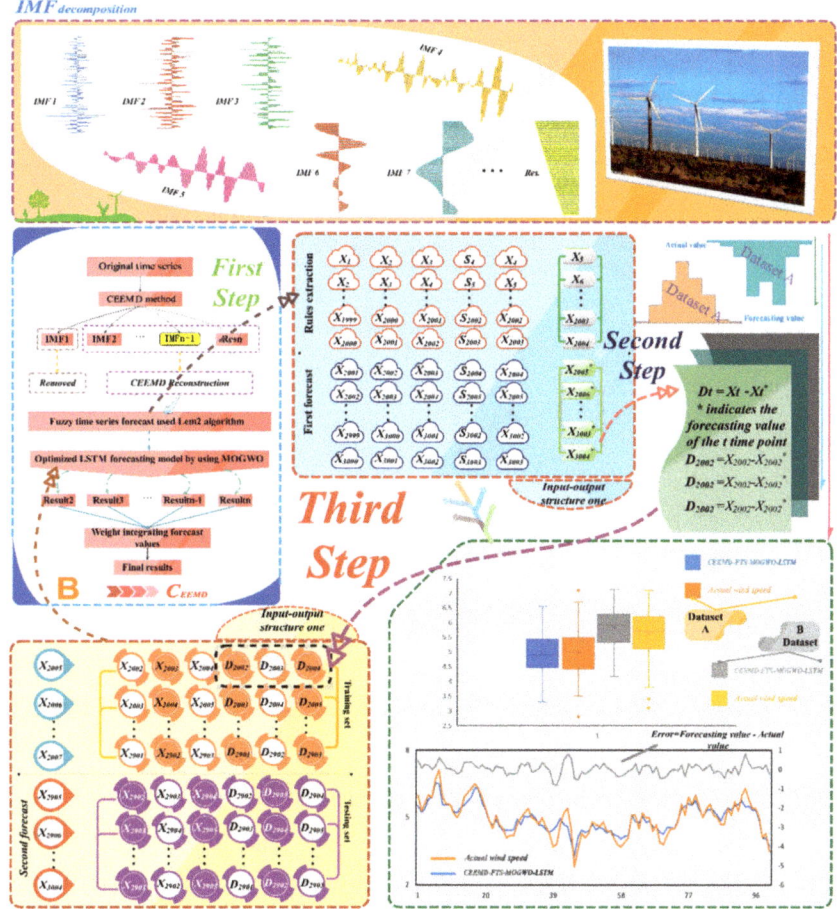

Figure 1. Explicit processes of data input and complementary ensemble empirical mode decomposition (CEEMD) parts of the CEEMD-fuzzy time series (FTS) multi-objective grey wolf optimizer (MOGWO)-LSTM (CFML) model.

Table 1. The selected input variables for long short-term memory (LSTM).

Factors	Explanation
X_t	The present value
LAG1	first-order lagged period X_{t-1}
LAG2	second-order lagged period X_{t-2}
D1	difference 1: $D_t = X_t - forecasted\ X_t$
D2	difference 2: $D_{t-1} = X_{t-1} - forecasted\ X_{t-1}$
D2	difference 3: $D_{t-2} = X_{t-2} - forecasted\ X_{t-2}$

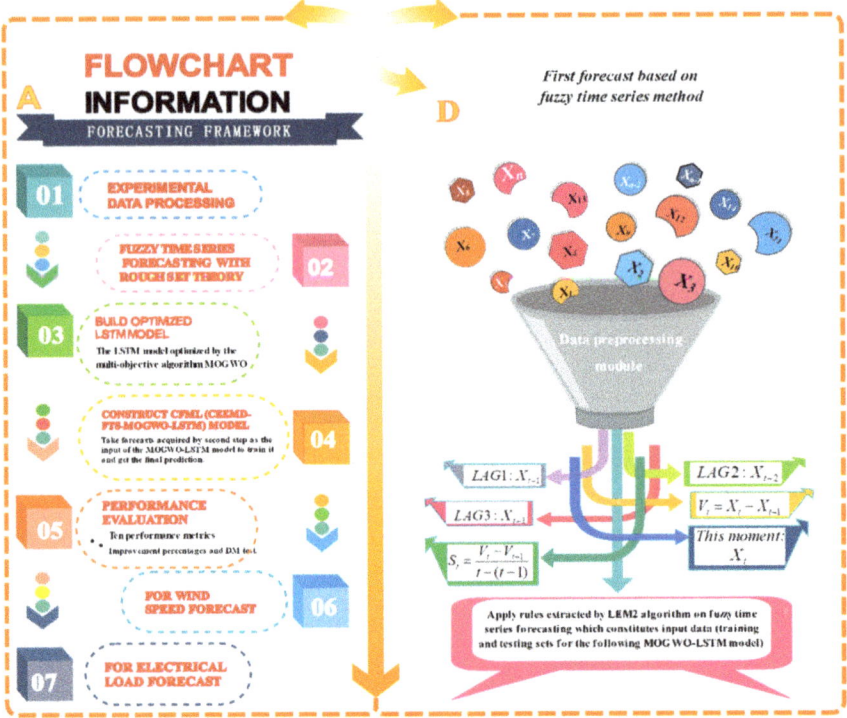

Figure 2. Flowchart of the paper and the input data of the first forecasting.

2.2. Data Preprocessing Module

The CEEMD algorithm, proposed by Yeh et al. [49], is the modified version of the EEMD and EMD. According to Anbazhagan et al. [50], the primary steps of this algorithm are as follows:

Step 1: Add white noise pairwise with the identical amplitude and the opposite phase to the raw data sequence $v(t)$, after which we can obtain a pair of polluted signals:

$$\begin{cases} P_{ni} = v(t) + W_{ni}(t) \\ N_{ni} = v(t) - W_{ni}(t) \end{cases} \quad (1)$$

where P_{ni} denotes the positive noise of i-th trial, N_{ni} is the negative noise of i-th trial, and W_{ni} represents the noise with identical amplitude and phase.

Step 2: Decompose the polluted signal pairs (P_{ni}, N_{ni}) into a finite set including IMF components:

$$\begin{cases} P_{ni}(t) = \sum_{j=1}^{M} u_{ij}^{+}(t) \\ N_{ni}(t) = \sum_{j=1}^{M} u_{ij}^{-}(t) \end{cases} \quad (2)$$

where u_{ij}^{-} and u_{ij}^{+} are the j-th intrinsic mode functions of the i-th trial with negative and positive noise. Furthermore, M signifies the number of IMFs.

Step 3: Two sets of IMF components, i.e., the negative noise set of the first IMF component $\left\{u_{ij}^-(t)\right\}_{i=1,j=1}^{T,M}$ and positive noises $\left\{u_{ij}^+(t)\right\}_{i=1,j=1}^{T,M}$, are obtained by performing the above two steps T times with different amounts of white noise.

Step 4: The component of the j-th IMF $u_j(t)$ can be calculated as follows in order to get the ensemble means of whole IMFs:

$$u_j(t) = \frac{1}{2T}\sum_{i=1}^{T}\left(u_{ij}^+(t) + u_{ij}^-(t)\right) \quad (3)$$

2.3. Rough Set Theory (RST) and LEM2

In this part, the fuzzy forecasting module of the proposed new hybrid model CFML which contains the rough set theory and the more detailed rule induction algorithm called LEM2 is introduced in brief.

Pawlak and Skoworn proposed RST [51], and it has been acknowledged as one of the most effective mathematical techniques for dealing with uncertainty as well as vagueness. The premise of Rough Set Philosophy is that, due to the lack of information in the discourse space related to each object, the few information objects distinguished by the same information cannot be distinguished. The set of all indistinguishable objects is regarded as the basic set and creates the basic particles of cosmic knowledge. Any union of elementary sets is accepted as an exact set; otherwise, the set is called a rough set. RST includes the utilization of indiscernibility relations to approximately approach the sets of objects by upper and lower approximations [52]. This rough set theory is widely used to acquire more accurate rules to predict objects, and the LEM2 algorithm is usually adopted as a way of applying rough set theory to the induction of rules.

LEM2 [53], a rough set rule induction algorithm, is most frequently adopted as it has better results in most cases. In this study, the formed rules are generated in an "if-then" manner through composing several fuzzy decision values as well as fuzzy conditional values. Moreover, "supports" indicate how many records are archived in the dataset that matches the generated decision rules. LEM2 computes a local covering and then converts it into a rule set. LEM2 learns a discriminant rule set; it learns the smallest set of minimal rules describing a concept. This algorithm can generate both certain and possible rules from a decision table. The rough set induction LEM2 algorithm has several advantages because of the application of rough set theory, as follows:

1. Rough sets can discern hidden facts and make it possible for us to understand these facts in natural language, which contributes a great deal to decision making;
2. Rough sets take the background information of decision makers into account;
3. Rough sets can deal with both qualitative and quantitative attributes;
4. Rough sets enable machines to extract certain rules in a relatively short time, which means it reduces the time cost of discovering hidden rules.

The detailed process of how LEM2 works is briefly demonstrated as follows: For an attribute–value pair $(e;u) = o$, a block of n which is signified by $[o]$, is a set of instances belonging to H so that, for an attribute, e has a value u. For a concept represented by the decision–value pair $(n;p)$, B is a nonempty upper or lower approximation of it. Set K consists of a set of attribute–value pairs $o = (e;u)$, which is called set T only under the condition that $\emptyset \neq [T] = \cap_{o \in T}[o] \subseteq K$, where set T is a minimal complex of K only under the condition that K depends on set T and that there are no subsets of T such that K depends on the subset. Symbol C is a nonempty collection of nonempty attribute–value pair sets, and L is the local covering of K. A more detailed explanation can be found in the work of Grzymala-Busse [53].

Figure 3 demonstrates the pseudocode of LEM2 based on the study of Liu et al. [54].

Step 1. Compute all attribute–value pair blocks.
Step 2. Identify attribute–value pairs with the largest $|[(e;u)] \cap G|$.

Step 3. If the cardinality of the set $|[(e;u)] \cap G|$ is equal to another one, then select the attribute pair with the smallest block size.

Step 4. If necessary, we have to go through an additional internal loop in order to find the candidates for the minimal complex.

Step 5. Then, the following steps are used to find the second minimal complex and so on.

Step 6. Finally, we can get the local covering of a hidden fact, which may reveal the decision-making process.

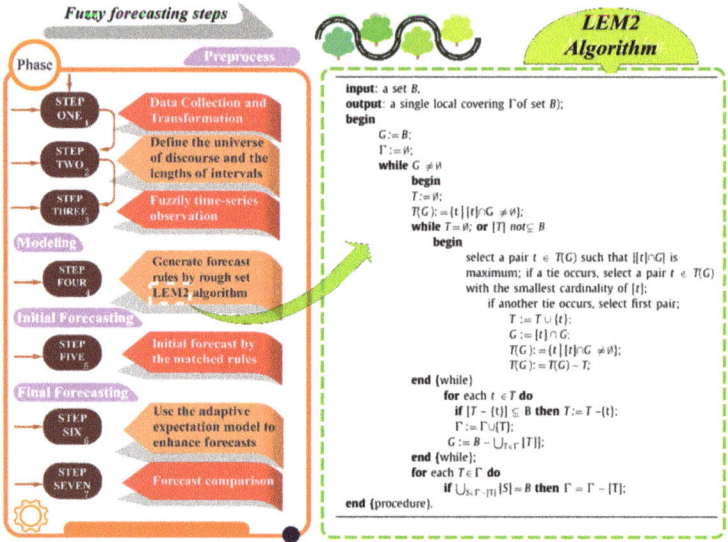

Figure 3. Flowchart of fuzzy time series forecasting.

2.4. Multi-Objective Grey Wolf Optimizer (MOGWO)

To get more accurate forecasts, we adopt the GWO (grey wolf optimizer) algorithm which is modified to deal with the multi-objective problems to optimize the main forecasting model LSTM. By using the multi-objective optimization theory, we can achieve both an accurate and a stable forecasting quality.

Mirjalili et al. proposed the grey wolf optimization algorithm [55], which was based on grey wolves' social leadership and hunting skills. In addition, the hunting process is led by three wolves (α, β, and δ). The rest of the wolves follow these three leaders throughout the whole search process to approach the global best solution.

The following formulas were proposed in an effort to emulate the encircling behaviors of grey wolves:

$$K = |B \times R^p(ite) - R(ite)| \qquad (4)$$

$$R(ite+1) = R_p(ite) - M \times K \qquad (5)$$

where K denotes the distance between the prey and the predator, *ite* refers to the current iteration, R denotes the position vector of wolves, R_p is the prey's position vector, and M and B are coefficient vectors:

$$M = 2c \times e_1 - c \qquad (6)$$

$$B = 2c \times e_2 - c \qquad (7)$$

where e_1 and e_2 are random vectors in $[0, 1]$ and the elements of c decrease linearly from 2 to 0 across all iterations.

The GWO algorithm archives the first three best results gained so far in each iteration and then imposes other agents, namely the rest of the wolves, to update the positions with respect to them. The following formulas are calculated constantly for each search agent [55] in order to mimic the hunting process, and the promising regions of the search space are also found in this process:

$$K_\alpha = |B_1 \times R_\alpha - R| \tag{8}$$

$$K_\beta = |B_2 \times R_\beta - R| \tag{9}$$

$$K_\delta = |B_3 \times R_\delta - R| \tag{10}$$

$$R_1 = R_\alpha - M_1 \times (K_\alpha) \tag{11}$$

$$R_2 = R_\beta - M_2 \times (K_\beta) \tag{12}$$

$$R_3 = R_\delta - M_3 \times (K_\delta) \tag{13}$$

$$R(t+1) = \frac{R_1 + R_2 + R_3}{3} \tag{14}$$

The B vector produces random values in $[0, 2]$. This will help the GWO algorithm show increased behavior in the whole optimization process and help to avoid and explore the local optimum. All these steps are illustrated in Figure 4. R_i is the position of wolf i, which also represents the initial weight and threshold of the LSTM model. That is to say, R_i is a vector and its dimension is determined by the number of initial weights and thresholds of the LSTM model and each element in this vector is a value of a threshold or a weight of LSTM.

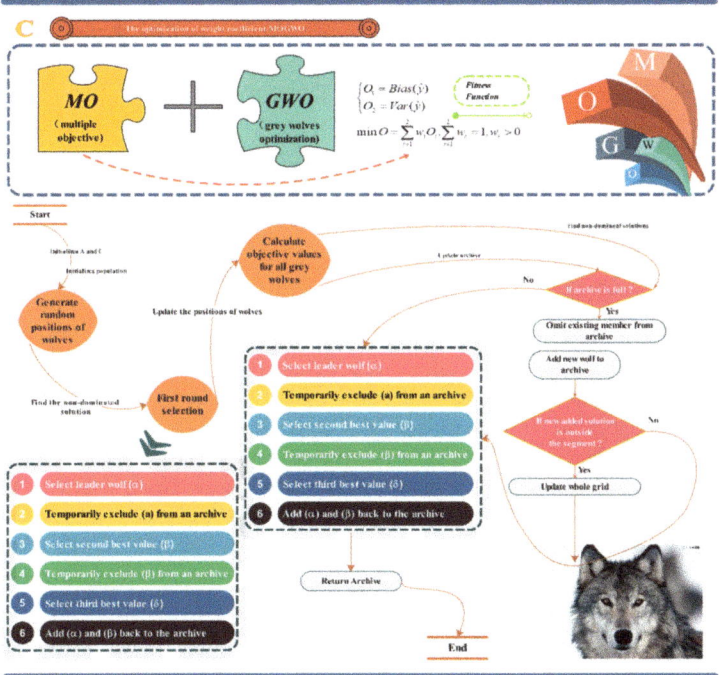

Figure 4. Position updating mechanism of search agents and the effects of A on it.

Attacking is the final stage of hunting, in which the wolf pack catches the prey and the prey stops moving. The process is determined by D. Grey wolves will continue to hunt when |D| < 1, and the wolves are obliged to leave the prey when |D| > 1.

2.5. Long Short-Term Memory (LSTM)

The LSTM model was developed by Schmidhuber and Horchreiter [56]. The harmless gradient in the network is truncated by forcing constant error flow through the constant error turntable in a special multiplication unit. In order to cope with these constant error flows, all of the nonlinear units are able to learn to close or open gates in this network.

The cell state is the key part of the LSTM structure. It runs directly along the entire chain, deleting or adding information to the cell state, carefully adjusted by structures called gates. These gates serve as optional entry points for this information. They consist of a pointwise multiplication operation and a sigmoid neural net layer (Figure 5).

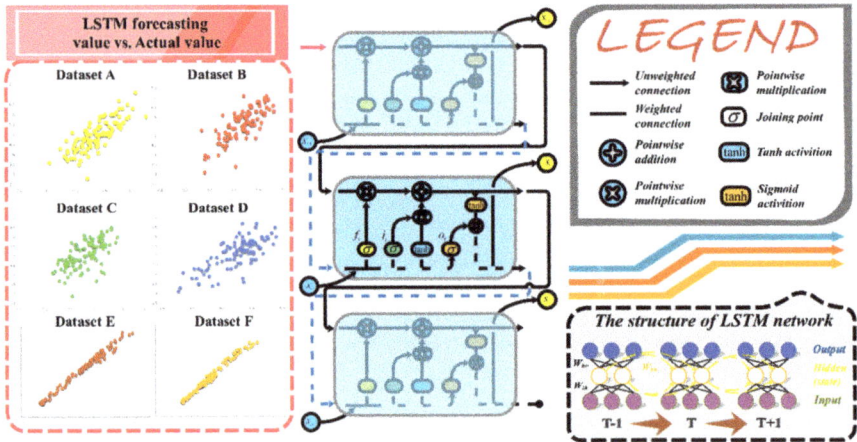

Figure 5. LSTM (long-short-term memory) structure.

An input at time i is (X_i), and the following formulas are used to compute the hidden state (S_i):

1. In the LSTM module, the first step is to determine which information will be discarded from the cell state. The forget gate (f_i) is in charge of making decisions, as follows:

$$f = \sigma(X_i \times T^f + S_{i-1} \times V^i + b_i) \qquad (15)$$

where σ is the sigmoid function which turns the input value into an outcome between 0 and 1. T signifies weight parameters, and b denotes bias parameters (i.e., T^f, T^j, T^c, and T^o and $b_{ii}, b_j, b_c,$ and b_o). In this part, the exponents of T and V are not power values; they are just notations used to illustrate which gate the parameters belong to. For instance, T^f represents the weight parameters belonging to the forget gate, namely gate f.

2. The next step is to determine which new information will be selected and stored in the cell state. This step has two sub-steps: The first one is the input gate ($Input_i$) layer that helps to determine which value is going to be updated. A tanh layer is the second one, which produces a vector composed of new candidate values C_i. Calculations are demonstrated as follows:

$$Input_i = \sigma(X_i \cdot T^{input} + S_{i-1} \cdot V^{input} + b_j) \qquad (16)$$

$$\widetilde{C}_i = tanh(X_i \cdot T^c + S_{i-1} \cdot V^c + b_c) \qquad (17)$$

where $\widetilde{C}_i$ is a candidate memory cell, which is similar to a memory cell, but uses a tanh function.

3. The next step is to update the old cell state C_{i-1} into the new cell state C_i, which can be described as follows:

$$C_i = C_{i-1} \otimes f_i \otimes Input_i \otimes \widetilde{C}_i \qquad (18)$$

In Equation (26), the symbol ⊗ represents pointwise multiplication.

4. The final step is to determine what is about to be generated and selected as the output. This output is a filtered version which is predicated on the cell state, during which the output gate (o_i) determines which final output will consist of a specific part of the cell state. After, the cell state runs through the tanh layer, which is multiplied by the output gate as follows:

$$o_i = \sigma(X_i \cdot T^o + S_{i-1} \cdot V^o + b_o) \qquad (19)$$

$$S_i = o_i \otimes tanh(C_i) \qquad (20)$$

Algorithm: MOGWO-LSTM

Objective function

$$\min \begin{cases} fitness_1 = |Bias(\hat{x})| \\ fitness_2 = Std(x - \hat{x}) \end{cases}$$

Input:
Training data: $x_t^{(0)} = \left(x^{(0)}(1), x^{(0)}(2), \ldots, x^{(0)}(p)\right)$
Testing data: $x_f^{(0)} = \left(x^{(0)}(p+1), x^{(0)}(p+2), \ldots, x^{(0)}(p+l)\right)$

Output:
$\hat{y}_f^{(0)} = \left(\hat{y}_f^{(0)}(p+1), \hat{y}_f^{(0)}(p+2), \ldots, \hat{y}_f^{(0)}(p+l)\right)$—a series of forecasting data

Parameters of MOGWO:

Iter—the maximum number of iterations	n—the number of grey wolves
t—the current iteration number	R_i—the position of wolf i
e_1—the random vector in [0, 1]	c—the constant vector in [0, 2]

Parameters of LSTM:

Iteration—the maximum number of iterations	Bias_input—the bias vector of the input gate in [0, 1]
Input_num—the knots of the input	Bias_forget—the bias vector of the forget gate in [0, 1]
Cell_num—the knots of the cell	Bias_output—the bias vector of the output gate in [0, 1]
Output_num—the knots of the output	yita—the rate of adjustment for the weight at each time
Cost_gate—the termination error cost	data_num-the number of columns of training data.

1:/*Set the parameters of **MOGWO** and **LSTM***/
2:/*Initialize the grey wolf population R_i (i = 1, 2, ..., n) randomly*/
3:/*Initialize c, **M**, and **B***/
4:/*Define the archive size*/
5: **FOR EACH** i: $1 \le i \le n$ **DO**
6: Evaluate the corresponding fitness function F_i for each search agent
7: **END FOR**
8: /*Find the non-dominated solutions and initialize the archive with them*/
9: R_α, R_β, R_δ = SelectLeader(archive)
10: **WHILE** (t < Iter) **DO**

11: **FOR EACH** i: $1 \leq i \leq n$ **DO**
12: /*Update the position of the current search agent*/
13: $\mathbf{K}_j = |\mathbf{B}_i \cdot \mathbf{R}_j - \mathbf{R}|$, $i = 1, 2, 3; j = \alpha, \beta, \delta$
14: $\mathbf{R}_i = \mathbf{R}_j - \mathbf{M}_i \cdot \mathbf{K}_j$, $i = 1, 2, 3; j = \alpha, \beta, \delta$
15: $\mathbf{R}(t + 1) = (\mathbf{R}_1 + \mathbf{R}_2 + \mathbf{R}_3)/3$
16: **END FOR**
17: /*Update **c**, **M**, and **B***/
18: $\mathbf{M} = 2 \cdot \mathbf{c} \cdot \mathbf{e}_{1\_c}$; $\mathbf{B} = 2 \cdot \mathbf{c} \cdot \mathbf{e}_{2\_c}$
19: /*Evaluate the corresponding fitness function $\mathbf{F}_i$ for each search agent*/
20: /*Find the non-dominated solutions*/
21: /*Update the archive with regard to the obtained non dominated solutions*/
22: **IF** the archive is full **DO**
23: /*Delete one solution from the current archive members*/
24: /*Add the new solution to the archive*/
25: **END IF**
26: **IF** any newly added solutions to the archive are outside the hypercubes **DO**
27: /*Update the grids to cover the new solution(s)*/
28: **END IF**
29: $\mathbf{R}_\alpha, \mathbf{R}_\beta, \mathbf{R}_\delta = SelectLeader(archive)$
30: $t = t + 1$
31: **END WHILE**
32: **RETURN** *archive*
33: **OBTAIN** $\mathbf{R}^* = SelectLeader(archive)$
34: Set $\mathbf{R}^*$ as the initial weight and threshold of **LSTM**
35: /*Standardize the training data and testing data*/
36: /*Initialize the structure of the LSTM network*/
37: /*Initialize cost_gate, bias_input, bias_forget, bias_output and the weight of the LSTM network*/
38: **FOR EACH** i: $1 \leq i \leq Iteration$ **DO**
39: yita=0.01
40: **FOR EACH** m: $1 \leq m \leq data\_num$ **DO**
41: **Equation (15) to Equation (20)**
42: /*Calculate the error cost of this round*/
43: error cost = $\sum_{t=1}^{l} (forecasted\ \hat{x}_t - actual\ x_t)^2$, l is the dimension of testing data
44: **IF** error cost < cost_gate **DO**
45: **Break**
46: **END IF**
47: /*Update the weight of all gates*/
48: **END FOR**
49: **IF** error cost < cost_gate **DO**
50: **Break**
51: **END IF**
52: **END FOR**
53: /* Learning process has been done/
54: Input the standardized historical data into **LSTM** to forecast the future changes
55: De-normalize the obtained forecasting outcomes and generate the final forecasting results

There are two commonly adopted criteria for verifying forecasting effectiveness, accuracy and stability. Also, we should not just focus on one objective. Both objectives—high accuracy and stability—should be studied simultaneously and implemented in the optimization part. Therefore, based on bias-variance framework, the fitness function should be defined as follows:

$$\begin{aligned} E(\hat{x} - x)^2 &= E[\hat{x} - E(\hat{x}) + E(\hat{x}) - x]^2 \\ &= E[\hat{x} - E(\hat{x})]^2 + [E(\hat{x}) - E(x)]^2 \\ &= Var(\hat{x}) + Bias^2(\hat{x}) \end{aligned} \quad (21)$$

where x is the actual value, $\hat{x}$ is the forecasted value, and E is the expectation value of the corresponding variable.

The bias equals the average difference between the actual and forecasted values, which represents forecasting accuracy. A smaller absolute value of the bias demonstrates a more accurate forecasting accuracy. A smaller variance value indicates a more stable forecasting performance. However, in the conduct of most experiments, it was found that the criteria are not suitable for issues that this paper seeks to address. Thus, the standard deviation of forecasting errors is selected as a substitute for fitness 2. Therefore, the fitness function in this paper is formulated as follows:

$$\min \begin{cases} fitness_1 = |Bias(\hat{x})| \\ fitness_2 = Std(x - \hat{x}) \end{cases} \quad (22)$$

Hence, the objectives of multi-objective optimization problems are usually conflicting. In that regard, the Pareto optimal solution set provides an answer since it represents the best trade-offs between different objectives. Our optimization problem in this study is a minimization issue, so the way we choose suitable solutions can be formulated as follows:

Minimize the following:

$$F(\mathbf{x}) = \{f_1(\mathbf{x}), f_2(\mathbf{x}), \cdots, f_o(\mathbf{x})\} \quad (23)$$

Subject to the following:

$$g_i(\mathbf{x}) \geq 0, \ i = 1, 2, \cdots, m \quad (24)$$

$$h_i(\mathbf{x}) \geq 0, \ i = 1, 2, \cdots, p \quad (25)$$

$$L_i \leq x_i \leq U_i, \ i = 1, 2, \cdots, n \quad (26)$$

where o denotes the number of objectives, m is the number of inequality constraints, p is the number of equality constraints, and L_i and U_i are the lower and upper boundaries of the i-th variables, respectively.

Also, several definitions regarding this problem is listed as follows:

Definition 1. *Pareto dominance.*

Suppose that there are two vectors: $x = (x_1, x_2, \cdots, x_k)$ and $y = (y_1, y_2, \cdots, y_k)$. Vector x dominates y, denoted as $x \succ y$, if

$$\forall i \{1, 2, \cdots, k\}, [f_i(x) \geq f_i(y)] \wedge [i \in 1, 2, \cdots, k : f_i(x)] \quad (27)$$

Definition 2. *Pareto optimality.*

The solution $x \in X$ is named a Pareto optimal if

$$\nexists y \in X | F(y) \succ F(x) \quad (28)$$

Two solutions are non-dominated with respect to each other if neither of them dominates the other.

Definition 3. *Pareto optimal set.*

The set including all non-dominated solutions is named a Pareto set as follows:

$$P_s := \{x, y \in X | \exists F(y) > F(x)\} \quad (29)$$

Definition 4. *Pareto optimal front.*

A set containing the corresponding values of Pareto optimal solutions in a Pareto optimal set is defined as a Pareto optimal front:

$$P_f := \{F(x) | x \in P_s\} \quad (30)$$

2.6. Evaluation Module

This section illustrates reasonable and scientific evaluating modules. In addition, some typical evaluation metric rules that are usually adopted in the relevant research are adopted to verify the forecasting performance; R^2 (Pearson's correlation coefficient) and DM test methods are also exploited in this paper.

2.6.1. Typical Performance Metric

As far as we know, there are no uniform and consistent criteria to test the validity of the prediction results or to compare the results with those of other models. In this study, we adopt lots of multifarious methods and metrics, which are all shown in Table 2. Here, N is the length of the dataset, A denotes the actual value, whereas F represents the forecasting value.

Table 2. Performance metric rules.

Metric	Definition	Equation
AE	Average error of N forecasting results	$AE = \frac{1}{N}\sum_{i=1}^{N}(A_i - F_i)$
MAE	Mean absolute error of N forecasting results	$MAE = \frac{1}{N}\sum_{i=1}^{N}|A_i - F_i|$
RMSE	Square root of average of the error squares	$RMSE = \sqrt{\frac{1}{N}\sum_{i=1}^{N}(A_i - F_i)^2}$
NMSE	The normalized average of the squares of the errors	$NMSE = \frac{1}{N}\sum_{i=1}^{N}\frac{(A_i - F_i)^2}{F_i A_i}$
MAPE	Average of N absolute percentage error	$0MAPE = \frac{1}{N}\sum_{i=1}^{N}\left|\frac{A_i - F_i}{A_i}\right| \times 100\%$
IA	Index of agreement of the forecasting results	$IA = 1 - \frac{\sum_{i=1}^{N}(A_i - F_i)^2}{\sum_{i=1}^{N}(|F_i - \overline{A}| + |A_i - \overline{A}|)^2}$
FB	Fractional bias of N forecasting results	$FB = 2 \times \frac{\overline{A} - \overline{F}}{\overline{A} + \overline{F}}$
U1	Theil U statistics 1 of forecasting results	$U1 = \frac{\sqrt{\frac{1}{N}\sum_{i=1}^{N}(A_i - F_i)^2}}{\sqrt{\frac{1}{N}\sum_{i=1}^{N}A_i^2} + \sqrt{\frac{1}{N}\sum_{i=1}^{N}F_i^2}}$
U2	Theil U statistics 2 of forecasting results	$U2 = \frac{\sqrt{\frac{1}{N}\sum_{i=1}^{N}\left(\frac{A_{i+1} - F_{i+1}}{A_i}\right)^2}}{\sqrt{\frac{1}{N}\sum_{i=1}^{N}\left(\frac{A_{i+1} - F_i}{A_i}\right)^2}}$
DA	Direction accuracy of the forecasting results	$DA = \frac{1}{l}\sum_{i=1}^{l}w_i, w_i = \begin{cases} 1, if(A_{i+1} - A_i) \cdot (F_{i+1} - A_i) > 0 \\ 0, otherwise \end{cases}$
INDEX	Improvement ratio of the index among different models	$INDEX = \frac{|F_i - A_i|_{compared} - |F_i - A_i|_{proposed}}{|F_i - A_i|_{proposed}}$
R	Pearson's correlation coefficient	$R = \frac{\sum_{i}^{N}(A_i - \overline{A})(F_i - \overline{F})}{\sqrt{\sum_{i}^{N}(A_i - \overline{A})^2 \sum_{i}^{N}(F_i - \overline{F})^2}}$

2.6.2. Diebold–Mariano Test

Considering α as the significance level, the null hypothesis H_0 indicates that there are no significant differences between the two different forecasting models. Otherwise, H_1 denotes the disagreement with H_0. The following formulas indicate the related hypotheses:

$$H_0 : E\left[Loss\left(e_i^1\right)\right] = E\left[Loss\left(e_i^2\right)\right] \tag{31}$$

$$H_1 : E\left[Loss\left(e_i^1\right)\right] \neq E\left[Loss\left(e_i^2\right)\right] \tag{32}$$

where $Loss$ represents the loss function of forecasting errors and e_i^p ($p = 1, 2$) are the forecasting errors of two comparison models.

Furthermore, the DM test statistics can be calculated as follows:

$$DM\ value = \frac{\sum_{i=1}^{n}\left(Loss\left(e_i^1\right) - Loss\left(e_i^2\right)\right)/n}{\sqrt{S^2/n}} s^2 \tag{33}$$

where s^2 is an estimation for the variance of $d_i = Loss\left(e_i^1\right) - Loss\left(e_i^2\right)$.

The DM test value is compared with $Z_{\alpha/2}$. H_0 will be rejected under the circumstance that the DM statistic falls outside the acceptance interval $[-Z_{\alpha/2}, Z_{\alpha/2}]$, which indicates that there is a significant difference between the comparison models and the forecasting performances of the proposed model, meaning we accept H_1.

3. Analysis and Experiments

In this part, three different experiments using four different wind speed datasets acquired from Liaotung peninsula and two different electrical power load datasets collected from QLD (Queensland) are carried out to test the proposed hybrid system.

3.1. Raw Data Description

In this study, four different 10-min wind speed datasets were collected from four sites (Figure 6), namely the four wind pour plants in the Liaotung peninsula: the Hengshan site (40°, 120°), Xianren island (40°, 122.5°), the Donggang site (42.5°, 122.5°), and the Danton site (40°, 125°).

Also, two additional electrical load datasets were applied to demonstrate the efficiency of the hybrid forecasting model. The total number of data points in each wind speed dataset was 9488, and that of the electrical load was 2544. Only the first 1000 observations were adopted to verify the model. Of the total 1000 observations, the first 900 observations were used as the training set, while the testing set contained the remaining 100 observations (Figure 6). Furthermore, some basic statistical information, i.e., minimum, average values, as well as maximum values, etc. of the dataset referred to above are demonstrated in Table 3.

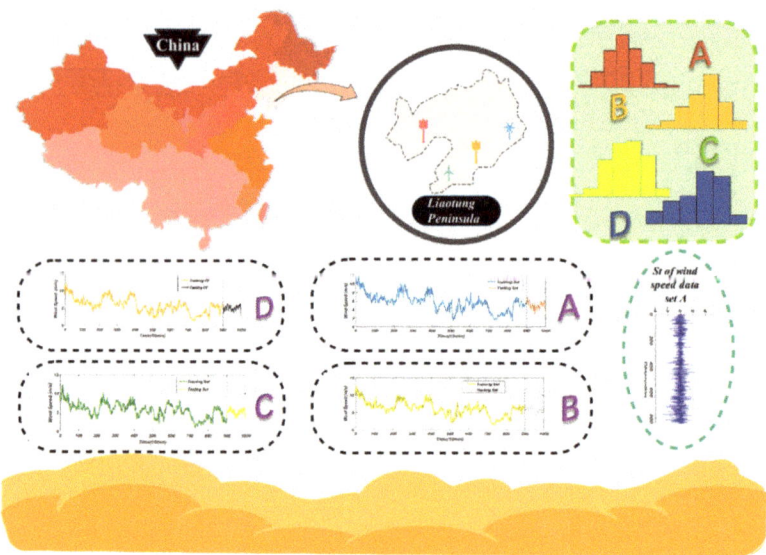

Figure 6. Four wind speed datasets with 10-min time intervals.

Table 3. Statistical values of each experiment dataset.

Data Set	Statistical Indicator					Data Set	Statistical Indicator				
	Mid.	Max.	Min.	Std	Mean		Mid.	Max.	Min.	Std	Mean
Dataset A						Dataset D					
All samples	4.9391	17.200	0.1000	2.7072	4.6000	All samples	4.8754	17.700	0.1000	2.6413	4.6000
Training	5.7401	11.800	1.2000	2.0136	5.8000	Training	5.6011	12.500	0.9000	1.8937	5.8000
Testing	4.9750	7.1000	2.8000	0.7774	5.0000	Testing	5.1120	6.7000	3.1000	0.7983	5.2500
Dataset B						Dataset E					
All samples	5.2674	28.800	0.1000	2.9040	4.9000	All samples	6043.4	8180.7	4488.0	841.07	6189.2
Training	6.1190	12.700	1.3000	2.0481	6.2000	Training	6065.9	8180.7	4488.0	849.28	6214.1
Testing	5.6190	7.1000	3.1000	0.8237	5.7000	Testing	5840.7	7221.2	4515.0	736.47	5981.9
Dataset C						Dataset F					
All samples	5.0718	22.100	0.1000	2.9000	4.6000	All samples	5515.5	7780.5	4357.8	684.29	5444.2
Training	5.8262	12.300	1.3000	2.0946	5.8000	Training	5542.3	7780.5	4357.8	693.79	5472.0
Testing	5.0920	6.5000	2.9000	0.7108	5.1000	Testing	5273.9	6416.3	4447.3	537.19	5170.9

3.2. Experiment I: Tests of MOGWO and LSTM

In this experiment, we present two subparts to verify the superiority of the MOGWO and LSTM forecasting algorithm, respectively.

3.2.1. Test of MOGWO

The four typical test functions that are demonstrated in Table 4 are commonly used to verify the superiority of the proposed optimizer and to deal with the multi-objective optimization issues [57–59]. NSGA-II and multi-objective dragonfly (MODA) were used in this study for comparison. The experimental parameters were as follows: the search agents' total number was 50, the archive size was 50, and the iteration number was 100. The inverted generational distance (IGD), a widely used metric, was adopted in this paper for the evaluation. Each test function was tested fifty times, and Table 5 shows the statistical values of the IGD. Moreover, Figure 7 demonstrates the Pareto optimal solutions which were acquired by different algorithms.

Table 4. Four test benchmark functions.

Kursawe	ZDT1
Minimize $f_1(x) = \sum_{i=1}^{2}\left[-10\exp\left[-0.2\sqrt{x_1^2+x_2^2}\right]\right]$	Minimize $f_1(x) = x_i$
Minimize $f_2(x) = \sum_{i=1}^{3}\left[\|x_i\|^{0.8} + 5\sin(x_i^3)\right]$	Minimize $f_2(x) = g(x) \times h(f_1(x), g(x))$
where $-5 \leq x_i \leq 5, 1 \leq i \leq 3$	where $G(x) = 1 + \frac{9}{N-1}\sum_{i=2}^{N}x_i$, $h(f_1(x), g(x)) = 1 - \sqrt{\frac{f_1(x)}{g(x)}}$, $0 \leq x_i \leq 1, 1 \leq i \leq 30$
ZDT2	ZDT3
Minimize $f_1(x) = x_i$	Minimize $f_1(x) = x_i$
Minimize $f_2(x) = g(x) \times h(f_1(x), g(x))$	Minimize $f_2(x) = g(x) \times h(f_1(x), g(x))$
where $G(x) = 1 + \frac{9}{N-1}\sum_{i=2}^{N}x_i$, $h(f_1(x), g(x)) = 1 - \left(\frac{f_1(x)}{g(x)}\right)^2$, $0 \leq x_i \leq 1, 1 \leq i \leq 30$	where $G(x) = 1 + \frac{9}{29}\sum_{i=2}^{N}x_i$, $h(f_1(x), g(x)) = 1 - \sqrt{\frac{f_1(x)}{g(x)}}$, $0 \leq x_i \leq 1, 1 \leq i \leq 30$

Table 5. Statistical values of the inverted generational distance (IGD) for four test functions.

Test Functions	IGD Values				
	Mean	Max.	Min.	Std.	Med.
Kursawe					
MODA	0.012500	0.021500	0.008500	0.003600	0.011500
NSGA-II	0.006500	0.015500	**0.004500**	0.002800	0.005900
MOGWO	**0.005200**	**0.005800**	0.004900	**0.000251**	**0.005200**
ZDT1					
MODA	0.014600	0.022300	0.007900	0.004800	0.014400
NSGA-II	0.015800	0.036400	**0.000375**	0.008800	0.013500
MOGWO	**0.006800**	**0.016400**	0.002100	**0.003800**	**0.005900**
ZDT2					
MODA	0.013900	0.022100	0.006900	**0.004600**	0.012100
NSGA-II	0.029200	0.060400	0.003300	0.013500	0.025600
MOGWO	**0.009000**	**0.019400**	**0.001200**	0.005500	**0.008100**
ZDT3					
MODA	0.018700	0.025900	0.007000	0.005200	0.019300
NSGA-II	0.011500	0.021500	0.004700	0.004700	0.011000
MOGWO	**0.005600**	**0.015000**	**0.001000**	**0.003000**	**0.005600**

The values in bold indicate the best value of each benchmark function.

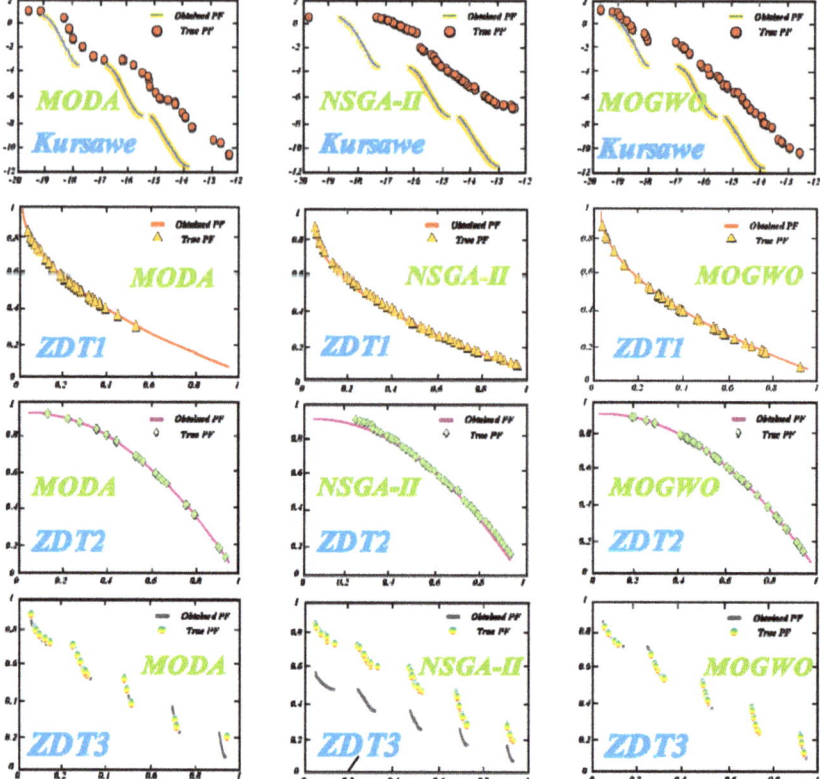

Figure 7. Obtained Pareto optimal solutions by NSGA-II, MODA, and MOGWO for the test functions: Kursawe, ZDT1, ZDT2, and ZDT3.

Based on the outcomes, two conclusions were made as follows:

1. The MOGWO algorithm obtained the best IGD outcomes among almost all optimizers for four test functions (Kursawe, ZDT1, ZDT2, and ZDT3) while performing worse than the Kursawe as well as ZDT1 algorithms in terms of the minimum value and worse than MODA regarding the standard deviation. From a whole perspective, these outcomes are strong enough to demonstrate the superior optimization ability of MOGWO algorithms compared with the others.
2. Figure 7 shows that the MOGWO algorithm was able to obtain more Pareto optimal solutions. In addition, the solutions found by the MOGWO algorithm were more evenly distributed on the true PF (pareto front) curve and were closer to the real Pareto optimal solutions.

Remark: The optimizing ability of MOGWO has been proven through the results and discussions of the aforementioned experiment comparison. Thus, MOGWO can be widely used to cope with multi-objective problems, thus being adopted as the best optimization model in the proposed CFML system.

3.2.2. Test of LSTM in CEEMD-FTS-MOGWO-LSTM

This subsection aims to compare LSTM, DBN, CNN, and SAE for the four wind speed datasets collected from four different wind farms with 10-min data. We set the parameters for each model based on the error and bias since there are no previous studies on how to set the optimal parameters. Also, to reduce the impact of randomness, we took the mean value of the experiments performed 50 times. The relative results and detailed values are listed in Table 6, and Figure 8 demonstrates the prediction outcomes of the aforementioned four models at the four wind speed sites. From the forecasting data, we drew several conclusions:

1. The LSTM model achieved almost the best results and the most accurate predictions of all four wind speed datasets with roughly the same run time and identical training and testing datasets. Namely, the adopted LSTM model outperformed the CNN, DBN, and SAE from a whole perspective and provided fairly competitive results.
2. For the data collected from the four different wind farms, the LSTM model worked better than the other three deep learning models, which means that the superiority of the LSTM forecasting algorithm remained, regardless of the different geographical distribution, to some extent.
3. The forecasting performance of different models was adequately reflected by the error metrics adopted by us in this part. That is to say, error measurement is effective and can be used to accurately evaluate the ability of the prediction models.

Table 6. Forecasting results of the four deep learning algorithms at four sites.

Sites	Models	AE	MAE	RMSE	NMSE	MAPE	IA	FB	r	U1	U2
Dataset A	CNN	−0.1466	0.5558	0.6871	0.0215	0.1143	0.9958	**0.0299**	0.5871	0.0693	0.845
	DBN	−0.2578	0.4917	0.6105	0.0169	0.0988	0.9967	0.0528	0.7122	0.0618	0.8078
	SAE	−0.2431	0.4891	0.6084	0.0165	0.0982	0.9967	0.0501	0.7083	0.062	0.7952
	LSTM	0.2706	**0.4364**	**0.5462**	**0.0138**	**0.0948**	**0.9973**	−0.0530	**0.7915**	**0.0529**	**0.6470**
Dataset B	CNN	0.1251	0.5515	0.7198	0.0191	0.1063	0.9963	−0.0220	0.5558	0.0628	0.8427
	DBN	0.2338	0.4853	0.6111	0.0115	0.0885	0.9974	−0.0402	0.7284	0.0521	0.8130
	SAE	−0.01814	0.5077	0.6337	0.0146	0.0947	0.9971	**0.0032**	0.6608	0.0560	0.7455
	LSTM	0.2034	**0.4448**	**0.5677**	**0.0122**	**0.0863**	**0.9977**	−0.0356	**0.7645**	**0.0492**	**0.6598**
Dataset C	CNN	−0.1974	0.5585	0.7095	0.0221	0.1288	0.9957	0.0394	0.5892	0.0700	0.8672
	DBN	0.1024	0.4765	0.6138	0.0154	0.0981	0.9968	−0.0197	0.5589	0.0587	0.7241
	SAE	−0.0451	0.4538	0.5808	**0.0145**	0.0936	0.9971	0.0089	**0.6481**	0.0568	0.6088
	LSTM	**0.0131**	**0.4419**	**0.5731**	0.0146	**0.0928**	0.9971	−0.0026	0.6241	**0.0557**	**0.6151**
Dataset D	CNN	−0.1974	0.5585	0.7095	0.0221	0.1132	0.9957	0.0394	0.5892	0.0700	0.8672
	DBN	−0.3784	0.5490	0.6827	0.0202	0.1077	0.9960	0.0772	0.7419	0.0688	0.8875
	SAE	−0.1586	0.4776	0.6025	0.0154	0.0958	0.9969	0.0315	0.7227	0.0592	0.7510
	LSTM	**−0.1168**	**0.4295**	**0.5565**	**0.0131**	**0.0868**	**0.9974**	0.0231	**0.7488**	**0.0544**	**0.7198**

The values in bold indicate the best values of each benchmark function.

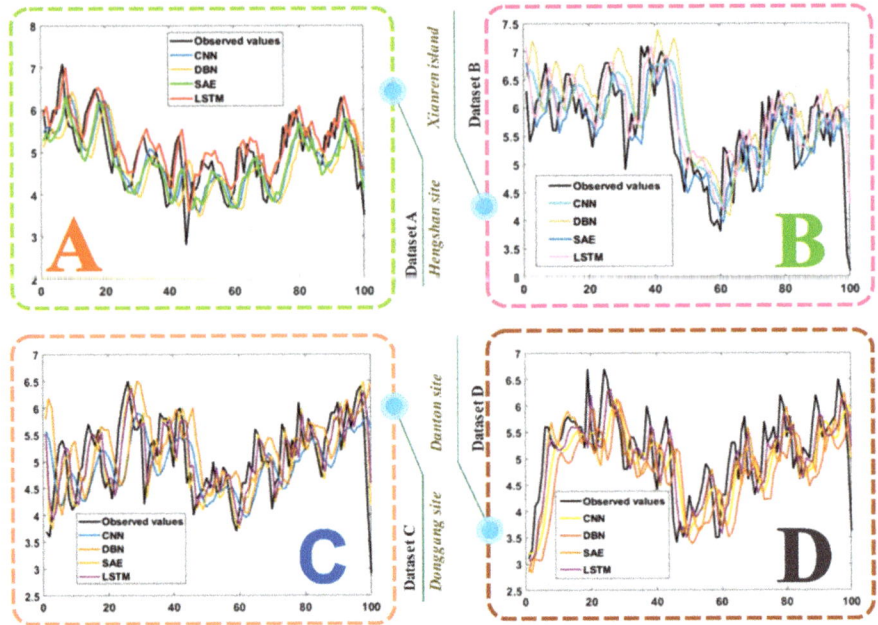

Figure 8. Forecasting results of the four deep learning algorithms.

Remark: For all four datasets, although the LSTM model performed more poorly than the other models on some metrics, the best values of the majority of error metrics, such as mean absolute error (MAE), square root of average of the error squares (RMSE), mean absolute percentage error (MAPE), index of agreement (IA), and so on, indicate that the adopted LSTM model can achieve excellent forecasting accuracy. That is also the reason why we chose LSTM as the main forecasting model in our proposed hybrid forecasting model.

3.3. Experiment II

The comparisons made in this experiment were conducted to demonstrate the specific improvements brought by the fuzzy time series forecasting part and the optimizer algorithm as well as the combination of MOGWO and FTS. Furthermore, an experiment to prove the enhancement in the forecasting ability of the combined model brought by CEEMD was made as well. Moreover, the comparisons between the proposed hybrid forecasting model and all the other models are also listed and analyzed in this part. Table 7 and Figure 9 demonstrate the relevant error metric values of the models mentioned above.

(1) For the first comparison, WNN, GRNN, ARIMA, and the LSTM models were built and compared with each other in order to determine the best one for performing wind speed forecasting, which was found to be the ARIMA. However, of all the neural network algorithms, LSTM was shown to be the best one, and Experiment I proved that LSTM is better than the other three deep learning models as well. Hence, the following steps and comparisons are all based on the basic and regular forecasting model—LSTM.

(2) In terms of R (Pearson's correlation coefficient), ARIMA failed to outdo LSTM in datasets A and B. In addition, we tried AR, MA, ARMA, and ARIMA with different parameters each, and we found that of all these settings, ARMA(2,1), ARIMA(3,1,2), and ARIMA(3,2,2), achieved almost the same forecasting accuracy at about 8% MAPE, which is apparently better than that of the other neural networks. The reason for this phenomenon is that the moving-average model that includes AR requires clear rhythm patterns and fairly linear data series trends, whereas wind speed datasets are neither seasonal nor regular, so all of these irregular features were almost removed by the moving-average method as a result of the differencing operation.

(3) From Table 7, for example, the MOGWO-LSTM achieved a MAPE value of 8.64%, while the basic LSTM model only achieved a MAPE value of 9.48% in the case of site A. Moreover, we tested the effectiveness of the fuzzy time series forecasting part. For example, in the case of site B, the MAPE value of FTS-LSTM was 7.91%, 8.34% lower than that of the LSTM model.

(4) According to Figure 8, the FTS-MOGWO-LSTM model achieved 8.02% in MAPE and 75.34% in r^2 from a mean perspective, although it failed to reach the highest r^2 value in datasets A and B. Next, the separate improvement on the forecasting ability brought by FTS or MOGWO varied in different datasets. For example, in the case of dataset A, FTS-LSTM was higher than MOGWO-LSTM, which means that MOGWO contributes more to forecasting.

(5) Apart from these comparisons, the decomposition algorithm was also tested in this part. In this paper, we tested several parameter configurations regarding the Nstd (signal noise ratio), NR (noise addition number), Maxiter (maximum number of iterations), and modes (number of IMFs) in the CEEMD algorithm. We tested the Nstd (0.05–0.4), NR (10–500), Maxiter (100–1000), and modes (9–13) to find the best configuration. Detailed parameter settings vary from dataset to dataset, so settings should be changed at any time when the dataset is changed. In this part, for instance, the best settings for dataset A were as follows: an Nstd of 0.2, an NR of 50, and a Maxiter of 500. The total IMF number was 12, and the best accuracy is acquired by 11 IMFs. Also, Table 8 shows that the CFML model achieved the highest r^2 value and the lowest MAPE in all four data sites, which demonstrates the improvements brought by CEEMD.

Remark: Through the aforementioned comparisons and conclusions, it is apparent that the proposed hybrid forecasting model achieves the best values in all the applied error metrics. Moreover, the outcomes prove that the adopted multi-objective optimizer MOGWO, the data decomposition approach CEEMD, and the fuzzy time series part can improve the forecasting ability of the original forecasting model LSTM to a great extent.

Table 7. Results of the developed forecasting framework and other models (Experiment II).

Sites	Models	AE	MAE	RMSE	NMSE	MAPE	IA	FB	U1	U2	DA	r²
Dataset A	ARIMA	0.0019	0.3995	0.4941	0.0115	0.0837	0.9978	-0.0004	0.0491	0.6576	0.4242	0.7830
	GRNN	0.1427	0.4650	0.5723	0.0154	0.1004	0.9970	-0.0283	0.0562	0.6984	0.4949	0.7057
	WNN	0.0089	0.4678	0.5812	0.0161	0.0994	0.9969	-0.0018	0.0578	0.7620	0.5152	0.6738
	LSTM	0.2706	0.4364	0.5462	0.0138	0.0948	0.9973	-0.0530	0.0529	0.6470	0.4343	0.7915
	MOGWO-LSTM	0.1142	0.4069	0.5007	0.0117	0.0864	0.9978	-0.0227	0.0492	0.6376	0.5152	0.7848
	FTS-LSTM	0.0599	0.4041	0.4966	0.0115	0.0852	0.9978	-0.0120	0.0491	0.6453	0.4848	0.7822
	FTS-MOGWO-LSTM	-0.0106	0.3962	0.4884	0.0110	0.0822	0.9979	0.0021	0.0483	0.6585	0.4343	0.7828
	CEEMD-FTS-MOGWO-LSTM	-0.0205	0.2314	0.2964	0.0041	0.0487	0.9992	0.0041	0.0296	0.7439	0.7374	0.9359
Dataset B	ARIMA	0.0129	0.4160	0.5344	0.0103	0.0768	0.9980	-0.0023	0.0470	0.6523	0.4848	0.7809
	GRNN	0.1744	0.4548	0.5907	0.0136	0.0889	0.9975	-0.0306	0.0514	0.7058	0.5859	0.7252
	WNN	0.1796	0.4394	0.5510	0.0118	0.0858	0.9978	-0.0315	0.0479	0.6692	0.4949	0.7726
	LSTM	-0.2642	0.4271	0.5487	0.0138	0.0863	0.9973	0.0545	0.0560	0.7711	0.5152	0.7855
	MOGWO-LSTM	-0.0291	0.4338	0.5521	0.0114	0.0803	0.9978	0.0052	0.0488	0.6925	0.5152	0.7519
	FTS-LSTM	-0.2094	0.4398	0.5700	0.0116	0.0791	0.9977	0.0380	0.0512	0.7650	0.5455	0.7632
	FTS-MOGWO-LSTM	-0.0980	0.4204	0.5356	0.0105	0.0773	0.9979	0.0176	0.0477	0.7189	0.5253	0.7663
	CEEMD-FTS-MOGWO-LSTM	-0.0532	0.2345	0.2850	0.0032	0.0439	0.9994	0.0095	0.0253	0.6145	0.7677	0.9737
Dataset C	ARIMA	-0.0031	0.4313	0.5485	0.0130	0.0893	0.9974	-0.0006	0.0534	0.5905	0.4343	0.6835
	GRNN	0.0932	0.4836	0.6393	0.0185	0.1038	0.9964	-0.0181	0.0617	0.6799	0.5051	0.5105
	WNN	0.0199	0.4727	0.6438	0.0186	0.1005	0.9964	-0.0039	0.0625	0.7129	0.4343	0.5528
	LSTM	0.0131	0.4419	0.5731	0.0146	0.0928	0.9971	-0.0026	0.0557	0.6154	0.5556	0.6241
	MOGWO-LSTM	0.1206	0.4315	0.5739	0.0146	0.0919	0.9971	-0.0234	0.0553	0.5967	0.5253	0.6341
	FTS-LSTM	-0.0550	0.4181	0.5416	0.0129	0.0868	0.9974	0.0109	0.0531	0.6260	0.5758	0.6515
	FTS-MOGWO-LSTM	0.0929	0.3892	0.5201	0.0121	0.0826	0.9976	-0.0181	0.0503	0.6041	0.6061	0.6905
	CEEMD-FTS-MOGWO-LSTM	-0.0189	0.2432	0.3085	0.0039	0.0488	0.9992	0.0037	0.0301	0.5552	0.7677	0.9154
Dataset D	ARIMA	-0.0415	0.4194	0.5416	0.0121	0.0846	0.9975	0.0081	0.0525	0.6718	0.4242	0.7712
	GRNN	-0.1744	0.4986	0.6308	0.0173	0.1008	0.9966	0.0347	0.0621	0.7925	0.5051	0.6845
	WNN	-0.2658	0.4778	0.5979	0.0150	0.0943	0.9969	0.0534	0.0594	0.7722	0.4242	0.7516
	LSTM	-0.1168	0.4295	0.5565	0.0131	0.0868	0.9974	0.0231	0.0544	0.7198	0.4848	0.7488
	MOGWO-LSTM	-0.0652	0.4094	0.5411	0.0122	0.0831	0.9975	0.0128	0.0527	0.7009	0.5455	0.7516
	FTS-LSTM	-0.0447	0.4075	0.5263	0.0114	0.0825	0.9976	0.0088	0.0512	0.6954	0.5859	0.7582
	FTS-MOGWO-LSTM	0.0151	0.3825	0.5031	0.0106	0.0787	0.9978	-0.0030	0.0487	0.6923	0.5859	0.7740
	CEEMD-FTS-MOGWO-LSTM	-0.1282	0.2569	0.3272	0.0039	0.0491	0.9993	0.9991	0.0254	0.5921	0.7179	0.9280

127

Table 8. Experimental outcomes of the proposed forecasting system and other models (Experiment III, Wednesday).

Models	AE	MAE	RMSE	NMSE	MAPE	IA	FB	U1	U2	DA	R
GRNN	45.5683	196.0143	241.4824	0.0018	0.0347	0.9996	−0.0078	0.0204	0.7029	0.3535	0.9478
WNN	20.7296	168.5709	205.6567	0.0014	0.0302	0.9997	−0.0035	0.0174	0.7651	0.6667	0.9604
CNN	137.5887	229.2342	239.6551	0.0025	0.0403	0.9994	−0.0233	0.0247	0.7953	0.444	0.9362
DBN	19.7873	191.6701	243.2305	0.0019	0.0341	0.9996	−0.0034	0.0206	0.7248	0.2727	0.9444
SAE	101.5634	175.8853	214.9376	0.0013	0.0304	0.9997	−0.0173	0.0181	0.7351	0.4343	0.9652
LSTM	−161.6647	172.3742	205.9165	0.0011	0.0281	0.9997	0.0281	0.0177	0.7425	0.7576	0.9916
FTS-LSTM	47.6418	96.6102	115.9360	0.0004	0.0171	0.9999	−0.0081	0.0098	0.5328	0.7071	0.9904
MOGWO-LSTM	−83.5761	106.2048	129.7533	0.0004	0.0176	0.9999	0.0144	0.0111	0.5570	0.7677	0.9918
FTS-MOGWO-LSTM	26.9179	84.9093	104.1058	0.0003	0.0146	0.9999	−0.0046	0.0088	0.4629	0.7677	0.9903
EMD-FTS-MOGWO-LSTM	52.6362	67.7765	79.8200	0.0002	0.0116	1.0000	−0.0090	0.0068	0.4940	0.7374	0.9968
EEMD-FTS-MOGWO-LSTM	11.3961	55.9408	69.4255	0.0001	0.0096	1.0000	−0.0020	0.0059	0.4142	0.8283	0.9957
CEEMD-FTS-MOGWO-LSTM	−29.7311	47.5537	64.3627	0.0001	0.0083	1.0000	0.0051	0.0055	0.4030	0.9293	0.9970

The values in bold indicate the best values of each benchmark function.

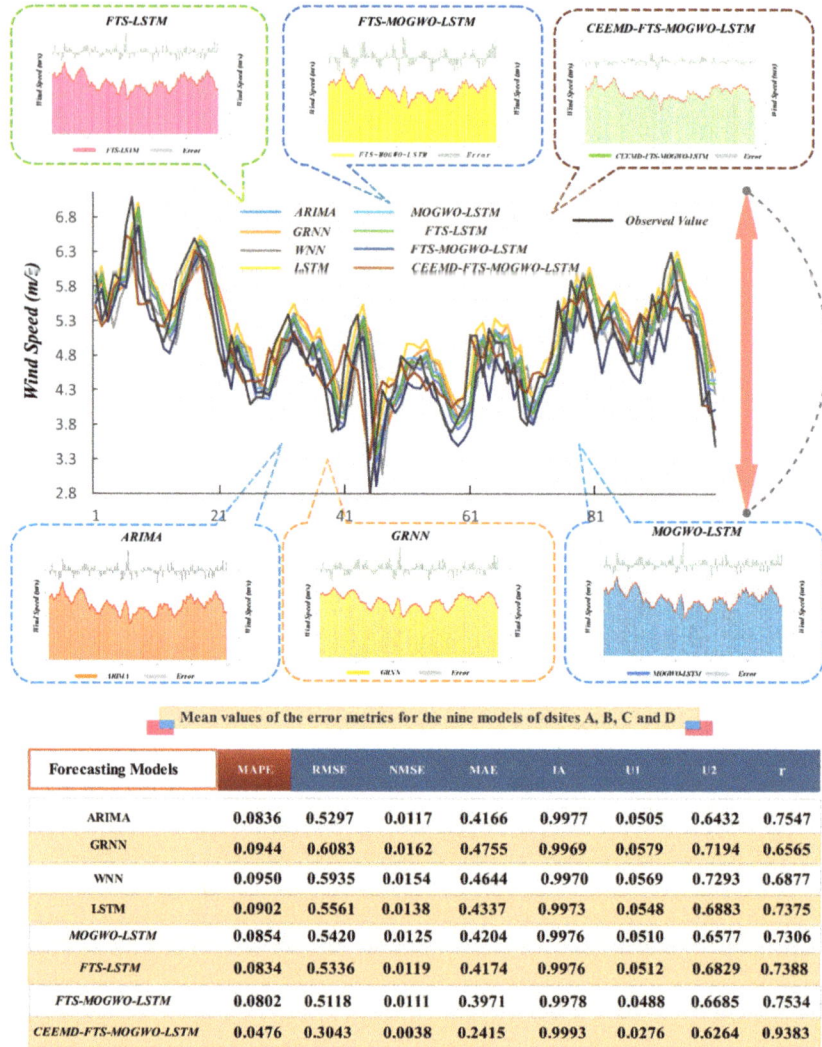

Figure 9. Forecasting results of the developed forecasting system and the other compared models (Experiment II).

3.4. Experiment III: Tested with Electrical Load Data

The third experiment aims to verify the performance of the proposed CFML forecasting model in QLD (Queensland) electrical power load forecasting (Figure 10). Due to the similarity in weekdays or weekends and the noticeable differences between the load data from weekdays and weekends, the data from Wednesday was randomly selected as a representative of weekdays and the data from Sunday was chosen to represent weekends [60]. Tables 8 and 10 list the experimental outcomes. All forecasting results from Wednesday and Sunday are depicted in Figure 10. In addition, the basic datasets from Wednesday and Sunday in QLD are shown in Figure 10, and both of these datasets were collected from Queensland in Australia. The specific results of electrical load forecasts are presented and shown clearly in this subsection, from which the following conclusions were drawn:

(1) Regarding the electrical power load data from Wednesday and all forecasting steps, the proposed hybrid forecasting system performed the best among all the other models. Moreover, among all the single models involved in this experiment, the single model that performed best was the WNN algorithm, while the worst was the CNN model. However, this may be a result of the data features, which does not mean that the CNN constantly performs more poorly than the WNN model. Since the regular form of the CNN model is designed to deal with figure data, to perform unidimensional time series forecasting, it should be first transformed into a matrix in which each row contains many observations, such as 128 or 256, just like the grey scale image data to some extent. Otherwise, it is also reasonable and practical to let each row represent the number you would like to use as input data, but a compromise in the accuracy may arise on some occasions.

(2) For the test of the optimization part and the verification of the fuzzy forecasting part, comparisons between MOGWO-LSTM and LSTM and comparisons between FTS-LSTM and LSTM are obviously shown in the aforementioned tables and figures, respectively. For instance, on Wednesday, the regular LSTM model achieved a MAPE of 2.81%, which is higher than the MAPE of FTS-LSTM by 39.14%. Moreover, the MOGWO-LSTM increased by 37.36% in terms of the MAPE of 1.76%. Also, the FTS-MOGWO-LSTM model possessed a MAPE of 1.46%, lower than that of the single LSTM combined with FTS or MOGWO. Noticeably, although this combined model did not have that highest r^2, it was not obviously lower than that of other compared models. Moreover, it was apparently higher than that of regular networks such as GRNN, WNN, DBN, SAE, and so on.

(3) All comparisons for the electrical power load data on Wednesday and Sunday demonstrate that the decomposition methods achieved the best forecasting results. In this study, we tested different parameter settings regarding the Nstd, NR, Maxiter, and modes for EMD, EEMD, and CEEMD. The following outcomes were all acquired based on the best parameter settings for each decomposition algorithm. Tables 9 and 10 show that the CEEMD method apparently outweighs the EEMD and EMD methods, which explains why the CEEMD was selected by us and employed in this research. Also, from Figure 10, the forecasts gained by the CEEMD model corresponded most to the real data on both Wednesday and Sunday.

Remark: Based on the three experiments mentioned above, the strong applicability of the developed model in these two electrical power load signals and in different wind data sites, which feature different characteristics, reasonably and convincingly demonstrates that the CEEMD-FTS-MOGWO-LSTM model has universal applicability. Also, the CFML model performs better than all other compared benchmark models.

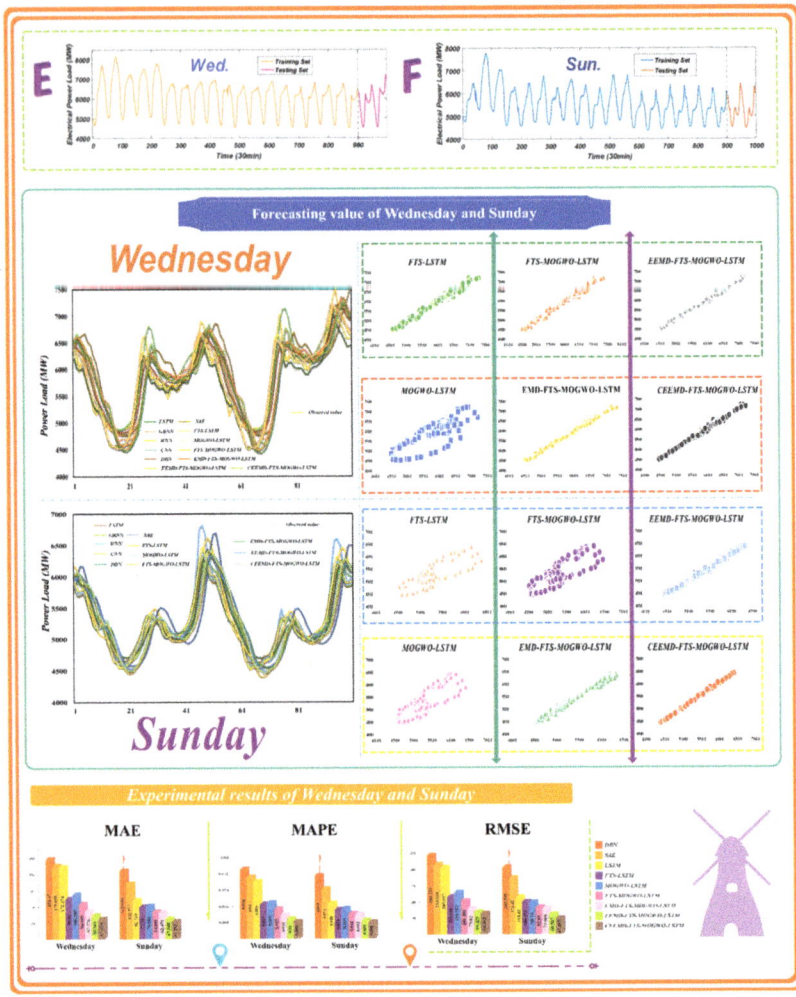

Figure 10. The forecasting results from Wednesday and Sunday as well as the basic data descriptions.

Table 9. Results for the Diebold–Mariano (DM) test.

Models	Dataset A	Dataset B	Dataset C	Dataset D	Dataset E	Dataset F	Average
GRNN	3.9575	3.6231 *	4.0912 *	5.1216 *	6.8446 *	6.3102 *	7.4871 *
WNN	4.2354 *	3.8835 *	4.0655 *	5.3478 *	7.0481 *	5.5907 *	5.0285 *
CNN	6.4340 *	4.4792 *	5.4704 *	5.1895 *	6.6125 *	6.8757 *	5.8436 *
DBN	5.8905 *	5.1538 *	4.0607 *	5.7001 *	5.7287 *	6.2989 *	5.4721 *
SAE	5.9415 *	4.7566 *	4.7852 *	5.5428 *	7.7388 *	6.3725 *	5.8563 *
LSTM	4.0334 *	3.8478 *	4.3132 *	4.4067 *	7.9982 *	6.4910 *	5.1817 *
FTS-LSTM	4.9204 *	4.6690 *	5.3686 *	4.1885 *	5.1504 *	4.8412 *	4.8064 *
MOGWO-LSTM	3.6338 *	3.8032 *	3.9883 *	4.0228 *	5.4912 *	5.5515 *	4.4151 *
FTS-MOGWO-LSTM	4.4712 *	4.1507 *	3.8489 *	3.8727 *	4.0104 *	4.5032 *	4.1429 *
EMD-FTS-MOGWO-LSTM	-	-	-	-	1.9867 *	4.7634 *	3.3751 *
EEMD-FTS-MOGWO-LSTM	-	-	-	-	0.8353	2.5458 *	1.6901 *
CEEMD-FTS-MOGWO-LSTM	-	-	-	-	-	-	-

* Indicates the 1% significance level.

Table 10. Experimental outcomes of the proposed forecasting system and other models (Experiment III, Sunday).

Models	AE	MAE	RMSE	NMSE	MAPE	IA	FB	U1	U2	DA	R
GRNN	17.5396	149.6115	190.1444	0.0013	0.0284	0.9997	−0.0033	0.0179	0.6929	0.3838	0.9376
WNN	38.7488	103.6095	137.2156	0.0006	0.0194	0.9998	−0.0073	0.0129	0.6450	0.7071	0.9711
CNN	16.6657	162.4187	200.3068	0.0013	0.0302	0.9997	−0.0032	0.0189	0.7094	0.3737	0.9308
DBN	8.2873	163.9351	205.5054	0.0015	0.0310	0.9996	−0.0016	0.0194	0.7268	0.3232	0.9234
SAE	6.4847	132.5766	173.3199	0.0010	0.0244	0.9998	−0.0012	0.0163	0.6732	0.4949	0.9487
LSTM	−2.8595	92.739	113.8205	0.0004	0.0175	0.9999	0.0005	0.0107	0.6788	0.8081	0.9916
FTS-LSTM	−20.6497	77.1604	100.2723	0.0003	0.0143	0.9999	0.0039	0.0095	0.5844	0.8485	0.9910
MOGWO-LSTM	−4.2641	78.6017	98.7397	0.0003	0.0148	0.9999	0.0008	0.0093	0.6091	0.8485	0.9917
FTS-MOGWO-LSTM	**1.9840**	64.8811	82.8495	0.0002	0.0122	0.9999	**−0.0004**	0.0078	0.5073	0.8586	0.9907
EMD-FTS-MOGWO-LSTM	−6.8800	62.4585	79.6677	−0.0002	0.0118	0.9999	0.0013	0.0075	0.5218	0.7778	0.9904
EEMD-FTS-MOGWO-LSTM	−8.9363	47.3082	60.5872	0.0001	0.0088	**1.0000**	0.0017	0.0057	0.4453	0.8586	0.9960
CEEMD-FTS-MOGWO-LSTM	−40.7260	**41.1810**	**47.4667**	**0.00008**	**0.0079**	**1.0000**	0.0078	**0.0045**	**0.3802**	**0.8687**	**0.9990**

The values in bold indicates the best values of each benchmark function.

4. Discussion

In this section, based on the Diebold–Mariano test (DM test), we discuss and analyze the forecasting model's statistical significance, after which we adopt the Pearson's correlation coefficient to discuss the association strength. Then, to verify the contributions of our CFML model, the improvement percentages between different combinations of basic models are also discussed in this section. Also, the multistep-ahead forecasting of the developed model and a sensitivity analysis are conducted.

4.1. Discussion I: Statistical Significance

The DM test is widely used to demonstrate the significance of the improvement brought by the developed CFML forecasting system compared with other algorithms. Table 9 lists the specific DM test outcomes, which demonstrates that we are able to reject the null hypothesis at the 1% significance level because all of the compared models' DM test outcomes were greater than the critical 1% significance value for all four wind speed datasets and the two electrical power load data series. Hence, we are convinced that the proposed CFML forecasting system obviously outweighs the other compared algorithms. According to this, we are able to conclude reasonably that the hybrid forecasting framework displays a significant difference in terms of the statistical level. Furthermore, this proves that the proposed CFML model is superior to the other models mentioned above and involved in wind speed forecasting.

4.2. Discussion II: Association Strength

The Pearson test can reveal the correlation strength between the predicted and actual values, which was proposed by scientist Karl Pearson. In this section, the correlation strength is discussed based on the Pearson test to prove the superiority of the proposed hybrid prediction model and all other comparative models. Specifically, if the Pearson's correlation coefficient is equal to 0, there is no linear relationship between the two sets of data and, if the Pearson's correlation coefficient is equal to 1, there is a linear relationship between the actual value and the predicted value. Table 11 demonstrates the outcomes of the Pearson's test, from which we were able to obtain the conclusion that the values of all other comparative models were lower than that of the proposed CFML forecasting model, which shows that the forecasting values of the CFML model possess higher association strengths to some extent.

Table 11. Results for the Pearson's test.

Models	Dataset A	Dataset B	Dataset C	Dataset D	Dataset E	Dataset F	Average
GRNN	0.7830	0.7252	0.5105	0.6845	0.9478	0.9376	0.7648
WNN	0.6738	0.7726	0.5528	0.7516	0.9504	0.9711	0.7787
CNN	0.5871	0.5558	0.2078	0.5892	0.9362	0.9308	0.6345
DBN	0.7122	0.7284	0.5589	0.7419	0.9444	0.9234	0.7682
SAE	0.7083	0.6608	0.6481	0.7227	0.9652	0.9487	0.7756
LSTM	0.7915	0.7855	0.6241	0.7488	0.9916	0.9916	0.8221
FTS-LSTM	0.7822	0.7632	0.6515	0.7582	0.9904	0.9910	0.8228
MOGWO-LSTM	0.7848	0.7663	0.6341	0.7515	0.9918	0.9917	0.8200
FTS-MOGWO-LSTM	0.7828	0.7663	0.6905	0.7740	0.9903	0.9907	0.8324
EMD-FTS-MOGWO-LSTM	-	-	-	-	0.9968	0.9904	0.9936
EEMD-FTS-MOGWO-LSTM	-	-	-	-	0.9957	0.9960	**0.9959**
CEEMD-FTS-MOGWO-LSTM	**0.9369**	**0.9737**	**0.9154**	**0.928**	**0.9970**	**0.9990**	0.9583

The values in bold indicate the best values of each benchmark function.

4.3. Discussion III: Improvement Percentage

In order to fully and clearly demonstrate the superiority of the proposed hybrid prediction system, this section discusses the percentage improvements in MAPE, RMSE, MAE, and direction accuracy (DA) between the developed system and other comparative models. These comparisons analyze and quantify how each component works in the overall prediction framework. Table 12 demonstrates the outcomes of the improvement percentages, taking dataset B and the electrical load power on Wednesday as examples, which shows the following conclusions:

(1) By contrasting the improvement percentage between FTS-MOGWO-LSTM with FTS-LSTM and MOGWO-LSTM, we drew the conclusion that the combination of MOGWO and FTS contributes more than either FTS-LSTM or MOGWO-LSTM to the forecasting ability of the whole presented hybrid CFML forecasting model.

(2) The comparison between the CEEMD-FTS-MOGWO-LSTM and the FTS-MOGWO-LSTM models obviously revealed the improvement brought by the addition of the decomposition approach CEEMD.

(3) On average, all improvement percentages were positive and significant, except for the percentages of FTS-MOGWO-LSTM, as it fluctuated according to different datasets with different features. This can be studied in the future. Regardless of the fluctuations, all values revealed that FTS-MOGWO-LSTM does perform better than the regular one.

Table 12. Results for the discussion of improvement percentages.

Improvement Percentages	Dataset B	Wednesday	Average	Dataset B	Wednesday	Average
	MOGWO-LSTM vs. LSTM			FTS-LSTM vs. LSTM		
MAE	−1.568719	38.387067	18.409174	−2.973542	43.953213	20.489836
RMSE	−0.619646	36.98742	18.183887	−3.881903	43.697567	19.907832
MAPE	6.952491	37.366548	22.15952	8.34299	39.145907	23.744449
U2	10.180262	24.983165	17.581714	0.791078	28.242424	14.516751
Improvement Percentages	FTS-MOGWO-LSTM vs. LSTM			FTS-MOGWO-LSTM vs. MOGWO-LSTM		
MAE	1.568719	50.741294	26.155007	3.088981	20.051354	11.570168
RMSE	2.387461	49.442711	25.915086	2.988589	19.766357	11.377473
MAPE	10.428737	48.042705	29.235721	3.73599	17.045455	10.390723
U2	6.76955	37.656566	22.213058	−3.797286	16.894075	6.5483945
Improvement Percentages	FTS-MOGWO-LSTM vs. FTS-LSTM			CEEMD-FTS-MOGWO-LSTM vs. MOGWO-LSTM		
MAE	4.411096	12.111454	8.261275	45.94283	55.224528	50.58368
RMSE	6.035088	10.204078	8.119583	48.37892	50.396098	49.387508
MAPE	2.275601	14.619883	8.447742	45.33001	52.840909	49.085461
U2	5.804507	13.119369	9.461938	11.27635	27.648115	19.462233
Improvement Percentages	CEEMD-FTS-MOGWO-LSTM vs. FTS-MOGWO-LSTM			CEEMD-FTS-MOGWO-LSTM vs. LSTM		
MAE	44.219791	43.99471	44.107251	45.09483	72.412519	58.753673
RMSE	46.788648	38.175683	42.482166	48.05905	68.743301	58.401175
MAPE	43.208279	43.150685	43.179482	49.13094	70.462633	59.796786
U2	14.522187	12.94016	13.731174	20.30865	45.723906	33.016278

4.4. Discussion IV: Multistep-Ahead Forecasting

Now, we consider that the one-step forecasting model is sometimes insufficient to ensure the controllability and reliability of the electrical power load or wind speed forecasting system. Therefore, to test the multistep performance of the developed CFML system, the multistep prediction in this study used the two datasets listed in Table 3 (i.e., dataset A and the electrical power load on Sunday as representatives).

Table 13 illustrates the forecasting outcomes of those comparative models (i.e., GRNN, LSTM, and EEMD-FTS-MOGWO-LSTM) and the proposed CEEMD-FTS-MOGWO-LSTM forecasting model. It can be observed that for one-step, two-step, and three-step predictions using electrical power load data or wind speed data, the proposed model always achieved the lowest MAPE value in the test models. That is to say, the developed framework effectively carried out multistep-ahead forecasting in electrical power load prediction or wind speed prediction (through effective error index measurements).

4.5. Discussion V: Sensitivity Analysis

The hybrid forecasting model has two essential parameters, namely the number of iterations and the number of search agents. Hence, in this subsection, we explore the effects of these two parameters on the prediction performance of wind speed dataset A. That is, the other parameters' values were unchanged, while the number of search agents and iterations changed. Specifically, we set the search agents as 5, 10, 15, 20, 25, and 30, and then, we kept the search agent at the value of 10, changing the values of iterations to 5, 10, 20, 30, 40, and 50. Tables 14 and 15 illustrate the experimental outcomes of dataset A. The following conclusions were drawn:

(1) The value of MAPE first decreased as the number of search agents increased. Then, it declined to the minimum value with 10 search agents, after which it started increasing and fluctuated at a high level except for a decrease at 25 search agents. Overall, we can see that the proposed hybrid CFML forecasting model performed the best with 10 search agents.

(2) Keeping the number of search agents at the best value of 10, we changed the number of iterations in order to check the influence caused by the iterations on the performance of the presented model. We almost drew a similar conclusion to that of the search agents to some degree. We can see that, as the number of iterations increased from 5 to 30, the accuracy measured by various metrics, especially MAPE, first fell to the minimum value with 10 iterations and then rose gradually as the number of iteration increased. According to these two conclusions, we set the number of search agents and the number of iterations to 10 in our experiment.

(3) It was found through the comparisons that the number of those two parameters would worsen the performance of the CEEMD-FTS-MOGWO-LSTM system proposed in this study if either they were too small or too big. In addition, different prediction conditions were shown to depend to a large extent on the decision-making process. Therefore, it is important to figure out the optimal parameters under different application conditions.

Table 13. Results for the multistep-ahead forecasting.

Data	Multistep Ahead	Forecasting Models	MAE	RMSE	NMSE	MAPE	IA	FB	U1	U2	DA	r
Dataset A	One-step ahead	GRNN	0.4650	0.5723	0.0154	0.1004	0.9970	−0.0283	0.0562	0.6984	0.4949	0.7057
		LSTM	0.4364	0.5462	0.0138	0.0948	0.9973	−0.0530	0.0529	0.6470	0.4343	0.7915
		EEMD-FTS-MOGWO-LSTM	0.2513	0.3215	0.0048	0.0524	0.9990	0.0101	0.0322	0.7000	0.7778	0.9478
		CEEMD-FTS-MOGWO-LSTM	0.2314	0.2964	0.0041	0.0487	0.9992	0.0041	0.0296	0.7439	0.7374	0.9359
	Two-step ahead	GRNN	0.5546	0.6748	0.0203	0.1170	0.9959	−0.0149	0.0666	0.8160	0.3232	0.5548
		LSTM	0.4980	0.6034	0.0175	0.1058	0.9967	0.0023	0.0600	0.8169	0.4545	0.6754
		EEMD-FTS-MOGWO-LSTM	0.3725	0.4655	0.0090	0.0730	0.9980	0.0586	0.0477	0.7563	0.6263	0.8897
		CEEMD-FTS-MOGWO-LSTM	0.3121	0.3930	0.0072	0.0667	0.9986	−0.0169	0.0387	0.5739	0.6566	0.8691
	Three-step ahead	GRNN	0.5688	0.7183	0.0239	0.1262	0.9954	−0.0601	0.0694	0.8542	0.4545	0.5725
		LSTM	0.5449	0.6986	0.0213	0.1076	0.9956	0.0716	0.0719	0.8715	0.3535	0.6332
		EEMD-FTS-MOGWO-LSTM	0.4327	0.5276	0.0122	0.0877	0.9975	0.0546	0.0539	0.7566	0.6162	0.8082
		CEEMD-FTS-MOGWO-LSTM	0.3818	0.4891	0.0116	0.0840	0.9978	−0.0405	0.0478	0.7496	0.5859	0.8332
Dataset F	One-step ahead	GRNN	149.6115	190.1444	0.0013	0.0284	0.9997	−0.0033	0.0179	0.6929	0.3838	0.9376
		LSTM	92.7390	113.8205	0.0004	0.0175	0.9999	0.0005	0.0107	0.6788	0.8081	0.9916
		EEMD-FTS-MOGWO-LSTM	47.3082	60.5872	0.0001	0.0088	1.0000	0.0017	0.0057	0.4453	0.8586	0.996
		CEEMD-FTS-MOGWO-LSTM	41.1810	47.4667	0.00008	0.0079	1.0000	0.0078	0.0045	0.3802	0.8687	0.999
	Two-step ahead	GRNN	192.6101	244.0532	0.0021	0.0368	0.9995	−0.0069	0.0230	0.7653	0.3535	0.8958
		LSTM	137.3114	171.6678	0.0010	0.0258	0.9998	0.0032	0.0162	0.6710	0.4848	0.9708
		EEMD-FTS-MOGWO-LSTM	109.3356	151.5123	0.0007	0.0202	0.9998	−0.0096	0.0142	0.6495	0.6061	0.9685
		CEEMD-FTS-MOGWO-LSTM	56.0655	72.4324	0.0002	0.0105	1.0000	−0.0010	0.0068	0.4913	0.7879	0.9909
	Three-step ahead	GRNN	225.4602	287.1460	0.0029	0.0429	0.9993	−0.0092	0.0270	0.8026	0.2525	0.8480
		LSTM	225.4602	287.1460	0.0029	0.0429	0.9993	−0.0092	0.0270	0.8026	0.2525	0.8480
		EEMD-FTS-MOGWO-LSTM	139.4634	177.1613	0.0012	0.0272	0.9997	−0.0209	0.0165	0.7375	0.5859	0.9673
		CEEMD-FTS-MOGWO-LSTM	107.3264	133.4660	0.0007	0.0208	0.9999	−0.0120	0.0125	0.6643	0.6364	0.9779

Table 14. Sensitivity analysis of different search agent numbers based on MOGWO.

Metrics	The Value of Search Agent Number					
	5	10	15	20	25	30
AE	−0.583443	**−0.020492**	−0.480544	−1.462529	−0.670987	−1.334932
MAE	0.613591	**0.231376**	0.492307	1.462529	0.680333	1.334932
RMSE	0.680007	**0.296408**	0.540443	1.483524	0.730494	1.349639
NMSE	0.019238	**0.004058**	0.011898	0.127156	0.022886	0.105523
MAPE	0.119743	**0.048723**	0.096181	0.294995	0.133244	0.271309
IA	0.995908	**0.999202**	0.997397	0.983123	0.995343	0.985745
FB	0.124580	**0.004128**	0.101493	0.344632	0.144625	0.309906
U1	0.071900	**0.029562**	0.056484	0.172524	0.077915	0.154439
U2	0.974610	0.743881	0.851054	**1.010876**	0.974186	1.003426
DA	0.575758	**0.737374**	0.626263	0.484848	0.565657	0.484848
r	0.925713	0.935871	0.969081	0.964314	0.955029	**0.970766**

The values in bold indicate the best values of each benchmark function.

Table 15. Sensitivity analysis of the different iteration numbers based on MOGWO.

Metrics	The Value of Iteration Number					
	5	10	20	30	40	50
AE	−0.372790	**−0.020492**	0.288276	0.091318	0.133480	−0.398180
MAE	0.40222	**0.231376**	0.310034	0.350980	0.355459	0.409639
RMSE	0.474841	**0.296408**	0.362281	0.419625	0.438289	0.464493
NMSE	0.008926	**0.004058**	0.006453	0.008568	0.009241	0.009084
MAPE	0.077856	**0.048723**	0.068445	0.076189	0.077642	0.080769
IA	0.997962	**0.999202**	0.998823	0.998390	0.998213	0.998088
FB	0.077850	0.004128	−0.05631	**−0.01819**	−0.02647	0.083373
U1	0.049091	**0.029562**	0.035048	0.041391	0.043116	0.048082
U2	0.767918	0.743881	0.716270	0.726236	0.744410	**0.779216**
DA	0.656566	**0.737374**	0.666667	0.666667	0.646465	0.676768
r	0.947467	0.935871	**0.969309**	0.850194	0.883903	0.955046

The values in bold indicate the best values of each benchmark function.

Remark: According to Discussions I to V, we can draw the conclusion that the proposed hybrid forecasting system, namely CEEMD-FTS-MOGWO-LSTM, possesses a more effective and stable forecasting ability, regarding not only the wind speed but also the electrical power load, than other models in terms of a lot of aspects, such as the correlation strength, statistical significance, and forecasting accuracy. Also, the small number of iterations and search agents demonstrates the superiority and convenience of the proposed model.

5. Conclusions

Accurate wind speed electrical power load forecasting is crucial for power grid safety management, power system operation, and the power market. However, due to the nonlinearity and randomness of wind speed data and electrical power load series, it is still a difficult and challenging task to establish an effective forecasting framework to deal with this problem. In this study, a new hybrid prediction system was developed in order to obtain stability and accuracy simultaneously. Four wind speed datasets and two electrical power load datasets were adopted to test the effectiveness of the hybrid forecasting framework. The outcomes show that our proposed system outperformed all other comparative benchmark models on many indicators. Firstly, a data preprocessing decomposition approach, named CEEMD, was successfully applied in this study to enhance the forecasting ability of the CFML forecasting model. Secondly, an effective multi-objective optimization algorithm, MOGWO, was successfully combined and used to find out the optimal initial parameters. It not only achieved better results in testing functions than the other two optimization models (NSGA-II and MODA) but also showed the best optimization capability. Moreover, fuzzy time series forecasting with the rough set induction rule, which is based on the LEM2 algorithm to build rule sets, was successfully combined with MOGWO and the deep learning algorithm, called LSTM, in this paper. It was shown that the addition of the FTS part, the MOGWO part, and the data decomposition part all bring improvements in the performance of the hybrid forecasting framework. Also, a similar method can be applied in other fields, for example, the electrical power load, which was verified in this paper. Finally, the forecasting models CEEMD, FTS, and MOGWO showed the ability to carry the strength of each component and to effectively improve the forecasting ability of the CFML forecasting model in terms of stability and accuracy.

Author Contributions: Conceptualization, D.W. and J.W.; Methodology, J.W.; Software, D.W.; Validation, J.W., K.N. and G.T.; Formal Analysis, D.W. and J.W.; Investigation, K.N. and G.T.; Resources, D.W.; Data Curation K.N. and G.T.; Writing-Original Draft Preparation, D.W.; Writing-Review & Editing, D.W. and J.W.; Visualization, D.W. and J.W.; Supervision, J.W.; Project Administration, D.W.; Funding Acquisition, J.W.

Funding: This work was supported by the National Natural Science Foundation of China (grant number 71671029).

Conflicts of Interest: The authors declare that there is no conflict of interest regarding the publication of this paper.

Abbreviations

	List of Abbreviations		
		FB	The fractional bias
		U1	The Theil U statistic 1
CFML	CEEMD-FTS-MOGWO-LSTM	U2	The Theil U statistic 2
WNN	Wavelet Neutral Network	DA	The direction accuracy
GRNN	Generalized Regression Neural Network	INDEX	The improvement ratio of the index among different models
SAE	Sparse Autoencoder	R^2	The Pearson's correlation coefficient
LSTM	Long Short-Term Memory	DM	Diebold–Mariano test
DBN	Deep Belief Network	H^0	The null hypothesis
CNN	Convolutional Neural Network	H^1	The alternative hypothesis
IGD	The inverted generational distance	α	The confidence level
FTS	Fuzzy time series	X^t	An input at time t
LEM2	Learning from examples module version two	S^t	The hidden state

AR	Autoregressive model	MA	Moving-average model
ARIMA	Autoregressive Integrated Moving Average	ARMA	Autoregressive moving average model
MODA	Multi-objective dragonfly	S^{t-1}	The previous time step
MOGWO	Multi-objective grey wolf	f^t	The forget gate
NSGA-II	Non-dominated sorted genetic algorithm-II	i^t	The input gate
K^α	The distance between wolf α and the prey	R^1	The position of wolf α at time $ite+1$
K^β	The distance between wolf β and the prey	R^2	The position of wolf β at time $ite+1$
K^δ	The distance between wolf δ and the prey	R^3	The position of wolf δ at time $ite+1$
QLD	Queensland	C_{t-1}	The old cell state
P^{ni}	Positive noise	N^{ni}	Negative noise
AE	The average error	W^{ni}	Noise with identical amplitude and phase
MAE	The mean absolute error	O^t	The output gate
RMSE	The root-mean-square error	g^j	The j-th inequality constraint
NMSE	The normalized average of the squares of error	h^j	The j-th equality constraint
MAPE	The mean absolute percentage error	RST	Rough set theory
IMF	Intrinsic mode function	IA	The index of agreement
ZDT2	Zitzler–Deb–Thiele's function N. 2	ZDT1	Zitzler–Deb–Thiele's function N. 1
Kursawe	Kursawe function	ZDT3	Zitzler–Deb–Thiele's function N. 3
EMD	Empirical Mode Decomposition		
EEMD	Ensemble Empirical Mode Decomposition		
CEEMD	Complete Ensemble Empirical Mode Decomposition		

References

1. Ou, T.C. A novel unsymmetrical faults analysis for microgrid distribution system. *Int. J. Electr. Power Energy Syst.* **2012**, *43*, 1017–1024. [CrossRef]
2. Ou, T.C. Ground fault current analysis with a direct building algorithm for microgrid distribution. *Int. J. Electr. Power Energy Syst.* **2013**, *53*, 867–875. [CrossRef]
3. Lin, W.M.; Ou, T.C. Unbalanced distribution network fault analysis with hybrid compensation. *IET Gener. Transm. Distrib.* **2010**, *5*, 92–100. [CrossRef]
4. Ou, T.C.; Lu, K.H.; Huang, C.J. Improvement of transient stability in a hybrid power multi-system using a designed NIDC (novel intelligent damping controller). *Energies* **2017**, *10*, 488. [CrossRef]
5. Ye, S.; Zhu, G.; Xiao, Z. Long term load forecasting and recommendations for china based on support vector regression. *Energy Power Eng.* **2012**, *4*, 380–385. [CrossRef]
6. He, Q.; Wang, J.; Haiyan Lu, H. A hybrid system for short-term wind speed forecasting. *Appl. Energy* **2018**, *226*, 756–771. [CrossRef]
7. Yang, W.; Wang, J.; Lu, H. Hybrid wind energy forecasting and analysis system based on divide and conquer scheme: A case study in China. *J. Clean. Prod.* **2019**, *222*, 942–959. [CrossRef]
8. Abdel-Aal, R.E.; Elhadidy, M.A.; Shaahid, S.M. Modeling and forecasting the mean hourly wind speed time series using GMDH-based abductive networks. *Renew. Energy* **2009**, *34*, 1686–1699. [CrossRef]
9. Wang, J.; Niu, T.; Lu, H.; Yang, W.; Du, P. A Novel Framework of Reservoir Computing for Deterministic and Probabilistic Wind Power Forecasting. *IEEE Trans. Sustain. Energy* **2019**. [CrossRef]
10. Ma, L.; Luan, S.Y.; Jiang, C.W.; Liu, H.L.; Zhang, Y. A review on the forecasting of wind speed and generated power. *Renew. Sustain. Energy Rev.* **2009**, *13*, 915–920.
11. Cardenas-Barrera, J.L.; Meng, J.; Castillo-Guerra, E.; Chang, L. A neural networkapproach to multi-step-ahead, short-term wind speed forecasting. *IEEE* **2013**, *2*, 243–248.

12. Torres, J.L.; García, A.; Blas, M.D.; Francisco, A.D. Forecast of hourly average wind speed with arma models in navarre (Spain). *Sol. Energy* **2005**, *79*, 65–77. [CrossRef]
13. Liu, H.; Tian, H.Q.; Li, Y.F. An emd-recursive arima method to predict wind speed for railway strong wind warning system. *J. Wind Eng. Ind. Aerodynam.* **2015**, *141*, 27–38. [CrossRef]
14. Kavasseri, R.G.; Seetharaman, K. Day-ahead wind speed forecasting using arima models. *Renew. Energy* **2009**, *34*, 1388–1393. [CrossRef]
15. Yang, D.; Sharma, V.; Ye, Z.; Lim, L.I.; Zhao, L.; Aryaputera, A.W. Forecasting of global horizontal irradiance by exponential smoothing, using decompositions. *Energy* **2015**, *81*, 111–119. [CrossRef]
16. Li, Y.; Ling, L.; Chen, J. Combined grey prediction fuzzy control law with application to road tunnel ventilation system. *J. Appl. Res. Technol.* **2015**, *13*, 313–320. [CrossRef]
17. Barbounis, T.G.; Theocharis, J.B. A locally recurrent fuzzy neural network with application to the wind speed prediction using spatial correlation. *Neurocomputing* **2007**, *70*, 1525–1542. [CrossRef]
18. Guo, Z.H.; Wu, J.; Lu, H.Y.; Wang, J.Z. A case study on a hybrid wind speed forecasting method using BP neural network. *Knowl. Based Syst.* **2011**, *24*, 1048–1056. [CrossRef]
19. Li, G.; Shi, J. On comparing three artificial neural networks for wind speed forecasting. *Appl. Energy* **2010**, *87*, 2313–2320. [CrossRef]
20. Jiang, P.; Liu, F.; Song, Y.L. A hybrid forecasting model based on date-framework strategy and improved feature selection technology for short-term load forecasting. *Energy* **2017**, *119*, 694–709. [CrossRef]
21. Hao, Y.; Tian, C. The study and application of a novel hybrid system for air quality early-warning. *Appl. Soft Comput.* **2019**, *74*, 729–746. [CrossRef]
22. Zhang, X.; Wang, J.; Gao, Y. A hybrid short-term electricity price forecasting framework: Cuckoo search-based feature selection with singular spectrum analysis and SVM. *Energy Econ.* **2019**, *81*, 899–913. [CrossRef]
23. Lago, J.; Ridder, F.D.; Schutter, B.D. Forecasting spot electricity prices: Deep learning approaches and empirical comparison of traditional algorithms. *Appl. Energy* **2018**, *221*, 386–405. [CrossRef]
24. Hinton, G.E.; Osindero, S.; Teh, Y.W. A fast learning algorithm for deep belief nets. *Neural Comput.* **2006**, *18*, 1527–1554. [CrossRef] [PubMed]
25. Ni, K.L.; Wang, J.; Tang, G.J.; Wei, D.X. Research and Application of a Novel Hybrid Model Based on a Deep Neural Network for Electricity Load Forecasting: A Case Study in Australia. *Energies* **2019**, *12*, 2467. [CrossRef]
26. Fischer, T.; Krauss, C. Deep learning with long short-term memory networks for financial market predictions. *Eur. J. Oper. Res.* **2018**, *270*, 654–669. [CrossRef]
27. Khatami, A.; Khosravi, A.; Nguyen, T.; Lim, C.P.; Nahavandi, S. Medical image analysis using wavelet transform and deep belief networks. *Expert Syst. Appl.* **2017**, *86*, 190–198. [CrossRef]
28. Hinton, G.; Deng, L.; Yu, D.; Dahl, G.; Mohamed, A.R.; Jaitly, N.; Senior, A.; Vanhoucke, V.; Nguyen, P.; Sainath, T.; et al. Deep neural networks for acoustic modeling in speech recognition: The shared views of four research groups. *Signal Process. Mag.* **2012**, *29*, 82–97. [CrossRef]
29. Peris, A.; Domingo, M.; Casacuberta, F. Interactive neural machine translation. *Comput. Speech Lang.* **2017**, *45*, 201–220. [CrossRef]
30. Wang, H.Z.; Li, G.Q.; Wang, G.B.; Peng, J.C.; Jiang, H.; Liu, Y.T. Deep learning based ensemble approach for probabilistic wind power forecasting. *Appl. Energy* **2017**, *188*, 56–70. [CrossRef]
31. Fan, C.; Xiao, F.; Zhao, Y. A short-term building cooling load prediction method using deep learning algorithms. *Appl. Energy* **2017**, *195*, 222–233. [CrossRef]
32. Kong, X.; Xu, X.; Yan, Z.; Chen, S.; Yang, H.; Han, D. Deep learning hybrid method for islanding detection in distributed generation. *Appl. Energy* **2018**, *210*, 776–785. [CrossRef]
33. Coelho, I.; Coelho, V.; Luz, E.; Ochi, L.; Guimarães, F.; Rios, E. A GPU deep learning metaheuristic based model for time series forecasting. *Appl. Energy* **2017**, *201*, 412–418. [CrossRef]
34. Hong, Y.Y.; Chang, H.L.; Chiu, C.S. Hour-ahead wind power and speed forecasting using simultaneous perturbation stochastic approximation (spsa) algorithm and neural network with fuzzy inputs. *Energy* **2010**, *35*, 3870–3876. [CrossRef]

35. Mohandes, M.A.; Halawani, T.O.; Rehman, S.; Hussain, A.A. Support vector machines for wind speed prediction. *Renew. Energy* **2004**, *29*, 939–947. [CrossRef]
36. Zhou, J.; Shi, J.; Li, G. Fine tuning support vector machines for short-term wind speed forecasting. *Energy Convers. Manag.* **2011**, *52*, 1990–1998. [CrossRef]
37. He, J.M.; Wang, J.; Xiao, L.Q. A hybrid approach based on the Gaussian process with t-observation model for short-term wind speed forecasts. *Renew. Energy* **2017**, *114*, 670–685.
38. Hao, Y.; Tian, C. A novel two-stage forecasting model based on error factor and ensemble method for multi-step wind power forecasting. *Appl. Energy* **2019**, *238*, 368–383. [CrossRef]
39. Niu, T.; Wang, J.; Lu, H.; Du, P. Uncertainty modeling for chaotic time series based on optimal multi-input multi-output architecture: Application to offshore wind speed. *Energy Convers. Manag.* **2018**, *156*, 597–617. [CrossRef]
40. Wang, J.; Li, H.; Lu, H. Application of a novel early warning system based on fuzzy time series in urban air quality forecasting in China. *Appl. Soft Comput. J.* **2018**, *71*, 783–799. [CrossRef]
41. Bates, J.M.; Granger, C.W.J. The combination of forecasts. *Oper. Res. Q.* **1969**, *20*, 451–468. [CrossRef]
42. Xiao, L.; Qian, F.; Shao, W. Multi-step wind speed forecasting based on a hybrid forecasting architecture and an improved bat algorithm. *Energy Convers. Manag.* **2017**, *143*, 410–430. [CrossRef]
43. Xiao, L.; Wang, J.; Hou, R.; Wu, J. A combined model based on data pre-analysis and weight coefficients optimization for electrical load forecasting. *Energy* **2015**, *82*, 524–549. [CrossRef]
44. Wang, J.; Du, P.; Lu, H.; Yang, W.; Niu, T. An improved grey model optimized by multi-objective ant lion optimization algorithm for annual electricity consumption forecasting. *Appl. Soft Comput. J.* **2018**, *72*, 321–337. [CrossRef]
45. Li, H.; Wang, J.; Li, R.; Lu, H. Novel analysis-forecast system based on multi-objective optimization for air quality index. *J. Clean. Prod.* **2019**, *208*, 1365–1383. [CrossRef]
46. Liu, H.; Tian, H.Q.; Pan, D.F.; Li, Y.F. Forecasting models for wind speed using wavelet, wavelet packet, time series and artificial neural networks. *Appl. Energy* **2013**, *107*, 191–208. [CrossRef]
47. Liu, H.; Tian, H.Q.; Li, Y.F. Comparison of new hybrid FEEMD-MLP, FEEMD-ANFIS, Wavelet Packet-MLP and Wavelet Packet-ANFIS for wind speed predictions. *Energy Convers. Manag.* **2014**, *89*, 11. [CrossRef]
48. Afshar, K.; Bigdeli, N. Data analysis and short term load forecasting in Iran electricity market using singular spectral analysis (SSA). *Energy* **2011**, *36*, 2620–2627. [CrossRef]
49. Yeh, J.R.; Shieh, J.S.; Huang, N.E. Complementary ensemble empirical mode decomposition: A novel noise enhanced data analysis method. *Adv. Adapt. Data Anal.* **2010**, *2*, 135–156. [CrossRef]
50. Anbazhagan, S.; Kumarappan, N. Day-ahead deregulated electricity market price forecasting using recurrent neural network. *IEEE Syst. J.* **2013**, *7*, 866–872. [CrossRef]
51. Pawlak, Z.; Skoworn, A. Rudiments of rough sets. *Inf. Sci.* **2007**, *177*, 3–27. [CrossRef]
52. Stefanowski, J. On rough set based approaches to induction of decision rules. *Rough Sets Knowl. Discov.* **1998**, *1*, 500–529.
53. Grzymala-Busse, J.W. A new version of the rule induction system LERS. *Fundam. Inform.* **1997**, *31*, 27–39.
54. Liu, L.; Wiliem, A.; Chen, S.; Lovell, B.C. Automatic Image Attribute Selection for Zero-Shot Learning of Object Categories. In Proceedings of the Twenty Second International Conference on Pattern Recognition, Stockholm, Sweden, 24–28 August 2014; pp. 2619–2624.
55. Mirjalili, S.; Saremi, S.; Mirjalil, S.M.; Coelho, L.S. Multi-objective grey wolf optimizer: A novel algorithm for multi-criterion optimization. *Energy* **2016**, *47*, 106–119. [CrossRef]
56. Hochreiter, S.; Schmidhuber, J. Long Short-Term Memory. *Neural Comput.* **1997**, *9*, 1735–1780. [CrossRef] [PubMed]
57. Yang, W.; Wang, J.; Niu, T. A hybrid forecasting system based on a dual decomposition strategy and multi-objective optimization for electricity price forecasting. *Appl. Energy* **2019**, *235*, 1205–1225. [CrossRef]
58. Zhou, Q.G.; Wang, C.; Zhang, G.F. Hybrid forecasting system based on an optimal model selection strategy for different wind speed forecasting problems. *Appl. Energy* **2019**, *250*, 1559–1580. [CrossRef]

59. Jiang, P.; Liu, Z. Variable weights combined model based on multi-objective optimization for short-term wind speed forecasting. *Appl. Soft Comput.* **2019**, *82*, 105587. [CrossRef]
60. Zhang, X.; Wang, J.; Zhang, K. Short-term electric load forecasting based on singular spectrum analysis and support vector machine optimized by Cuckoo search algorithm. *Electr. Power Syst. Res.* **2017**, *146*, 270–285. [CrossRef]

© 2019 by the authors. Licensee MDPI, Basel, Switzerland. This article is an open access article distributed under the terms and conditions of the Creative Commons Attribution (CC BY) license (http://creativecommons.org/licenses/by/4.0/).

Article

Forecasting Daily Crude Oil Prices Using Improved CEEMDAN and Ridge Regression-Based Predictors

Taiyong Li [1,2,*], Yingrui Zhou [1], Xinsheng Li [3,*], Jiang Wu [1] and Ting He [4]

1. School of Economic Information Engineering, Southwestern University of Finance and Economics, Chengdu 611130, China; 217020204201@2017.swufe.edu.cn (Y.Z.); wuj_t@swufe.edu.cn (J.W.)
2. Sichuan Province Key Laboratory of Financial Intelligence and Financial Engineering, Southwestern University of Finance and Economics, Chengdu 611130, China
3. College of Computer Science, Sichuan University, Chengdu 610064, China
4. Architectural Design Institute, Nuclear Power Institute of China, Chengdu 610213, China; cdhet@163.com
* Correspondence: litaiyong@gmail.com (T.L.); lixinsheng@scu.edu.cn (X.L.)

Received: 8 August 2019; Accepted: 18 September 2019; Published: 20 September 2019

Abstract: As one of the leading types of energy, crude oil plays a crucial role in the global economy. Understanding the movement of crude oil prices is very attractive for producers, consumers and even researchers. However, due to its complex features of nonlinearity and nonstationarity, it is a very challenging task to accurately forecasting crude oil prices. Inspired by the well-known framework "decomposition and ensemble" in signal processing and/or time series forecasting, we propose a new approach that integrates the improved complete ensemble empirical mode decomposition with adaptive noise (ICEEMDAN), differential evolution (DE) and several types of ridge regression (RR), namely, ICEEMDAN-DE-RR, for more accurate crude oil price forecasting in this paper. The proposed approach consists of three steps. First, we use the ICEEMDAN to decompose the complex daily crude oil price series into several relatively simple components. Second, ridge regression or kernel ridge regression is employed to forecast each decomposed component. To enhance the accuracy of ridge regression, DE is used to jointly optimize the regularization item, the weights and parameters of each single kernel for each component. Finally, the predicted results of all components are aggregated as the final predicted results. The publicly available West Texas Intermediate (WTI) daily crude oil spot prices are used to validate the performance of the proposed approach. The experimental results indicate that the proposed approach can achieve better performance than some state-of-the-art approaches in terms of several evaluation criteria, demonstrating that the proposed ICEEMDAN-DE-RR is very promising for daily crude oil price forecasting.

Keywords: crude oil prices; time series forecasting; improved complete ensemble empirical mode decomposition with adaptive noise (ICEEMDAN); kernel learning; kernel ridge regression; differential evolution (DE)

---

1. Introduction

Crude oil is one of the leading types of energy that has great impacts on the global economy. Trying to accurately expect changes in crude oil prices benefits the producers and consumers of crude oil. However, the prices are affected by many factors, such as climate, exchange rate, supply and demand, speculation activities, geopolitics and so on, and they have fluctuated drastically in the last decades [1,2]. For example, the prices of West Texas Intermediate (WTI) reached over 145 USD/barrel in July 2008 and then quickly reduced to about 30 USD/barrel in the next five months. Crude oil prices have shown significant nonlinearity and nonstationarity in the last three decades. The complex fluctuation of crude oil prices makes it a very challenging task to accurately predict crude oil prices.

Despite this, many researchers have contributed to building automatic models to forecast crude oil prices accurately.

The task of forecasting crude oil prices is to expect future prices using existing data. From the perspective of the input of the forecasting task, it can be divided into two groups: multivariate forecasting and univariate forecasting. The former usually feeds the data associated with types of variables, such as macroeconomic variables, exchange rates, sentiment analysis, inventory variables, previous crude oil prices, and so on, to the predictors [1–7], while the latter uses the previous prices only [8–12]. These are two different perspectives for studying crude oil price forecasting. In practical applications, the former is usually used to forecast long-term crude oil prices, for example, monthly prices or weekly prices, while the latter is for daily prices in most cases. In the task of forecasting crude oil prices, the predictors can be mainly categorized into two classes: statistical models (econometric models) and artificial intelligence (AI) models. Mirmirani and Li employed vector auto-regression (VAR) to forecast the movements of U.S. oil prices [13]. Murat and Tokat found that a vector error correction model (VECM) with crack spread futures outperformed the traditional random walk (RW) model [14]. Moshiri and Foroutan applied auto-regressive integrated moving average (ARIMA) and another statistical model, generalized autoregressive conditional heteroskedasticity (GARCH), to forecasting daily crude oil futures prices [15]. Some extensions of GARCH have also been employed in recent years [16–18]. In Lyocsa and Molnar's study, the authors investigated whether the heterogeneous autoregressive (HAR) model can improve the results of forecasting the volatility of crude oil prices by using information from related energy commodity, and the experimental results demonstrated that such information can not improve the volatility forecasting [19]. Lv studied the performance of the HAR model of realized volatility (HAR-RV) for forecasting crude oil futures price volatility [20]. Naser found that the dynamic model averaging (DMA) model showed better performance in forecasting crude oil prices than all the other alternative models, and it could also achieve better results of forecasting spot prices than futures prices [21]. Azevedo and Campos combined ARIMA, exponential smoothing, and dynamic regression to forecast WTI and Brent crude oil spot prices, and the experimental results indicated that the combined model was promising for crude oil price forecasting [22].

The statistical models are usually built on the assumption of linearity and stationarity of the predicted time series. However, most research has shown that crude oil prices are highly nonlinear and nonstationary [8,12,23], so such characteristics limit the accuracy of statistical models for forecasting crude oil prices. To cope with the complex characteristics of crude oil prices, more and more scholars use AI models to forecast crude oil prices. The most popular AI models include artificial neural network (ANN) [12,24–27], support vector regression (SVR) [28,29] and least squares SVR (LSSVR) [2,10,30], sparse Bayesian learning (SBL) [31,32], extreme learning machine (ELM) [23,33,34], extreme gradient boosting (XGBoost) [8], random vector functional link (RVFL) network [11], long short-term memory (LSTM) [35], and so on. Yu et al. used a feed-forward neural network (FNN) to forecast each decomposed component from the raw series of crude oil prices, and then integrated the results of all components as the final forecasting result by an adaptive linear neural network (ALNN) [12]. Xiong et al. also used FNN to conduct multi-step-ahead weekly crude oil spot price forecasting [25]. Barunik and Malinska found that a focused time-delay NN could achieve higher accuracy than the compared models when forecasting monthly crude oil prices [26]. Extensive research has demonstrated that the kernel-based methods, such as SVR, LSSVR and relevance vector machine, are promising for forecasting crude oil prices [2,10,28–30,36]. Very recently, the LSTM, an artificial recurrent NN architecture widely used in deep learning, has been applied to forecasting crude oil prices. Owing to its power in processing sequences of data, the LSTM-based approach has yielded very promising forecasting results [35]. Chiroma et al. presented an extensive review of the research that applied AI-based models to crude oil price forecasting [37].

Due to the nonlinearity and nonstationarity of crude oil price series, statistical models and AI models usually cannot achieve satisfactory results by conducting forecasting with the raw crude oil prices directly. A simple but effective way is to adopt the "divide and conquer" strategy, that is, to decompose the complex signal into several relatively simple components and then extract relevant features or handle each component for further work. Typical applications of such strategy include fault diagnosis [38,39], biosignal analysis [40,41], time series forecasting [42,43], and so on [44–46]. Following this strategy, a "decomposition and ensemble" framework has become very popular in the field of energy forecasting, such as wind speed forecasting [47,48], load forecasting [49–51] and price forecasting [8,11,52,53] in recent years. Ren et al. integrated empirical mode decomposition (EMD) and SVR to forecast wind speed. Specifically, EMD was used to decompose the raw wind speed series into a couple of components (a residue and a few intrinsic mode functions (IMFs)). After that, SVR was used to build an individual forecasting model for each component. At last, the predicted values of all the components were aggregated as the final forecasting result [47]. Similarly, Li et al. utilized an extended EMD, namely, ensemble EMD (EEMD), and random forests (RF) for electricity consumption forecasting [31], and Yang and Wang applied complementary EEMD (CEEMD) and back propagation NN (BPNN) to forecast wind speed [54]. All the research indicates that the approaches following the framework of "decomposition and ensemble" is capable of significantly improving the accuracy of energy forecasting.

Regarding the decomposition methods, although EMD, EEMD and CEEMD have the ability of improving accuracy, they may introduce new noise into the recovered signal and still suffer from the "mode mixing" problem [55,56]. To solve this problem, a complete EEMD with adaptive noise (CEEMDAN) and an improved CEEMDAN (ICEEMDAN) were proposed [57,58]. The existing study has demonstrated the power of CEEMDAN/ICEEMDAN in energy forecasting [8,59]. As far as the forecasting method for each component, so-called individual forecasting, any regression methods can be selected for this purpose in theory. Besides the above-mentioned methods such as SVR, ANN, ELM, LSTM and so on, ridge regression (RR) is a simple but powerful regression for forecasting. Moreover, the accuracy of regression can be further improved by introducing kernels into RR (KRR), and the KRR has been successfully applied in wind speed forecasting [60,61], object tracking [62], and preheat temperature prediction [63]. The basic idea of the kernel trick is to map the features of the low-dimensional space to the high-dimensional space to obtain more representative features. Naik et al. used wavelet kernel RR and low rank multi-kernel RR to forecast the components of wind speed and wind power decomposed by EMD and variational mode decomposition (VMD), respectively [61,64]. The low rank multi-kernel RR in their approach was a simple linear combination by a polynomial kernel and a wavelet kernel, that is to say, the multi-kernel was actually a combination of two simple kernels [64]. The number and type of kernels may limit the performance of the proposed approach. Qian et al. used multi-kernel RR for object tracking, where the final kernel included one linear kernel, five polynomial kernels and five Gaussian kernels, and the parameter of each kernel was specified in advance and the optimization process was only to optimize the weight of each kernel [62]. Regarding multi-kernel learning, an ideal way is to optimize the weights and the parameters of each kernel together. The nature-inspired algorithms, such as particle swarm optimization (PSO) [65–67], differential evolution (DE) [68,69], ant colony optimization [70,71] and so on, can be applied to optimizing both the weights and the parameters of the multi-kernel learning. Among the algorithms, DE has proven to be very powerful for numerical optimization.

Motivated by the potential of ICEEMDAN in signal decomposition, RR in regression and DE in numerical optimization, we proposed a novel approach integrating ICEEMDAN, DE and RR, namely, ICEEMDAN-DE-RR, for crude oil price forecasting in this paper. Specifically, the ICEEMDAN-DE-RR consists of three steps. First, ICEEMDAN is employed to decompose the raw daily crude oil price series into several relatively simple components. Second, we use RR or KRR optimized by DE to forecast each component individually. Finally, the predicted results from each component are aggregated as the final forecasting result.

The main contributions of this paper lie in the following:

(1) We propose a new framework of multiple kernel learning, which simultaneously optimizes the weights and parameters of kernels using nature-inspired optimization.
(2) We forecast crude oil prices by integrating ICEEMDAN, DE and RR, following the "decomposition and ensemble" framework. To the best of our knowledge, it is the first time that this combination is used for forecasting tasks.
(3) The experimental results indicate that the proposed approach is effective for crude oil price forecasting.

It is worth pointing out that although there have existed lots of models following the "decomposition and ensemble" framework for energy forecasting, the proposed models are different from them in several aspects. First, it is an attempt to use RR to forecast crude oil prices for the first time. Existing research focuses on using RR to forecast wind speed, hydrologic time series, real estate appraisal and so on [60,72,73], not including crude oil prices. Second, a new multiple kernel learning framework is proposed using DE to optimize the parameters and/or weight of each base kernel, as well as the regularization item simultaneously. The experimental results demonstrate the effectiveness of the proposed approach. Third, the integration of ICEEMDAN, DE and RR is used to forecast time series for the first time.

The novelty of this paper is three-fold: (1) Based on the power of ICEEMDAN, DE, and RR in signal decomposition, numerical optimization, and regression, respectively, a novel combination of these three methods is proposed for time series forecasting; (2) To improve the representability of kernels, a novel multiple kernel learning framework using DE to simultaneously optimize the weights and parameters of every single kernel is proposed, which can be applied to both classification and regression; (3) The proposed ICEEMDAN-DE-RR approaches are firstly applied to forecasting crude oil prices and the results demonstrate the effectiveness of the approaches.

The remainder of this paper is structured as follows. In Section 2, we briefly introduce ICEEMDAN, DE and RR. Section 3 formulates the proposed ICEEMDAN-DE-RR method in detail. To evaluate the proposed ICEEMDAN-DE-RR, we report and analyze the experimental results in Section 4. Finally, we conclude the paper in Section 5.

2. Methods

2.1. Improved Complete Ensemble Empirical Mode Decomposition with Adaptive Noise (ICEEMDAN)

ICEEMDAN was originated from EMD proposed by Huang et al. [55–58]. EMD is an adaptive method for time-space analysis, which decomposes a raw sequence that is non-linear and non-stationary into several IMFs and one residue. The main steps of EMD are described as follows:

Step 1: Find out all local extrema of the raw data $x(t), t = 1, 2, 3, \cdots, T$;
Step 2: Link all local minima and local maxima to construct the lower envelopes $x_{low}(t)$ and upper envelopes $x_{up}(t)$, respectively;
Step 3: Compute the local mean, i.e., $m(t) = \frac{x_{up}(t) + x_{low}(t)}{2}$;
Step 4: Extract the first IMF and residue by $IMF_1(t) = x(t) - m(t)$ and $R_1(t) = m(t)$, respectively;
Step 5: For $i = 1, 2, 3, \cdots, n$, if find out more than two local extrema of $R_i(t)$, go back to step 2 and get $IMF_{i+1}(t)$ and $R_{i+1}(t)$.

In EMD, it was found that there were similar parts of signals existing at the same corresponding position in different IMFs, which was called mode mixing. Because of it, IMFs have lost their physical meanings [55]. To cope with this issue, Wu and Huang proposed Ensemble EMD (EEMD) by performing EMD many times on the time series with added white noises [56]. The new time series with white noises $x^i(t)$ can be formulated as Equation (1):

$$x^i(t) = x(t) + w^i(t), \qquad (1)$$

where $x(t)$ represents the raw data series and $w^i(t)$ is the i-th white noise, $i = 1, 2, 3, \cdots, n$.

Then, when every $x^i(t)$ is decomposed, we can get the corresponding $IMF_k^i(t)$. To compute the real k-th IMF, $\overline{IMF_k}$, EEMD calculates the average of the $IMF_k^i(t)$, which can remove the effect of the white noises. However, in practice, one of the limitations of EEMD is that the recovered signal will include residual noise. To solve this problem, Torres et al. proposed a new extension of EEMD, termed as CEEMDAN for signal decomposition [57]. For $k = 2, 3, \cdots, K$, the k-th IMF and residue can be computed as Equations (2) and (3):

$$\overline{IMF_k} = 1/I \sum_{i=1}^{I} (E_1(r_{k-1}[t]) + \varepsilon_{k-1} E_1(w^i[t])), \tag{2}$$

$$r_k[t] = r_{k-1}[t] - \overline{IMF_k}, \tag{3}$$

where $E_1(.)$ represents the first IMF decomposed from the series, and ε_i is used to set the signal-to-noise (SNR) at each stage.

In 2014, Colominas et al. found that the IMFs of CEEMDAN contained some residual noise and some "spurious" modes. Thus, they further proposed a method to improve CEEMDAN (ICEEMDAN) [57,58], whose main steps can be described as follows:

Step 1: Add the first IMF of the given white noises to the original series $x(t)$, as shown in following:

$$x^i(t) = x(t) + \beta_0 E_1(w^i(t)), \tag{4}$$

where β_0 is the level of noise.

Step 2: Find out the local means $M(.)$ of $x^i(t)$ and calculate the average of local means to get the following residue:

$$r_1(t) = \frac{1}{N} \sum_{i=1}^{N} M(x^i(t)). \tag{5}$$

Step 3: Then, we can get the first IMF, as shown in Equation (6):

$$IMF_1 = x(t) - r_1(t). \tag{6}$$

Step 4: For $k = 2, 3, \cdots, K$, the residue and the k-th IMF can be computed by Equation (7) and Equation (8):

$$r_k(t) = \frac{1}{N} \sum_{i=1}^{N} M(r_{k-1}(t) + \varepsilon_{k-1} E_k(w^i(t))), \tag{7}$$

$$IMF_k = r_{k-1}[t] - r_k[t], \tag{8}$$

In this paper, the ICEEMDAN is used to decompose the original data series into several IMFs and one residue, standing for local physical features of original signals. The difficult task of forecasting the original signals is now becoming several relatively simple sub-tasks.

2.2. Kernel Ridge Regression (KRR)

Ridge regression (RR) is a typical linear regression that uses a sum-of-squares error function and regularization technique to control the bias variance trade-off, whose purpose is to discover the linear structures hidden in the data [74]. Kernel ridge regression (KRR) is an extension of RR by introducing a kernel function that maps the input data in a low dimensional space to a high one. The kernel function k is defined on an input space $\mathcal{X} \subseteq \mathbb{R}^d$ and is with the formula: $k : \mathcal{X} \times \mathcal{X} \to \mathbb{R}$. The kernel function is actually a feature map from d dimensional space into a high-dimensional Hilbert Space $\mathcal{H}_k$, $\Psi : \mathcal{X} \to \mathcal{H}_k$ such that $k(x_i, x_j) = \langle \Psi(\mathbf{x_i}), \Psi(\mathbf{x_j}) \rangle_{\mathcal{H}_k}$ [75–77]. The most popular kernel functions include:

- Linear kernel: $k_L(x_i, x_j) = x_i^T x_j$.
- Polynomial kernel: $k_P(x_i, x_j) = (a(x_i^T x_j) + b)^c$, where a, b, and c are the coefficient, constant and degree of k_P, respectively..
- Sigmoid kernel: $k_S(x_i, x_j) = \tanh(d(x_i^T x_j) + e)$, where d and e are the coefficient and constant, respectively.
- Radial basis function (RBF) kernel: $k_R(x_i, x_j) = e^{-f\|x_i - x_j\|^2}$, where f is related to the width of the kernel.

With the kernel functions and n data samples $(x_1, y_1), (x_2, y_2), \cdots, (x_n, y_n) \in \mathcal{X} \times \mathcal{Y}$ (y_i is the target value of corresponding x_i, $i = 1, 2, \cdots, n$), we can construct the kernel matrix as Equation (9):

$$\mathbf{K} = \begin{bmatrix} k(\mathbf{x}_1, \mathbf{x}_1) & k(\mathbf{x}_1, \mathbf{x}_2) & \ldots & k(\mathbf{x}_1, \mathbf{x}_n) \\ k(\mathbf{x}_2, \mathbf{x}_1) & k(\mathbf{x}_2, \mathbf{x}_2) & \ldots & k(\mathbf{x}_2, \mathbf{x}_n) \\ \ldots & \ldots & \ldots & \ldots \\ k(\mathbf{x}_n, \mathbf{x}_1) & k(\mathbf{x}_n, \mathbf{x}_2) & \ldots & k(\mathbf{x}_n, \mathbf{x}_n) \end{bmatrix}. \tag{9}$$

Then the KRR problem can be formulated as Equation (10):

$$\min_w \|\mathbf{Y} - \mathbf{K}w\|^2 + \lambda \|w\|^2, \tag{10}$$

where $\mathbf{Y}$ is the target vector of all the n data samples, w is the unknown vector to be found, and $\lambda \geq 0$ is a regularization item to avoid a large range of w. The solution in terms of w can be easily given in a closed-from manner as Equation (11):

$$w = (\mathbf{K} + \lambda \mathbf{I}_n)^{-1} \mathbf{Y}, \tag{11}$$

where $\mathbf{I}_n$ is an $n \times n$ identity matrix with ones on the main diagonal and zeros elsewhere.

Kernel types and parameters are two important factors for KRR. Some existing research used only a single kernel with specified parameters or simple combinations of several kernels with a fixed weight of every kernel in practical problems, limiting the forecasting performance of KRR. To improve the performance, an ideal solution is to adaptively optimize the weight and/or the parameters of each single kernel using some nature-inspired optimization algorithms. In this paper, we use differential evolution (DE) to optimize such weights and/or parameters for kernels.

2.3. Differential Evolution (DE)

Differential evolution (DE) is a member of the family of nature-inspired algorithms, and it has been demonstrated that DE is very powerful in solving various science and engineering problems [68]. The main idea of DE is to optimize a problem by using a few operations to iteratively improve a set of candidate solutions with evaluation criteria. Basically, the evolutionary process of DE consists of four stages/operations: initialization, mutation, crossover, and selection.

2.3.1. Initialization

For a D-dimensional optimization problem, given the population size P, evolutionary generation G, and the lower and upper bounds of each decision variable $X_{min} = [x_{1,min}, x_{2,min}, \cdots, x_{D,min}]$ and $X_{max} = [x_{1,max}, x_{2,max}, \cdots, x_{D,max}]$ respectively, the d-th decision variable of the i-th individual ($i = 1, 2, \cdots, P$) can be initialized as Equation (12):

$$I_{i,d}^1 = x_{d,min} + rand(0,1) \times (x_{d,max} - x_{d,min}), \tag{12}$$

where the "1" at the right-up corner of I represents the current evolutionary generation, and $rand(0,1)$ generates a random real number between 0 and 1.

The initialization produces a population with P individuals/solutions/vectors, and the $d-$th decision variable in each individual is in the range of $[x_{d,min}, x_{d,max}]$.

2.3.2. Mutation

The purpose of mutation is to generate a new vector V_i^g, so-called mutant vector, from several existing vectors/individuals with respect to each vector I_i^g, so-called target vector, in the population of the $g-$th generation. Some popular mutation strategies are shown as follows:

$$V_i^g = I_{r1}^g + F \times (I_{r2}^g - I_{r3}^g), \tag{13}$$

$$V_i^g = I_b^g + F \times (I_{r1}^g - I_{r2}^g), \tag{14}$$

$$V_i^g = I_b^g + F \times (I_{r1}^g - I_{r2}^g) + F \times (I_{r3}^g - I_{r4}^g), \tag{15}$$

$$V_i^g = I_i^g + F \times (I_b^g - I_i^g) + F \times (I_{r1}^g - I_{r2}^g), \tag{16}$$

where $r1 - r4$ are mutually random indices of the individuals, F is a preset parameter for scaling the difference vector, and I_b^g is the best individual at the $g-$th generation.

2.3.3. Crossover

The purpose of crossover is to generate a trial vector $U_i^g = \{U_{i,1}^g, U_{i,2}^g, \cdots, U_{i,D}^g\}$ from the target vector I_i^g and its corresponding mutant vector V_i^g with the following strategy:

$$U_{i,j}^g = \begin{cases} V_{i,j}^g, & \text{if } rand(0,1) \leq Cr \text{ or } j = j_{\text{rand}} \\ I_{i,j}^g, & \text{otherwise} \end{cases}, \tag{17}$$

where Cr is a user-defined crossover rate that satisfies $Cr \in [0,1]$, and j_{rand} is a random integer in $[1, D]$ to ensure that at least one decision variable in V_i^g can be passed to U_i^g directly.

2.3.4. Selection

The selection operation is to select the better vector from the target vector I_i^g and its corresponding trial vector U_i^g for the next generation with evaluation by fitness function f. The selection strategy is mathematically shown in Equation (18):

$$I_i^g = \begin{cases} U_i^g, & \text{if } f\left(U_i^g\right) \leq f\left(I_i^g\right) \\ I_i^g, & \text{otherwise} \end{cases}. \tag{18}$$

3. The Proposed ICEEMDAN-DE-RR Approach

3.1. Ridge Regression by DE

For any types of RR, the regularization item is an important parameter to be optimized. Kernel is a very powerful trick in machine learning, which maps the data that are linearly inseparable in the input space into a higher dimensional space where the mapped data are linearly separable using kernel functions. Regarding kernel Ridge regression (KRR), besides the regularization item in Equation (10), the parameters $a - f$ for the single kernels k_P, k_S and k_R need to be optimized. To further explore the ability of multiple kernel RR (MKRR) for crude oil price forecasting, we build a multiple kernel that consists of one k_L, one k_P, one k_S and n k_Rs, as shown in Equation (19),

$$k_M(x_i, x_j) = w_1 k_L(x_i, x_j) + w_2 k_P(x_i, x_j) + w_3 k_S(x_i, x_j) + \sum_{l=4}^{n+3} w_l k_R(x_i, x_j)$$
$$= w_1 x_i^T x_j + w_2 (a(x_i^T x_j) + b)^c + w_3 \tanh(d(x_i^T x_j) + e) + \sum_{l=4}^{n+3} w_l e^{-f_{l-3}\|x_i - x_j\|^2}, \quad (19)$$

where $w_1, w_2, \cdots, w_{n+3}$ are the weights of each single kernel, and $a - e$ and $f_1 - f_n$ are parameters for each single kernel.

In our approach, we use DE to optimize the regularization item λ in RR, λ and $a - f$ for each single kernel, and λ, weights and $a - e, f_1 - f_n$ for k_M, respectively. The weights for k_M, $w_i (i = 1, 2, \cdots, n-3)$, are generated from $n + 3$ real values $x_j (j = 1, 2, \cdots, n - 3)$ optimized by DE to meet $\sum_{i=1}^{n+3} = 1$ by Equation (20):

$$w_i = \frac{x_i}{\sum_{j=1}^{n+3} x_j}. \quad (20)$$

3.2. The Proposed ICEEMDAN-DE-RR Approach

The proposed ICEEMDAN-DE-RR approach is a typical form of "decomposition and ensemble", which consists of three stages, i.e., decomposition, individual forecasting, and ensemble forecasting, as shown in Figure 1.

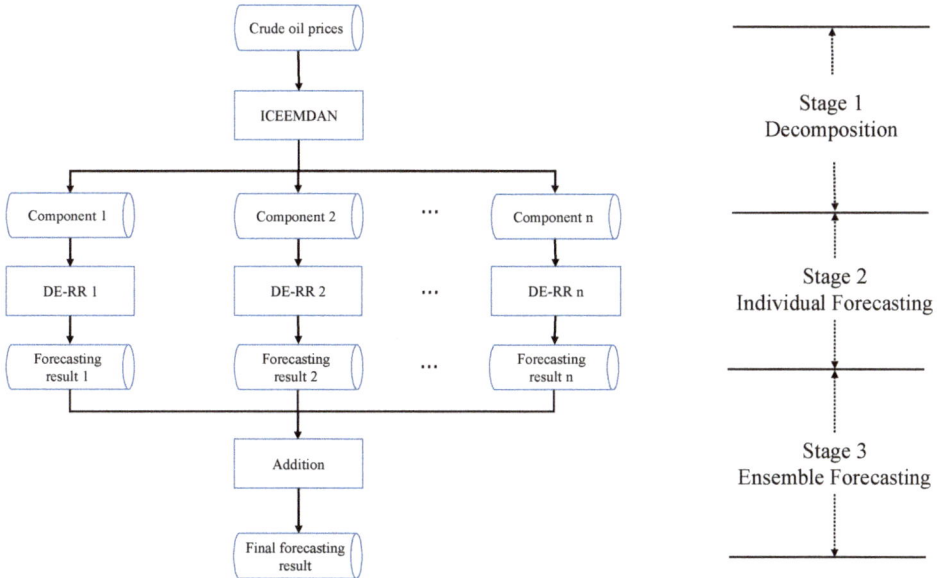

Figure 1. The flowchart of the proposed ICEEMDAN-DE-KRR.

The details of each stage are as follows:

Stage 1: **Decomposition.** The daily raw crude oil price series is decomposed into two groups of components: several IMFs and one residue.

Stage 2: **Individual forecasting.** The data samples in each component are divided into training set, validation set, and test set. The training set and validation set are used to build RR models, and then the test set is applied to evaluate the models. For each model, we use DE to optimize the regularization item, corresponding kernel parameters, and possible weights.

Stage 3: **Ensemble forecasting.** The individual forecasting results of all the components in Stage 2 are aggregated as the final forecasting results by addition.

The proposed ICEEMDAN-DE-RR adopts the typical "divide-and-conquer" strategy, which divides the complexly non-linear and non-stationary crude oil prices into several relatively simple components and then handles each component with a relatively simple DE-based RR predictor. With the strategy, the tough task of forecasting raw crude oil price series becomes several relatively simple sub-tasks of forecasting each component.

It is worth pointing out that although there is a lot of work on energy forecasting following the framework of "decomposition and ensemble", our proposed work is very different from the work in several aspects: (1) RR and KRR are first applied to crude oil forecasting; (2) a novel multiple kernel RR (MKRR) optimized by DE is proposed and it can be applied in other fields; and (3) the ICEEMDAN, DE and RR are integrated to forecast daily crude oil prices for the first time.

4. Experimental Results and Comparative Analysis

4.1. Data Description

To validate the effectiveness of the proposed approach, we select the West Texas Intermediate (WTI) daily crude oil spot closing prices from 2 January 1986 to 4 February 2019 as an experimental dataset. There are 8342 samples in total, and the daily crude oil prices from 2 January 1986 to 14 June 2012, with 6673 samples accounting for 80% of the total samples, are chosen as the training set, while the rest are for testing. Within the training set, 5338 (80%) and 1335 (20%) samples are used for training and validation, respectively.

The WTI daily crude oil spot prices and corresponding decomposed components by ICEEMDAN are shown in Figure 2. We can see that the complex raw crude oil prices are decomposed into two groups: high-frequency group (IMF1-IMF5) and low-frequency group (IMF6-IMF11 and residue). The high-frequency components fluctuate within a narrow range of amplitude while the low-frequency ones fluctuate within a wide range of amplitude, making forecasting crude oil prices with the components easier than with the raw crude oil prices.

We conduct several types of multi-step-ahead forecasting with a lag of L in the experiments. A type of m-step-ahead prediction means forecasting the crude oil prices on the $(t+m)$-th day with the L price samples before the t-th day but including the t-th day.

For a fair comparison, each decomposed component is scaled to $[0,1]$ using the min-max normalization, as formulated by Equation (21).

$$x'_t = \frac{x_t - x_{min}}{x_{max} - x_{min}}, \qquad (21)$$

where x_t and x'_t are crude oil price series before and after normalization respectively, and x_{max} and x_{min} are the maximum value and the minimum value of the time series, respectively.

4.2. Evaluation Criteria

We use a set of criteria to evaluate the proposed approach as well as the compared models. Specifically, the selected criteria include the mean absolute percent error (MAPE), the root-mean-square error (RMSE), and the directional statistic (Dstat). The MAPE, RMSE and Dstat are defined as Equations (22)–(24):

$$MAPE = \frac{1}{N}\sum_{i=1}^{N}|\frac{y_t - \hat{y}_t}{y_t}|, \qquad (22)$$

$$RMSE = \sqrt{\frac{1}{N}\sum_{i=1}^{N}(y_t - \hat{y}_t)^2}, \qquad (23)$$

$$Dstat = \frac{1}{N}\sum_{i=1}^{N} d_i \times 100\%, \qquad (24)$$

where y_t and $\hat{y}_t$ are the actual and predicted values at time t respectively, N is the size of the prediction, and $d_i = 1$ if $(\hat{y}_{t+1} - y_t)(y_{t+1} - y_t) \geq 0$; otherwise $d_i = 0$. The smaller the values of MAPE and RMSE, the better the model. In contrast, a higher Dstat means a better forecasting model.

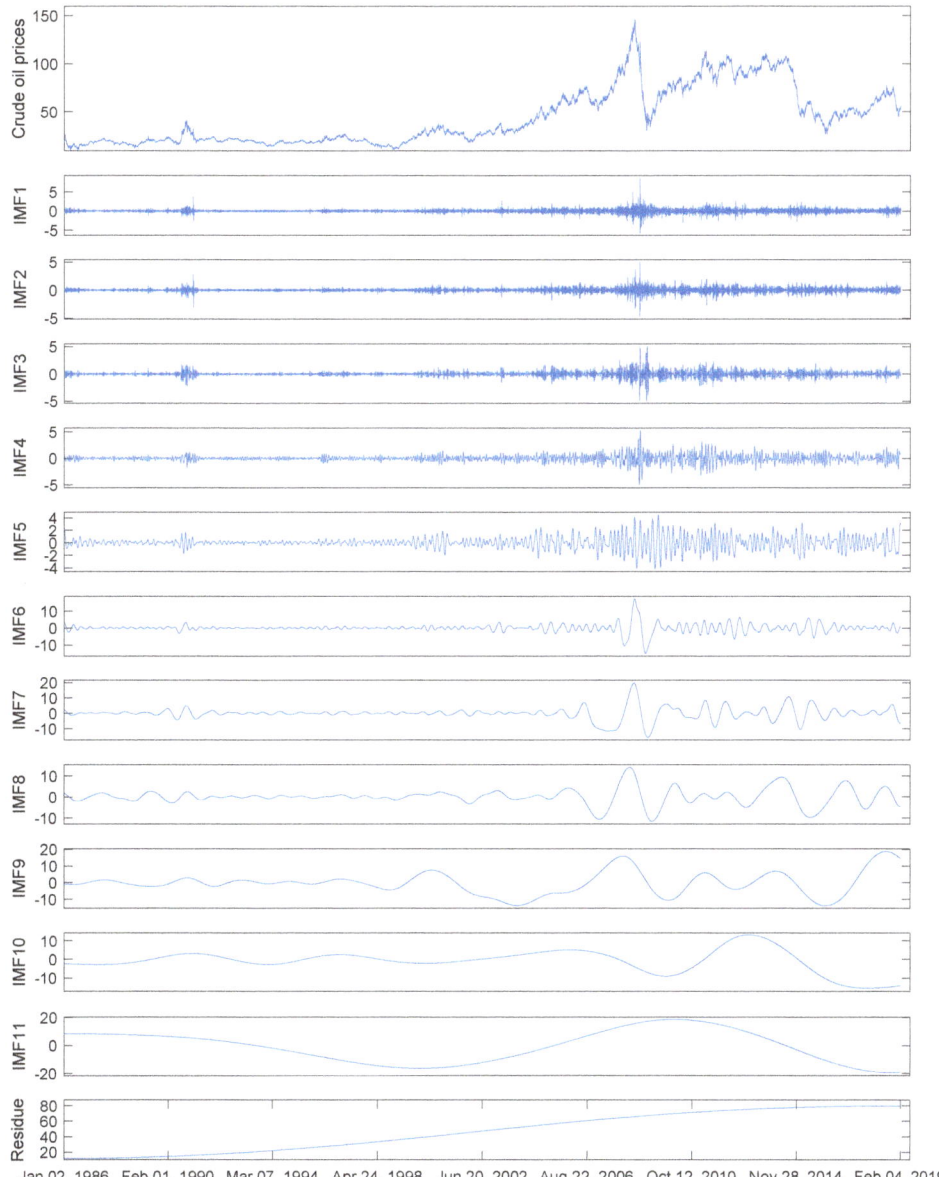

Figure 2. The daily WTI crude oil prices and the corresponding decomposed components by ICEEMDAN.

Besides, we take the Diebold–Mariano (DM) test to compare the statistic difference of the accuracy of prediction between pairs of models. At first, we compute the difference of the prediction of pairs of models at time t as Equation (25):

$$d_t = \sum_{t=1}^{N}(y_t - \hat{y_{t,a}})^2 - \sum_{t=1}^{N}(y_t - \hat{y_{t,b}})^2, \qquad (25)$$

where $\hat{y_{t,a}}$ is the prediction of model a at time t and $\hat{y_{t,b}}$ is the prediction of model b at time t. Then, the DM statistic can be defined as Equation (26):

$$DM = \frac{\bar{d}}{\sqrt{V_d/N}}, \qquad (26)$$

where

$$\bar{d} = \frac{1}{N}\sum_{t=1}^{N}d_t, \qquad (27)$$

$$V_d = cov(d_t, d_t) + 2\sum_{l=1}^{\infty}cov(d_t, d_{t-l}), \qquad (28)$$

where cov is a covariance matrix.

If the value of the DM test is negative and statistically significant (e.g., p-value ≤ 0.05), it is proven that there is a significant difference between the predictive accuracy of pairs of models [78].

4.3. Experimental Settings

We forecast daily crude oil prices from the raw price series and decomposed components, so-called single models and ensemble models, respectively. As for single models, we compare the RR-based methods (RR, LinRR, PolyRR, SigRR, RbfRR and MKRR in Table 1) with two state-of-the-art AI models: LSSVR and BPNN, as well as two classical statistical methods: ARIMA and RW. Regarding ensemble models, we compare ICEEMDAN with EEMD to show the power of decomposition, and all the forecasting methods with single models except for ARIMA are applied to ensemble models. The parameters in the experiments are shown in detail in Table 1. Note that for the MKRR, we use 23 single kernels, i.e., one linear kernel, one polynomial kernel, one Sigmoid kernel and 20 RBF kernels, to build the multiple kernel, and both the weight and parameters of each single kernel are optimized by DE. The values or the ranges of some parameters are from existing literature [8,31]. In addition, we use RMSE as the fitness function to evaluate the individuals in DE.

All the experiments were performed by Matlab R2016b on a PC with 64-bit Windows 10, a 3.6 GHz i7 CPU and 32 GB RAM.

4.4. Results and Analysis

4.4.1. Single Models

The single models are performed on the raw daily crude oil prices directly. We compared the RR-based methods with LSSVR, BPNN and ARIMA. The experimental results are reported in Table 2, with the best and the worst results being shown in bold and underline, respectively, in terms of each criterion with each horizon.

Table 1. The settings for the parameters.

Method	Description	Parameters
EEMD	Ensemble empirical mode decomposition	Noise standard deviation: 0.2; Number of realizations: 100.
ICEEMDAN	Improved complete EEMD with adaptive noise	Noise standard deviation: 0.05; Number of realizations: 500; Maximum number of sifting iterations allowed: 5000.
RR	Ridge Regression	λ: [0.001, 0.2].
LinRR	RR with a linear kernel	λ: [0.001, 0.2].
PolyRR	RR with a polynomial kernel	λ: [0.001, 0.2]; a: [0, 2]; b: [0, 10]; c: {1,2,3,4}
SigRR	RR with a Sigmoid kernel	λ: [0.001, 0.2]; d: [0, 4]; e: [0, 8].
RbfRR	RR with a radial basis functional kernel	λ: [0.001, 0.2]; f: $[2^{-10}, 2^{12}]$.
MKRR	RR with multiple kernels as formulated in Equation (19)	λ: [0.001, 0.2]; $a - e$: the same as the above single kernel; n: 20, number of the RBF kernels; $f_1 - f_{20}$: $[2^{-10}, 2^{12}]$; $w_1 - w_{23}$: [0, 1] s.t. $\sum_{i=1}^{23} w_i = 1$.
LSSVR	Least square support vector regression with a RBF kernel	Regularization parameter: $2^{\{-10,-9,\cdots,11,12\}}$; Width of the RBF kernel: $2^{\{-10,-9,\cdots,11,12\}}$.
BPNN	Back propagation neural network	Size of the hidden layer: {10, 20, 50, 100}; Maximum training epochs: {100, 1000, 10000}; Learning rate: {0.001, 0.01, 0.05, 0.1}.
ARIMA	Autoregressive integrated moving average	Akaike information criterion (AIC) to determine parameters (p-d-q) [79].
DE	Differential Evolution	Population size: 20; Number of iterations: 40; Crossover probability: 0.2.

Table 2. Results of single models.

Horizon	Criterion	RR	LinRR	PolyRR	SigRR	RbfRR	MKRR	LSSVR	BPNN	ARIMA	RW
1	MAPE	0.0154	0.0154	0.0154	0.0154	0.0156	0.0154	0.0154	0.0161	0.0157	0.0156
	RMSE	**1.2454**	1.2462	1.2473	1.2483	1.2567	1.2472	1.2481	1.3050	1.2701	1.2700
	Dstat	0.5000	0.4940	0.5132	0.5156	**0.5186**	0.5162	0.5102	0.5132	0.4868	0.5054
3	MAPE	**0.0262**	0.0263	0.0264	0.0264	0.0265	0.0263	0.0266	0.0264	0.0274	0.0272
	RMSE	**2.0627**	2.0689	2.0708	2.0701	2.0754	2.0767	2.0801	2.0797	2.1713	2.1645
	Dstat	0.4988	0.4988	0.4964	0.4958	0.5000	**0.5090**	0.4952	0.4994	0.4982	0.4952
6	MAPE	**0.0377**	0.0379	0.0381	0.0381	0.0381	0.0380	0.0379	0.0394	0.0408	0.0401
	RMSE	**2.8977**	2.9101	2.9209	2.9208	2.9239	2.9149	2.9128	2.9943	3.1824	3.1195
	Dstat	0.4952	0.4958	0.4862	0.4898	0.4922	0.4964	0.4910	**0.4976**	0.4916	0.4928

From the table, we can find that the AI models outperform the statistical models in 6 out of 9 cases. Among the AI models, BPNN obtains two worst results: the MAPE value of 0.0161 as well as the RMSE value of 1.3050 with Horizon 1, while LSSVR and PolyRR obtain the worst values once: the Dstat value of 0.4592 and 0.4862 with Horizon 3 and 6, respectively. Overall, the RR-based single models outperform other models in most cases. In particular, RR achieves the best results in 6 out of 9 cases, showing that it is superior to other single models. Regarding the statistical models, RW is very close to but slightly better than ARIMA. In terms of MAPE and RMSE, for each model, the results become worse and worse when the horizon increases.

Regarding directional statistics, RbfRR, MKRR and BPNN achieve the highest values of 0.5186, 0.5090 and 0.4976 with Horizon 1, 3, and 6, respectively. In contrast, ARIMA and PolyRR obtain the worst values of 0.4868 and 0.4862 with Horizon 1 and 6, respectively. For Horizon 3, both LSSVR and RW obtain the worst Dstat values of 0.4952. The intervals of the best values and the corresponding worst values are so narrow that all the results of all cases are around 0.5, just like the result of random guessing, showing that it is a tough task to forecast the direction using single models.

To further compare the single models, we report the DM test results in Table 3, with the statistics and the corresponding p-values (in brackets). From this table, we have some findings. First, compared with the statistical model ARIMA and RW, the statistics of all the AI models in all cases except for BPNN with Horizon 1 are far below -2.000 and the corresponding p-values are much less than 0.01, indicating that the AI models significantly outperform ARIMA and RW. ARIMA and RW have very similar results. Second, LSSVM and BPNN underperform RR-based approaches in most cases, showing that the RR-based predictors are more effective than the statistical AI models (LSSVM and BPNN) for forecasting raw crude oil prices, to some extent. Third, as for RR-based models, the RR, PolyRR and MKRR have very close performance, which are superior to LinRR, SigRR and RbfRR. All the findings confirm the analysis on MAPE, RMSE and Dstat.

Table 3. The Diebold-Mariano (DM) test results of single models.

Horizon	Tested Model	LinRR	PolyRR	SigRR	RbfRR	MKRR	LSSVR	BPNN	ARIMA	RW
1	RR	−1.1025 (0.2704)	−0.7203 (0.4714)	−1.5290 (0.1265)	−2.0533 (0.0402)	−0.6405 (0.5219)	−1.3788 (0.1681)	−5.5601 (0.0000)	−3.4678 (0.0005)	−3.4585 (0.0004)
	LinRR		−0.4701 (0.6383)	−1.3435 (0.1793)	−1.6807 (0.0930)	−0.3852 (0.7001)	−1.3221 (0.1863)	−5.6817 (0.0000)	−3.3577 (0.0008)	−3.2647 (0.0007)
	PolyRR			−0.4864 (0.6268)	−1.3044 (0.1923)	0.2103 (0.8334)	−0.4205 (0.6742)	−5.7019 (0.0000)	−2.8226 (0.0048)	−2.7642 (0.0000)
	SigRR				−1.2372 (0.2162)	0.5057 (0.6132)	0.1453 (0.8845)	−5.7208 (0.0000)	−2.8937 (0.0039)	−2.3072 (0.0002)
	RbfRR					1.3294 (0.1839)	1.2083 (0.2271)	−3.4277 (0.0006)	−1.3067 (0.1915)	−1.2796 (0.0142)
	MKRR						−0.4335 (0.6647)	−5.7099 (0.0000)	−2.8012 (0.0052)	−2.7326 (0.0312)
	LSSVR							−5.8110 (0.0000)	−2.8584 (0.0043)	−2.6057 (0.0147)
	BPNN								2.6579 (0.0079)	2.1439 (0.0001)
	ARIMA									0.0996 (0.1206)
3	RR	−2.4997 (0.0125)	−1.6877 (0.0916)	−2.0321 (0.0423)	−2.8803 (0.0040)	−2.3015 (0.0215)	−3.2386 (0.0012)	−2.7039 (0.0069)	−5.6427 (0.0000)	−4.9664 (0.0000)
	LinRR		−0.2930 (0.7696)	−0.2368 (0.8129)	−2.0401 (0.0415)	−1.0401 (0.2984)	−2.9172 (0.0036)	−1.3601 (0.1740)	−5.1351 (0.0000)	−5.1652 (0.0000)
	PolyRR			0.1966 (0.8442)	−0.6415 (0.5213)	−1.6590 (0.0973)	−1.1121 (0.2662)	−2.1367 (0.0328)	−4.6340 (0.0000)	−4.9189 (0.0000)
	SigRR				−1.0601 (0.2893)	−1.6399 (0.1012)	−1.6464 (0.0999)	−1.8857 (0.0595)	−4.8619 (0.0000)	−4.6375 (0.0000)
	RbfRR					−0.1690 (0.8658)	−3.6421 (0.0003)	−0.5004 (0.6169)	−4.4865 (0.0000)	−4.4237 (0.0000)
	MKRR						−0.4004 (0.6889)	−0.5933 (0.5530)	−4.3286 (0.0000)	−3.3925 (0.0000)
	LSSVR							0.0403 (0.9679)	−4.2520 (0.0000)	−3.8976 (0.0000)
	BPNN								−4.4861 (0.0000)	−4.3547 (0.0001)
	ARIMA									0.7708 (0.1300)
6	RR	−2.6901 (0.0072)	−3.0491 (0.0023)	−3.1495 (0.0017)	−3.2282 (0.0013)	−1.4575 (0.1452)	−2.4926 (0.0128)	−5.1039 (0.0000)	−7.6069 (0.0000)	−7.9403 (0.0000)
	LinRR		−1.3345 (0.1822)	−1.2552 (0.2096)	−2.1339 (0.0330)	−0.3964 (0.6919)	−0.3807 (0.7035)	−4.2189 (0.0000)	−7.0961 (0.0000)	−6.8125 (0.0000)
	PolyRR			0.0718 (0.9428)	−0.6199 (0.5354)	0.6465 (0.5180)	2.4994 (0.0125)	−4.9939 (0.0000)	−6.4072 (0.0000)	−6.0013 (0.0000)
	SigRR				−0.5182 (0.6044)	0.6242 (0.5326)	2.2295 (0.0259)	−5.2852 (0.0000)	−6.3341 (0.0000)	−6.1752 (0.0000)
	RbfRR					0.8653 (0.3870)	2.6871 (0.0073)	−4.0728 (0.0000)	−6.3042 (0.0000)	−6.4841 (0.0000)
	MKRR						0.2139 (0.8307)	−4.9976 (0.0000)	−6.4398 (0.0000)	−5.8925 (0.0000)
	LSSVR							−5.0705 (0.0000)	−6.6890 (0.0000)	−6.5482 (0.0001)
	BPNN								−4.0592 (0.0001)	−3.7692 (0.0002)
	ARIMA									0.7134 (0.2304)

Due to the nonlinearity and nonstationarity, the performance of directly forecasting on raw crude oil price series needs to be improved. To cope with this issue, we use ICEEMDAN to decompose the raw series into several components each of which shows relatively simple characteristics when compared with the raw series, and then each component is predicted using an AI model individually. At last, the predicted results of all components are aggregated as the final result.

4.4.2. Ensemble Models

To demonstrate the effectiveness of ICEEMDAN, we also use EEMD as one of the decomposition methods for comparison. For the forecasting methods, we compare RR-base predictors with two state-of-the-art AI methods: LSSVR and BPNN. The values of MAPE, RMSE and Dstat with ensemble models are shown in Table 4.

Table 4. Results of ensemble models.

Decomposition	Horizon	Criterion	RR	LinRR	PolyRR	SigRR	RbfRR	MKRR	LSSVR	BPNN	RW
EEMD	1	MAPE	**0.0084**	0.0089	**0.0084**	**0.0084**	0.0088	0.0085	0.0090	0.0200	0.0186
		RMSE	0.6401	0.6827	**0.6399**	**0.6399**	0.6799	0.6467	0.6805	1.6044	1.7455
		Dstat	0.8213	0.8112	**0.8231**	0.8189	0.7980	0.8135	0.8076	0.7344	0.5084
	3	MAPE	**0.0096**	0.0111	0.0097	0.0097	0.0107	0.0100	0.0118	0.0195	0.0296
		RMSE	0.7569	0.8702	0.7583	**0.7560**	0.8410	0.7803	0.9406	1.5599	2.5344
		Dstat	0.7746	0.7314	0.7728	**0.7794**	0.7500	0.7710	0.7272	0.6847	0.5000
	6	MAPE	**0.0120**	0.0146	0.0121	0.0122	0.0147	0.0122	0.0126	0.0210	0.0396
		RMSE	**0.9440**	1.1602	0.9547	0.9704	1.1560	0.9666	0.9896	1.6297	3.1068
		Dstat	0.7146	0.6607	0.7140	0.7002	0.6625	**0.7290**	0.6924	0.6265	0.4976
ICEEMDAN	1	MAPE	**0.0043**	0.0050	**0.0043**	**0.0043**	0.0048	**0.0043**	0.0044	0.0051	0.0175
		RMSE	0.3458	0.4039	0.3469	**0.3441**	0.3901	0.3505	0.3528	0.3964	1.6209
		Dstat	0.9101	0.8939	0.9101	**0.9113**	0.8975	0.9083	0.9071	0.8945	0.5228
	3	MAPE	**0.0073**	0.0089	0.0074	0.0076	0.0087	0.0074	0.0075	0.0092	0.0286
		RMSE	**0.5926**	0.7170	0.5953	0.6067	0.7001	0.5984	0.6044	0.7022	2.4296
		Dstat	**0.8453**	0.8040	0.8399	0.8417	0.8124	0.8393	0.8333	0.8100	0.4862
	6	MAPE	**0.0102**	0.0138	**0.0102**	0.0107	0.0130	0.0103	0.0104	0.0187	0.0400
		RMSE	**0.8027**	1.0977	0.8100	0.8513	1.0276	0.8137	0.8236	1.3531	3.1926
		Dstat	0.7590	0.6661	0.7584	0.7530	0.6847	**0.7626**	0.7578	0.6865	0.4982

As far as MAPE and RMSE with EEMD are concerned, the results of different forecasting models except for BPNN and RW are significantly superior to those of the corresponding single models. For example, the best (lowest) MAPE, and RMSE with Horizon 1 are improved from 0.0154 to 0.0084, and from 1.2454 to 0.6399, respectively. Regarding Dstat, the best/worst value except those by RW is 0.8231/0.7344, which is far greater than the values of single models. Among the forecasting methods, RR-based predictors achieve all the best values while BPNN and RW obtain all the worst results. Specifically, RR, SigRR and PolyRR achieve the best values 4, 4 and 3 out of 9 times, respectively. Except for the values of MAPE and RMSE with Horizon 1, the ensemble models by BPNN are advantageous over single BPNN. Another finding is that RW obtains the worst values 8 out of 9 times. In particular, the Dstat values by RW are always around 0.5, and the possible reason is that RW performs poorly in forecasting high-frequency components. The experimental results indicate that the ensemble models except for RW can significantly improve the forecasting effectiveness when compared with the single models.

When we look at the results with ICEEMDAN and AI models in Table 4, we can see a significant improvement in the forecasting ability. As for MAPE, the value of each model with ICEEMDAN is superior to that of its competitor with EEMD. Specifically, RR achieves the best (lowest) MAPE for all the horizons, while BPNN obtains the worst values for the same horizons. For Horizon 1, PolyRR, SigRR and MKRR also achieve the best MAPE (0.0043) as RR does. The results of RMSE show similar characteristics that all the models with ICEEMDAN exceed those with EEMD. The best values of RMSE with Horizon 1, 3, and 6 are achieved by SigRR, RR, and RR, respectively. In contrast, LinRR, LinRR and BPNN obtain the worst RMSEs with Horizon 1, 3 and 6, respectively. It is worth pointing out that the directional statistics is significantly improved by ICEEMDAN. The best Dstat (0.9113) is achieved by SigRR with Horizon 1, and the other models achieve very close Dstat, indicating that this metric is very stable with ICEEMDAN. The worst (lowest) value of Dstat is 0.6661, which is much higher than the best one by single models (0.5186). Therefore, the models with ICEEMDAN and AI models are able to effectively improve the results of directional statistics. Regarding the results with ICEEMDAN and RW models, they still perform poorly and obtain the nine worst values, although RW models with ICEEMDAN perform slightly better than those with EEMD for Horizon 1 and 2.

For the models with both EEMD and ICEEMDAN, most results of MAPE, RMSE and Dstat will become worse when the horizon increases, showing that it is more difficult to forecast crude oil prices with a long horizon than with a short one.

We still apply the DM test to compare the ensemble models, and the results are shown in Table 5. From this table, we can see that when the forecasting methods with ICEEMDAN are compared with those with EEMD, the statistical values are far below zero and the p-value is very close to zero (usually less than 0.0001) with Horizon 1 and 3, indicating that the former significantly outperforms the latter with these two horizons. Regarding Horizon 6, the forecasting methods, except for BPNN with ICEEMDAN, still outperform the corresponding methods with EEMD. For each decomposition, the RR-based methods are usually superior to LSSVR and BPNN. Among the RR-based predictors, RR and SigRR have the best forecasting ability, followed by MKRR and PolyRR, while RbfRR and LinRR have a slightly worse predictive power. In addition, the models with AI are all superior to the corresponding models with RW, showing that the forecasting effectiveness does not stem from luck but by the forecasting superiority of the proposed approaches. All the DM test results confirm that ICEEMDAN and RR-based predictors are very effective for forecasting daily crude oil prices. The proposed approach that integrates ICEEMDAN and RR is capable of improving the results of crude oil price forecasting.

4.5. Discussion

In this subsection, we will discuss the impact of the parameter settings of the ICEEMDAN, the impact of the lag orders and the result of each individual component. Since the above results and analysis have shown that RR and SigRR usually outperform the other models, we will take both RR and SigRR as examples to discuss the following.

4.5.1. The Impact of the Parameter Settings of the ICEEMDAN

When we use the ICEEMDAN to decompose the daily crude oil price series, we need to add noises to the series and decompose the series many times. Therefore, the noise standard deviation *nsd* and the number of realizations *nr* are two important parameters. To study the impact of *nsd* on forecasting, we run the proposed approach with a variable *nsd* in the range of {0.01, 0.03, 0.05, 0.08, 0.1, 0.15, 0.2, 0.3, 0.4} while fixing other parameters. The experimental results are shown in Figure 3. Likewise, we use a variable *nr* in the range of {20, 50, 100, 200, 300, 500, 800, 1000, 1500, 2000} and fixed other parameters to study the impact of the number of realizations, as shown in Figure 4.

Table 5. The Diebold-Mariano (DM) test results of ensemble models.

Horizon	Decomposition	Tested Model	ICEEMDAN									EEMD								
			LinRR	PolyRR	SigRR	RbfRR	MKRR	LSSVR	BPNN	RW	RR	LinRR	PolyRR	SigRR	RbfRR	MKRR	LSSVR	BPNN	RW
1	ICEEMDAN	RR	−7.6331 (0.0000)	−0.6142 (0.5392)	0.9695 (0.3324)	−7.5172 (0.0000)	−1.9834 (0.0475)	−3.3554 (0.0004)	−12.8611 (0.0000)	−5.5386 (0.0000)	−21.3654 (0.0000)	−22.2857 (0.0000)	−21.2054 (0.0000)	−21.2416 (0.0000)	−21.3583 (0.0000)	−20.9534 (0.0000)	−22.0337 (0.0000)	−16.7261 (0.0000)	−4.0125 (0.0001)
		LinRR		8.0753 (0.0000)	7.8183 (0.0000)	1.8874 (0.0593)	6.9073 (0.0000)	6.8284 (0.0000)	0.9153 (0.3602)	−5.4460 (0.0000)	−17.1007 (0.0000)	−19.9938 (0.0000)	−17.0228 (0.0000)	−17.1490 (0.0000)	−18.1073 (0.0000)	−17.0138 (0.0000)	−18.4270 (0.0000)	−16.4052 (0.0000)	−3.9545 (0.0001)
		PolyRR			2.1682 (0.0303)	−7.7155 (0.0000)	−1.7738 (0.0763)	−3.6728 (0.0002)	−12.0394 (0.0000)	−5.5375 (0.0000)	−21.3854 (0.0000)	−22.4548 (0.0000)	−21.3348 (0.0000)	−21.3959 (0.0000)	−21.4127 (0.0000)	−21.0541 (0.0000)	−22.1490 (0.0000)	−16.7245 (0.0000)	−4.0116 (0.0001)
		SigRR				−8.3841 (0.0000)	−2.7328 (0.0063)	−5.2931 (0.0000)	−12.1439 (0.0000)	−5.5416 (0.0000)	−21.3483 (0.0000)	−22.3840 (0.0000)	−21.2987 (0.0000)	−21.3724 (0.0000)	−21.5018 (0.0000)	−21.0097 (0.0000)	−22.1334 (0.0000)	−16.7370 (0.0000)	−4.0142 (0.0001)
		RbfRR					6.1499 (0.0000)	6.7789 (0.0000)	−0.8816 (0.3781)	−5.4706 (0.0000)	−18.2902 (0.0000)	−20.4238 (0.0000)	−18.2305 (0.0000)	−18.4002 (0.0000)	−20.0042 (0.0000)	−18.1252 (0.0000)	−19.5005 (0.0000)	−16.5070 (0.0000)	−3.9687 (0.0001)
		MKRR						−0.7986 (0.4246)	−11.7816 (0.0000)	−5.5313 (0.0000)	−21.1164 (0.0000)	−22.0611 (0.0000)	−21.0784 (0.0000)	−21.0921 (0.0000)	−20.9704 (0.0000)	−20.7933 (0.0000)	−21.8257 (0.0000)	−16.7113 (0.0000)	−4.0080 (0.0001)
		LSSVR							−10.4989 (0.0000)	−5.5281 (0.0000)	−20.9187 (0.0000)	−22.0006 (0.0000)	−20.8537 (0.0000)	−20.9486 (0.0000)	−21.1186 (0.0000)	−20.6389 (0.0000)	−21.8183 (0.0000)	−16.6977 (0.0000)	−4.0058 (0.0001)
		BPNN								−5.4562 (0.0000)	−17.9970 (0.0000)	−19.3554 (0.0000)	−17.9211 (0.0000)	−17.9391 (0.0000)	−18.2960 (0.0000)	−17.8094 (0.0000)	−19.1642 (0.0000)	−16.4971 (0.0000)	−3.9608 (0.0001)
		RW									4.8947 (0.0000)	4.7746 (0.0000)	4.8956 (0.0000)	4.8959 (0.0000)	4.7796 (0.0000)	4.8761 (0.0000)	4.7762 (0.0000)	0.1120 (0.9109)	−0.4916 (0.6231)
	EEMD	RR										−5.9878 (0.0000)	0.0981 (0.9218)	0.0921 (0.9266)	−5.8039 (0.0000)	−1.9935 (0.0464)	−7.2864 (0.0000)	−14.8109 (0.0000)	−3.6137 (0.0003)
		LinRR											5.8354 (0.0000)	6.0493 (0.0000)	0.3207 (0.7485)	4.6149 (0.0000)	0.2467 (0.8052)	−14.3910 (0.0000)	−3.5387 (0.0004)
		PolyRR												0.0195 (0.9844)	−5.7741 (0.0000)	−2.2603 (0.0239)	−7.7598 (0.0000)	−14.8346 (0.0000)	−3.6141 (0.0003)
		SigRR													−5.8048 (0.0000)	−2.4071 (0.0162)	−8.0538 (0.0000)	−14.8512 (0.0000)	−3.6144 (0.0003)
		RbfRR														4.6221 (0.0000)	−0.1080 (0.9140)	−14.4850 (0.0000)	−3.5431 (0.0004)
		MKRR															−7.2584 (0.0000)	−14.8197 (0.0000)	−3.6027 (0.0003)
		LSSVR																−14.5725 (0.0000)	−3.5415 (0.0004)
		BPNN																	−0.6384 (0.5233)

Table 5. Cont.

Horizon	Decomposition	Tested Model	ICEEMDAN								EEMD							
			LinRR	PolyRR	SigRR	RbfRR	MKRR	LSSVR	BPNN	RW	RR	LinRR	PolyRR	SigRR	RbfRR	MKRR	LSSVR	BPNN	RW
3	ICEEMDAN	RR	−9.9325 (0.0000)	−1.4417 (0.1496)	−3.7747 (0.0002)	−9.4380 (0.0000)	−2.4333 (0.0151)	−4.2254 (0.0000)	−13.4240 (0.0000)	−8.2617 (0.0000)	−12.9322 (0.0000)	−15.5357 (0.0000)	−13.0108 (0.0000)	−12.8337 (0.0000)	−14.9758 (0.0000)	−13.9333 (0.0000)	−16.8289 (0.0000)	−14.1737 (0.0000)	−8.1352 (0.0000)
		LinRR		10.0119 (0.0000)	9.7840 (0.0000)	1.8443 (0.0653)	9.5078 (0.0000)	9.0895 (0.0000)	1.0852 (0.2780)	−8.0440 (0.0000)	−2.6337 (0.0085)	−12.5877 (0.0000)	−2.7454 (0.0061)	−2.6451 (0.0082)	−8.2937 (0.0000)	−4.0327 (0.0001)	−10.8639 (0.0000)	−13.0047 (0.0000)	−7.9386 (0.0000)
		PolyRR			−4.4570 (0.0000)	−9.4540 (0.0000)	−1.1594 (0.2465)	−3.0217 (0.0026)	−13.1060 (0.0000)	−8.2580 (0.0000)	−12.5752 (0.0000)	−15.5953 (0.0000)	−12.7567 (0.0000)	−12.6621 (0.0000)	−14.8334 (0.0000)	−13.6041 (0.0000)	−16.7324 (0.0000)	−14.1551 (0.0000)	−8.1320 (0.0000)
		SigRR				−9.3379 (0.0000)	1.9688 (0.0491)	0.5195 (0.6035)	−10.9649 (0.0000)	−8.2399 (0.0000)	−11.3756 (0.0000)	−15.2838 (0.0000)	−11.5825 (0.0000)	−11.6158 (0.0000)	−14.3842 (0.0000)	−12.4692 (0.0000)	−16.2315 (0.0000)	−14.0525 (0.0000)	−8.1157 (0.0000)
		RbfRR					8.7712 (0.0000)	8.8140 (0.0000)	−0.1757 (0.8605)	−8.0736 (0.0000)	−3.7902 (0.0002)	−11.6173 (0.0000)	−3.9565 (0.0001)	−3.9195 (0.0001)	−11.1253 (0.0000)	−5.2578 (0.0000)	−11.7123 (0.0000)	−13.2845 (0.0000)	−7.9644 (0.0000)
		MKRR						−1.6406 (0.1011)	−12.7449 (0.0000)	−8.2505 (0.0000)	−12.6415 (0.0000)	−15.4153 (0.0000)	−12.7391 (0.0000)	−12.5443 (0.0000)	−14.6474 (0.0000)	−13.6362 (0.0000)	−16.5479 (0.0000)	−14.1136 (0.0000)	−8.1265 (0.0000)
		LSSVR							−13.4650 (0.0000)	−8.2427 (0.0000)	−11.9772 (0.0000)	−14.9897 (0.0000)	−12.1661 (0.0000)	−12.0859 (0.0000)	−14.6889 (0.0000)	−13.4358 (0.0000)	−16.4904 (0.0000)	−14.0859 (0.0000)	−8.1157 (0.0000)
		BPNN								−8.0500 (0.0000)	−3.9068 (0.0001)	−9.2782 (0.0000)	−4.1170 (0.0000)	−3.9602 (0.0001)	−8.0800 (0.0000)	−5.6840 (0.0000)	−11.3597 (0.0000)	−13.3170 (0.0000)	−7.9423 (0.0000)
		RW									7.9299 (0.0000)	7.7031 (0.0000)	7.9259 (0.0000)	7.9322 (0.0000)	7.7496 (0.0000)	7.8725 (0.0000)	7.4621 (0.0000)	5.0472 (0.0000)	−0.5382 (0.5905)
	EEMD	RR										−8.0803 (0.0000)	−0.6800 (0.4966)	0.2481 (0.8041)	−7.6514 (0.0000)	−4.8069 (0.0000)	−12.0032 (0.0000)	−12.7901 (0.0000)	−7.8385 (0.0000)
		LinRR											7.9869 (0.0000)	8.2376 (0.0000)	2.2903 (0.0221)	−7.659 (0.0002)	5.9929 (0.0000)	−3.7962 (0.0002)	−11.4198 (0.0000)	−7.6264 (0.0000)
		PolyRR												1.1239 (0.2612)	−7.659 (0.0000)		−4.7817 (0.0000)	−11.8134 (0.0000)	−12.8335 (0.0000)	−7.8359 (0.0000)
		SigRR													−8.2380 (0.0000)		−4.8751 (0.0000)	−12.0577 (0.0000)	−12.8268 (0.0000)	−7.8411 (0.0000)
		RbfRR															5.3608 (0.0000)	−7.2419 (0.0000)	−11.9950 (0.0000)	−7.6714 (0.0000)
		MKRR																−10.3296 (0.0000)	−12.6636 (0.0000)	−7.7891 (0.0000)
		LSSVR																	−10.7944 (0.0000)	−7.4217 (0.0000)
		BPNN																		−5.2626 (0.0000)

Table 5. Cont.

Horizon	Decomposition	Tested Model	ICEEMDAN										EEMD										
			LinRR	PolyRR	SigRR	RbfRR	MKRR	LSSVR	BPNN	RW			RR	LinRR	PolyRR	SigRR	RbfRR	MKRR	LSSVR	BPNN	RW		
6	ICEEMDAN	RR	−13.9660 (0.0000)	−2.1767 (0.0296)	−6.0937 (0.0000)	−12.9968 (0.0000)	−2.4287 (0.0153)	−4.9536 (0.0000)	−22.6250 (0.0000)	−14.1579 (0.0000)			−12.3204 (0.0000)	−15.3905 (0.0000)	−12.0345 (0.0000)	−12.7060 (0.0000)	−15.1929 (0.0000)	−12.4624 (0.0000)	−13.2884 (0.0000)	−19.3882 (0.0000)	−17.6734 (0.0000)		
		LinRR		14.3951 (0.0000)	14.3875 (0.0000)	4.9217 (0.0000)	13.1664 (0.0000)	13.1583 (0.0000)	−9.0778 (0.0000)	−13.5116 (0.0000)			7.7778 (0.0000)	−4.3984 (0.0000)	7.4146 (0.0000)	6.9775 (0.0000)	−3.0020 (0.0027)	6.0234 (0.0000)	5.4957 (0.0000)	−13.2753 (0.0000)	−16.9797 (0.0000)		
		PolyRR			−7.2407 (0.0000)	−13.3457 (0.0000)	−0.7001 (0.4840)	−2.9388 (0.0033)	−22.1291 (0.0000)	−14.1522 (0.0000)			−11.6702 (0.0000)	−15.6854 (0.0000)	−11.7628 (0.0000)	−12.7550 (0.0000)	−15.3002 (0.0000)	−11.7487 (0.0000)	−13.1322 (0.0000)	−19.3071 (0.0000)	−17.6775 (0.0000)		
		SigRR				−12.8356 (0.0000)	4.1760	3.6412 (0.0003)	−20.1380 (0.0000)	−14.0771 (0.0000)			−7.3939 (0.0000)	−14.8116 (0.0000)	−8.1197 (0.0000)	−9.6893 (0.0000)	−14.2892 (0.0000)	−7.9142 (0.0000)	−10.1005 (0.0000)	−18.4915 (0.0000)	−17.5994 (0.0000)		
		RbfRR					11.8646 (0.0000)	12.5228 (0.0000)	−12.1621 (0.0000)	−13.6712 (0.0000)			5.1460 (0.0000)	−6.9781 (0.0000)	4.6379 (0.0000)	3.9114 (0.0001)	−9.3717 (0.0000)	3.4358 (0.0006)	2.4569 (0.0141)	−14.7236 (0.0000)	−17.1397 (0.0000)		
		MKRR						−1.5720 (0.1161)	−22.1601 (0.0000)	−14.1246 (0.0000)			−10.9045 (0.0000)	−14.7753 (0.0000)	−10.8633 (0.0000)	−11.5082 (0.0000)	−14.4164 (0.0000)	−11.3219 (0.0000)	−12.0115 (0.0000)	−19.2344 (0.0000)	−17.6322 (0.0000)		
		LSSVR							−22.0285 (0.0000)	−14.1061 (0.0000)			−10.1588 (0.0000)	−14.5608 (0.0000)	−10.2971 (0.0000)	−11.2871 (0.0000)	−14.9082 (0.0000)	−10.9314 (0.0000)	−12.6866 (0.0000)	−18.7911 (0.0000)	−17.6113 (0.0000)		
		BPNN								−12.2361 (0.0000)			16.3390 (0.0000)	6.6381 (0.0000)	16.0747 (0.0000)	15.2332 (0.0000)	6.7072 (0.0000)	16.0034 (0.0000)	14.0536 (0.0000)	−7.3185 (0.0000)	−15.2268 (0.0000)		
		RW											13.8085 (0.0000)	13.2857 (0.0000)	13.7910 (0.0000)	13.7611 (0.0000)	13.2775 (0.0000)	13.7266 (0.0000)	13.6873 (0.0000)	11.0380 (0.0000)	0.7513 (0.4526)		
	EEMD	RR												−11.9133 (0.0000)	−2.8917 (0.0039)	−5.0101 (0.0000)	−11.8544 (0.0000)	−3.3420 (0.0009)	−7.1119 (0.0000)	−17.4323 (0.0000)	−17.2382 (0.0000)		
		LinRR													11.6342 (0.0000)	11.3981 (0.0000)	0.2374 (0.8124)	9.5491 (0.0000)	9.4853 (0.0000)	−12.3880 (0.0000)	−16.6841 (0.0000)		
		PolyRR														−4.2271 (0.0000)	−11.7039 (0.0000)	−1.5927 (0.1114)	−5.6236 (0.0000)	−17.1205 (0.0000)	−17.2187 (0.0000)		
		SigRR															−11.6910 (0.0000)	0.4412 (0.6591)	−3.2085 (0.0014)	−16.7302 (0.0000)	−17.1929 (0.0000)		
		RbfRR																9.9300 (0.0000)	11.0223 (0.0000)	−12.7276 (0.0000)	−16.6240 (0.0000)		
		MKRR																	−2.6530 (0.0081)	−16.3767 (0.0000)	−17.1081 (0.0000)		
		LSSVR																		−16.6247 (0.0000)	−17.0843 (0.0000)		
		BPNN																			−13.4903 (0.0000)		

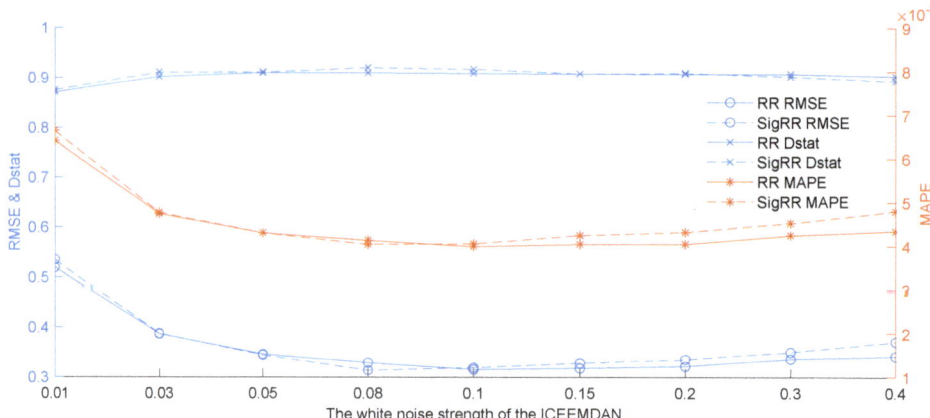

Figure 3. The impact of the white noise strength in the ICEEMDAN by RR and SigRR.

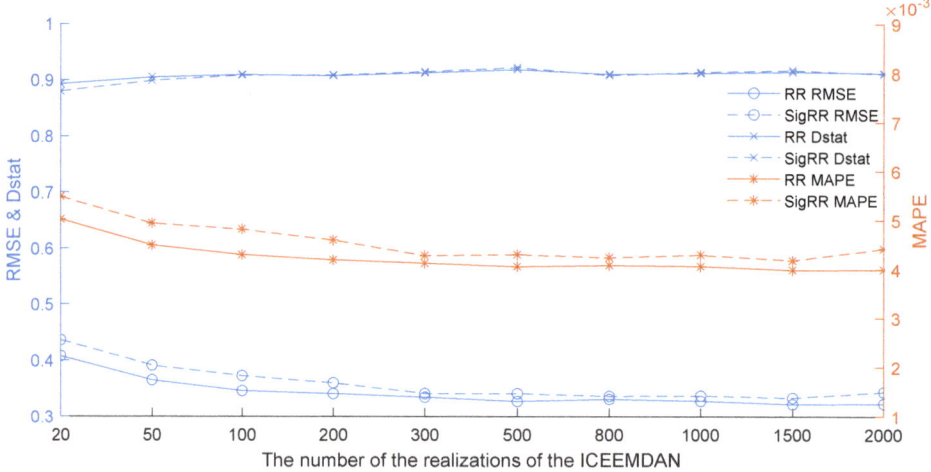

Figure 4. The impact of the number of the realizations in the ICEEMDAN by RR and SigRR.

It can be seen from Figure 3 that the results in terms of RMSE, MAPE and Dstat are gradually improved when *nsd* increases from 0.01 to 0.08. In contrast, after that, all the evaluation indicators are getting worse and worse with the increase of noise strength when *nsd* is greater than 0.1. Both RR and SigRR have similar trends, and one of the two models is alternatively better than the other. The results show that the white noise strength has great impact on the forecasting performance and an ideal white noise strength is between 0.05 and 0.1.

When we look at Figure 4, we can find that when the number of the realization is 20, the results of RMSE, MAPE and Dstat are all rather bad. When the number of realization increases from 20 to 500, all the results become better and better. Specifically, the Dstat reaches the best values for both RR and SigRR when the number of realization equals 500, while the results of RMSE and MAPE are very close to the best values. After that, the values of the three indicators are very stable when the number of realization varies from 500 to 2000. The results indicate that 500 is very ideal for the number of realizations.

4.5.2. The Impact of the Lag Orders

Lag orders refer to the length of recent data points treated as explanatory variables to build time series models. We further investigate the impact of variable lag orders from 1 to 20 with horizon 1, and the results are shown in Figure 5. When the lag order is equal to 1, the results of the evaluation indicators are the worst. However, when it varies from 1 to 6, the corresponding results are all becoming better and better. After that, the results have remained almost unchanged for the lag order from 6 to 20. Therefore, the best lag order is 6 because it can provide satisfactory results with less input, which confirms the previous study [12,31].

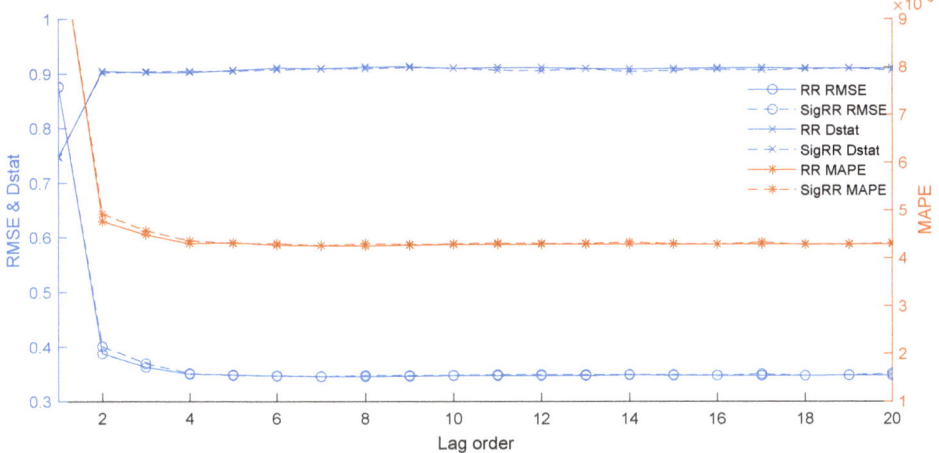

Figure 5. The impact of the lag orders by RR and SigRR.

4.5.3. The Result of Each Individual Component

Each decomposed component by the ICEEMDAN shows either high-frequency or low-frequency characteristics. In general, it is harder to forecasting a high-frequency component than a low-frequency one. We plot the predicted values and raw data of each component and the raw crude oil prices by RR and sigRR in Figures 6 and 7, respectively.

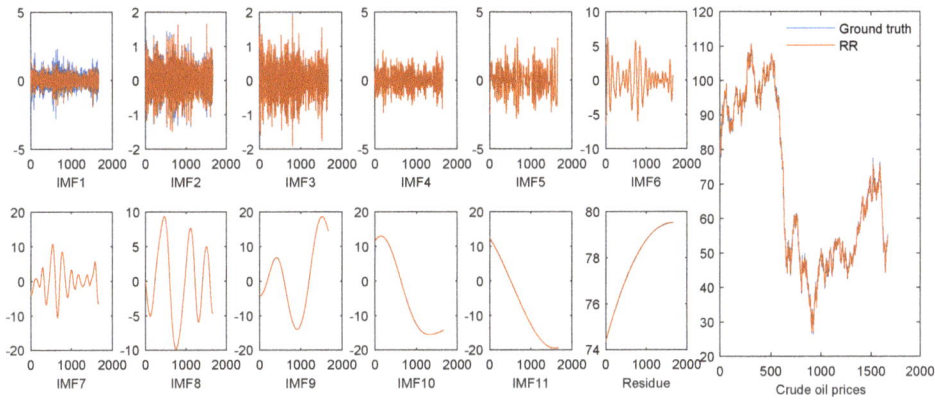

Figure 6. The individual and final forecasting results by RR.

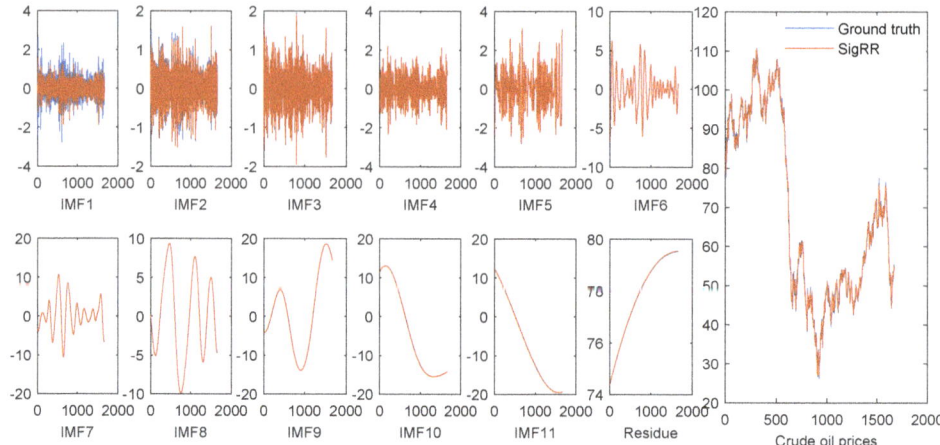

Figure 7. The individual and final forecasting results by SigRR.

It can be seen from these figures that both RR and SigRR are able to forecast the high-frequency components (IMF6-IMF11 as well as the residue) very well, and the predicted errors mainly come from the high-frequency components (IMF1-IMF5), especially from IMF1. Since the volatility of the hight-frequency components is relatively narrow, the forecasting errors from such components might be restricted. This is one of the possible reasons why the framework of "decomposition and ensemble" is effective for time series forecasting.

5. Summary and Conclusions

Forecasting daily crude oil prices is an important but challenging task. To improve the forecasting performance, a series of approaches using ICEEMDAN, DE and RR, termed as ICEEMDAN-DE-RR, are proposed in this paper. The proposed approaches firstly use ICEEMDAN to decompose the complex original crude oil prices into several components, and then each component is forecasted individually by DE-based RR predictors. In the end, the sum of the predicted results of all the components is taken as the final result. The extensive experiments demonstrated the proposed approaches can outperform some state-of-the-art methods.

Especially from the experimental results, we have the following interesting findings: (1) It is a very difficult task to accurately forecast daily crude oil prices with the raw price series because of its nonlinearity and nonstationarity; (2) AI-models usually outperform statistical methods when forecasting crude oil prices; (3) RR-based predictors with DE optimizing the parameters have good forecasting ability; (4) The framework of "decomposition and ensemble" can significantly improve the performance of forecasting daily crude oil prices; ICEEMDAN is advantageous over EEMD for the forecasting tasks; (5) The proposed ICEEMDAN-DE-RR approach outperforms the competitive methods in terms of several evaluation metrics, indicating that it is promising for daily crude oil price forecasting. (6) Regarding RR-based predictors, RR and SigRR with DE optimizing parameters can achieve very promising forecasting results in terms of several criteria.

In the future, we will apply the proposed approaches to forecasting other types of energy time series, such as natural gas prices, wind speed, wind power and electricity load.

Author Contributions: Formal analysis, T.L. and X.L.; Funding acquisition, X.L.; Investigation, J.W. and T.H.; Methodology, T.L.; Resources, T.H.; Software, T.L. and Y.Z.; Supervision, T.L. and X.L.; Writing—original draft, T.L. and Y.Z.; Writing—review & editing, T.L. and Y.Z.

Funding: This work was supported by the Fundamental Research Funds for the Central Universities (Grant No. JBK1902029), the Ministry of Education of Humanities and Social Science Project (Grant No. 19YJAZH047), Sichuan Science and Technology Program (Grant No. 2019YFG0117) and the Scientific Research Fund of Sichuan Provincial Education Department (Grant No. 17ZB0433).

Conflicts of Interest: The authors declare no conflict of interest.

References

1. Miao, H.; Ramchander, S.; Wang, T.; Yang, D. Influential factors in crude oil price forecasting. *Energy Econ.* **2017**, *68*, 77–88. [CrossRef]
2. Naderi, M.; Khamehchi, E.; Karimi, B. Novel statistical forecasting models for crude oil price, gas price, and interest rate based on meta-heuristic bat algorithm. *J. Pet. Sci. Eng.* **2019**, *172*, 13–22. [CrossRef]
3. Ye, M.; Zyren, J.; Shore, J. A monthly crude oil spot price forecasting model using relative inventories. *Int. J. Forecast.* **2005**, *21*, 491–501. [CrossRef]
4. Movagharnejad, K.; Mehdizadeh, B.; Banihashemi, M.; Kordkheili, M.S. Forecasting the differences between various commercial oil prices in the Persian Gulf region by neural network. *Energy* **2011**, *36*, 3979–3984. [CrossRef]
5. Zhang, Y.; Ma, F.; Shi, B.; Huang, D. Forecasting the prices of crude oil: An iterated combination approach. *Energy Econ.* **2018**, *70*, 472–483. [CrossRef]
6. Wen, F.; Gong, X.; Cai, S. Forecasting the volatility of crude oil futures using HAR-type models with structural breaks. *Energy Econ.* **2016**, *59*, 400–413. [CrossRef]
7. Li, J.; Zhu, S.; Wu, Q. Monthly crude oil spot price forecasting using variational mode decomposition. *Energy Econ.* **2019**, *83*, 240–253. [CrossRef]
8. Zhou, Y.; Li, T.; Shi, J.; Qian, Z. A CEEMDAN and XGBOOST-Based Approach to Forecast Crude Oil Prices. *Complexity* **2019**, *2019*, 4392785. [CrossRef]
9. He, K.; Yu, L.; Lai, K.K. Crude oil price analysis and forecasting using wavelet decomposed ensemble model. *Energy* **2012**, *46*, 564–574. [CrossRef]
10. Yu, L.; Dai, W.; Tang, L.; Wu, J. A hybrid grid-GA-based LSSVR learning paradigm for crude oil price forecasting. *Neural Comput. Appl.* **2016**, *27*, 2193–2215. [CrossRef]
11. Tang, L.; Wu, Y.; Yu, L. A non-iterative decomposition-ensemble learning paradigm using RVFL network for crude oil price forecasting. *Appl. Soft. Comput.* **2018**, *70*, 1097–1108. [CrossRef]
12. Yu, L.; Wang, S.; Lai, K.K. Forecasting crude oil price with an EMD-based neural network ensemble learning paradigm. *Energy Econ.* **2008**, *30*, 2623–2635. [CrossRef]
13. Mirmirani, S.; Li, H.C. A comparison of VAR and neural networks with genetic algorithm in forecasting price of oil. *Appl. Artif. Intell. Financ. Econ.* **2004**, *19*, 203–223.
14. Murat, A.; Tokat, E. Forecasting oil price movements with crack spread futures. *Energy Econ.* **2009**, *31*, 85–90. [CrossRef]
15. Moshiri, S.; Foroutan, F. Forecasting nonlinear crude oil futures prices. *Energy J.* **2006**, *27*, 81–95. [CrossRef]
16. Herrera, A.M.; Hu, L.; Pastor, D. Forecasting crude oil price volatility. *Int. J. Forecast.* **2018**, *34*, 622–635. [CrossRef]
17. Nademi, A.; Nademi, Y. Forecasting crude oil prices by a semiparametric Markov switching model: OPEC, WTI, and Brent cases. *Energy Econ.* **2018**, *74*, 757–766. [CrossRef]
18. Zhang, Y.J.; Yao, T.; He, L.Y.; Ripple, R. Volatility forecasting of crude oil market: Can the regime switching GARCH model beat the single-regime GARCH models? *Int. Rev. Econ. Financ.* **2019**, *59*, 302–317. [CrossRef]
19. Lyocsa, S.; Molnar, P. Exploiting dependence: Day-ahead volatility forecasting for crude oil and natural gas exchange-traded funds. *Energy* **2018**, *155*, 462–473. [CrossRef]
20. Lv, W. Does the OVX matter for volatility forecasting? Evidence from the crude oil market. *Phys. A* **2018**, *492*, 916–922. [CrossRef]
21. Naser, H. Estimating and forecasting the real prices of crude oil: A data rich model using a dynamic model averaging (DMA) approach. *Energy Econ.* **2016**, *56*, 75–87. [CrossRef]
22. Azevedo, V.G.; Campos, L.M.S. Combination of forecasts for the price of crude oil on the spot market. *Int. J. Prod. Res.* **2016**, *54*, 5219–5235. [CrossRef]

23. Tang, L.; Dai, W.; Yu, L. A Novel CEEMD-Based EELM Ensemble Learning Paradigm for Crude Oil Price Forecasting. *Int. J. Inf. Technol. Decis. Mak.* **2015**, *14*, 141–169. [CrossRef]
24. Tehrani, R.; Khodayar, F. A hybrid optimized artificial intelligent model to forecast crude oil using genetic algorithm. *Afr. J. Bus. Manag.* **2011**, *5*, 13130–13135. [CrossRef]
25. Xiong, T.; Bao, Y.; Hu, Z. Beyond one-step-ahead forecasting: Evaluation of alternative multi-step-ahead forecasting models for crude oil prices. *Energy Econ.* **2013**, *40*, 405–415. [CrossRef]
26. Barunik, J.; Malinska, B. Forecasting the term structure of crude oil futures prices with neural networks. *Appl. Energy* **2016**, *164*, 366–379. [CrossRef]
27. Ding, Y. A novel decompose-ensemble methodology with AIC-ANN approach for crude oil forecasting. *Energy* **2018**, *154*, 328–336. [CrossRef]
28. Fan, L.; Pan, S.; Li, Z.; Li, H. An ICA-based support vector regression scheme for forecasting crude oil prices. *Technol. Forecast. Soc. Chang.* **2016**, *112*, 245–253. [CrossRef]
29. Yu, L.; Zhang, X.; Wang, S. Assessing Potentiality of Support Vector Machine Method in Crude Oil Price Forecasting. *Eurasia J. Math. Sci. Technol. Educ.* **2017**, *13*, 7893–7904. [CrossRef]
30. Zhang, Y.; Zhang, J. Volatility forecasting of crude oil market: A new hybrid method. *J. Forecast.* **2018**, *37*, 781–789. [CrossRef]
31. Li, T.; Hu, Z.; Jia, Y.; Wu, J.; Zhou, Y. Forecasting Crude Oil Prices Using Ensemble Empirical Mode Decomposition and Sparse Bayesian Learning. *Energies* **2018**, *11*, 1882. [CrossRef]
32. Wu, J.; Chen, Y.; Zhou, T.; Li, T. An Adaptive Hybrid Learning Paradigm Integrating CEEMD, ARIMA and SBL for Crude Oil Price Forecasting. *Energies* **2019**, *12*, 1239. [CrossRef]
33. Yu, L.; Dai, W.; Tang, L. A novel decomposition ensemble model with extended extreme learning machine for crude oil price forecasting. *Eng. Appl. Artif. Intell.* **2016**, *47*, 110–121. [CrossRef]
34. Wang, J.; Athanasopoulos, G.; Hyndman, R.J.; Wang, S. Crude oil price forecasting based on internet concern using an extreme learning machine. *Int. J. Forecast.* **2018**, *34*, 665–677. [CrossRef]
35. Wu, Y.X.; Wu, Q.B.; Zhu, J.Q. Improved EEMD-based crude oil price forecasting using LSTM networks. *Phys. A* **2019**, *516*, 114–124. [CrossRef]
36. Li, T.; Zhou, M.; Guo, C.; Luo, M.; Wu, J.; Pan, F.; Tao, Q.; He, T. Forecasting Crude Oil Price Using EEMD and RVM with Adaptive PSO-Based Kernels. *Energies* **2016**, *9*, 1014. [CrossRef]
37. Chiroma, H.; Abdul-kareem, S.; Noor, A.S.M.; Abubakar, A.I.; Safa, N.S.; Shuib, L.; Hamza, M.F.; Gital, A.Y.; Herawan, T. A Review on Artificial Intelligence Methodologies for the Forecasting of Crude Oil Price. *Intell. Autom. Soft Comput.* **2016**, *22*, 449–462. [CrossRef]
38. Deng, W.; Zhang, S.; Zhao, H.; Yang, X. A Novel Fault Diagnosis Method Based on Integrating Empirical Wavelet Transform and Fuzzy Entropy for Motor Bearing. *IEEE Access* **2018**, *6*, 35042–35056. [CrossRef]
39. Zhao, H.; Yao, R.; Xu, L.; Yuan, Y.; Li, G.; Deng, W. Study on a Novel Fault Damage Degree Identification Method Using High-Order Differential Mathematical Morphology Gradient Spectrum Entropy. *Entropy* **2018**, *20*, 682. [CrossRef]
40. Bajaj, V.; Pachori, R.B. Classification of Seizure and Nonseizure EEG Signals Using Empirical Mode Decomposition. *IEEE Trans. Inf. Technol. Biomed.* **2012**, *16*, 1135–1142. [CrossRef] [PubMed]
41. Li, T.; Zhou, M. ECG Classification Using Wavelet Packet Entropy and Random Forests. *Entropy* **2016**, *18*, 285. [CrossRef]
42. Zhang, H.; Wang, X.; Cao, J.; Tang, M.; Guo, Y. A multivariate short-term traffic flow forecasting method based on wavelet analysis and seasonal time series. *Appl. Intell.* **2018**, *48*, 3827–3838. [CrossRef]
43. Pannakkong, W.; Sriboonchitta, S.; Huynh, V.N. An Ensemble Model of Arima and Ann with Restricted Boltzmann Machine Based on Decomposition of Discrete Wavelet Transform for Time Series Forecasting. *J. Syst. Sci. Syst. Eng.* **2018**, *27*, 690–708. [CrossRef]
44. Li, T.; Yang, M.; Wu, J.; Jing, X. A novel image encryption algorithm based on a fractional-order hyperchaotic system and DNA computing. *Complexity* **2017**, *2017*, 9010251. [CrossRef]
45. Li, T.; Shi, J.; Li, X.; Wu, J.; Pan, F. Image encryption based on pixel-level diffusion with dynamic filtering and DNA-level permutation with 3D Latin cubes. *Entropy* **2019**, *21*, 319. [CrossRef]
46. Li, X.; Xie, Z.; Wu, J.; Li, T. Image encryption based on dynamic filtering and bit cuboid operations. *Complexity* **2019**, *2019*, 7485621. [CrossRef]

47. Ren, Y.; Suganthan, P.N.; Srikanth, N. A Novel Empirical Mode Decomposition with Support Vector Regression for Wind Speed Forecasting. *IEEE Trans. Neural Netw. Learn. Syst.* **2016**, *27*, 1793–1798. [CrossRef] [PubMed]
48. Yang, Z.S.; Wang, J. A combination forecasting approach applied in multistep wind speed forecasting based on a data processing strategy and an optimized artificial intelligence algorithm. *Appl. Energy* **2018**, *230*, 1108–1125. [CrossRef]
49. Abdoos, A.; Hemmati, M.; Abdoos, A.A. Short term load forecasting using a hybrid intelligent method. *Knowl.-Based Syst.* **2015**, *76*, 139–147. [CrossRef]
50. Fan, G.F.; Peng, L.L.; Hong, W.C.; Sun, F. Electric load forecasting by the SVR model with differential empirical mode decomposition and auto regression. *Neurocomputing* **2016**, *173*, 958–970. [CrossRef]
51. Qiu, X.H.; Ren, Y.; Suganthan, P.N.; Amaratunga, G.A.J. Empirical Mode Decomposition based ensemble deep learning for load demand time series forecasting. *Appl. Soft. Comput.* **2017**, *54*, 246–255. [CrossRef]
52. Sun, W.; Zhang, C.C. Analysis and forecasting of the carbon price using multi resolution singular value decomposition and extreme learning machine optimized by adaptive whale optimization algorithm. *Appl. Energy* **2018**, *231*, 1354–1371. [CrossRef]
53. Wang, D.Y.; Luo, H.Y.; Grunder, O.; Lin, Y.B.; Guo, H.X. Multi-step ahead electricity price forecasting using a hybrid model based on two-layer decomposition technique and BP neural network optimized by firefly algorithm. *Appl. Energy* **2017**, *190*, 390–407. [CrossRef]
54. Yang, Z.S.; Wang, J. A hybrid forecasting approach applied in wind speed forecasting based on a data processing strategy and an optimized artificial intelligence algorithm. *Energy* **2018**, *160*, 87–100. [CrossRef]
55. Huang, N.E.; Shen, Z.; Long, S.R. A new view of nonlinear water waves: the Hilbert Spectrum 1. *Annu. Rev. Fluid Mech.* **1999**, *31*, 417–457. [CrossRef]
56. Wu, Z.; Huang, N.E. Ensemble empirical mode decomposition: A noise-assisted data analysis method. *Adv. Adapt. Data Anal* **2009**, *1*, 1–41. [CrossRef]
57. Torres, M.E.; Colominas, M.A.; Schlotthauer, G.; Flandrin, P. A complete ensemble empirical mode decomposition with adaptive noise. In Proceedings of the 2011 IEEE international conference on acoustics, speech and signal processing (ICASSP), Prague, Czech Republic, 22–27 May 2011; pp. 4144–4147.
58. Colominas, M.A.; Schlotthauer, G.; Torres, M.E. Improved complete ensemble EMD: A suitable tool for biomedical signal processing. *Biomed. Signal Process. Control* **2014**, *14*, 19–29. [CrossRef]
59. Dai, S.; Niu, D.; Li, Y. Daily peak load forecasting based on complete ensemble empirical mode decomposition with adaptive noise and support vector machine optimized by modified grey Wolf optimization algorithm. *Energies* **2018**, *11*, 163. [CrossRef]
60. Douak, F.; Melgani, F.; Benoudjit, N. Kernel ridge regression with active learning for wind speed prediction. *Appl. Energy* **2013**, *103*, 328–340. [CrossRef]
61. Naik, J.; Satapathy, P.; Dash, P.K. Short-term wind speed and wind power prediction using hybrid empirical mode decomposition and kernel ridge regression. *Appl. Soft. Comput.* **2018**, *70*, 1167–1188. [CrossRef]
62. Qian, C.; Breckon, T.P.; Li, H. Robust visual tracking via speedup multiple kernel ridge regression. *J. Electron. Imaging* **2015**, *24*, 053016. [CrossRef]
63. Maalouf, M.; Homouz, D.; Abutayeh, M. Accurate Prediction of Preheat Temperature in Solar Flash Desalination Systems Using Kernel Ridge Regression. *J. Energy Eng.* **2016**, *142*, E4015017. [CrossRef]
64. Naik, J.; Bisoi, R.; Dash, P.K. Prediction interval forecasting of wind speed and wind power using modes decomposition based low rank multi-kernel ridge regression. *Renew. Energy* **2018**, *129*, 357–383. [CrossRef]
65. Kennedy, J. Particle swarm optimization. In *Encyclopedia of Machine Learning*; Springer: Berlin, Germany, 2010; pp. 760–766.
66. Deng, W.; Zhao, H.; Yang, X.; Xiong, J.; Sun, M.; Li, B. Study on an improved adaptive PSO algorithm for solving multi-objective gate assignment. *Appl. Soft. Comput.* **2017**, *59*, 288–302. [CrossRef]
67. Deng, W.; Yao, R.; Zhao, H.; Yang, X.; Li, G. A novel intelligent diagnosis method using optimal LS-SVM with improved PSO algorithm. *Soft Comput.* **2019**, *23*, 2445–2462. [CrossRef]
68. Storn, R.; Price, K. Differential evolution—A simple and efficient heuristic for global optimization over continuous spaces. *J. Glob. Optim.* **1997**, *11*, 341–359. [CrossRef]
69. Das, S.; Suganthan, P.N. Differential Evolution: A Survey of the State-of-the-Art. *IEEE Trans. Evol. Comput.* **2011**, *15*, 4–31. [CrossRef]

70. Dorigo, M.; Blum, C. Ant colony optimization theory: A survey. *Theor. Comput. Sci.* **2005**, *344*, 243–278. [CrossRef]
71. Deng, W.; Xu, J.; Zhao, H. An Improved Ant Colony Optimization Algorithm Based on Hybrid Strategies for Scheduling problem. *IEEE Access* **2019**, 20281–20292. [CrossRef]
72. Yu, X.; Liong, S.Y. Forecasting of hydrologic time series with ridge regression in feature space. *J. Hydrol.* **2007**, *332*, 290–302. [CrossRef]
73. Ahn, J.J.; Byun, H.W.; Oh, K.J.; Kim, T.Y. Using ridge regression with genetic algorithm to enhance real estate appraisal forecasting. *Expert Syst. Appl.* **2012**, *39*, 8369–8379. [CrossRef]
74. Zhang, S.; Hu, Q.; Xie, Z.; Mi, J. Kernel ridge regression for general noise model with its application. *Neurocomputing* **2015**, *149*, 836–846. [CrossRef]
75. Saunders, C., Gammerman, A., Vovk, V. Ridge Regression Learning Algorithm in Dual Variables. In Proceedings of the Fifteenth International Conference on Machine Learning, Madison, WI, USA, 24–27 July 1998; Morgan Kaufmann Publishers Inc.: San Francisco, CA, USA, 1998; pp. 515–521.
76. Maalouf, M.; Barsoum, Z. Failure strength prediction of aluminum spot-welded joints using kernel ridge regression. *Int. J. Adv. Manuf. Technol.* **2017**, *91*, 3717–3725. [CrossRef]
77. Avron, H.; Clarkson, K.L.; Woodruff, D.P. Faster kernel ridge regression using sketching and preconditioning. *SIAM J. Matrix Anal. Appl.* **2017**, *38*, 1116–1138. [CrossRef]
78. Diebold, F.; Mariano, R. Comparing predictive accuracy. *J. Bus. Econ. Stat.* **2002**, *20*, 134–144. [CrossRef]
79. Sakamoto, Y.; Ishiguro, M.; Kitagawa, G. *Akaike Information Criterion Statistics*; Reidel, D., Ed.; Springer: Dordrecht, The Netherlands, 1986; Volume 81.

© 2019 by the authors. Licensee MDPI, Basel, Switzerland. This article is an open access article distributed under the terms and conditions of the Creative Commons Attribution (CC BY) license (http://creativecommons.org/licenses/by/4.0/).

Article

A Novel Prediction Approach for Short-Term Renewable Energy Consumption in China Based on Improved Gaussian Process Regression

Yuansheng Huang [1], Lei Yang [1,*], Chong Gao [2], Yuqing Jiang [2] and Yulin Dong [2]

[1] School of Economics and Management, North China Electric Power University, Beijing 102206, China; hys2656@allyun.com

[2] School of Economics and Management, North China Electric Power University, Baoding 071003, China; 51851114@ncepu.edu.cn (C.G.); 2182218063@ncepu.edu.cn (Y.J.); 2182218022@ncepu.edu.cn (Y.D.)

* Correspondence: 1162106026@ncepu.edu.cn; Tel.: +86-186-317-28689

Received: 9 September 2019; Accepted: 30 October 2019; Published: 1 November 2019

Abstract: Energy consumption issues are important factors concerning the achievement of sustainable social development and also have a significant impact on energy security, particularly for China whose energy structure is experiencing a transformation. Construction of an accurate and reliable prediction model for the volatility changes in energy consumption can provide valuable reference information for policy makers of the government and for the energy industry. In view of this, a novel improved model is developed in this article by integrating the modified state transition algorithm (MSTA) with the Gaussian processes regression (GPR) approach for non-fossil energy consumption predictions for China at the end of the 13th Five-Year Project, in which the MSTA is utilized for effective optimization of hyper-parameters in GPR. Aiming for validating the superiority of MSTA, several comparisons are conducted on two well-known functions and the optimization results show the effectiveness of modification in the state transition algorithm (STA). Then, based on the latest statistical renewable energy consumption data, the MSTA-GPR model is utilized to generate consumption predictions for overall renewable energy and each single renewable energy source, including hydropower, wind, solar, geothermal, biomass and other energies, respectively. The forecasting results reveal that the proposed improved GPR can promote the forecasting ability of basic GPR and obtain the best prediction effect among all the other comparison models. Finally, combined with the forecasting results, the trend of each renewable energy source is analyzed.

Keywords: renewable energy consumption; Gaussian processes regression; state transition algorithm; five-year project; forecasting

1. Introduction

The energy industry provides an important impetus for the advancement of society and has a significant impact on sustainable development [1–5], power safety [6,7], and environmental changes [8,9]. Aiming to alleviate the pressure brought by energy problems, developing renewable energy has been considered as an effective approach by more and more scholars at home and abroad [10]. In China, renewable energies refer to the energies that can be continuously regenerated in nature, for instance, hydropower, wind, solar, biomass, geothermal and so on. The latest statistics obtained form British Petroleum (BP) Statistical Review of World Energy 2019 displays that the renewable energy consumption in China has reached the amount of 391.67 million tons oil equivalent (Mtoe), which experienced a huge promotion over the past decades. China's overall non-fossil energy consumption in 2018 increased 8.1% compared with that of 2017. During the past year, the hydropower has promoted by 3.2%, the wind energy consumption has increased by 24.1%, the solar energy consumption has grown by 50.7%, and geothermal, biomass and other energy has been promoted by 14%. According to the collected data, the consumption and the corresponding proportion of different renewable energies in the past ten years are exhibited in Figure 1.

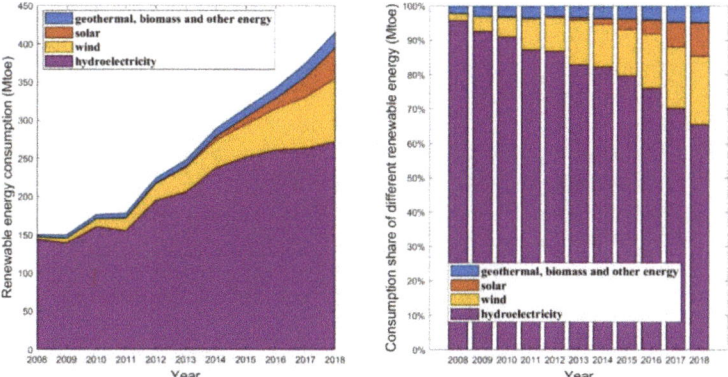

Figure 1. The composition of renewable energy consumption in China.

As displayed in Figure 1, dramatic changes can be observed in the composition of non-fossil energy consumption of China during the past few years owing to a series of incentive policies implementations, especially during the twelfth Five-Year Project which was from 2011 to 2015. Hydropower, with the consumption of 144.1 Mtoe, accounts for 95.77% of the overall renewable energy consumption in 2008. However, due to the development of other renewable energies, the share of hydropower has fallen to 79.73% during the late years of the twelfth Five-Year Project, and further decreased to 69.47% by the year-end of 2018. Meanwhile, the wind energy accounts for the biggest growth share in renewable consumption, which increased from 1.97% in 2008 to 10.93% in 2018, and the corresponding consumption amount increased from 2.96 Mtoe to 82.82 Mtoe. The share of solar energy in the overall renewable consumption grew from 0.02% in 2008 to 9.66% in 2018, with the corresponding growth from 0.03 Mtoe to 40.16 Mtoe. The share of geothermal, biomass and other energy consumption in the overall renewable consumption grew from 2.24% in 2008 to 4.94% in 2018, with the corresponding growth from 3.37 Mtoe to 20.53 Mtoe. Presently, aiming at realizing sustainable development, China is focusing on modifying the traditional energy supply structure dominated by fossil fuels and encouraging the utilization of non-fossil energy in power generation. Thus, the establishment of a reliable and accurate foreseeing for China's non-fossil energy consumption at the end of thirteenth Five-Year Project (2016–2020) and afterwards is of practical significance, offering valuable references to contribute for the healthy and steady growth of China's energy and economy.

In aiming for obtaining a satisfactory forecasting performance, a number of approaches have been developed to predict energy consumption, for instance: time series analysis [11], the Long-range Energy Alternatives Planning System (LEAP) [12,13], the Nanoelectromechanical systems approach (NEMS) [14,15], computational intelligence technology [16] and hybrid forecasting systems [17,18]. However, although the models listed above have strong non-linear modeling ability, they cannot capture the characteristics of small-scale samples very well. Aiming to solve this problem, Gaussian process regression is developed as the perfect intelligence approach for low-dimensional and small sample regression problems [19].

Owing to the properties of flexibility, non-linearity, inherent non-parametric factors, and so on, GPR has been utilized by numerous scholars in various fields including chemistry [20], astrophysics [21], materials [22], and so on. For example, estimation of diffusion coefficients in the voltammetric signals was obtained by Bogdan et al., [23] with the application of GPR which is utilized to analyze the electroanalytical experimental data. In aiming to forecast the export content of the flue gas, GPR was conducted to obtain the design optimization of combustion systems utilizing real time flame figures in [24]. Furthermore, there are also researches involving GPR in the prediction of wind speed [25]. Wang et al. [26] proposed a hybrid approach which combines four different models including Extreme Learning Machine, Support Vector Machine, Least Squares Support Vector Machine and GPR to gain the probabilistic predictions for wind speed in the short term. Based on the features of renewable energy consumption, it is appropriate to utilize GPR for the acquirement of renewable energy consumption prediction. Nevertheless, through the review of the previous studies, it can be noticed that few researches have been investigated in this domain by now.

In the construction of GPR, the choice of hyper-parameters is of great influence on the forecasting capacity. Thus, it is of extreme significance to find a proper value for the hyper-parameter of GPR. As a traditional measure, the conjugate gradient (CG) has been conducted as the optimization operator for parameters selection [27]. Nevertheless, the performance of this measure is affected by the basic guess selection, and it is hard to determine the proper iteration amount. Furthermore, in most instances, the estimation of hyper-parameters for GPR is a non-convex issue, where measures on basis of the gradient have troubles in finding the global optimal value [28,29]. To aim at solving this problem, intelligent optimization measures, including the particle swarm optimization (PSO) [30–32] and the genetic algorithm (GA) [33–35], are found to be better choices for optimal parameters selection in model training process. Among these models mentioned, it is validated that the state transition algorithm (STA) is effective in numerous complicated optimization issues and shows wonderful ability for nonlinear optimization in contrast with GA and PSO [36]. However, the original STA utilizes the space framework of objective function and seeks the best answers with the application of its unique state transformation operators. Additionally, the seeking range of state transformation operators is primarily decided by the corresponding transformation factors. If the transformation factor takes a large value, the global search ability of the model will be stronger. Conversely, as the value of the transformation factor is small, the local search ability of the model will be better. The transformation factor in the traditional structure of STA often takes an invariant value, which will add extra computations in the later period of optimization and cannot contribute for the optimization result improvement. Aiming for calculation complexity reduction and optimization result promotion, it is needed to consider parameter optimization for the transformation factor to find harmony between the global search and local search for the basic STA.

According to the analysis above, in this paper, a GPR model integrated with modified STA is put forward to make predictions of China's overall renewable energy consumption and its respective components consumption. In the proposed model, the parameter selection for STA and the parameter optimization for GPR are considered at the same time. Additionally, the latest renewable energy consumption data published by the BP statistical Review of World Energy 2019 are utilized to test the proposed model. The prediction outcomes prove that the proposed modified state transition algorithm (MSTA)-GRP model displays the optimal prediction effect in contrast with all the other prediction approaches. The major contributions can be described as follows: (1) A novel integration forecasting model MSTA-GPR model is proposed. The MSTA is integrated into the GPR for the hyper-parameters optimization to improve the forecasting performance. (2) Two well-known functions are utilized to validate the optimization effect against traditional optimization algorithms, such as GA and PSO. (3) The proposed MSTA-GPR is utilized to make consumption predictions of China's renewable energy at the end of the thirteenth Five-Year Project. The final result proves the satisfactory forecasting performance of the MSTA-GPR model and provides both a deterministic and an interval prediction for the renewable energy consumption development.

This passage is arranged with the following framework: Section 2 provides the description of the GPR, MSTA and the proposed MSTA-GPR model; Section 3 provides two validation cases to test the optimization performance of the modification in the basic STA; Section 4 shows applications of the proposed MSTA-GPR model for the consumption prediction of the overall renewable energy and its corresponding components; finally, the conclusions are obtained in Section 5.

2. Methodology

2.1. Gaussian Process Regression

Gaussian process (GP) is a kind of stochastic process in probability theory and mathematical statistics. It is a combination of a series of random variables obeying normal distribution in an exponential set. GP has two important components, one is the average function, and the other is the covariance function, which can describe the GP in form of Equation (1).

$$f(x) \sim GP(a(x), C(x, x')) \qquad (1)$$

The form of average function is described in Equation (2), and the form of covariance equation is represented by Equation (3) [37].

$$a(x) = E[f(x)], \qquad (2)$$

$$C(x, x') = E[(f(x) - a(x))(f(x') - a(x'))]. \qquad (3)$$

Generally, the squared-exponential covariance equation is considered as a widely applied covariance function. Assume that there is a data set with noise for training, which is in form of Equation (4):

$$D = \{x^{(i)}, y^{(i)} | i = 1, 2, \ldots, n\} \qquad (4)$$

then, we apply the GPR method to make predictions for the output value of y^* with the future input value x^* in way of studying a function from the data set given, which relates to a presupposed prior Gaussian function.

The posterior distribution can be acquired for the $(n+1)$ GP results according to Bayers rule, when the distribution for a novel value is calculated. As an examination input x^{n+1} and the corresponding training set D are given, the forecasting outcomes follow normal distribution by adjusting the observed values of the training set, which is shown from Equation (4) to Equation (6).

$$P(y^{(n+1)} | D, x^{(n+1)}) \sim N(\mu_{y^{(n+1)}}, \sigma^2_{y^{(n+1)}}), \qquad (4)$$

$$\mu_{y^{(n+1)}} = a^T Q^{-1} y, \qquad (5)$$

$$\sigma^2_{y^{(n+1)}} = C(x^{(n+1)}, x^{(n+1)}) - \alpha^T Q^{-1} \alpha. \qquad (6)$$

In the above equations, $\mu_{y^{(n+1)}}$ represents the mean, and $\sigma^2_{y^{(n+1)}}$ means the variance. Q_{pq} and α_p are given in equations below:

$$Q_{pq} = C(x^{(p)}, x^{(q)}) + r^2 \theta_{pq}, \qquad (7)$$

$$\alpha_p = C(x^{(n+1)}, x^{(q)}), p = 1, 2, \ldots, n. \qquad (8)$$

Mentioned by the previous paragraphs, covariance function $C(x_p, x_q; \Theta)$ along with hyper-parameters Θ has a great effect in GPR as it decides the smoothness of the data in evaluating the new function. As mentioned in [38], the log likelihood can be maximized to choose the optimal hyper-parameters for GPR, which is described in Equation (9):

$$\begin{aligned} \log P(D|\Theta) &= \log P(y^{(1)}, y^{(2)}, \ldots, y^{(n)} | x^{(1)}, x^{(2)}, \ldots, x^{(n)}, \Theta) \\ &= -\tfrac{1}{2} \log \det C - \tfrac{1}{2} y^T C^{-1} y - \tfrac{n}{2} \log 2\pi \end{aligned} \qquad (9)$$

2.2. Improved State Transition Algorithm

2.2.1. Original State Transition Algorithm

Firstly, an equation to be optimized with no limitations is described as follow:

$$\min_{x \in R^n} f(x) \tag{10}$$

where, $f(x)$ denotes an objective function mapping from R^n to R. Assume the potential solution as a state, and the objective problem is solved through updating the optimal solution found by now with iterations, which is considered as sate transition. The procedure of STA is expressed as below:

$$\begin{cases} s_{k+1} = A_k s_k + B_k u_k \\ y_{k+1} = f(s_{k+1}) \end{cases} \tag{11}$$

where, a state is represented by s_k; the state transition matrices are represented by A_k and B_k; the function of s_k and the previous states are represented by u_k; and the objective function is described utilizing the symbol of f. Additionally, the solutions of the continuous objective function of the STA are searched for with four different state transformation operators below.

(1) Rotation transformation:

$$s_{k+1} = s_k + \alpha \frac{1}{n \|s_k\|_2} R_r s_k \tag{12}$$

where, the rotation factor is positive and represented by α. A random matrix which belongs to $R^{n \times n}$ is denoted by R_r with elements distributed in $[-1,1]$. $\|x\|$ defines the L2-norm of a vector. Utilization of the rotation transformation can contribute to the search in the hypersphere.

(2) Translation transformation:

$$s_{k+1} = s_k + \beta R_t \frac{s_k - s_{k-1}}{\|s_k - s_{k-1}\|_2} \tag{13}$$

where, the translation factor is a fixed positive value and represented by β. R_t belonging to R defines a stochastic variable and the corresponding elements of R_t take value between $[0,1]$. Application of the translation transformation can contribute to the line search along between x_{k-1} and x_k.

(3) Expansion transformation:

$$s_{k+1} = s_k + \gamma R_e x_k \tag{14}$$

where, the expansion factor is a fixed positive value which is represented by γ. A stochastic diagonal matrix is represented by $R_e \in R^{n \times n}$ with elements obeying normal distribution. Application of expansion transformation can contribute to the whole space search which spreads the element in x_k to the range of infinite.

(4) Axesion transformation:

$$s_{k+1} = s_k + \delta R_a x_k \tag{15}$$

where, the axesion factor is a fixed positive value and defined by δ; a stochastic diagonal matrix which is represented by $R_a \in R^{n \times n}$ with elements generated form normal distribution. Moreover, these is only one nonzero stochastic element in R_a. Utilization of the axesion transformation can contribute to the search along the direction of axes.

Furthermore, the search enforcement (SE) is a parameter which is utilized to control the amount of each transformation during the implementation of four different transformation operators.

The major steps of the basic STA can be described as follow [39]:

1:    repeat
2:      repeat if $\alpha < \alpha_{\min}$ then
3:        $\alpha \leftarrow \alpha_{\min}$
4:      end if
5:      $Optimal \leftarrow \exp ansion(fun, Optimal, SE, \beta, \gamma)$
6:      $Optimal \leftarrow rotation(fun, Optimal, SE, \alpha, \beta)$
7:      $Optimal \leftarrow axesion(fun, Optimal, SE, \beta, \delta)$
8:      $\alpha \leftarrow \frac{\alpha}{fc}$

where, lessening of the coefficient α is decided by fc which takes a fixed value. Once a better solution is found, the translation operator will be activated.

2.2.2. Modification for the Original State Transition Algorithm

Compared with models on basis of the gradient, the STA has one advantage which is to search in all orientations and at any length. But there are also limitations for the STA. For example, decided by the transformation factor, the search area of the rotation and translation transformation is limited in a hpersphere or a line. To improve this situation, a parameter set $\Omega = \{1, 10^{-1}, 10^{-2}, 10^{-3}, 10^{-4}, 10^{-5}, 10^{-6}, 10^{-7}, 10^{-8}\}$ is considered in the basic STA for the optimal value selection of transformation factor [40]. The parameter which can obtain the best value for the objective function is selected as the optimal parameter. The optimal parameter $\widetilde{a}^*$ is given as the equation below:

$$\widetilde{a}^* = \underset{\widetilde{a}^* \in \Omega}{\arg\min} f(x_k + \widetilde{a}_k \widetilde{d}_k). \tag{16}$$

Aiming for a more complete utilization of the parameters, each parameter chosen is held for a certain period, which is represented as T_p. Then the rotation function in the modified STA is described as follow:

1:    $[Optimal, \alpha] \leftarrow update\_alpha(fun, Optimal, SE, \Omega)$
2:    for $i \leftarrow 1, T_p$ do
3:      $Optimal \leftarrow rotation(fun, Optimal, SE, \alpha)$
4:    end for

where, the realization of optimal parameter selection for the rotation factor is conducted by equation update alpha. In this way, the common periodical reduction of the transformation factors is abandoned. The parameter to be optimized is chosen for each state transformation with the exception of the translation operator and the best parameter selected is held within a certain period.

2.2.3. Prediction Process of Improved GPR on Basis of Modified STA (MSTA-GPR)

Three steps are carried out to realize the proposed MSTA-GPR model: Step 1. Initialization; Step 2. The selection of optimal hyper-parameters. The description of the fitness function is shown as Equation (9); Step 3. Forecasting. The flowchart of MSTA-GPR is shown in Figure 2.

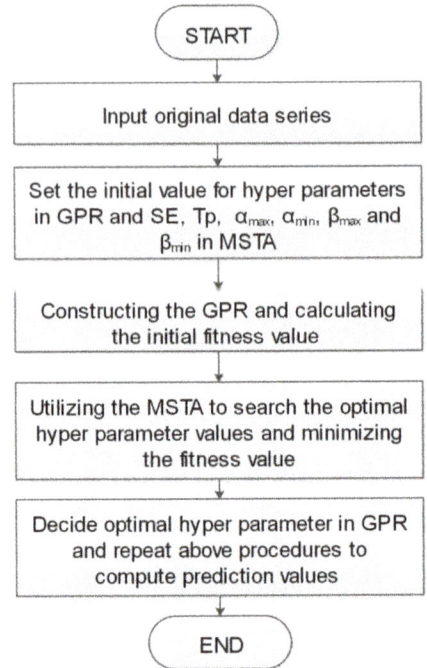

Figure 2. The implementation steps of the proposed modified state transition algorithm-Gaussian processes regression model (MSTA-GPR).

The details of each step are described as follow:

Step 1. (Initialization): The training set is built to form the input and the covariance function is selected for GPR.

Step 2. (Selection of optimal hyper-parameters):

Step 2.1. Parameter setting: A random initial solution $Optimal_0$ is created in the searching space. Parameters for MSTA are set: $\alpha = \alpha_{max}, \alpha_{min}, \beta = \beta_{max}, \beta_{min}, \gamma, T_p, fun$, and SE. The max function estimations are set to $5e4 * n * \log(n)$ and n is the amount of the decision variables.

Step 2.2. Expansion: Create SE potential solutions with the expansion transformation operator on basis of the optimal solution $Optimal_k$ found so far. Renew the optimal solution when $Optimal_k$ is promoted. After that, translation transformation operator is applied and the optimal solution is renewed; otherwise not.

Step 2.3. Rotation: Create SE potential solutions with the rotation transformation operator on basis of the optimal solution $Optimal_k$ found so far. Renew the optimal solution when $Optimal_k$ is promoted. After that, the translation transformation operator is applied and the optimal solution is renewed; otherwise not.

Step 2.4. Optimal parameter selection for STA: the optimal transformation factors are selected for STA according to the description in Section 2.2.2.

Step 2.5. Termination: If α or β is beyond the upper or lower bound, they will be set as the corresponding value of the upper or lower bound. The iteration continues until the corresponding termination is achieved. Thus, the optimal hyper-parameters of GPR are found.

Step 3. (Prediction): The new data are introduced to form the corresponding input of the MSTA-GPR model for prediction. Finally, the forecasting results are obtained.

3. Validation of MSTA Optimization

In this section, the global optimization ability of MSTA is investigated with two famous equations, which can validate the effectiveness of the modification in basic STA. The test equations are shown as follow:

(1) Rosenbrock function:

$$f_1 = \sum_{i=1}^{n} \left(100(x_{i+1} - x_i^2)^2 + (x_i - 1)^2\right). \quad (17)$$

The constrain for the equation above is $x_i \in [0, \pi]$, $i = 1, 2, \ldots, n$. The optimal solution is $x_{op} = (0, \ldots, 0)$ and the corresponding optimal value for the function is 0.

(2) Michalewicz function:

$$f_2 = -\sum_{i=1}^{n} \sin(x_i) \sin\left(\frac{i x_i^2}{\pi}\right)^{20}. \quad (18)$$

The constrain for the equation above is that $x_i \in [0, \pi]$, $i = 1, 2, \ldots, n$. And the corresponding optimal value for the equation is not known.

The basic STA and two widely used optimization approaches, which are PSO and GA, are utilized to form comparisons for MSTA. The corresponding parameter setting recommended for the algorithms involved are shown in Table 1. The dimension for decision variable is investigated at 20, 30, and 50. Aiming for comparisons in the same situation, all programs are coded in Matlab 2018a on a personal computer with 8 GB RAM under a Windows environment and the computation procedures are conducted 20 times.

Table 1. Parameter setting for each optimization model involved. GA, genetic algorithm; PSO, particle swarm optimization.

Prediction Approaches	Parameter	Value
MSTA	SE	20
	T_p	10
	Range	$[10^{-3} \times \text{Dim}, 1000 \times \text{Dim}]$
STA [36]	SE	20
	Rotation factor scope	$[10^{-4}, 1]$
	Translation factor	1
	Expansion factor	1
	Axesion factor	1
GA [41]	Population	20
	Crossover rate	0.95
	Tournament size	2
	Mutation rate	0.05
PSO [42]	Swarm size	30
	Inertia range	[0.1,1.1]
	Self-adjustment weight	1.49
	Social-adjustment weight	1.49
	Minimum neighborhood size	0.25 × swam size

It can be known from Table 2 that, in the case of the Rosenbrock function, the optimization performance of MSTA is validated to be the best compared with the other three comparison optimization algorithms regardless of the best, worst, or mean situation. And even as the dimension of the independent variable increases, the MSTA can still achieve a satisfactory result which is superior to the optimization outcomes of STA, GA, or PSO. Moreover, in the case of the Michalewicz function, as the global optimal solution is not known, the optimization capacity of each algorithm can be better explored one step further on. It can still be seen that from Table 2, the optimal outcomes obtained by MSTA are the best among all the optimization algorithms under different situations and dimensions, which again proves the superiority of MSTA optimization. For example, when the dimension takes 20, compared with STA, GA, and PSO, the mean optimal value promotion of MSTA is 8.15%, 9.94% and 97.32%, respectively. Conclusively, the two validation cases show the effectiveness of the modification for the basic STA. Integrated with the optimal parameter selection, the performance of MSTA is thus improved significantly and is better than that of the basic STA and the two traditional optimal algorithms, which makes it a better choice for hyper parameter optimization in GPR.

Table 2. Validation comparisons of different optimization algorithms.

Fun		f_1			f_2		
Dim		20	30	50	20	30	50
MSTA	Best	6.06×10^{-7}	8.40×10^{-7}	1.84×10^{-6}	−19.96	−29.95	−49.97
	Worst	1.10×10^{-6}	1.88×10^{-6}	2.87×10^{-6}	−19.78	−29.87	−49.93
	Mean	8.03×10^{-7}	1.26×10^{-6}	2.16×10^{-6}	−19.91	−29.91	−49.95
STA	Best	11.17	23.75	36.91	−19.60	−29.53	−49.39
	Worst	13.57	24.66	45.34	−17.60	−27.51	−46.51
	Mean	12.94	24.10	42.34	−18.41	−28.82	−47.85
GA	Best	0.49	0.04	0.08	−18.11	−28.86	−41.26
	Worst	0.49	0.04	0.08	−18.11	−28.86	−41.26
	Mean	0.49	0.04	0.08	−18.11	−28.86	−41.26
PSO	Best	13.26	1.48	13.24	10.09	−15.76	−7.97
	Worst	13.26	1.48	13.24	10.09	−15.76	−7.97
	Mean	13.26	1.48	13.24	10.09	−15.76	−7.97

4. Application of MSTA-GPR for Overall Renewable Energy Consumption Prediction in China

In this Section, the MSTA-GPR approach is applied for the renewable energy consumption prediction in China. Aiming for validation of the superiority of MSTA-GPR approach, the corresponding forecasting results are compared with that of PSO-GPR [43], GPR [44] and the autoregressive integrated moving average ARIMA model [45]. The basic data are offered by the BP statistical Review of World Energy 2019. The training set is formed utilizing observations obtained from 2008 to 2015 to train each forecasting model involved, and the first three years of the thirteenth Five-Year Project (2016–2020) are considered to validate the corresponding prediction effect. All the original data are listed in Table 3.

Table 3. The consumption data for China's renewable energy from 2006 to 2018.

Year	Overall	Hydropower	Wind	Solar	Geothermal Biomass and Other
2006	101.08	98.61	0.84	0.02	1.61
2007	113.30	109.80	1.24	0.03	2.23
2008	150.49	144.13	2.96	0.03	3.36
2009	150.33	139.30	6.25	0.06	4.72
2010	176.86	160.97	10.10	0.16	5.63
2011	178.46	155.69	15.91	0.59	6.27
2012	224.66	195.23	21.72	0.81	6.90
2013	248.10	205.82	31.95	1.89	8.44
2014	288.99	237.85	35.32	5.32	10.50
2015	316.31	252.19	42.03	9.86	12.23
2016	342.62	260.96	53.64	13.96	14.06
2017	375.04	263.63	66.75	26.65	18.01
2018	415.59	272.08	82.82	40.16	20.53

Besides, aiming for the prediction performance evaluation, the mean absolute percent error (MAPE) is computed for the forecasting outcome of each model involved. The equation of MAPE is described as follow:

$$MAPE = \frac{1}{Y}\sum_{y=1}^{Y}\left|\frac{p^{true}(y) - p^{forecast}(y)}{p^{true}(y)}\right| \times 100\% \quad (19)$$

where, $p^{true}(y)$ means the data recorded at year y, $p^{forecast}(y)$ means the prediction of year y, and Y is the amount of all the values to be predicted.

4.1. Overall Renewable Energy Consumption

The suggested MSTA-GPR approach is utilized in this part to investigate the overall renewable energy consumption prediction in China. The predictions and corresponding indexes are displayed in Table 4. Figure 3 displays the interval prediction for the overall renewable energy consumption in China from 2016 to 2018. And in the interval prediction, the 95% upper bound and the 95% lower bound reveal the maximum values and minimum values respectively that can be obtained by GPR when the confidence level of the regression prediction result is 95%.

Table 4. Consumption prediction for overall renewable energy of China from 2006 to 2018 (Mtoe). ARIMA, autoregressive integrated moving average; MAPE, mean absolute percent error.

Year	Real Data	MSTA-GPR Value	Error (%)	PSO-GPR Value	Error (%)	GPR Value	Error (%)	ARIMA Value	Error (%)
2016	342.62	347.08	1.30	348.39	1.68	348.88	1.83	343.72	0.32
2017	375.04	375.04	0.00	374.40	0.17	374.70	0.09	371.17	1.03
2018	415.59	405.29	2.48	401.07	3.49	400.94	3.53	398.66	4.07
MAPE			1.26		1.78		1.81		1.81

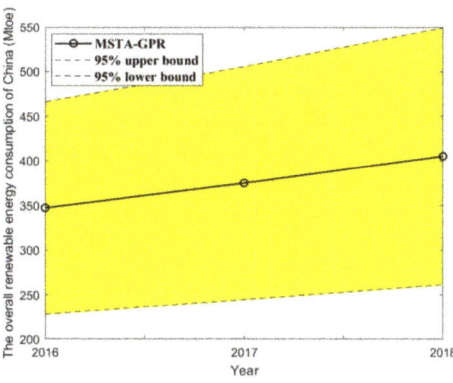

Figure 3. The interval prediction result of MSTA-GPR for overall renewable energy consumption in China.

From Table 4 and Figure 3, it can be observed that the prediction outcomes reveal that the MSTA-GPR approach offers a more satisfactory forecasting accuracy than the other approaches in consumption predicting of the overall renewable energy in China. It can be obtained from the historical data that in recent years, the development of China's overall renewable energy consumption is close to linear growth. Hence, GPR and ARIMA have similar prediction performance. Compared with GPR and ARIMA, the MSTA-GPR approach has promoted each forecasting accuracy by 30.39%. Optimized by PSO, the prediction performance of PSO-GPR is slightly better than that of basic GPR. Compared with PSO-GPR, the MSTA-GPR approach has promoted the forecasting accuracy by 29.21%. This comparison result indicates that the global ability of MSTA is better than that of PSO. As can be seen from Table 4, the trend of overall renewable energy consumption in China keeps growing in the last few years and will continue to maintain in the future. According to the latest published statistics, by the first half of 2019, the amount of electricity generated by renewable energy has reached 887.9 billion kWh, which increases 14% compared with that of last year.

4.2. Hydroelectricity Consumption in China

This part investigates the prediction of China's hydroelectricity consumption. The prediction outcomes of each model and corresponding errors are displayed in Table A1 of Appendix A. Furthermore, the interval prediction for China's hydroelectricity consumption is described in Figure A1 of Appendix A.

From Table A1 and Figure A1, it can be observed that the prediction outcomes reveal that the MSTA-GPR approach offers a more satisfactory forecasting performance than the other approaches in predicting the hydroelectricity consumption of China. As can be obtained from the historical data, the growth trend of hydroelectricity is not continuous. The forecasting performance of ARIMA is the worst of all. Compared with ARIMA, the MSTA-GPR approach has promoted the forecasting accuracy by 91.08%. GPR offers a better forecasting result than that of ARIMA by recognizing the non-linear features in the historical data. However, the prediction performance of GPR is not the best because the hyper-parameters are not optimized. Compared with GPR, the MSTA-GPR approach has promoted the forecasting accuracy by 66.67%. Combined with PSO, the forecasting accuracy of PSO-GPR is further promoted than basic GPR. But PSO is easy to fall into the local optimum in the process of searching the optimal solution. Compared with PSO-GPR, the MSTA-GPR approach has promoted the forecasting accuracy by 29.54%. In recent years, the growth rate of hydropower has slowed down, but still accounts for the largest proportion of renewable energy consumption in China. The latest published statistics shows that, by the first half year of 2019, the amount of electricity generated by hydropower is 513.8 billion kWh, which has promoted by 11.8% compared with that of last year.

4.3. Wind Power Consumption in China

This Section explores the prediction of China's wind power consumption. Prediction outcome of each model and corresponding errors are displayed in Table A2 of Appendix A. Additionally, the interval prediction for China's wind power consumption is described in Figure A2 of Appendix A.

From Table A2 and Figure A2, it can be observed that the prediction outcomes reveal that the MSTA-GPR approach offers a more satisfactory forecasting performance than the other approaches in predicting the wind power consumption of China. According to historical data, the consumption of wind power has increased rapidly in recent years. As a traditional time series forecasting method, ARIMA cannot capture the nonlinear growth trend of wind power consumption well, which results in a poor forecasting result. Compared with ARIMA, the MSTA-GPR approach has promoted the forecasting accuracy by 36.81%. Owning to the advantage of recognizing non-linear features in data, both PSO-GPR and GPR can obtain better forecasting results than ARIMA. However, due to the lack of a more effective hyper parameter optimization method, their forecasting performances are not good as that of MSTA-GPR. Compared with PSO-GPR and GPR, the MSTA-GPR approach has promoted the forecasting accuracy by 7.98% and 25.07%, respectively. In recent years, with the gradual maturity of technology, wind power generation has been vigorously developed, and the amount generated by wind power is increasing year by year. By the first half year of 2019, the wind power generation in China has achieved 214.5 billion kWh, which has promoted by 11.5% compared with that of last year.

4.4. Solar Power Consumption in China

The solar power consumption prediction of China is investigated in this Section utilizing the MSTA-GPR approach. The prediction outcomes of each model and corresponding errors are displayed in Table A3 of Appendix A. Additionally, the interval prediction for China's solar power consumption is described in Figure A3 of Appendix A.

From Table A3 and Figure A3, it can be observed that the prediction outcomes reveal that the MSTA-GPR approach offers a more satisfactory forecasting performance than the other approaches in predicting the solar power consumption of China. The solar power consumption experiences a rapid growth in recent years. But ARIMA cannot follow the rapid changes of solar power consumption, which results in a low prediction accuracy. Compared with ARIMA, the MSTA-GPR approach has promoted the forecasting accuracy by 63.15%. In contrast, PSO-GPR and GPR can adapt to the rapid changes of solar power consumption in the short term and get better prediction results. But their forecasting accuracy is not the best. Compared with PSO-GPR and GPR, the MSTA-GPR approach has promoted the forecasting accuracy by 0.58% and 29.89%, respectively. With the implementation of the renewable energy incentive policy, solar power generation has been vigorously promoted, and its proportion in renewable energy consumption has also increased year by year. According to the latest data published, by the first half year of 2019, the solar power generation has reached 106.7 billion kWh, which has promoted by 30% compared with that of last year.

4.5. Geothermal, Biomass and Other Energy Consumption Prediction in China

This Section explores the predictions of China's geothermal, biomass and other energy consumption. The prediction outcomes of each model and corresponding errors are displayed in Table A4 of Appendix A. Additionally, the corresponding interval prediction is described in Figure A4 of Appendix A.

From Table A4 and Figure A4, it can be observed that the prediction outcomes reveal that the MSTA-GPR approach offers a more satisfactory forecasting performance than the other approaches in predicting the geothermal, biomass and other types of energy consumption of China. Compared with PSO-GPR, GPR and ARIMA, the MSTA-GPR approach has promoted the forecasting accuracy by 1.94%, 20.98% and 67.49%, respectively. The results show that, compared with the other models, the proposed MSTA-GPR model has better nonlinear feature recognition ability and more effective parameter optimization ability in small sample data set. The geothermal, biomass and other types of energy consumption in China have enriched the diversity of the energy supply structure and have experienced steady development in recent years. For example, biomass power generation has reached 52.9 billion kWh, which has increased 21.3% compared with that of last year.

4.6. Discussion

In contrast with PSO-GPR, GPR and ARIMA, the proposed MSTA-GPR displays a better forecasting result, owning to the effective parameter optimization of MSTA in hyper parameter selection for GPR. The forecasting outcomes reveal the changes of future energy consumption development in China. As obtained from the data in previous sections, the overall renewable energy consumption will grow at a mean rate of 8.25% during the thirteenth Five-Year Project, and the consumption of China's hydroelectricity will slightly grow at a mean rate of 1.60%. Additionally, the mean increase rate for China's wind power, solar power and geothermal, biomass and other types of energy consumption are 20.36%, 58.76% and 16.73%, respectively.

As far as we know, with the steady and rapid development of the economy, China's energy consumption will maintain a sustained growth momentum in the future. However, China's energy consumption system is still dominated by fossil fuels right now. The dependency on fossil fuel consumption is not sustainable, and serious environmental problems may occur owing to fossil fuel combustion, such as the greenhouse effect, acid rain, and others. China's renewable energy consumption will continue to grow at a steady speed, and the composition of the overall energy consumption will be more reasonable and balanced along with the application of corresponding energy policies. The prediction outcomes of this paper can offer useful information for the decision maker to foresee the future changes of renewable energy development and handle the environmental pollution problems, which can contribute for a smooth transition towards the 14th Five-Year Project and sustainable development in the future.

5. Conclusions

By integrating the modified state transition algorithm into Gaussian process regression, a novel approach MSTA-GPR is developed to make predictions more effective for China's renewable energy consumption. The main contribution of this article is to promote the forecasting performance of GPR with the application of MSTA in optimal hyper parameter selection. The superiority of MSTA in global optimization is validated with two well-known functions against the basic STA, GA and PSO. The suggested MSTA-GPR model is applied with the real data from 2008 to 2015 to make predictions of renewable energy consumption in China for the first three years of 13th Five-Year Project (2016–2020) to test the prediction performance.

The suggested approach can be easily applied and proved to be effective for short period prediction of time series. The forecasting outcomes reveal that compared with PSO-GPR, GPR and ARIMA, the MAPE of forecasting outcomes obtained by MSTA-GPR is superior to that of the other forecasting methods. This proves that the proposed MSTA-GPR is a better approach for renewable energy consumption and the forecasting performance of MSTA-GPR is better than hybrid model PSO-GPR, the basic GPR, and the traditional time series forecasting method ARIMA. Furthermore, the proposed MSTA-GPR approach is also supposed to deal with other complicated energy problems with various influence factors, for instance the price of electricity [46], solar radiation [47], and so on.

Author Contributions: L.Y. put forward the original idea in this paper and wrote the original manuscript; Y.J. and Y.D. offered the model technical support; Y.H. and C.G. reviewed and offered modification suggestions.

Funding: This investigation was funded by Baoding Low Carbon Economy Industry Research Institute Construction Project (2016BD0056).

Acknowledgments: The authors want to give thanks to the support of Baoding Low Carbon Economy Industry Research Institute Construction Project (2016BD0056).

Conflicts of Interest: The authors state that there is no conflict of interest.

Appendix A

Table A1. Consumption prediction for hydroelectricity of China from 2016 to 2018 (Mtoe).

Year	Real Data	MSTA-GPR		PSO-GPR		GPR		ARIMA	
		Value	Error (%)	Value	Error (%)	Value	Error (%)	Value	Error (%)
2016	260.96	260.96	0.00	257.65	1.27	261.97	0.39	267.82	2.63
2017	263.63	268.54	1.86	267.27	1.38	272.20	3.25	284.06	7.75
2018	272.08	272.08	0.00	272.08	0.00	277.34	1.93	300.58	10.47
MAPE			0.62		0.88		1.86		6.95

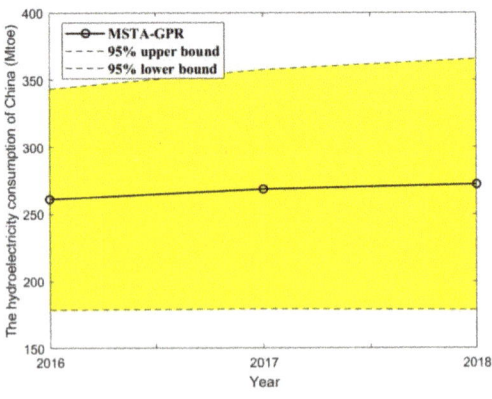

Figure A1. The interval prediction result of MSTA-GPR for China's hydroelectricity consumption.

Table A2. Wind power consumption data for China from 2016 to 2018 (Mtoe).

Year	Real Data	MSTA-GPR Value	Error (%)	PSO-GPR Value	Error (%)	GPR Value	Error (%)	ARIMA Value	Error (%)
2016	53.64	49.81	7.15	49.65	7.45	48.92	8.80	49.03	8.59
2017	66.75	61.32	8.14	60.79	8.94	59.59	10.74	56.28	15.69
2018	82.82	75.42	8.93	74.59	9.94	73.36	11.42	63.72	23.06
MAPE			8.07		8.77		10.32		15.78

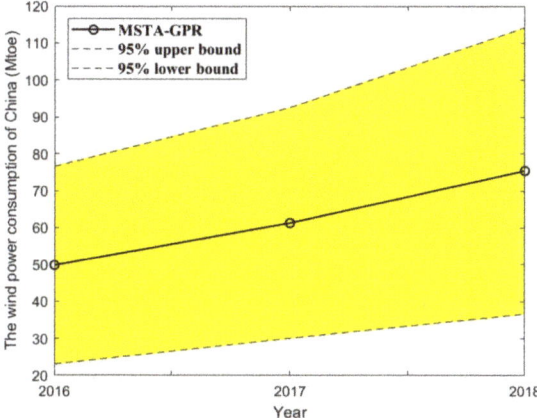

Figure A2. The interval prediction result of MSTA-GPR for China's wind power consumption.

Table A3. Solar power consumption data for China from 2016 to 2018 (Mtoe).

Year	Real Data	MSTA-GPR Value	Error (%)	PSO-GPR Value	Error (%)	GPR Value	Error (%)	ARIMA Value	Error (%)
2016	13.96	15.40	10.36	15.47	10.84	16.71	19.72	14.60	4.62
2017	26.66	22.58	15.31	22.66	15.00	24.61	7.68	19.56	26.62
2018	40.16	40.16	0.00	40.16	0.00	43.88	9.26	24.73	38.44
MAPE			8.56		8.61		12.21		23.23

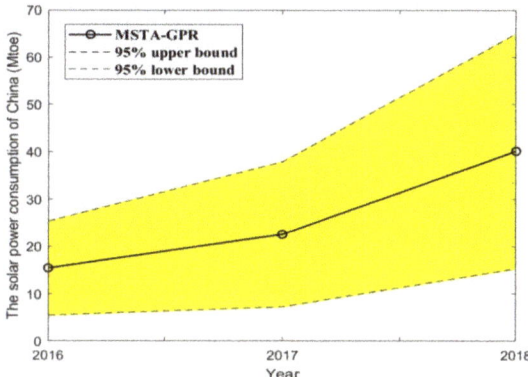

Figure A3. The interval prediction result of MSTA-GPR for China's solar power consumption.

Table A4. Consumption prediction for geothermal, biomass and other energy from 2016 to 2018 (Mtoe).

Year	Real Data	MSTA-GPR Value	Error (%)	PSO-GPR Value	Error (%)	GPR Value	Error (%)	ARIMA Value	Error (%)
2016	14.06	14.22	1.13	14.08	0.17	14.36	2.13	13.88	1.28
2017	18.01	16.30	9.48	16.09	10.66	16.54	8.14	15.46	14.16
2018	20.53	20.53	0.00	20.53	0.00	21.18	3.19	16.99	17.22
MAPE			3.54		3.61		4.48		10.89

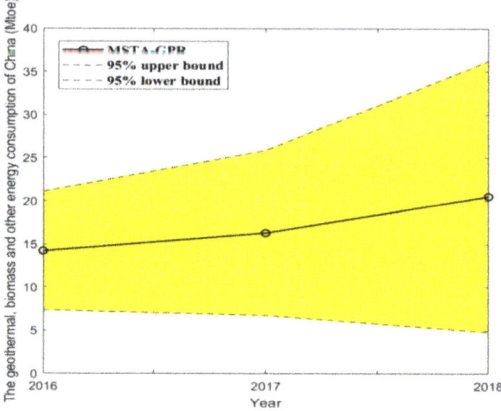

Figure A4. The interval prediction result of MSTA-GPR for China's geothermal, biomass and other energy consumption.

References

1. Divina, F.; Gilson, A.; Goméz-Vela, F.; García Torres, M.; Torres, J. Stacking ensemble learning for short-term electricity consumption forecasting. *Energies* **2018**, *11*, 949. [CrossRef]
2. Pahle, M.; Pachauri, S.; Steinbacher, K. Can the Green Economy deliver it all? Experiences of renewable energy policies with socio-economic objectives. *Appl. Energy* **2016**, *179*, 1331–1341. [CrossRef]
3. Singh, S.; Yassine, A. Big data mining of energy time series for behavioral analytics and energy consumption forecasting. *Energies* **2018**, *11*, 452. [CrossRef]
4. Chang, Y.; Zheng, F.; Li, Y. Renewable energy policies in promoting financing and investment among the East Asia Summit countries: Quantitative assessment and policy implications. *Energy Policy* **2016**, *95*, 427–436. [CrossRef]
5. Wang, Q. Effects of urbanisation on energy consumption in China. *Energy Policy* **2014**, *65*, 332–339. [CrossRef]
6. Qiang, W.; Kan, Z. A framework for evaluating global national energy security. *Appl. Energy* **2017**, *188*, 19–31.
7. Ang, B.W.; Choong, W.L.; Ng, T.S. A framework for evaluating Singapore's energy security. *Appl. Energy* **2015**, *148*, 314–325. [CrossRef]
8. Bauer, N.; Mouratiadou, I.; Luderer, G.; Baumstark, L.; Brecha, R.J.; Edenhofer, O.; Kriegler, E. Global fossil energy markets and climate change mitigation—An analysis with REMIND. *Clim. Change* **2016**, *136*, 69–82. [CrossRef]
9. Dirks, J.A.; Gorrissen, W.J.; Hathaway, J.H.; Skorski, D.C.; Scott, M.J.; Pulsipher, T.C.; Huang, M.; Ying, L.; Rice, J.S. Impacts of climate change on energy consumption and peak demand in buildings: A detailed regional approach. *Energy* **2015**, *79*, 20–32. [CrossRef]
10. Dai, H.; Xie, X.; Yang, X.; Jian, L.; Masui, T. Green growth: The economic impacts of large-scale renewable energy development in China. *Appl. Energy* **2015**, *162*, 435–449. [CrossRef]
11. Martínez-Álvarez, F.; Troncoso, A.; Riquelme, J. Recent Advances in Energy Time Series Forecasting. *Energies* **2017**, *10*, 809. [CrossRef]
12. Schnaars, S.P. How to develop and use scenarios. *Long Range Plan.* **1987**, *20*, 105–114. [CrossRef]

13. Dong, K.Y.; Sun, R.J.; Li, H.; Jiang, H.D. A review of China's energy consumption structure and outlook based on a long-range energy alternatives modeling tool. *Pet. Sci.* **2017**, *14*, 214–227. [CrossRef]
14. Soroush, R.; Koochi, A.; Keivani, M.; Abadyan, M. A Bilayer Model for Incorporating the Coupled Effects of Surface Energy and Microstructure on the Electromechanical Stability of NEMS. *Int. J. Struct. Stab. Dyn.* **2017**, *17*, 1771005. [CrossRef]
15. Gabriel, S.A.; Kydes, A.S.; Whitman, P. The national energy modeling system: A large-scale energy-economic equilibrium model. *Oper. Res.* **2001**, *49*, 14–25. [CrossRef]
16. Meenal, R.; Selvakumar, A.I. Assessment of SVM, empirical and ANN based solar radiation prediction models with most influencing input parameters. *Renew. Energy* **2018**, *121*, 324–343. [CrossRef]
17. Cai, W.; Lai, K.H.; Liu, C.; Wei, F.; Ma, M.; Jia, S.; Jiang, Z.; Lv, L. Promoting sustainability of manufacturing industry through the lean energy-saving and emission-reduction strategy. *Sci. Total Environ.* **2019**, *665*, 23–32. [CrossRef]
18. Pei, D.; Wang, J.; Yang, W.; Tong, N. Multi-step ahead forecasting in electrical power system using a hybrid forecasting system. *Renew. Energy* **2018**, *122*, 533–550.
19. Rasmussen, C.E.; Nickisch, H. Gaussian Processes for Machine Learning (GPML) Toolbox. *J. Mach. Learn. Res.* **2010**, *11*, 3011–3015.
20. Jie, Y.; Chen, K.; Rashid, M.M. A Bayesian model averaging based multi-kernel Gaussian process regression framework for nonlinear state estimation and quality prediction of multiphase batch processes with transient dynamics and uncertainty. *Chem. Eng. Sci.* **2013**, *93*, 96–109.
21. Nair, R.; Jhingan, S.; Jain, D. Testing the consistency between cosmological measurements of distance and age. *Phys. Lett. B* **2015**, *745*, 64–68. [CrossRef]
22. Baraldi, P.; Mangili, F.; Zio, E. A belief function theory based approach to combining different representation of uncertainty in prognostics. *Inf. Sci.* **2015**, *303*, 134–149. [CrossRef]
23. Bogdan, M.; Brugger, D.; Rosenstiel, W.; Speiser, B. Estimation of diffusion coefficients from voltammetric signals by support vector and gaussian process regression. *J. Cheminform.* **2014**, *6*, 30. [CrossRef] [PubMed]
24. Chen, J.; Chan, L.L.T.; Cheng, Y.C. Gaussian process regression based optimal design of combustion systems using flame images. *Appl. Energy* **2013**, *111*, 153–160. [CrossRef]
25. Peng, K.; Feng, G.; Guan, X. Sparse online warped Gaussian process for wind power probabilistic forecasting. *Appl. Energy* **2013**, *108*, 410–428.
26. Wang, J.; Hu, J. A robust combination approach for short-term wind speed forecasting and analysis—Combination of the ARIMA (Autoregressive Integrated Moving Average), ELM (Extreme Learning Machine), SVM (Support Vector Machine) and LSSVM (Least Square SVM) forecasts us. *Energy* **2015**, *93*, 41–56. [CrossRef]
27. He, Z.K.; Liu, G.B.; Zhao, X.J.; Wang, M.H. Overview of Gaussian process regression. *Control Decis.* **2013**, *28*, 1121–1129.
28. Xiong, Z.H.; Huang, G.H.; Shao, H.H. Comparison and Application Research on Soft Sensor Modeling Based on Gaussian Processes and Support Vector Machines. *Inf. Control* **2004**, *33*, 754–757.
29. Liu, K.; Liu, B.; Chong, X.U. Intelligent analysis model of slope nonlinear displacement time series based on genetic-gaussian process regression algorithm of combined kernel function. *Chin. J. Rock Mech. Eng.* **2009**, *28*, 2128–2134.
30. Yu, S.; Ke, W.; Wei, Y.M. A hybrid self-adaptive Particle Swarm Optimization–Genetic Algorithm–Radial Basis Function model for annual electricity demand prediction. *Energy Convers. Manag.* **2015**, *91*, 176–185. [CrossRef]
31. Rahmani, R.; Yusof, R.; Seyedmahmoudian, M.; Mekhilef, S. Hybrid technique of ant colony and particle swarm optimization for short term wind energy forecasting. *J. Wind Eng. Ind. Aerodyn.* **2013**, *123*, 163–170. [CrossRef]
32. Bahrami, S.; Hooshmand, R.A.; Parastegari, M. Short term electric load forecasting by wavelet transform and grey model improved by PSO (particle swarm optimization) algorithm. *Energy* **2014**, *72*, 434–442. [CrossRef]
33. Hui, L.; Tian, H.; Liang, X.; Li, Y. New wind speed forecasting approaches using fast ensemble empirical model decomposition, genetic algorithm, Mind Evolutionary Algorithm and Artificial Neural Networks. *Renew. Energy* **2015**, *83*, 1066–1075.

34. Hui, L.; Tian, H.Q.; Chao, C.; Li, Y.F. An experimental investigation of two Wavelet-MLP hybrid frameworks for wind speed prediction using GA and PSO optimization. *Int. J. Electr. Power Energy Syst.* **2013**, *52*, 161–173.
35. Da, L.; Niu, D.; Hui, W.; Fan, L. Short-term wind speed forecasting using wavelet transform and support vector machines optimized by genetic algorithm. *Renew. Energy* **2014**, *62*, 592–597.
36. Miao, H.; Zhou, X.; Huang, T.; Yang, C.; Gui, W. Dynamic optimization based on state transition algorithm for copper removal process. *Neural Comput. Appl.* **2017**, *31*, 2827–2839.
37. Rasmussen, C.E.; Williams, C.K.I. *Gaussian Processes for Machine Learning (Adaptive Computation and Machine Learning)*; The MIT Press: Cambridge, MA, USA, 2005; pp. 69–106.
38. Fang, D.; Zhang, X.; Yu, Q.; Jin, T.C.; Tian, L. A novel method for carbon dioxide emission forecasting based on improved Gaussian processes regression. *J. Clean. Prod.* **2018**, *173*, 143–150. [CrossRef]
39. Zhou, X.; Yang, C.; Gui, W. Nonlinear system identification and control using state transition algorithm. *Appl. Math. Comput.* **2014**, *226*, 169–179. [CrossRef]
40. Zhou, X.; Yang, C.; Gui, W. A Statistical Study on Parameter Selection of Operators in Continuous State Transition Algorithm. *IEEE Trans. Cybern.* **2019**, *49*, 3722–3730. [CrossRef]
41. Tran, T.D.; Jin, G.G. Real-coded genetic algorithm benchmarked on noiseless black-box optimization testbed. In Proceedings of the 12th Annual Conference Companion on Genetic and Evolutionary Computation, Portland, OR, USA, 7–11 July 2010; ACM: New York, NY, USA, 2010; pp. 1731–1738.
42. Iadevaia, S.; Lu, Y.; Morales, F.C.; Mills, G.B.; Ram, P.T. Identification of optimal drug combinations targeting cellular networks: Integrating phospho-proteomics and computational network analysis. *Cancer Res.* **2010**, *70*, 6704–6714. [CrossRef]
43. Guo, J.; Chen, F.; Xu, C. Traffic Flow Forecasting for Road Tunnel Using PSO-GPR Algorithm with Combined Kernel Function. *Math. Probl. Eng.* **2017**, *2017*, 2090783. [CrossRef]
44. Gao, W.; Karbasi, M.; Hasanipanah, M.; Zhang, X.; Guo, J. Developing GPR model for forecasting the rock fragmentation in surface mines. *Eng. Comput.* **2018**, *34*, 339–345.
45. Karmy, J.P.; Maldonado, S. Hierarchical Time Series Forecasting via Support Vector Regression in the European Travel Retail Industry. *Expert Syst. Appl.* **2019**, *137*, 59–73. [CrossRef]
46. Yang, W.; Wang, J.; Niu, T.; Du, P. A hybrid forecasting system based on a dual decomposition strategy and multi-objective optimization for electricity price forecasting. *Appl. Energy* **2019**, *235*, 1205–1225. [CrossRef]
47. Fan, J.; Wu, L.; Zhang, F.; Cai, H.; Zeng, W.; Wang, X.; Zou, H. Empirical and machine learning models for predicting daily global solar radiation from sunshine duration: A review and case study in China. *Renew. Sustain. Energy Rev.* **2019**, *100*, 186–212. [CrossRef]

© 2019 by the authors. Licensee MDPI, Basel, Switzerland. This article is an open access article distributed under the terms and conditions of the Creative Commons Attribution (CC BY) license (http://creativecommons.org/licenses/by/4.0/).

Article

A Test of Using Markov-Switching GARCH Models in Oil and Natural Gas Trading

Oscar V. De la Torre-Torres [1], Evaristo Galeana-Figueroa [1,*] and José Álvarez-García [2]

[1] Faculty of Accounting and Management, Saint Nicholas and Hidalgo Michoacán State University (UMSNH), 58030 Morelia, Mexico; oscar.delatorre.torres@gmail.com
[2] Financial Economy and Accounting Department, Faculty of Business, Finance and Tourism, University of Extremadura, 10071 Cáceres, Spain; pepealvarez@unex.com
* Correspondence: e_galeana@hotmail.com

Received: 18 November 2019; Accepted: 17 December 2019; Published: 26 December 2019

Abstract: In this paper, we test the use of Markov-switching (MS) GARCH (MSGARCH) models for trading either oil or natural gas futures. Using weekly data from 7 January 1994 to 31 May 2019, we tested the next trading rule: to invest in the simulated commodity if the investor expects to be in the low-volatility regime at t + 1 or to otherwise hold the risk-free asset. Assumptions for our simulations included the following: (1) we assumed that the investors trade in a homogeneous (Gaussian or t-Student) two regime context and (2) the investor used a time-fixed, ARCH, or GARCH variance in each regime. Our results suggest that the use of the MS Gaussian model, with time-fixed variance, leads to the best performance in the oil market. For the case of natural gas, we found no benefit of using our trading rule against a buy-and-hold strategy in the three-month U.S. Treasury bills.

Keywords: Markov-switching; Markov-switching GARCH; energy futures; commodities; portfolio management; active investment; diversification; institutional investors; energy price hedging

1. Introduction

Energy futures, such as oil and natural gas, are a widely used means for hedging the commodity price risk and also for investing and speculation. Given their close relationship with economic activity and general prices, energy commodities (especially oil) have also been a source of portfolio diversification. Nowadays, given electronic trading, as well as global flow of capital, it is possible for institutional investors to diversify their investments, given the expected correlations of commodities with securities such as stocks and bonds. Some related tests about the benefits of diversification with alternative assets (such as commodities) are found in [1–3]. Nevertheless, there are some issues with the correlations between commodities and conventional assets that need to be addressed. The first issue is the level of the contagion effect (i.e., higher positive correlations), given the corresponding increase of the demand in alternative assets such as commodities [4,5]. An alternative asset, in terms of the investment industry, is different from the three types of conventional securities which include: money market instrument, fixed income, and equity. The second issue to be addressed is that investing in a commodity index adds little mean-variance efficiency to a portfolio [6]. In other words, the diversification benefit for a portfolio is observed only with agricultural commodities [4] and other types of alternative assets, such as real estate [5], hedge funds [6], volatility futures [3], or clean-energy (technology) stocks [7]. Despite this, the issue of a diversified portfolio has been tested in several academic reviews, such as in [2,8,9] which are some of the most recent ones.

Among the potential causes of limited diversification benefits in commodities, is the fact that the correlation between the commodities and conventional securities increases significantly in distress time periods. This is a phenomenon known as "correlation clustering" and implies that the correlation levels are not always negative or close to zero and tend to increase during bad-performing time periods in financial markets.

Confirmation of the presence of correlation clustering has been probed by several studies such as [10–14] which are some of the most recent and closely related studies to this paper. Additionally, [15–17] found evidence of correlation clustering, by measuring this effect in two regimes. In these cases, similar to this paper, the authors split the states of nature (or regimes) into two regimes, as follows:

1. A $k = 1$, "normal", good-performing, or low volatility regime, in which the price fluctuations are narrow, and the expected returns tend to be positive;
2. A $k = 2$, "distress", bad-performing, or high volatility regime, in which the price fluctuations tend to be wider than the ones in $k = 1$. In addition, it is expected to have negative returns in this regime.

Therefore, and as detailed in the methodology section, it is expected that the standard deviation in the second regime is higher than the observed in the first regime: $\sigma_{k=2} > \sigma_{s=1}$.

Given the marginal diversification benefits of commodities in a portfolio, trading activities in energy commodities could be more appropriate for active trading purposes. Therefore, we aim to test a trading strategy in the following most traded energy commodities futures in the U.S. [18]: The one-month West Texas Intermediate (henceforth OIL) and Henry Hub delivered natural gas (NATGAS).

Departing from the motivation that an energy commodity index in a portfolio could lead to marginal risk-return benefits [4,5], an interesting question to answer is, "What would the performance of a given investor have been if she followed the next active trading strategy at t?"

1. To invest in a risk-free asset (such as three-month U.S. Treasury bill or USTBILL) if the investor expects to be in the "distress" ($k = 2$) regime at $T + 1$;
2. To otherwise invest in an energy commodity (OIL or NATGAS).

Our position is that an investor could achieve an outstanding performance if this strategy was followed as compared with a "buy-and-hold" or "passive" strategy, that is, a strategy in which the investor holds her proceedings unchanged in the OIL, the NATGAS, or the USTBILL through time. In addition, we assume that an active trading strategy, such as the previous one, could help to reduce risk exposure and increase mean-variance (i.e., risk-return) efficiency.

A key step, in the previous trading strategy, is to estimate the probability, $\xi_{k=2,T+1}$, of being in the distress ($k = 2$) regime at $T + 1$. For this purpose, we suggest the use of a time series method known as Markov-switching (MS) model [19,20]. Sometimes this model is also known as Hamilton's filter. With this type of model, the returns' (r_t) generating stochastic process can be estimated with a K, location (mean) and scale (standard deviation) parameters. Another interesting feature of the MS model is the fact that the investor or trader can estimate the smoothed probability, $\xi_{k=i,t}$, of being in each k regime at t. In addition, the transition probabilities, $\pi_{k=j,k=i}$, of changing (or staying) from regime $k = i$ at t, to regime $k = j$ at $t + 1$ are part of this model's outputs. With these transition probabilities, the investor is able to forecast the smoothed probabilities for $t + s$ ($s \geq 1$) and to perform the previous investment strategy.

As described below, MS models, as originally proposed by Hamilton, assume a time-fixed scale (standard deviation, $\sigma_{k=i}$) parameter in each regime. Given this, some extensions [21–24] have been made in order to incorporate a generalized, autoregressive conditional heteroskedastic (GARCH) process [25,26] in a MS model. This led to the development of the Markov-switching GARCH (MSGARCH) model, a model that allows a more precise estimation of the time-varying standard deviations, $\sigma_{k=i,t}$, in each regime at t.

The trading strategy that we propose herein is based on the one proposed by Brooks and Persand [27] for U.K. equities and fixed income securities (as risk-free assets). This trading strategy and the use of MS models for trading have been extended and tested in other equity markets [28–31] or in the optimal pension fund selection in Mexico [32].

To our knowledge and based on a detailed literature review of the most important and well-known academic journal databases, nothing has been written about the practical use of MS models for trading in energy commodity markets. The only related reference to this work is a very interesting paper by Alizadeh et al. [33], who proposed the calculation of MS hedge ratios. They proposed to use MS models in order to determine how much of the portfolio must be placed in OIL, gasoline, or heating oil futures and how much of it in the corresponding spot delivered underlying commodity. Although this interesting work is somewhat related to the present one, our purposes are different. We state this due to the fact that our trading strategy is to buy the energy commodity if the investor expects a "normal" or low volatility regime at $T + 1$, or otherwise buy a risk-free asset. As a research method, we started from the databases of Scopus and the Web of Science and continued with other repositories such as EBSCO, Jstor, Econpapers, Ideas-Repec, and finally, Google scholar.

Our results contribute significantly to the existing literature because almost all previous studies (including [27]) use a time-fixed or "constant" variance scale parameter and do not use MSGARCH models. Our first purpose is to determine if it is more appropriate to use MSGARCH models instead of the time-fixed MS models. In addition, we extend the literature by testing the potential use of this trading strategy in other types of markets such as OIL and NATGAS.

Among the potential benefits of our results among practitioners, we find that an energy commodity trader could decide to hold a long position from t to $T + 1$, or liquidate the commodity if the probability, $\xi_{s\,=\,2,t+1}$, of being in a distress regime at $T + 1$ is known. In addition, an institutional investor could use our results in order to enhance portfolio energy commodity positions, more specifically, to enhance total portfolio performance. In a similar manner, a futures trader or underwriter could use this strategy to determine if it is necessary to hold OIL, or NATGAS positions, during low volatility periods, as a coverage of the issued OIL or NATGAS derivatives.

Given the theoretical and practical goals of this paper, we tested, from a U.S. dollar-based agent's point of view, the following hypothesis: "The use of the suggested trading strategy with MSGARCH models leads to a better performance in the OIL and NATGAS market as compared with a buy-and-hold strategy".

For a more detailed and introductory review about the difference between a trader, speculator, or investor, please refer to [34].

Having presented our main goals and purposes, we organized the remainder of this paper as follows: In the next section, we present our literature review and an introductory review of MSGARCH models, for the unrelated reader and to link the use of MSGARCH models in the simulated trading rule. In Section 3, we describe the MS model fitting of the input data and we present the pseudocode used in our simulations, followed by a review of the simulation results in OIL and NATGAS. Finally, in the last section, we present our concluding remarks and guidelines for further research.

2. Literature Review and the Use of MSGARCH Models in Our Simulations

2.1. Review of the Previous Literature That Motivates Our Tests

The use of MS models has been tested and suggested in several fields of research in economics, finance, and even meteorology or energy (turbine) engineering [10,11,35,36]. The first test was the estimation of the probabilities that a given country is in a recession regime ($k = 2$) or expansion regime ($k = 1$) at $t + n$ [12,13] and, closely related, these models were used to test the potential presence of common changes in economic cycles [13,15–17]. Other noneconomic applications are the modeling of temperature or wind speed modeling and forecasting [37–40]. From the studies more related to the present one and, as an application of MS models in financial time series, we mention the tests made in developed countries' stock markets. A good example is by Klein [41], who tested the presence of time-varying herd behavior in the U.S. and Euro area stock markets. With the use of

MS models, the author found that there is a notable deviation from rational asset pricing in distress or periods of high volatility, because the behavior of market agents was more rational in normal or low volatility periods than during distress periods. Another related paper is by Areal et al. [42] who tested the performance of a "vice" or non-socially responsible portfolio against a socially responsible portfolio, in the U.S. stock markets. Contrary to the claims in the literature, they found that the vice fund is an underperformer during distress or high volatility time periods. Finally, for the developing stock markets case, we mention the work of Zheng and Zuo [43] who used MS models to measure the "spillover" or contagion effect between stock markets of the U.S., the U.K., Germany, Japan, and Hong Kong and found that there is a spillover effect between markets, and that this effect is higher during distress time periods.

In our literature review, we also found increasing literature related to testing the use of MS, GARCH, and MSGARCH models in European and emerging stock markets [41,44,45] (Reference [28] makes a first review of the benefits of time-varying GARCH variances in the European Emerging stock markets and found the benefits of their use in Value at Risk calculation.). For a more detailed definition of the typology of markets (i.e., frontier, emerging, or developed), please refer to the classification and methodology document of MSCI [46]. This document is made in association with Standard & Poor Dow Jones LLC.

Among the closely-related works that test the use of MS models in emerging markets, we mention Rotta and Valls Pereira [14] who extended the regime-switching dynamic conditional correlation model with asymmetric GARCH variances. By using the model in the U.S., the U.K., Brazil, and South Korea, they found that their model was appropriate to model the volatility clustering effect, due to the time-varying properties of the correlation among markets, but also given their tested regime-switching framework. With respect to emerging stock markets, we mention the works of Cabrera et al. [47] and Sosa, Ortiz and Cabello [48] who tested the use of either MS or MSGARCH models in Latin American stock markets. Their results were in agreement in that it was appropriate to use either two regime MS models [48] or three regime MSGARCH models [47] in order to characterize the performance of these markets. In addition, they suggested that these models could be useful to measure the spillover effect and the potential presence of a "Latin American stock market common cycle".

For the specific case of the use of MS models in Asian stock markets, we mention the work of Lin [49] who tested the co-movements of some of the main Asian stock markets (India, Indonesia, Korea, the Philippines, Thailand, and Taiwan) as well as their currencies. The author found that the co-movement is higher during distress time periods. Related also to this paper and as a test to the random walk stochastic process, the study by Shen and Holmes [50] showed that the use of non-switching unit root tests is not appropriate in the Asian stock markets. They favored the use of a two-regime switching test and suggested the presence of a higher mean-reverting effect in normal or low-volatility time periods.

For the midwest stock markets, Balcilar et al. [51] showed the presence of three regimes (low, high, and crash volatilities) in the integration of the stock markets of Abu Dhabi, Dubai, Kuwait, Qatar, and Saudi Arabia. In a similar fashion, the works of Boamah [52] and Bundoo [53] tested the presence of herding and stock market integration during non-normal or high volatility time periods, in a two or three regime context.

Up to this point we have presented literature that mostly relates to the use of MS models for time series characterization. The characterization of the stock index time series in two or more regimes is crucial for the appropriateness of MS models in investment decisions. Up to now, the previous references have shown the benefits of using MS models in these stock markets. Given this, we found strong evidence in favor of these models. Next, we continue with the literature review related to the proper use of MS models in other types of time series.

From the perspective of the use of MS and MSGARCH models in other types of time series, we found the works of Alexander and Kaeck [54] and Ma and Deng [55]. These authors searched for the determinants of credit default swaps (CDS), in developed or emerging economies, and their behavior in the context of two regimes. Both papers characterized properly the two-regime behavior of CDS and found a close relationship of CDS with interest rate levels and stock index performance.

For the specific case of the use of MS or MSGARCH models in commodity markets, we can mention the paper of Valera and Lee [56] who also tested the random-walk and informational efficiency hypothesis in the rice market of the following six Asian countries: China, Hong Kong, Indonesia, Malaysia, Philippines, and Singapore. Their test also showed that the use of a single regime unit root test is not appropriate, and therefore the Asian rice prices do not follow a conventional (single regime) random walk. Instead, the authors found that it is appropriate to model the stochastic process with a MS random walk, that is, to use the assumption that the random walk process is generated and inferred with a two regime MS model.

Among all the references mentioned herein, the previous study relates closely to this paper because it reviews the benefits of MS models for commodity time series characterization in commodities. However, the paper does not review the use of MS models in an investment decision process. Next, we mention some of the works that review this use of MS models (investment decisions).

As noted in this detailed but not exhaustive literature review, due to issues of space, most of the literature related to the benefits of MS or MSGARCH models focused on determining if these appropriately characterize the number of regimes, to measure contagion (spillover) effects between markets or to estimate the risk exposure. For the specific case of using MS models in investment decisions, little has been written. Brooks and Persand [27] were the first to propose using MS models for investment decisions. In a Gaussian, two regime context and by using the $T+1$ forecasted smoothed probabilities ($\xi_{k,T+1}$) of the gilt-equity ratio, the authors determined how much to invest, (ω_{Gilt}), at t, in the U.K. gilts (as the risk-free asset) or in the FTSE-100 ($\omega_{FTSE100}$, as the risky one). In order to determine this investment level (ω_i), they used the aforementioned probabilities as follows:

$$w = \begin{bmatrix} \omega_{Gilt} \\ \omega_{FTSE100} \end{bmatrix} = \begin{bmatrix} \xi_{k=2,T+1} \\ \xi_{k=1,T+1} \end{bmatrix} \quad (1)$$

Their simulations show that their active trading strategy in these two assets lead to a better performance than a passive or buy-and-hold strategy in the gilts or the FTSE-100.

It is worth noting that this paper was the main motivation for this review. The key difference between the tests made in [27] and this paper, is the fact that the simulated trader decides to invest in the risky asset only if a normal or low volatility time period is expected at $T+1$. In addition, we test the use of MS and MSGARCH models with Gaussian and t-Student probability density functions (pdfs), whereas [27] uses only a time-fixed variance, i.e., MS model with Gaussian pdf.

After the original proposal by [27], little has been written about the use of MS or MSGARCH models for investment purposes [57–59]. Only the works of Hauptmann et al. [28] and Engel, Wahl and Zagst [31] extended the use of MS models with time-varying (logit regression) smoothed probabilities. More specifically, these works estimated sequentially three regime MS models. Given the influence of economic and financial factors, they forecasted the probability of being in each regime and made investment decisions with these forecasts. Their results in the U.S., Euro, and Asian markets showed an overperformance of their simulated portfolio against a buy-and-hold strategy. A result that is related to the results of our paper.

Following a rationale similar to that of [27], De la Torre, Galeana-Figueroa, and Álvarez-García [29] extended the use of the Gaussian and t-Student MS models to the U.K., U.S., Italian, and Mexican stock markets. In addition, [30] extended the use of the test of MS to MSGARCH models in the Andean region countries (Chile, Colombia, and Peru) and [32] to the informed and mean-variance efficient pension fund selection in Mexico.

Despite these extensions, nothing has been written about the use of MS or MSGARCH models in commodities and, more specifically, energy commodities. With this in mind, it is necessary to review the benefits of using the Gaussian or t-Student MS or MSGARCH in the active trading of these commodities.

As previously mentioned in the introduction, Alizadeh et al. [33] tested the use of MS models for the calculation of hedge ratios in the OIL futures market, as a hedging strategy that was tested only for fitting purposes and not for active trading activities.

On the basis of this literature review, we want to explain the rationale behind MS and MSGARCH models and how we used these in our simulations.

As mentioned previously, the active trading strategy that we test in this paper uses the forecast of the smoothed probability, $\xi_{k=2,t+1}$, of the high volatility regime. Because this is the key parameter to use in the decision process, it is of interest for us to present a brief and introductory review of MS and MSGARCH models for the unrelated reader.

2.2. The Rationale of MS and MSGARCH Models and Their Use in Our Simulations

MS models were primarily proposed by Hamilton [19,20,60] using a straightforward rationale, i.e., "the stochastic process of a (return) time series r_t can be modeled with a set of K number of location (mean) and scale (variance) parameters. This, given the k probability density functions (pdf) of k hidden and unobserved regimes". Because these k number of regimes are unobserved, they can be modeled with a Markovian chain with k number of states (or regimes), a chain that has a $k \times k$ transition probability matrix Π. Each entrance of this matrix corresponds to the transition probability ($\pi_{i,j}$) of transiting from one state $k = i$, at $t - 1$, to another one $k = j$ at t. This means that, as is the case of a non-absorbing Markovian chain, there is a probability of migrating from one regime to another ($\pi_{i,j}$ or $\pi_{j,i}$) or staying in it ($\pi_{i,i}$ or $\pi_{j,j}$). For the case of interest (a two-regime scenario) we represent the 2×2 transition probability matrix Π as follows:

$$\Pi = \begin{bmatrix} \pi_{i,i} & \pi_{i,j} \\ \pi_{j,i} & \pi_{j,j} \end{bmatrix}, \pi_{i,j} = P(k_{t+1} = j | k_t = i, r_t, \theta) \quad (2)$$

where θ is the likelihood function parameter set and θ is estimated using a Bayesian method known as the E-M algorithm [61], in which the analyst starts with an assumed value of θ and the pdf parameters (including Π). Then, the algorithm maximizes the log-likelihood function (the sum of natural logarithm of the assumed pdf in each regime at t) and, then, filters the maximized parameters with the data. This last step is done in order to have more suitable (better fitted) parameters for the data. For further reference and for a straight-forward review of the estimation algorithm of the MS models, please refer to [60].

In order to estimate the transition probability matrix in the second step (the filtering process), Hamilton proposes to filter (from the time series r_t) the probability that a given realization of r_t is generated from regime k. This can be done with a Gaussian or a t-Student pdf for the purposes of this paper:

$$p_{k,t} = \frac{1}{\sqrt{2\pi}\sigma_k} e^{-\frac{1}{2}\left(\frac{\varepsilon_t}{\sigma_k}\right)^2} \quad (3)$$

$$p_{k,t} = \frac{\Gamma\left(\frac{v_k+1}{2}\right)}{\sqrt{(v_k-2)\pi}\Gamma\left(\frac{v_k}{2}\right)} \left(1 + \frac{\left(\frac{\varepsilon_t}{\sigma_k}\right)^2}{(v_k-2)}\right)^{-\frac{v_k+1}{2}} \quad (4)$$

Once the filtered probabilities have been estimated for each regime in each realization, one can estimate the location ($\mu_{k=i}$) and scale ($\sigma_{k=i}$) parameters for each regime and also the transition probability matrix Π in Equation (2). As a complementary estimation, the k-th regime filtered probabilities can be smoothed (by using Kim's [62] algorithm) to avoid abrupt changes in the regime probability at t. This last process leads to a smoothed regime probability, $\xi_{k=i,t}$, for each regime and each realization of r_t. These are presented in a $T \times K$ smoothed probability matrix $\mathbf{p} = [\xi_{k=1,t}, \xi_{k=2,t}]$.

With this matrix, the application of a MS model to the time series r_t leads to the next parameter set:

$$\theta = \left[\mu_{k=i}, \sigma_{k=i}, \Pi, \mathbf{p} = \left[\xi_{k=i,t}, \xi_{k=i,t}\right]\right] \quad (5)$$

From this set, the transition probability matrix Π and the last realization of the smoothed regime probabilities matrix (**p**) at $t = T$, $\mathbf{sp_T} = \left[\xi_{k=i,T}, \xi_{k=i,T}\right]$ are of primary interest. These two parameters allowed us to forecast the probability of being in each regime at $T + 1$ as shown next:

$$\begin{bmatrix} \xi_{k=1,T+1} \\ \xi_{k=2,T+1} \end{bmatrix} = \Pi \cdot \mathbf{sp}'_T = \Pi \cdot \begin{bmatrix} \xi_{k=1,T} \\ \xi_{k=2,T} \end{bmatrix} \quad (6)$$

Finally, from this vector, we are interested in the forecasted smoothed probability of the distress ($k = 2$) regime $\xi_{k=2,T+1}$, in order to determine the probability of being in this regime at $T + 1$.

Among the assumptions of the MS model, as originally proposed by Hamilton [19,20], we mention that the transition probability matrix Π and the location ($\mu_{k=i}$) and scale ($\sigma_{k=i}$) parameters are time fixed.

Despite this, some extensions were made to the original MS model in order to allow the scale ($\sigma_{k=i}$) parameter to be a time-varying parameter. The need for time-varying variances has two practical motivations as follows:

1. Because one of the applications of MS models is market risk measurement, the assumption of a time-fixed standard deviation through time is very limiting for risk management. As an example, an OIL futures trader could incorporate the effect of the change of regime, but the estimation of potential losses could be over or underestimated if the variance is time fixed, which causes the trader's financial institution to save higher or lower risk capital reserves than needed.
2. An energy derivatives trader or a clearance chamber in an energy derivatives market needs a more reliable risk measure (i.e., a proper variance), given the actual state of nature (or regime) in the market. This suggest, as appropriate for derivatives pricing and clearance, the use of a regime dependent time-varying scale parameter ($\sigma_{k=i,t}$).

As one answer to these previous practical needs, the generalized autoregressive conditional heteroskedastic (GARCH) models were proposed by Engle [63] and Bollerslev [64]. These models estimate the variance as a time-varying one and also forecast it in future time periods ($T + n$). The general functional form of a GARCH model is the following:

$$\sigma_t^2 = \omega + \sum_{p=1}^{P} \beta_p \cdot \varepsilon_{t-p}^2 + \sum_{q}^{Q} \gamma_q \cdot \sigma_{i,t-q}^2 + v_t \quad (7)$$

In the previous expression, the actual (or even forecasted) value of the volatility σ_t^2 depends of the squared lagged values of the residuals ($\varepsilon_t = r_t - \bar{r}$) and also from past values of the estimated volatility. The lagged squared values in the second term of (7) correspond to the ARCH (autoregressive conditional heteroskedastic) effect and the lagged values of the estimated variance to the generalization of the ARCH equation (GARCH term). This is a necessary generalization for faster and more efficient estimation purposes. The limitation of the GARCH model and his extensions such as the ones proposed by [65–67], is the presence of the persistence effect. This means that $\sum_{p=1}^{P} \beta_p + \sum_{q}^{Q} \gamma_q \approx 1$ in some market circumstances, leads also to an over estimation of the variance and the risk exposure.

On the basis of the previous motivations and the persistence effect in GARCH models, a potential solution to this effect is to estimate the GARCH model (7) in a Markov-switching context. This is supported by the fact that the potential presence of the persistence effect is due to the presence of breaks or regimes in the behavior of the time series [21–24]. With this in mind, Markov-switching models with GARCH variance (henceforth MSGARCH) are a natural extension of the GARCH model in (6):

$$\sigma_{i,t,k}^2 = \omega_k + \sum_{p=1}^{P} \beta_{p,k} \cdot \varepsilon_{t-p}^2 + \sum_{q}^{Q} \gamma_{q,k} \cdot \sigma_{i,t-q,k}^2 + v_t \quad (8)$$

Given this, the theoretical and practical motivation of this paper is to determine if it is appropriate to use either MS or MSGARCH models to estimate the expected variance (or standard deviation). This, in order to estimate a more accurate forecast of the smoothed probability at $T+1$. It is necessary to test this because the use of a time-fixed (σ_k) or a time-varying GARCH ($\sigma_{k,t}$) standard deviation leads to different estimations of the smoothed probabilities with (3) or (4).

Given the previous review of MS and MSGARCH models, if a trader estimates the forecasted second regime smoothed probability ($\xi_{k\,=\,2,T+1}$) with a time-fixed or a GARCH variance, it is expected to have different probability values. Given these different probability values, the trader could perform a different trading decision in each case. With this rationale, there are practical and theoretical reasons to test our two aforementioned hypotheses, that is, to demonstrate that it is better to use a MSGARCH model, than a MS model for trading decisions in the OIL and NATGAS markets.

As a methodological note, the MSARCH or MSGARCH model can be estimated with the following two possible Bayesian inference methods [25,26,68]: The E-M [61] algorithm previously described or Makov chain Monte Carlo simulation methods such as the Metropoli–Hastings [69] sampler. In our simulations, we estimated the three types of models (MS, MSARCH, and MSGARCH) with the E-M algorithm, through the simplification suggested by Viterbi [70] (please refer to Ardia [25] for further details of the algorithm). We estimated the models with the MSGARCH R library [71].

Next, we review the input data, how we conducted our simulations, and the main findings in our results.

3. Methodology

3.1. Input Data Processing and Simulation Dates

Since we have reviewed how the MSGARCH models are used in the simulated decision-making process, next, we briefly describe the input data. First, we will start with a description of our sources, along with the input data processing, followed by a fitting test of the MS and MSGARCH models in the time series of interest.

For the intended purposes, we used the weekly historical data of the OIL and NATGAS continuous one-month future price, as summarized in Table 1. We used these historical weekly close prices from 6 April 1990 to 31 May 2019.

Table 1. Summary of the time series used as input in our simulations, their tickers, price-contract size relation and source.

Refinitiv™ RIC®	Source	Index Name	Ticker in the Paper	Trading Units
CLc1	Refinitiv™ Eikon™	CME-NYMEX WTI continous 1-month commodity future	Oil	USD per barrel
NGc1	Refinitiv™ Eikon™	CME-NYMEX Henry Hub Natural Gas continous 1-month commodity future	Natural gas	USD per BTU (1 BTU = 27.05 cubic meters)
UST3MT = RR	Refinitiv™ Eikon™	US 3-month treasury bill	USTBILL	USD

Source: Own elaboration with data of Refinitiv Eikon [72].

With the historical price (p_t) of each simulated commodity, we calculated the continuous time return or continuous time percentage variation of each energy future each week (leading to a total of 1521 observations):

$$r_{i,t} = ln(P_{i,t}) - ln(P_{i,t-1}) \qquad (9)$$

Our portfolio trading simulations started from 7 January 1994 and ended 31 May 2019 ($T = 1326$ weeks) but we used the historical return data from 7 April 1990 to the simulated date (t) for estimation purposes.

Once we simulated all six aforementioned scenarios in the 1326 weeks of interest, we compared the performance of the simulated portfolio with the "buy-and-hold" strategy, in OIL, NATGAS, and USTBILL.

We calculated the accumulated return of the simulated portfolios and the buy-and-hold strategies as follows:

$$\Delta\%_{accumulated} = \left(\left(\frac{\text{Portfolio, commodity or USTBILL fund value at T}}{\text{Portfolio, commodity or USTBILL fund value at } t-1}\right) - 1\right) \times 100 \quad (10)$$

We also summarized the performance of the portfolios by calculating the continuous time percentage variation return ($\Delta\%_{portfolio,commodity \text{ or USTBILL at } t} = \frac{\ln(\text{Portfolio, commodity or USTBILL fund value at } t)}{\ln(\text{Portfolio, commodity or USTBILL fund value at } t-1)}$). With these returns, we calculated the observed mean return, its standard deviation, the maximum potential loss (defined as the minimum or lowest return value), the Sharpe [73] ratio (SR) as in (11) and the 95% and 98% confidence conditional value at risk (CVaR) as in (12). The Sharpe ratio (SR) is a performance measure that estimates how much risk premia (extra return from a risk-free asset) the investor receives, given each 1.00% of risk exposure taken in a given investment. The higher the SR, the better.

$$SR = \frac{mean(\Delta\%\text{Portfolio}_{i,t} - rf_t)}{\sigma(\Delta\%\text{Portfolio}_{i,t} - rf_t)} \quad (11)$$

In the previous expression, $\Delta\%Portfolio_{i,t}$ is the percentage variation of the portfolio value at t and rf_t represents the corresponding observed weekly equivalent rate of the USTBILL.

$$CVaR = \int_{-\infty}^{q=\alpha} \Delta\%\text{Portfolio}_{i,q} \cdot P\left(\Delta\%\text{Portfolio}_{i,q}\right) d\Delta\%\text{Portfolio}_{i,tq}, \Delta\%\text{Portfolio}_{i,tq} \leq \alpha \quad (12)$$

As an additional methodology note, we ran our simulations in the following six scenarios:

1. The simulation of the two commodities of interest using the MS model with homogeneous Gaussian pdf and time-fixed variance. We denote this scenario as [commodity name]-MS-Gaussian (e.g., "Oil-MS-Gaussian");
2. The use of the MS model with homogeneous t-Student pdf and time-fixed variance ([commodity]-MS-tStud);
3. The simulation with a MS model with homogeneous Gaussian pdf and ARCH variance ([commodity]-MSARCH-Gaussian);
4. The use of a t-Student MSARCH model ([commodity]-MSARCH-tStud);
5. The scenario of the MS model with homogeneous Gaussian pdf and GARCH variance as (4). Denoted as [commodity]-MSGARCH-Gaussian;
6. The simulation of the homogeneous t-student MSGARCH ([commodity]-MSGARCH-tStud).

First, we explain the simulation process and data processing and, then, review the appropriateness of using MS or MSGARCH models in the two commodities. For this purpose, we estimated the models in the entire time series of both commodities (the 1521 dates) and then we estimated the LLF in each of the six scenarios as follows:

$$LLF = \sum_t^T \ln\left(\sum_{k=1}^K \pi_k \cdot p_{k,t}\right) \quad (13)$$

In the previous expression, $p_{k,t}$ is the filtered Gaussian (3) or t-Student (4) pdf and π_k is a regime mixture law that measures the proportion of the k-th regime in the entire LLF ($\pi_k = \left(\sum_{t=1}^T p_{k,t}\right) \cdot T^{-1}$).

With these *LLF* values, we estimated the Akaike information criterion (AIC) [14] and determined, as "the best" model or scenario, the one with lowest AIC. Our results are summarized in Table 2.

Table 2. Single and multiple regime AIC fitting test for the three commodities' time series of interest.

Model or Scenario	Oil	Natural Gas
Single-Gaussian	−4840.63	−3750.07
Single-tStud	−4992.30	−3824.21
MS-Gaussian	−5054.02	−3882.19
MS-tStud	−5048.80	−3873.38
MSARCH-Gaussian	−5044.06	−3870.25
MSARCH-tStud	−5043.92	−3861.60
MSGARCH-Gaussian	−5067.62 [Best fit]	−3885.0747 [Best fit]
MSGARCH-tStud	−5053.89	−3875.72

Source: Own elaboration with results of our simulations and data from Refinitiv Eikon [72].

The results, shown in Table 2, suggest that the two regime, Gaussian MSGARCH, is the best model to fit the time series of the two simulated commodities. A result that preliminarily confirms our first hypothesis. In order to test the validity of this result through time, we ran the recursive estimation of the six MS tested models (with constant, ARCH or GARCH variance). This, in each of the 1326 weeks of the simulation since 7 January 2000 to 31 May 2019. After this, we calculated the mean AIC value. The results are summarized in Table 3.

Table 3. Single and multiple regime recursive AIC fitting test for the three commodities' time series of interest.

Model or Scenario	Oil	Natural Gas
Single-Gaussian	−2711.1544	−2077.9385
Single-tStud	−2807.7203	−2127.7972
MS-Gaussian	−2841.9781 [Best fit]	−2147.2707 [Best fit]
MS-tStud	Not feasible	Not feasible
MSARCH-Gaussian	−2829.7621	−2135.5721
MSARCH-tStud	−2823.6334	−2127.4305
MSGARCH-Gaussian	−2825.6056	−2133.9354
MSGARCH-tStud	−2818.5195	−2125.1552

Source: Own elaboration with results of our simulations and data from Refinitiv Eikon [72].

As noted, given the inference algorithm used for estimation purposes and the nature of the data, the MS-tStud scenario in both commodities is marked as "not feasible". This is because, in some of the dates (The unfeasible dates are 24 April 2009 and 19 June 2009 in the OIL market and 31st December 2010 and 12 June 2015 for the NATGAS.), the use of Hamilton's [19,20] filter with the Viterbi [70] algorithm did not converge and it did not found a feasible solution. For this reason, we excluded, from our trading simulations, the MS-tStud scenario.

In addition, from Table 3, we found a result that looks contradictory to the results in Table 2, in terms of fitting. If we compared the results of Table 3 with those of Table 2, the MS model with Gaussian pdf and constant variance showed the best fit in oil and natural gas.

Despite these contradictory results, we ran our investment simulations in the feasible scenarios of Table 3. Up to this review of results, the full time series and the recursive MS and MSGARCH analysis prove that the time series of the three commodities can be modeled with two regime MS, or MSGARCH models.

Next, we provide a brief description of the pseudocode used in our simulations.

3.2. The Pseudocode and Assumptions Used in Our Simulations

As previously mentioned, from all the parameters in the parameter set of MS or MSGARCH models, we are interested in the smoothed probabilities of being in each regime, $\xi_{k\,=\,1,t}$, and also in the transition probability matrix Π. With these two parameters and by using (8), we can forecast the smoothed probability of being in both regimes at $T\,+\,1$. Contrary to [27], we do not use both regimes' smoothed probabilities. We pay special attention to the forecasted smoothed probability of the second regime, $(S\xi_{k\,=\,2,T+1})$. As a methodological note, the MSGARCH library sorts the k regimes from the regime with the lowest ($k\,=\,1$) to the highest ($k\,=\,2$) standard deviation, in order to perform the next indicator function of the forecasted regime at $T+1$ as follows:

$$k_{T+1} = \begin{cases} 1, if \xi_{k\,=\,2,T+1} \leq 0.5 \\ 2, if \xi_{k\,=\,2,T+1} > 0.5 \end{cases} \tag{14}$$

It is of methodological importance to mention that we estimated the MSGARCH, MSARCH, and MS models only with the residuals as recommended by Haas et al. [24]. In order to estimate these residuals, we detrended the historical return time series with the arithmetic single regime mean as follows:

$$\varepsilon_{i,t} = r_{i,t} - \bar{r}_i \tag{15}$$

With the forecasted regime at $T\,+\,1$ (k_{T+1}), we ran the simulations of the investment process by following the next pseudocode in each simulation date ($t\,=\,7$ January 1994 and $T\,=\,31$ May 31 2019) as follows:

For date 1 to T in the simulation:

1. To determine the actual balance in the portfolio (cash balance and market value of holdings);
2. To execute the Markov-switching model analysis in (4) with either GARCH, ARCH, or constant variance and also a Gaussian (6) or t-Student (7) pdf;
3. To determine the expected regime (k_{T+1}) at $t\,+\,1$ with (9);
4. With k_{T+1}, to perform the next trading decision rule:

    a. To invest in the energy commodity if $k_{T+1}\,=\,1$,
    b. To invest in the risk-free asset if $k_{T+1}\,=\,2$;

5. To value the portfolio with a mark-to-market procedure.

End

In order to run our simulations, we used the following assumptions in the portfolio and its trading activities:

1. We simulated the performance of a USD 100,000.00 theoretical fund that only invests in the following two possible assets:

    a. A theoretical ETF that tracks the performance of the simulated energy commodity. An ETF that has a starting value of USD 100.00 and zero tracking error as assumption.
    b. A theoretical fund that pays the three-month U.S. Treasury bill rate each week. This fund also has a USD 100.00 theoretical starting value.

2. This portfolio is not allowed to make short sales and only has the following two accounts:

    a. A cash balance account,
    b. A security custody account in which the energy commodity futures are saved.

3. In order to simplify the simulations and given the potential heterogeneity in the trading fees among institutional investors, we are assuming that the simulated portfolio has no trading costs or taxes to pay.

Next, we review of our simulations, starting with the buy-and-hold strategy.

3.3. Passive or "Buy-and-Hold" Investment Strategy Results

In Table 4, we present the results that a given investor or commodity trader would have had, had she performed a "buy-and-hold" strategy during the simulated period. As noted, the passive investment strategy in OIL paid an accumulated return of 249.21%. A return that is equivalent to a yearly return (in brackets) of 9.77%. As noted, this value is higher than the 90.50% accumulated return paid by the USTBILL (3.54% yearly). With this in mind, investing in OIL has a proper risk return or mean-variance relation as shown in the Sharpe ratio. The result of this measure suggests that investing in OIL paid a weekly 0.0097% (0.13% yearly) of risk premium for each 1.00% risk exposure in this energy commodity.

Table 4. Performance of a passive or "buy-and-hold" investment strategy in the two simulated energy commodities and the U.S. Treasury bills.

Model or Scenario	Accumulated Return	Mean Return	Return Std. Dev.	Max Drawdown
Oil	249.2167 [9.7732]	0.0944 [4.9088]	4.9222 [35.4945]	−31.218
Natural Gas	13.8219 [0.542]	0.0098 [0.5096]	7.125 [51.3791]	−42.6905
USTBILL	90.502 [3.5491]	0.0546 [2.8392]	0.0449 [0.3238]	-

Model or scenario	CVaR (95%)	CVaR (98%)	Sharpe ratio
Oil	−11.8377 [−85.3629]	−15.3773 [−110.8873]	0.0097 [0.1383]
Natural Gas	−15.7226 [−113.3773]	−19.8391 [−143.0618]	−0.0052 [0.0099]
USTBILL	-	-	

Note: All the values are presented in % with the exception of the Sharpe ratio. In addition, all the values are shown in weekly terms with the exception of the accumulated return that is measured for the whole simulation period. The equivalent yearly values are presented in brackets. Source: Own elaboration with results of our simulations and data from Refinitiv Eikon [72].

A different situation is observed in the passive investment in NATGAS. As noted in the same table, the passive investment strategy in this commodity paid only a 13.82% of accumulated return in the whole simulation period (a 0.54% in a yearly basis). This return is lower than the observed one in USTBILL.

For the case of the risk measures (max drawdown and CVaR) in the two simulated commodities, we compared the observed results for these two passive strategies with their corresponding active trading scenarios in OIL and NATGAS.

3.4. Results of the Markov-Switching Active Investment Strategy in the WTI Oil Market

For the particular case of OIL futures, we present the performance results of our simulations in Table 5. As noted, all the simulated scenarios paid a higher accumulated return than their corresponding passive or buy-and-hold strategy.

In addition, the MS and MSGARCH models led to better results if they are used in active investment strategies, with the Gaussian MS scenario paying the highest return. This result does not entirely fulfill our first hypothesis, due to the fact that the best model for the intended purposes is not an MSGARCH.

Had an investor used this type of MS model in their investment strategy, they would have earned a 1097.49% return (43.03% in yearly basis). This result is higher than the Gaussian MSGARCH that paid the second-best accumulated return in our simulations (788.00% or 30.90% yearly).

By comparing the risk exposure measures in Table 4 (buy-and-hold strategy), it can be observed that the max drawdown and the potential loss (CVaR) in the simulated portfolios are lower than the ones in Table 4 for OIL.

Table 5. Performance of the Markov-switching active investment strategy applied in the continuous one-month WTI oil future price contract.

Model or Scenario	Accumulated Return	Mean Return	Return Std. Dev.	Max Drawdown
Oil-MS-Gaussian	1097.49 [43.0388]	0.1874 [9.7448]	3.7326 [26.9162]	−13.7099
Oil-MS-tStud	Not feasible	Not feasible	Not feasible	Not feasible
Oil-MSARCH-Gaussian	762.0588 [29.8847]	0.1626 [8.4552]	3.5678 [25.7278]	−13.7099
Oil-MSARCH-tStud	123.3836 [4.8386]	0.0607 [3.1564]	3.1883 [22.9912]	−15.8776
Oil-MSGARCH-Gaussian	788.0043 [30.9021]	0.1648 [8.5696]	3.8678 [27.8911]	−27.353
Oil-MSGARCH-tStud	624.3021 [24.4824]	0.1494 [7.7688]	3.2428 [23.3842]	−17.9683
Model or scenario	**CVaR (95%)**	**CVaR (98%)**	**Sharpe ratio**	**Mean risky exposure**
Oil-MS-Gaussian	−8.4109 [−60.6519]	−10.1399 [−73.1199]	0.0252 [0.3620]	0.902
Oil-MS-tStud	Not feasible	Not feasible	Not feasible	Not feasible
Oil-MSARCH-Gaussian	−8.124 [−58.583]	−9.7196 [−70.089]	0.0206 [0.3286]	0.8808
Oil-MSARCH-tStud	−7.9165 [−57.0867]	−9.7627 [−70.3998]	0.0041 [0.1378]	0.7323
Oil-MSGARCH-Gaussian	−9.2385 [−66.6198]	−12.0042 [−86.5635]	0.0256 [0.3072]	0.8032
Oil-MSGARCH-tStud	−8.052 [−58.0638]	−10.3119 [−74.3602]	0.0182 [0.3322]	0.6305

Note: The same presentation format as in Table 4. Source: Own elaboration with results of our simulations and data from Refinitiv Eikon [72].

Despite this, it is noted that the Gaussian MS scenario shows higher CVaR values than the MSGARCH scenarios. This result is important because, if a trader wants to use an MS or MSGARCH model for trading purposes, it is preferable to use a Gaussian time-fixed variance MS one. But, if a futures trader or a risk manager wants to measure more appropriately the risk exposure in the OIL position, it is better to use a Gaussian MSGARCH model.

This preliminary conclusion (the use of MS models for trading and the use of MSGARCH for risk management) is explained by the fact that the Gaussian (constant variance) MS model is more appropriate to make forecasts of the second regime at $T + 1$, leading to a proper trading sign of buying (selling) the OIL future during "calm" ("distress") forecasted periods. This statement is supported by the "mean risky exposure" field of Table 5, a result that shows a less conservative strategy than the one made in the other scenarios or MS models.

In Figure 1, we present the historical performance of the five simulated portfolios (lines), together with the performance of the passive or buy-and-hold portfolio in the simulated commodity (shaded area).

As noted, practically all the portfolios were sensitive to the increase in volatility in the next distress periods such as: the 2000 to 2001 technology companies crisis, the reputational and accounting issues of companies such as Enron (a closely-related event with these two commodities); the subprime credit crisis of 2007 to 2008, the European debt issues of 2011 to 2013, and the most recent issues of the U.S. negotiations with key trade partners (2018 to 2019). From the simulated scenarios, the one that used the Gaussian MS model was the most parsimonious in the rebalancing activities and the one that showed a good fit for these crisis episodes. This is noted in the "almost straight" behavior of the simulated portfolio during these periods. The bottom panel of the same Figure 1 shows the investment level in the simulated commodity at t. We present this panel in order to show the benefits of the use of MS, MSARCH, or MSGARCH modes. As noted, there are some differences in the estimation of the forecast of the second regime and this leads to different decisions in each simulated portfolio. More specifically, the reader can note that three best performing portfolios reduced to 0.00% their holdings in the oil futures in distress time periods. Examples of this are the subprime crisis of October 2008 to February

2009 or the mid 2013 European debt issues. For the specific case of the time-fixed variance MS model (with Gaussian pdf), this model was less sensitive to the changes on the volatility levels. The use of this model allowed long positions in the oil futures to be held when the most sensitive MSARCH and MSGARCH did not. This difference led the simulated oil trader to have a better performance result.

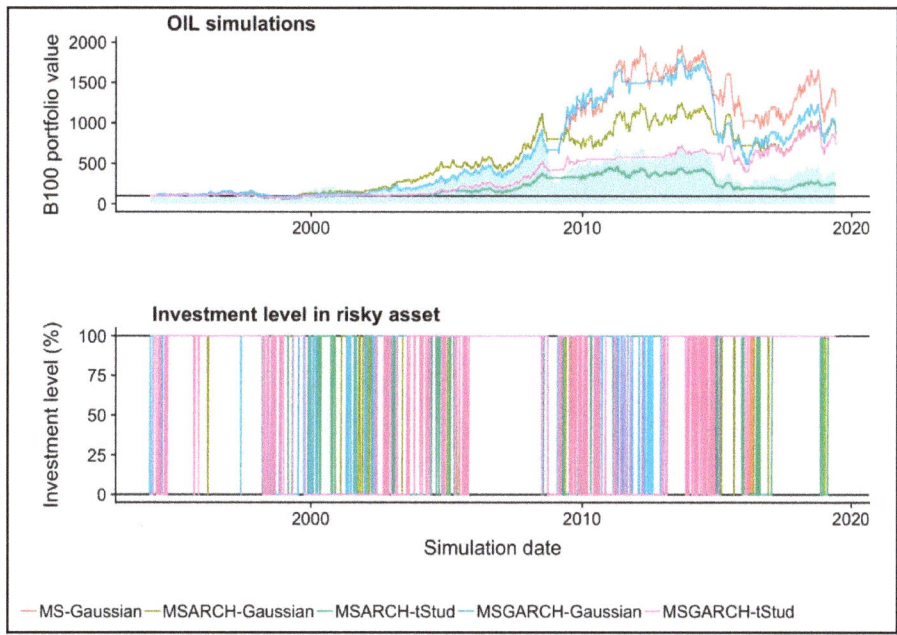

Figure 1. Historical performance of the five simulated scenarios of the investment strategy in the WTI oil continuous price one-month future and its historical investment level. Source: Own elaboration with results of our simulations and data from Refinitiv Eikon [72].

In order to strengthen the performance review of the simulated portfolios, we performed a one-way ANOVA test and a nonparametric Kruskal–Wallis test, with the five simulated portfolios and the performance of the buy-and-hold ones in OIL and USTBILL. The results of these two tests are shown in Table 6. As noted, the results of these tests suggest that there is no significant difference. This issue is due to the fact that the previous tests make a mean or median comparison between the simulated portfolios and do not differentiate the performance fluctuations and risk exposure. In addition, these tests do not differentiate the distance between the highest to the lowest observed return in each case.

Table 6. ANOVA and Kruskal–Wallis test of the observed weekly returns in the simulated portfolios of the OIL price and the USTBILL portfolio.

One-Way ANOVA Test				
Degrees of Freedom	**Squred Sums**	**Squared Means**	**F Value**	**Pr (>F)**
5.0000	0.0016	0.0003	0.2162	0.9558
7944.0000	11.4572	0.0014		
Kruskal-Wallis test		**K-W statistic**	**Degrees of Freedom**	**Pr (>Xi2)**
		2.7928	5.0000	0.7319

Source: Own elaboration with results of our simulations and data from Refinitiv Eikon [72].

In order to complete a deeper performance review of the simulated portfolios, we present the box plots of Figure 2. As noted by the reader, the box plots of the simulated portfolios are narrower than those of the buy-and-hold strategy in OIL. This gives support to our position that the use of our trading rule with MS models leads to a better performance, due to a lower risk exposure of the simulated portfolios and a potential good market timing.

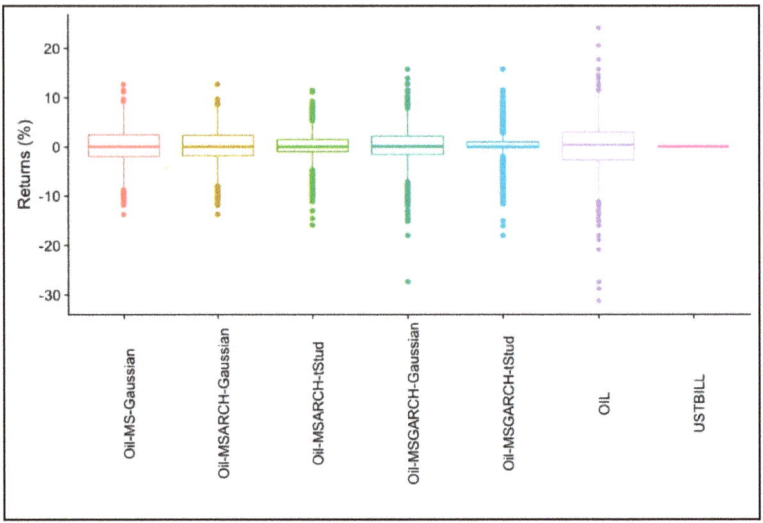

Figure 2. Box plot of the returns of five simulated scenarios in the WTI oil continuous. Source: Own elaboration with results of our simulations and data from Refinitiv Eikon [72].

In order to strengthen our position that the Gaussian MS model led to the best performance, we ran the next attribution and market timing test:

$$r_{i,t} = \alpha + \beta_1 \cdot r_{\text{commodity},t} + \beta_2 \cdot r^2_{\text{commodity},t} + \varepsilon_t \text{ commodity} \tag{16}$$

In the previous expression, $r_{\text{commodity},t}$ is the percentage variation of the buy-and-hold portfolio. With this term, we measured how much the commodity performance contributed to the simulated return each week. In the second term we added a nonlinearity to the generated return. This second term measures the market timing of the simulated portfolio. If the β_2 value is greater than zero, the trading rule enhanced market timing skills (our main purpose herein). The previous regression was made in the risk premiums of the simulated portfolios and OIL, that is, we are regressing only the difference between the return paid by the USTBILL and by each commodity and simulated portfolio. The results of this attribution and market timing test are shown in Table 7.

This test gives a stronger support to our results by the fact that, as expected, the α value is not significant, whereas that of β_2 is positive and significant. For the specific case of the Gaussian MS portfolio (the best performer from the simulated ones), we found evidence of good market timing. This, with a 0.9731 β_2 value that suggests that for each 1.00% increase in the OIL risk premium, the simulated trading rule generated an extra 0.9731%, given a good market timing. This is higher than the 0.6049% explained by β_1. This last constant suggests that each 0.6049% of the returns paid by the simulated portfolios is explained by a 1.00% OIL price increase.

Next, we proceed to the observed results in the NATGAS.

Table 7. Attribution and market timing test of the five simulated portfolios in the OIL market.

Simulated Portfolio	α	α p-Value	β₁	β₁ p-Value
Oil-MS-Gaussian	−0.0012	0.0794	0.6049	0.0000
Oil-MSARCH-Gaussian	−0.0012	0.1095	0.5511	0.0000
Oil-MSARCH-tStud	−0.0014	0.0593	0.4358	0.0000
Oil-MSGARCH-Gaussian	−0.0005	0.4508	0.6356	0.0000
Oil-MSGARCH-tStud	−0.0009	0.2301	0.4552	0.0000
Simulated portfolio	β_2	β_2 p-Value	R^2	
Oil-MS-Gaussian	0.9731	0.0000	0.5982	
Oil-MSARCH-Gaussian	0.8441	0.0000	0.5443	
Oil-MSARCH-tStud	0.5300	0.0000	0.4293	
Oil-MSGARCH-Gaussian	0.5807	0.0000	0.6262	
Oil-MSGARCH-tStud	0.6881	0.0000	0.4495	

Source: Own elaboration with results of our simulations and data from Refinitiv Eikon [72].

3.5. Results of the Markov-Switching Active Investment Strategy in the Natural Gas Market

In the case of the NATGAS trading simulations, no useful results were found for a NATGAS trader. We mention this due to the fact that the results are not as attractive as the ones observed in the OIL market. In Table 8, we present the performance results of the five feasible simulated scenarios. As noted, only the use of Gaussian MS or MS-ARCH models led to a positive accumulated return. Even if these two simulated portfolios generate alpha (higher returns than the buy-and-hold strategy), the observed values are not higher than the ones observed in the passive USTBILL portfolio (Table 4).

Table 8. Performance of the Markov-switching active investment strategy applied in the continuous one-month natural gas future price contract.

Model or Scenario	Accumulated Return	Mean Return	Return Std. Dev.	Max Drawdown
Natural gas-MS-Gaussian	80.607 [3.1611]	0.0446 [2.3192]	2.473 [17.8331]	−10.3716
Natural gas-MS-tStud	Not feasible	Not feasible	Not feasible	Not feasible
Natural gas-MSARCH-Gaussian	41.3346 [1.621]	0.0261 [1.3572]	2.4053 [17.3449]	−10.3692
Natural gas-MSARCH-tStud	−12.3048 [−0.4825]	−0.0099 [−0.5148]	2.4059 [17.3492]	−14.6584
Natural gas-MSGARCH-Gaussian	−61.2853 [−2.4033]	−0.0716 [−3.7232]	3.986 [28.7435]	−42.6652
Natural gas-MSGARCH-tStud	−3.8858 [−0.1524]	−0.003 [−0.156]	1.9494 [14.0573]	−9.642
Model or Scenario	CVaR (95%)	CVaR (98%)	Sharpe Ratio	Mean risky Exposure
Natural gas-MS-Gaussian	−6.4364 [−46.4135]	−7.9449 [−57.2915]	0.0027 [0.1301]	0.4412
Natural gas-MS-tStud	Not feasible	Not feasible	Not feasible	Not feasible
Natural gas-MSARCH-Gaussian	−6.383 [−46.0285]	−7.9212 [−57.1206]	−0.0005 [0.0782]	0.4118
Natural gas-MSARCH-tStud	−6.5453 [−47.1988]	−8.5821 [−61.8864]	−0.008 [−0.0297]	0.3145
Natural gas-MSGARCH-Gaussian	−9.572 [−69.0247]	−12.0872 [−87.162]	−0.0162 [−0.1295]	0.6599
Natural gas-MSGARCH-tStud	−5.4323 [−39.1729]	−6.8775 [−49.5944]	−0.0041 [−0.0111]	0.2481

Note: The same presentation format as in Tables 4 and 5. Source: Own elaboration with results of our simulations and data from Refinitiv Eikon [72].

Even if this result supports part of our working hypothesis of alpha generation, it is preferable to invest in a buy-and-hold strategy in USTBILL than trading with our strategy in natural gas.

We observe that this result is not due to the active investment strategy proposed herein, but because the NATGAS did not paid a higher return than the USTBILL. This leads us to observe that this commodity is not appropriate for trading purposes with a quantitative strategy.

For the specific case of the risk exposure in this commodity, practically all the scenarios show a significant reduction from the observed values in the buy-and-hold strategy and the CVaR values are lower than the ones of the passive investment scenario.

Figure 2 shows the historical performance of the simulated portfolios, along with the historical investment level in the NATGAS future. Even if the Gaussian MS model is the best for fitting the data recursively (Table 3), the accumulated return is not so attractive. As Figure 2 and Table 8 show, the mean risky investment level (or exposure) is lower than 50.00% in the simulations. This produced a more conservative strategy. In addition, in some periods, such as July 2007 to October 2008, the presence of the distress or high volatility periods was higher, and the price was subject to wider fluctuations. This led our trading algorithm to invest in the risk-free asset.

This last statement is proven in the historical investment level in the natural gas future, as shown in the lower panel of Figure 3. As noted, the Gaussian time-fixed and ARCH variance MS models were highly sensitive to changes in the high-volatility regime probability. This led to a sell of the natural gas futures position and to an increase in the risk-free asset. This behavior was of practical use in the 2009 to 2010 period in which the quantitative easing program of the U.S. Federal Reserve took effect which allowed a reduction in the speculative positions in this commodity and a price downfall. This change of regime was noted by these two models, resulting in a sell of the risky position in this future. This last decision was crucial, in order to generate an overperformance against the buy-and-hold strategy (shaded area). Despite the performance results observed in our simulations, the performance of the five simulated portfolios is not better than that of the USTBILL.

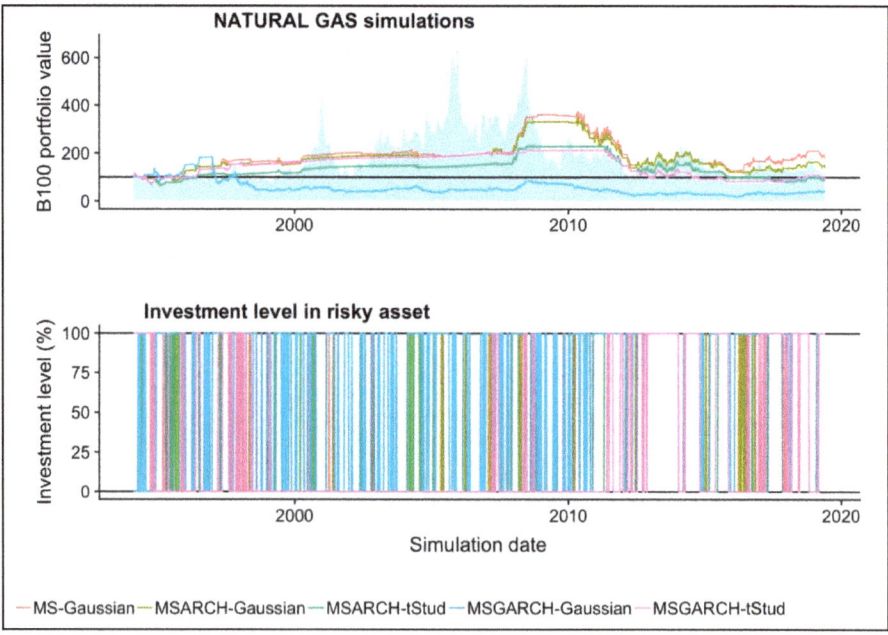

Figure 3. Historical performance of the five simulated scenarios of the investment strategy in the natural gas price one-month future and its historical investment level. Source: Own elaboration with results of our simulations and data from Refinitiv Eikon [72].

In order to make a more consistent review, we performed the one-way ANOVA and Kruskal–Wallis tests, along with the review of the returns box plots. The results are shown in Table 9 and Figure 4. As noted, there is no significant difference in the performance of the five simulated portfolios, even if the return fluctuation is narrower in these. This last result suggests that, even if the risk exposure is lower in the simulated portfolios, their performance is not so different between them.

Table 9. ANOVA and Kruskal–Wallis test of the observed weekly returns in the simulated portfolios of the NATGAS price and the USTBILL portfolio.

One-Way ANOVA Test				
Degrees of Freedom	Squred Sums	Squared Means	F Value	Pr (>F)
5	0.0010	0.0002	0.1444	0.9817
7944	11.6639	0.0014		
Kruskal–Wallis test		K-W statistic	Degrees of Freedom	Pr (>Xi2)
		10.8893	5.000	0.0536

Source: Own elaboration with results of our simulations and data from Refinitiv Eikon [72].

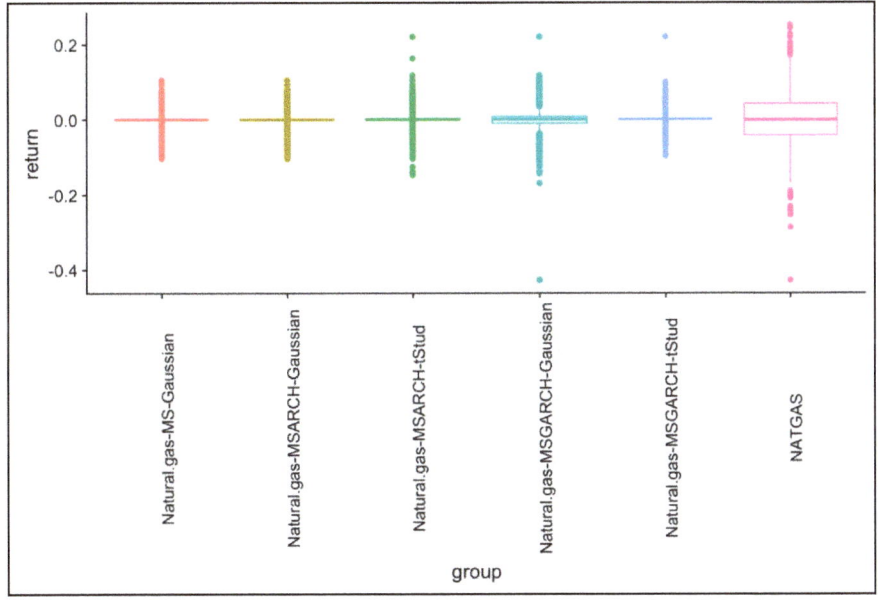

Figure 4. Box plot of the returns of five simulated scenarios in the natural gas continuous. Source: Own elaboration with results of our simulations and data from Refinitiv Eikon [72].

In order to verify if the observed performance results in the NATGAS are due to market timing skills with the simulated trading rule, we present the proper test results in Table 10. As noted, the values suggest that the performance in the simulations made in this commodity is due only to NATGAS price fluctuations. Only the β_1 values are significant and low. This gives stronger support to our conclusions related to this commodity; the commodity did not have a better performance than the USTBILL and, complementary to this our trading rule did not generate good market timing, that is, it did not work for the intended purposes.

Table 10. Attribution and market timing test of the five simulated portfolios in the NATGAS market.

Simulated Portfolio	α	α p-Value	β_1	β_1 p-Value
Oil-MS-Gaussian	−0.0001	0.8563	0.0402	0.0047
Oil-MSARCH-Gaussian	−0.0003	0.6503	0.0405	0.0034
Oil-MSARCH-tStud	−0.0007	0.3583	0.0415	0.0027
Oil-MSGARCH-Gaussian	−0.0019	0.1157	0.1455	0.0000
Oil-MSGARCH-tStud	−0.0006	0.2841	0.0270	0.0158
Simulated portfolio	**β_2**	**β_2 p-value**	**R^2**	
Oil-MS-Gaussian	0.0230	0.8485	0.0062	
Oil-MSARCH-Gaussian	0.0257	0.8261	0.0067	
Oil-MSARCH-tStud	0.0147	0.8998	0.0071	
Oil-MSGARCH-Gaussian	0.2118	0.2698	0.0305	
Oil-MSGARCH-tStud	0.0341	0.7194	0.0044	

Source: Own elaboration with results of our simulations and data from Refinitiv Eikon [72].

As a corollary of results, the use of MS models leads to a better performance if these are used for trading decision purposes in the oil market only. More specifically, the use of Gaussian, time-fixed variance MS models lead to the best performance in both commodities. This is an issue that does not completely fulfill our working hypothesis because the best performing model is the Gaussian with time-fixed variance and not a MSGARCH model. Despite this, we found that the use of MS models for trading is useful only in the oil market. We mention this, given the poor performance of the natural gas simulations against the U.S. Treasury bills and the poor market timing of the simulated trading rule in this case.

4. Concluding Remarks and Guidelines for Further Research

Markov-switching (MS) models have been used in several applications since their first proposal in [19,20]. From all these, we were interested in their use for active trading in the most traded energy commodities [18]: The West Texas Intermediate oil (OIL) and the Henry Hub delivered natural gas (NATGAS). More specifically, we were interested, for trading decision purposes, in the forecast of the distress or high volatility regime or time period for these two commodities.

The use of MS models for active trading was originally proposed by Brooks and Persand [27] in the U.K. gilt and stock markets, in a two regime and Gaussian probability density function (pdf) context. This test was later extended to other stock markets by [28,31,57–59] in a Gaussian, constant (or time-fixed) variance, and in a two or three-regime context. Only the work of [30] extend the use of MS models with a time-varying autoregressive conditional heteroscedasticity (ARCH) or a generalized autoregressive conditional heteroscedasticity (GARCH) variance (henceforth MSARCH and MASGARCH models, respectively).

By the fact there is no literature on studies that test the use of MS, MSARCH, or MSGARCH models for commodity trading, we extended the review of the practical usefulness of MS models in the following three ways:

1. The use of MS models for trading in the OIL and NATGAS markets;
2. The use of a two regime, t-Student pdf by comparing the observed results with the ones in a Gaussian context;
3. By using an ARCH or GARCH variance for the estimation of the MS model.

These energy commodities were of special interest to us, given their direct link in the economic activity and their use in the diversification practices in institutional investors such as mutual funds, pension funds, or insurance companies.

With weekly data from 6 April 1990 to 31 May 2019, we performed weekly simulations (from 7 January 1994 to the end of the dataset) of the next investment strategy which included:

1. To invest in the commodity future of interest if the investor expects to be in the "normal" or "calm" regime ($k = 1$) at $T + 1$;
2. To invest in the risk-free asset (the three-month U.S. Treasury bill or USTBILL) if the investor expects to be in the "distress" or "high volatility" time period.

This led us to test the following working hypotheses:

1. It is better to use a MSARCH or MSGARCH model in order to forecast the $T + 1$ the probability, $\xi_{k=2,t+1}$, of being in the distress regime in the OIL or NATGAS market;
2. The use of the suggested trading strategy with MS-GARCH models leads to a better performance in the OIL and NATGAS market. This compared with a passive or "buy-and-hold" one.

As a corollary of results of the simulations performed herein, we want to highlight that our first working hypothesis partially holds for OIL. That is, the use of MS models is appropriate for an active investment in the OIL market. We concluded this because the use of MS models leads to a proper $T + 1$ forecast of the distress regime probability and to a proper investment decision (proper market timing). Despite this, our position in our first hypothesis was that it is preferable to use a MSARCH or MSGARCH model instead. As part of our results, it is important to mention that the t-Student MSGARCH model is the best one for risk measurement (that is for energy market risk management purposes) but the constant variance MS model with Gaussian pdf is the best option for active trading in the OIL market. This last result is due to the 1097.49% accumulated return observed in this scenario.

For the specific case of the NATGAS market, we found that the accumulated results are lower than those of a buy-and-hold strategy in USTBILL, due to the fact that the NATGAS had a lower performance (accumulated return) than the USTBILL during the simulation period. Therefore, we conclude that the use of Gaussian or t-Student MS, MSARCH, or MSGARCH models does not lead to good performance results in this market, given the performance of the simulated commodity.

We believe that our results contribute to the existing literature about the practical usefulness of Markov-switching (MS) models in trading activities. In addition, our simulations lead us to suggest that the use of the proposed active investment strategy could help portfolio managers, energy traders, or individual investors to invest in these types of commodities, with an acceptable level of accuracy in the forecast of distress time periods.

Limitantions Found in Our Simulations and Guidelines for Further Research

Among the limitations (opportunity areas) that we found in our simulations is the fact that we used (due to space restrictions and for simplicity in the rhetoric situation) symmetric and homogeneous Gaussian and t-Student pdfs and, for the same exposition reasons, we used a two regime assumption and symmetric ARCH and GARCH models. Had we made our test in a symmetric vs. asymmetric pdf and GARCH models, we would have needed to present the results of not six but of 18 scenarios. This number of scenarios is reached had we used asymmetric Gaussian and t-Student pdfs [74] and the two most used asymmetric GARCH models, the T-GARCH [67] and the GJR-GARCH [66]. Related to this issue, we suggest testing the use of these pdfs and GARCH variances in similar simulations and to extend the study to the use of the generalized error distribution (GED) pdf.

Another limitation in our test is the fact that the MSARCH or MSGARCH can be estimated only in the residuals, because we estimated these with the arithmetic mean of the returns. We suggest extending our test by using other nonlinear mean models such as the ARMA model.

Finally, we used the assumption that the transition probability matrix (Π) is time fixed, the extension to time-varying transition probabilities and also the incorporation of external factors in the estimation of the MS models could be of potential interest.

Author Contributions: All authors contributed equally to this work. All authors wrote, reviewed, and commented on the manuscript. All authors have read and approved the final manuscript. All authors have read and agreed to the published version of the manuscript.

Funding: This research received funding from the Teacher's Development Program (PRODEP) of the Mexican Public Education Secretary (SEP), as part of its academic paper's publication sponsorship program.

Conflicts of Interest: The authors declare no conflict of interest with the analysis and tests made herein.

References

1. Jacobs, H.; Müller, S.; Weber, M. How Should Private Investors Diversify?—An Empirical Evaluation of Alternative Asset Allocation Policies to Construct A World Market Portfolio. *SSRN Electron. J.* **2011**. [CrossRef]
2. Christoffersen, P.; Errunza, V.; Jacobs, K.; Jin, X. Correlation dynamics and international diversification benefits. *Int. J. Forecast.* **2014**, *30*, 807–824. [CrossRef]
3. Alexander, C.; Korovilas, D.; Kapraun, J. Diversification with volatility products. *J. Int. Money Financ.* **2016**, *65*, 213–235. [CrossRef]
4. Bessler, W.; Wolff, D. Do commodities add value in multi-asset portfolios? An out-of-sample analysis for different investment strategies. *J. Bank. Financ.* **2015**, *60*, 1–20. [CrossRef]
5. Hung, K.; Onayev, Z.; Tu, C.C. Time-varying diversification effect of real estate in institutional portfolios: When alternative assets are considered. *J. Real Estate Portf. Manag.* **2008**, *14*, 241–261.
6. Jackwerth, J.C.; Slavutskaya, A. The total benefit of alternative assets to pension fund portfolios. *J. Financ. Mark.* **2016**, *31*, 25–42. [CrossRef]
7. Ahmad, W.; Rais, S. Time-Varying Spillover and the Portfolio Diversification Implications of Clean Energy Equity with Commodities and Financial Assets. *Emerg. Mark. Financ. Trade* **2018**, *54*, 1838–1856. [CrossRef]
8. Hoevenaars, R.; Molenaar, R.; Schotman, P.; Steenkamp, T. Strategic asset allocation with liabilities: Beyond stocks and bonds. *J. Econ. Dyn. Control* **2008**, *32*, 2939–2970. [CrossRef]
9. Yan, L.; Garcia, P. Portfolio investment: Are commodities useful? *J. Commod. Mark.* **2017**, *8*, 43–55. [CrossRef]
10. Guo, J.; Sun, Z.; Tang, H.; Jia, X.; Wang, S.; Yan, X.; Ye, G.; Wu, G. Hybrid Optimization Algorithm of Particle Swarm Optimization and Cuckoo Search for Preventive Maintenance Period Optimization. *Discr. Dyn. Nat. Soc.* **2016**. [CrossRef]
11. Zhang, Z.; Hong, W. Electric load forecasting by complete ensemble empirical model decomposition adaptive noise and support vector regression with quantum-based dragonfly algorithm. *Nonlinear Dyn.* **2019**, *98*, 1107–1136. [CrossRef]
12. Chauvet, M. An econometric characterization of business cycle dynamics with factor structure and regime switching. *Int. Econ. Rev. (Philadelphia)* **2000**, *10*, 127–142. [CrossRef]
13. Misas, M.; Ramírez, M.T. Depressions in the Colombian economic growth during the twentieth century: A Markov switching regime model. *Appl. Econ. Lett.* **2007**, *14*, 803–808. [CrossRef]
14. Rotta, P.N.; Valls Pereira, P.L. Analysis of contagion from the dynamic conditional correlation model with Markov Regime switching. *Appl. Econ.* **2016**, *48*, 2367–2382. [CrossRef]
15. Camacho, M.; Perez-Quiros, G. Commodity Prices and the Business Cycle in Latin America: Living and Dying by Commodities? *Emerg. Mark. Financ. Trade* **2014**, *50*, 110–137. [CrossRef]
16. Hamilton, J.; Lin, G. Stock Market Volatility and the Business Cycle. *J. Appl. Econom.* **1996**, *11*, 573–593. [CrossRef]
17. Dufrénot, G.; Keddad, B. Business cycles synchronization in East Asia: A Markov-switching approach. *Econ. Model.* **2014**, *42*, 186–197. [CrossRef]
18. Commodity Futures Trading Commission Commitments of Traders | U.S. COMMODITY FUTURES TRADING COMMISSION. Available online: https://www.cftc.gov/MarketReports/CommitmentsofTraders/index.htm (accessed on 22 April 2019).
19. Hamilton, J.D. A New Approach to the Economic Analysis of Nonstationary Time Series and the Business Cycle. *Econometrica* **1989**, *57*, 357–384. [CrossRef]
20. Hamilton, J.D. Analysis of time series subject to changes in regime. *J. Econom.* **1990**, *45*, 39–70. [CrossRef]
21. Lamoureux, C.G.; Lastrapes, W.D. Persistence in Variance, Structural Change, and the GARCH Model. *J. Bus. Econ. Stat.* **1990**, *8*, 225–234. [CrossRef]

22. Hamilton, J.D.; Susmel, R. Autoregressive conditional heteroskedasticity and changes in regime. *J. Econom.* **1994**, *64*, 307–333. [CrossRef]
23. Klaassen, F. Improving GARCH volatility forecasts with regime-switching GARCH. In *Advances in Markov-Switching Models*; Physica-Verlag HD: Heidelberg, Germany, 2002; pp. 223–254.
24. Haas, M.; Mittnik, S.; Paolella, M.S. A New Approach to Markov-Switching GARCH Models. *J. Financ. Econom.* **2004**, *2*, 493–530. [CrossRef]
25. Ardia, D. *Financial Risk Management with Bayesian Estimation of GARCH Models*; Springer: Belin/Heidelberg, Germany, 2008; Volume 612.
26. Ardia, D.; Bluteau, K.; Boudt, K.; Catania, L. Forecasting risk with Markov-switching GARCH models: A large-scale performance study. *Int. J. Forecast.* **2018**, *34*, 733–747. [CrossRef]
27. Brooks, C.; Persand, G. The trading profitability of forecasts of the gilt–equity yield ratio. *Int. J. Forecast.* **2001**, *17*, 11–29. [CrossRef]
28. Hauptmann, J.; Hoppenkamps, A.; Min, A.; Ramsauer, F.; Zagst, R. Forecasting market turbulence using regime-switching models. *Financ. Mark. Portf. Manag.* **2014**, *28*, 139–164. [CrossRef]
29. De la Torre, O.; Galeana-Figueroa, E.; Álvarez-García, J. Using Markov-Switching models in Italian, British, U.S. and Mexican equity portfolios: A performance test. *Electron. J. Appl. Stat. Anal.* **2018**, *11*, 489–505. [CrossRef]
30. De la Torre-Torres, O.V.; Aguilasocho-Montoya, D.; Álvarez-García, J. Active portfolio management in the Andean countries' stock markets with Markov-Switching GARCH models. *Rev. Mex. Econ. y Finanz.* **2019**, *14*, 601–616. [CrossRef]
31. Engel, J.; Wahl, M.; Zagst, R. Forecasting turbulence in the Asian and European stock market using regime-switching models. *Quant. Financ. Econ.* **2018**, *2*, 388–406. [CrossRef]
32. De la Torre-Torres, O.; Álvarez-García, J.; Santillán-Salgado, J.; López-Herrera, F. Potential improvements to pension funds performance in Mexico Mejoras potenciales al desempeño de los fondos de pensiones en México. *Rev. Espac.* **2019**, *40*, 26–41.
33. Alizadeh, A.H.; Nomikos, N.K.; Pouliasis, P.K. A Markov regime switching approach for hedging energy commodities. *J. Bank. Financ.* **2008**, *32*, 1970–1983. [CrossRef]
34. Bodie, Z.; Kane, A.; Marcus, A. *Investments Global Edition*, 10th ed.; Mc Graw-Hill: New York, NY, USA, 2014.
35. Hong, W.-C.; Li, M.-W.; Geng, J.; Zhang, Y. Novel chaotic bat algorithm for forecasting complex motion of floating platforms. *Appl. Math. Model.* **2019**, *72*, 425–443. [CrossRef]
36. Pant, T.; Han, C.; Wang, H. Examination of errors of table integration in flamelet/progress variable modeling of a turbulent non-premixed jet flame. *Appl. Math. Model.* **2019**, *72*, 369–384. [CrossRef]
37. Ailliot, P.; Monbet, V. Markov-switching autoregressive models for wind time series. *Environ. Model. Softw.* **2012**, *30*, 92–101. [CrossRef]
38. Elias, R.S.; Wahab, M.I.M.; Fang, L. Stochastics and Statistics A comparison of regime-switching temperature modeling approaches for applications in weather derivatives. *Eur. J. Oper. Res.* **2014**, *232*, 549–560. [CrossRef]
39. Ailliot, P.; Bessac, J.; Monbet, V.; Pène, F. Non-homogeneous hidden Markov-switching models for wind time series. *J. Stat. Plan. Inference* **2015**, *160*, 75–88. [CrossRef]
40. Monbet, V.; Ailliot, P. Sparse vector Markov switching autoregressive models. Application to multivariate time series of temperature. *Comput. Stat. Data Anal.* **2017**, *108*, 40–51. [CrossRef]
41. Klein, A.C. Time-variations in herding behavior: Evidence from a Markov switching SUR model. *J. Int. Financ. Mark. Institutions Money* **2013**, *26*, 291–304. [CrossRef]
42. Areal, N.; Cortez, M.C.; Silva, F. The conditional performance of US mutual funds over different market regimes: Do different types of ethical screens matter? *Financ. Mark. Portf. Manag.* **2013**, *27*, 397–429. [CrossRef]
43. Zheng, T.; Zuo, H. Reexamining the time-varying volatility spillover effects: A Markov switching causality approach. *North Am. J. Econ. Financ.* **2013**, *26*, 643–662. [CrossRef]
44. Sorin Gabriel, A. Evaluating the Forecasting Performance of GARCH Models. Evidence from Romania. *Procedia-Social Behav. Sci.* **2012**, *62*, 1006–1010. [CrossRef]
45. Ye, W.; Zhu, Y.; Wu, Y.; Miao, B. Markov regime-switching quantile regression models and financial contagion detection. *Insur. Math. Econ.* **2016**, *67*, 21–26. [CrossRef]
46. MSCI Inc. MSCI Global Investable Market Indexes Methodology. Available online: http://www.msci.com/eqb/methodology/meth_docs/MSCI_Jan2015_GIMIMethodology_vf.pdf (accessed on 2 May 2018).

47. Cabrera, G.; Coronado, S.; Rojas, O.; Venegas-Martínez, F. Synchronization and Changes in Volatilities in the Latin American'S Stock Exchange Markets. *Int. J. Pure Appl. Math.* **2017**, *114*. [CrossRef]
48. Sosa, M.; Ortiz, E.; Cabello, A. Dynamic Linkages between Stock Market and Exchange Rate in mila Countries: A Markov Regime Switching Approach (2003-2016). *Análisis Económico* **2018**, *33*, 57–74. [CrossRef]
49. Lin, C.-H. The comovement between exchange rates and stock prices in the Asian emerging markets. *Int. Rev. Econ. Financ.* **2012**, *22*, 161–172. [CrossRef]
50. Shen, X.; Holmes, M.J. Do Asia-Pacific stock prices follow a random walk? A regime-switching perspective. *Appl. Econ. Lett.* **2013**, *21*, 189–195. [CrossRef]
51. Balcilar, M.; Demirer, R.; Hammoudeh, S. Investor herds and regime-switching: Evidence from Gulf Arab stock markets. *J. Int. Financ. Mark. Institutions Money* **2013**, *23*, 295–321. [CrossRef]
52. Boamah, N.A.; Watts, E.J.; Loudon, G. Investigating temporal variation in the global and regional integration of African stock markets. *J. Multinatl. Financ. Manag.* **2016**, *36*, 103–118. [CrossRef]
53. Bundoo, S.K. Stock market development and integration in SADC (Southern African Development Community). *J. Adv. Res.* **2017**, *7*, 64–72. [CrossRef]
54. Alexander, C.; Kaeck, A. Regime dependent determinants of credit default swap spreads. *J. Bank. Financ.* **2007**, 1008–1021. [CrossRef]
55. Ma, J.; Deng, X.; Ho, K.-C.; Tsai, S.-B. Regime-Switching Determinants for Spreads of Emerging Markets Sovereign Credit Default Swaps. *Sustainability* **2018**, *10*, 2730. [CrossRef]
56. Valera, H.G.A.; Lee, J. Do rice prices follow a random walk? Evidence from Markov switching unit root tests for Asian markets. *Agric. Econ.* **2016**, *47*, 683–695. [CrossRef]
57. Ang, A.; Bekaert, G. International Asset Allocation With Regime Shifts. *Rev. Financ. Stud.* **2002**, *15*, 1137–1187. [CrossRef]
58. Ang, A.; Bekaert, G. How regimes affect asset allocation. *Financ. Anal. J.* **2004**, *60*, 86–99. [CrossRef]
59. Kritzman, M.; Page, S.; Turkington, D. Regime Shifts: Implications for Dynamic Strategies. *Financ. Anal. J.* **2012**, *68*, 22–39. [CrossRef]
60. Hamilton, J.D. *Time Series Analysis*; Princeton University Press: Princeton, NJ, USA, 1994.
61. Dempster, A.P.; Laird, N.M.; Rubin, D.B. Maximum Likelihood from Incomplete Data via the EM Algorithm. *J. R. Stat. Soc. Ser. B* **1977**, *39*, 1–38. [CrossRef]
62. Kim, C.-J. Dynamic linear models with Markov-switching. *J. Econom.* **1994**, *60*, 1–22. [CrossRef]
63. Engle, R. Autoregressive Conditional Heteroscedasticity with estimates of the variance of United Kingdom inflation. *Econometrica* **1982**, *50*, 987–1007. [CrossRef]
64. Bollerslev, T. Generalized Autorregresive Conditional Hetersoskedasticity. *J. Econom.* **1986**, *31*, 307–327. [CrossRef]
65. Nelson, D.B. Conditional Heteroskedasticity in Asset Returns: A New Approach. *Econometrica* **1991**, *59*, 347. [CrossRef]
66. Glosten, L.; Jaganathan, R.; Runkle, D.E. On the Relation between the Expected Value and the Volatility of the Nominal Excess Return on Stocks. *J. Finance* **1993**, *48*, 1779–1801. [CrossRef]
67. Zakoian, J.-M. Threshold heteroskedastic models. *J. Econ. Dyn. Control* **1994**, *18*, 931–955. [CrossRef]
68. Ardia, D.; Bluteau, K.; Boudt, K.; Trottier, D. Markov–Switching GARCH Models in R: The MSGARCH Package. *J. Stat. Softw.* **2019**, *91*, 38. [CrossRef]
69. Metropolis, N.; Rosenbluth, A.W.; Rosenbluth, M.N.; Teller, A.H.; Teller, E. Equation of State Calculations by Fast Computing Machines. *J. Chem. Phys.* **1953**, *21*, 1087–1092. [CrossRef]
70. Viterbi, A. Error bounds for convolutional codes and an asymptotically optimum decoding algorithm. *IEEE Trans. Inf. Theory* **1967**, *13*, 260–269. [CrossRef]
71. Ardia, D.; Bluteu, K.; Boudt, K.; Catania, L.; Ghalanos, A.; Peterson, B.; Trottier, D.-A. Package "MSGARCH" Title Markov-Switching GARCH Models. Available online: https://cran.r-project.org/web/packages/MSGARCH/index.html (accessed on 21 November 2018).
72. Refinitiv Refinitiv Eikon. Available online: https://eikon.thomsonreuters.com/index.html (accessed on 3 June 2019).

73. Sharpe, W. Mutual fund performance. *J. Bus.* **1966**, *39*, 119–138. [CrossRef]
74. Fernández, C.; Steel, M.F.J. On Bayesian Modeling of Fat Tails and Skewness. *J. Am. Stat. Assoc.* **1998**, *93*, 359–371. [CrossRef]

© 2019 by the authors. Licensee MDPI, Basel, Switzerland. This article is an open access article distributed under the terms and conditions of the Creative Commons Attribution (CC BY) license (http://creativecommons.org/licenses/by/4.0/).

Review

Review and Comparison of Intelligent Optimization Modelling Techniques for Energy Forecasting and Condition-Based Maintenance in PV Plants

Jesús Ferrero Bermejo [1], Juan Francisco Gómez Fernández [2], Rafael Pino [3], Adolfo Crespo Márquez [2,*] and Antonio Jesús Guillén López [2]

1. Magtel Operaciones, 41940 Seville, Spain; jesus.ferrero@magtel.es
2. Department of Industrial Management, Escuela Técnica Superior de Ingenieros, 41092 Sevilla, Spain; juan.gomez@iies.es (J.F.G.F.); ajguillen@us.es (A.J.G.L.)
3. Department of Statistics and Operations Research, Facultad de Matemáticas, Universidad de Sevilla, 41012 Sevilla, Spain; rafaelp@us.es
* Correspondence: adolfo@us.es; Tel.: +34-610-540-222

Received: 19 September 2019; Accepted: 29 October 2019; Published: 31 October 2019

Abstract: Within the field of soft computing, intelligent optimization modelling techniques include various major techniques in artificial intelligence. These techniques pretend to generate new business knowledge transforming sets of "raw data" into business value. One of the principal applications of these techniques is related to the design of predictive analytics for the improvement of advanced CBM (condition-based maintenance) strategies and energy production forecasting. These advanced techniques can be used to transform control system data, operational data and maintenance event data to failure diagnostic and prognostic knowledge and, ultimately, to derive expected energy generation. One of the systems where these techniques can be applied with massive potential impact are the legacy monitoring systems existing in solar PV energy generation plants. These systems produce a great amount of data over time, while at the same time they demand an important effort in order to increase their performance through the use of more accurate predictive analytics to reduce production losses having a direct impact on ROI. How to choose the most suitable techniques to apply is one of the problems to address. This paper presents a review and a comparative analysis of six intelligent optimization modelling techniques, which have been applied on a PV plant case study, using the energy production forecast as the decision variable. The methodology proposed not only pretends to elicit the most accurate solution but also validates the results, in comparison with the different outputs for the different techniques.

Keywords: artificial intelligence techniques; energy forecasting; condition-based maintenance; asset management

1. Introduction

Within the field of soft computing, intelligent optimization modelling techniques include various major techniques in artificial intelligence [1] pretending to generate new business data knowledge transforming sets of "raw data" into business value. In the Merriam-Webster dictionary data mining is defined as "the practice of searching through large amounts of computerized data to find useful patterns or trends", so we can then say that intelligent optimization modelling techniques are data mining techniques.

Nowadays, connections among industrial assets and integrating information systems, processes and operative technicians [2] are the core of the next-generation of industrial management. Based on the industrial Internet of Things (IoT), companies have to seek intelligent optimization modelling techniques (advanced analytics) [3] in order to optimize decision-making, business and social value. These techniques are preferred to fall inside the soft computing category, with the idea of solving real complex problems with inductive reasoning like humans, searching for probable patterns, being less precise, but adaptable to reasonable changes and easily applicable and obtainable [4].

To be able to implement these advanced techniques requires a comprehensive process sometimes named "intelligent data analysis" (IDA) [5], which is a more extensive and non-trivial process to identify understandable patterns from data. Within this process, the main difficulty is to identify valid and correct data for the analysis [3] from the different sources in the company. Second, efforts must be developed to create analytic models that provide value by improving performance. Third, a cultural change has to be embraced for companies to facilitate the implementation of the analytical results. In addition to this, since accumulation of data is too large and complex to be processed by traditional database management tools (the definition of "big data" in the Merriam-Webster dictionary), new tools to manage big data must be taking into consideration [6].

Under these considerations IDA can be applied to renewable energy production, as one of the most promising fields of application of these techniques [7]. The stochastic nature of these energy sources, and the lack of a consolidated technical background in most of these technologies, make this sector very susceptible for the application of intelligent optimization modelling techniques. The referred stochastic nature is determined by circumstances in the generation sources, but also by the existing operational conditions. That is, the natural resources have variations according to weather with a certain stationarity but with difficulties in forecasting behaviours. In addition, depending on the operational and environmental stresses in the activities, they will be more likely to fail. Consequently, the analysis of renewable energy production must consider adaptability to dynamic changes that can yield results [8].

The identification and prediction of potential failures can be improved using advanced analytics as a way to search proactively and reduce risk in order to improve efficiency in energy generation. Algorithms, such as machine learning, are now quite extended in renewable energy control systems. These kinds of facilities are characterized by the presence of a great number of sensors feeding the SCADA systems (supervisory control and data acquisition systems), usually very sophisticated systems including a control interface and a client interface (the plant's owner, distribution electric network administrator, etc.). Power and energy production measures are two of the most important variables managed by the SCADA. As principal system performance outputs, they can be exploited through data mining techniques to control system failures, since most of the systems failures directly affect the output power and the energy production efficiency [7].

A sample process for a comprehensive IDA, applied to the improvement of assets management in renewable energy, is presented in Figure 1.

In Figure 1 the green box describes the generic IDA process phases, phases which need to be managed inside an asset management condition-based maintenance (CBM) framework, in order to make sustainable and well-structured decisions, to obtain developments and to keep and improve solutions over time. In order to take rapid and optimal decisions, the challenge is to structure the information from different sources, synchronizing it properly in time, in a sustainable and easily assimilable way, reducing the errors (avoiding dependencies among variables, noise, and interferences) and valuing real risks. A clear conceptual framework allows the permanent development of current and new algorithms, corresponding to distinct data behaviour-anomalies with physical degradation patterns of assets according to their operation and operation environment conditions and their effects on the whole plant [11].

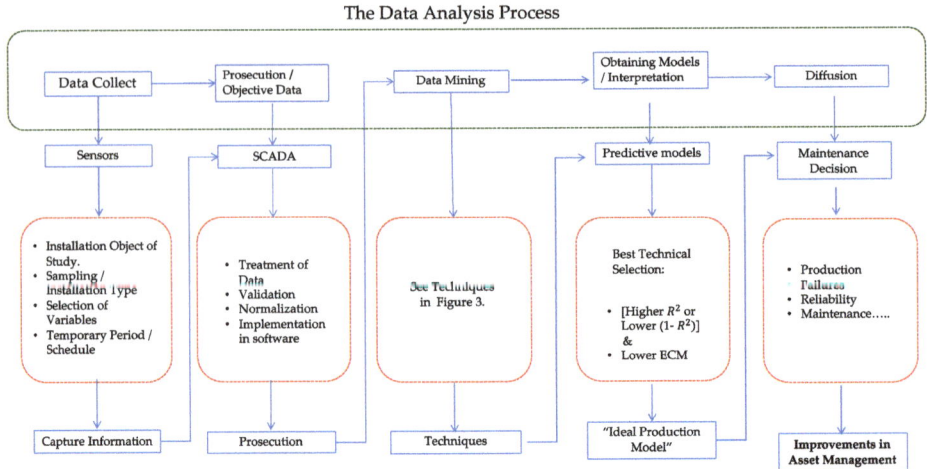

Figure 1. IDA phases for a renewable energy case study [9,10].

Each one of these IDA phases are interpreted, in the red boxes, for a PV energy production data system [9,10] showing a flow-chart for practical implementation. In this paper we will focus on the central phase in Figure 1, the analysis of different techniques of data mining (DM). Different techniques can be applied. We will concentrate in the selection of advanced DM techniques, comparing their results when applied to a similar case study. This issue is often not addressed when applying certain complex intelligent optimization modelling techniques, and no discussion emerges concerning this issue. This is because, often, the computational effort to apply a certain method is very important in order to be able to benchmark the results of several methods [12]. In the future, assuming more mature IDA application scenarios, the selection of DM techniques will likely be crucial to generating well-informed decisions.

Accepting this challenge, a review of the literature, the selection of techniques and a benchmark of their results are presented in this paper. According to the previous literature, most representative techniques of data mining [13,14] are presented and applied to a case study in a photovoltaic plant (see other examples where these techniques were applied in Table 1).

Artificial neural networks (ANN) have been largely developed in recent years. Some authors [15–20] have focused on obtaining PV production predictions through a behavioural pattern that is modelled by selected predictor variables. A very interesting topic is how these results can be applied in predictive maintenance solutions. In [7] these models are used to predict PV system's faults before they occur, improving the efficiency of PV installations, allowing programming in advance of suitable maintenance tasks. Following a similar approach, the rest of DM techniques are implemented to validate, or even improve, the good results obtained with the ANN in terms of asset maintenance and management.

Table 1. References of DM techniques analysed.

Techniques	References
Data mining	[13,21–25]
Artificial neural networks	[7,26–32]
Support vector machine	[33–37]
Decision trees	[14,21,38–43]

In general terms, the results obtained using DM or machine learning to follow and predict PV critical variables, like solar radiation [21], are good enough to use as inputs in decision-making processes, like maintenance decisions [7]. However, not all of the techniques have the same maturity level as ANNs. SVM, Random Forest and Boosting, as techniques to predict the yield of a PV plant, should be studied in greater depth in the coming years [22].

2. Background

2.1. Data Mining Techniques

Data mining techniques are in constant development by combining the use of the diverse techniques available over a wide range of application fields. The search of behavioural patterns or predictions based on various predictive variables that allow us to know the future or expected outcome to improve key decision-making is being extended by researching the most diverse application fields. For example, in [23] the assessment of credit ratings from a risk perspective, using different data mining techniques and hybrid models, are proposed, analysing the advantages and disadvantages of each. In a completely different application field, [24,25] present models of distribution of solar spectral radiation based on data mining techniques, using solar irradiance, temperature and humidity as input variables.

In [14] a classification of predictive techniques in the photovoltaic sector is presented (Figure 2). These results show how data mining techniques are becoming increasingly relevant, since they represent 61% (ANN, SVM, RF) of the total of the studies. Another interesting classification study is included in [25].

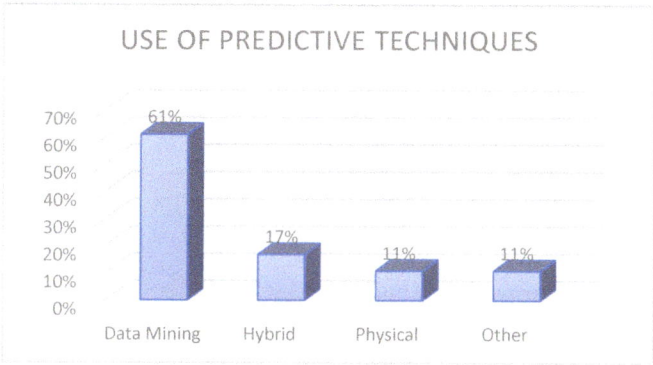

Figure 2. Predictive technique type classification [14].

For their part, the authors [21] make a review of the different techniques of machine learning for predicting solar radiation, which depends on the accuracy of the data. Although these are recent techniques that require more research, they are improving the conventional methods, concluding that the ones that should be used in the future are those of SVM, decision trees and Random Forest.

Making a general and deep presentation of different predictive and DM techniques is a very interesting task that goes well beyond the aims of this paper. Figure 3 presents a basic classification of the data mining techniques, including those that are going to be compared in this paper by applying them to the same case study. In the section below a brief literature review introducing these techniques is included.

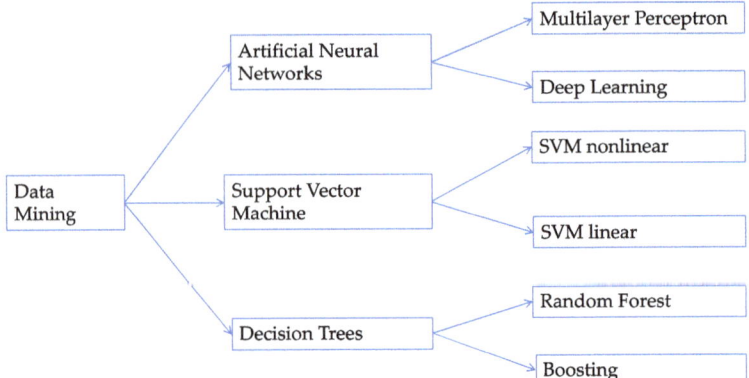

Figure 3. Classification of DM techniques included in this paper.

Table 1 summarize employed references in the paper corresponding to DM techniques analysed.

A comparison of techniques is made using the values of the correlation coefficient and the mean square error to measure the quality of the results of alternative models and techniques [34,43].

2.1.1. Artificial Neural Networks (ANN)

In estimations about renewable energies, ANN techniques are widely utilized and, more particularly, the field of photovoltaic systems has been continuously developing them in recent years [26–28]. There are various ANN models, and a particular architecture widely extended is multilayer perceptron (MLP) [44].

In [29] a study is presented to obtain with greater precision the production of electrical and thermal energy from a photovoltaic and thermal concentration system, using a neural network (multilayer perceptron) to predict solar radiation and irradiance. In a maintenance application, in [7] the authors go further in their study using the predictive model obtained with the multilayer perceptron neuronal network trained with the backpropagation algorithm to anticipate the occurrence of failures and, thus, improve the efficiency of the final production.

Deep learning neural networks are multilayer and feedforward neural networks that consist of multiple layers of interconnected neuron units with the aim of construing better level features, from lower layers to a proper output space. The application of deep learning techniques provides a fairly accurate prediction in renewable energies, and the authors [31] use a deep learning model to try to mitigate the risks of uncertainty in the production of a wind farm, testing this model in several wind farms in China. The result obtained with this technique improves those obtained with others, and avoids the uncertainty of energy production due to climate change. As for hydrological predictions, there are few studies using deep learning techniques, and the authors present their results [32]; while they are a beginning, the results are promising.

2.1.2. Support Vector Machine (SVM)

Inside the supervised machine learning techniques, support vector machines (SVM) [45] are properly related to classification and regression problems, representing in a space two classes, maximally separated through a hyperplane with high dimensionality (defined as a vector between two points of each class), that permit the classification of new data in one or both classes. Regarding the application of SVM techniques, the authors [33] present a study on the prediction for cooling of an office building in Guangzhou, China. For this purpose, they use the comparison of different neural network techniques (NNBR, NRBR, NRBR, NRBR) and NSRV, based on the results obtained in each of them from the mean square error and the relative mean (RMSE and MRE). This model of artificial intelligence

(SVM) is, in this case, the one that provides the best result, obtaining a high precision in the hourly prediction of the building's cooling and significantly improving the results of the neural networks.

Likewise, there are numerous references for the application of this technique in the renewable energy sector due to the good results obtained with them. The authors [34] use this technique to predict the average daily solar radiation using air temperature and analysing the result obtained by the highest correlation coefficient (0.969) and the lowest mean square error (0.833), which shows the promise of this new technique compared to traditional methods. The authors [35] attempt to predict the production of a wind farm in the short term, through wind speed, wind direction and humidity. They compare SVR techniques (multi-scale support vector regression) with a multilayer perceptron neural network, obtaining better results with SVR due to its speed and robustness. With regard to hydrological forecasting, there are also references, such as the [39], that use the RSVMG (recurrent support vector model) technique to predict the volume of rainfall during the typhoon season in Taiwan. Shi, J. in [36], for their part, use this technique to predict the output of a photovoltaic installation in China and verify the result through the RSME. Although it is a relatively recent technique, the results obtained are very promising and encourage further research in this field.

2.1.3. Decision Trees (DT)

As previously included, RF (Random Forest) is one of the most recent techniques we will apply in our case study and has obtained very good results. Some examples are presented below:

- Elyan, E. in [39] uses the RF technique to classify data, demonstrating that it is a very accurate method of classifying and obtaining results that improve accuracy over other techniques.
- Lin, Y. in [40] uses RF to improve the prediction of wind production in the short term, which is complicated by the stochastic nature of the wind and using the effects of seasonality. RF modelling obtains accurate results in this case.
- Moutis, P. [41] presents two applications of decision tree techniques: the planning of organized energy storage in microgrids and energy control within a PC through the optimal use of local energy resources, demonstrating through a case study the feasibility of this technique.
- Ren, L. in [42] use the DT technique to predict surface currents in a marine renewable energy environment in Galway Bay. The results obtained are very promising, obtaining a correlation coefficient higher than 0.89.

2.2. IDA for Maintenance Purposes: CBM Based on PHM

As we have mentioned, failure control based on condition monitoring needs to follow a sustainable and structured procedure in order to keep and improve solutions on time. Thus, failure detection, diagnostics and prediction, in networks of assets which co-operate among them to produce a certain purpose, demand an integrated approach, but that distinguish individual asset degradation behaviours. The logic of failure control has to manage not only reliability data but also operation and real-time internal and locational variables [11].

The use of CBM has increased significantly since the end of the 20th century, leading to more effective maintenance concepts [46]. The evolution of ICTs (intelligent sensors, digital devices, IoT, etc.), which have become more powerful and reliable technologies, while also becoming cheaper, has contributed to improving the performance of CBM plans [47,48]. The recent consolidation of PHM (prognostics and health management) as an engineering discipline, including the application of analytical techniques, such as data mining techniques, has promoted a new CBM by providing new capabilities and unprecedented potential to understand and obtain useful information on the deterioration of systems and their behaviour patterns over their lifetime [49–51], moreover deepening more effective and adaptable solutions according to changes [52]. In this evolution, new terms such as CBM + [53], CBM/PHM [50], or PdM (predictive maintenance) appear, differentiating predictive maintenance from CBM. In any case, this new vision of CBM, together with the concept of E-maintenance—which marks how the use of ICTs introduces the principles of collaboration, condition knowledge, intelligence, etc., constituting a vision focused on the new maintenance processes to which technology can give rise [54]—are the pillars of the development of modern maintenance [55]. In the current situation, despite this capacity development, there is still a significant gap for the implementation of this type of solution in an intensive manner in the industry, largely due to their complexity throughout their entire life cycle [48]. On the other hand, holistic models and frameworks are needed [51] that consider: the knowledge available on the degradation of systems and their behaviour in the face of failures, their dependencies on other systems, their external influences and the associated uncertainty.

Prognosis Approaches

An important aspect of describing PHM techniques is to analyse the types of approaches that can address the problem of prognosis. Three main types of prognostic approaches are recognized: physical model-based forecasting, data-based forecasting and hybrid forecasting [51]:

- Approaches based on physical models are focused on mathematical modelling of physical interactions between system components and the business processes. They also incorporate failure physics models (POF, physics of failure or PBM, physics-based model), searching the remaining useful life forecast (RUL) based on the degradation due to the participation in a determined processes.
- Data-based approaches (data-driven) use the recognition of statistical and learning patterns to detect changes in the data of descriptive process parameters, thus enabling diagnosis and prognosis. Behavioural patterns are recognized in the data monitoring to evaluate the health status of the system and the time to failure. Data mining techniques as are treated in this paper are the bases of this type of PHM method.
- Mergers or hybrids are forecasting methodologies that combine the strengths of the two previous approaches in order to estimate RUL, detect abnormal behaviour, identify failure precursors, etc. These methods have the greatest potential. Their application requires the definition of an application framework that supports the integration of physical models with data-driven models, simulating based on historical data to forecast in advance the remaining life according to each failure mode's circumstances.

All three models are useful. The current trend is very much towards the use of data-only models. This has undeniable benefits, but also many risks (lack of reliable data, lack of physical contrast and disconnection with the engineering interpretation of the problems raised, among others). In this sense a method allowing the understanding of the model is required and, in particular, the employed technique is valid or the results should, or can, be improved by the use of different techniques. The use of a single DM technique cannot be enough. The use of different technologies over the same data and use case could give us interesting results.

3. Election of DM Techniques: A Practical Methodology

PV plant maintenance management includes a large number of technical assets. If we think in real industrial cases, the technician is responsible for a large number of different PV plants' assets. Thus, the final goal of PHM DM solution development is to apply extensively to all the plants. Then, this paper's methodology objective is the use of more than one DM technique in order to show that can serve:

1. To know which technique produces better results depending on the application case. The application use case is composed by the following principal components:

    - Type of CBM output: Detection, diagnosis or prognosis;
    - Type of asset;

- Type of failure mode;
- Type of data available.

2. To co-validate the results of the different techniques. In other word, considering different techniques it is possible to detect uncertainties derived from our own mathematical models.
3. To extend the final results over the plant level or fleet level

The following figure (Figure 4) shows the methodology that we will apply for the selection of techniques whose behaviour pattern best suits the productive model of a given facility. To do this, we relate the different phases of the IDA (Figure 1) with the techniques of data mining (Figure 2), as well as the values for the best decision-making technique.

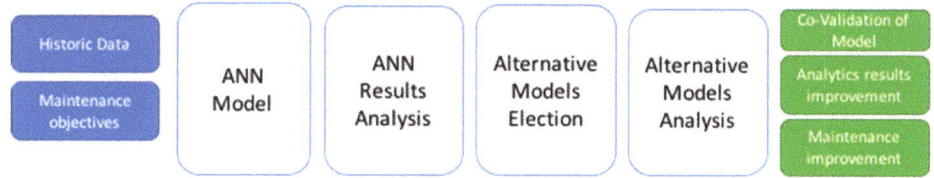

Figure 4. Methodology for using alternative DM techniques.

4. Case Study

We will apply the methodology set out on a photovoltaic installation with 6.1 Mw of rated power that is located in Córdoba and has been in operation since 2008. This facility is divided in 61,100 kW solar orchards. Applying the study on three of these orchards it has been verified that the results in all three are analogous, so we set out only one of them. Tables 2–4 show the information taken for the study.

Table 2. Temporary period for data collection for study.

Start Date	End Date	Data Collection	From	Until	Frequency
01/06/2011	30/09/2015	Hourly	8:00	17:00	10 daily data for each variable

Table 3. Selected variables/data for training and validation.

Inputs Variables	Outputs Variables	Selected Values	Training Set Percentage	Testing Set Percentage
Outdoor temperature, radiation, inside inverter temperature, operation hours	Time, production	In the absence of failures	75%	25%
			Same criteria for all techniques in order to establish the same comparison environment	

Table 4. Collected data in the study (treated and validated).

Outdoor Temp	Radiation	Indoor Temp	Operating Time	Production
303.25	490.3	312.1	9900	52
313.25	756.0	311	9901	74
319.25	860.8	314.7	9902	80
323.25	901.8	313.9	9903	82
325.25	918.0	315.5	9904	83
327.98	990.3	316.8	25,716	81
320.77	520.0	315.6	25,717	53
311.43	454.5	317.1	25,718	39
305.98	777.3	317.8	25,719	66

5. Employed DM Techniques

The employed DM techniques, for failure prediction, are presented below, using for comparison the mean square error to measure the quality of the results:

- ANN Models:
    - Multilayer Perceptron
    - Deep Learning
- Support Vector Machines:
    - SVM non-linear
    - SVM Lineal (Lib Linear)
- Random Forest
- Boosting

The practical implementation for each one of these techniques will now be introduced, describing the employed libraries, functions and transformation variables.

It is important to mention that unless learning is applied we cannot say that any DM model is intelligent. Therefore, for those situations when new data arrives after significant changes in an asset's location or operation, a learning period for the algorithms is required.

The error predicted by the model can also offer a good clue regarding potential scenario modifications and can be used to trigger and lead to a new phase of model actualization, or learning period. This will reduce reasonable worries about model validation and will give more confidence to support asset managers' decision-making regarding prediction and time estimation for the next failures. These ideas can also be programmed and automatically put into operation in the SCADA.

5.1. ANN Models: Multilayer Perceptron

For the case study, first, a three-layer perceptron is employed with the following activation functions: logistic and identity in the hidden layer ($g(u) = e^u/(e^u + 1)$) and in the output layer, respectively. If we denote w_h synaptic weights between the hidden layer and the output layer $\{w_h, h = 0, 1, 2, ..., H\}$, H as the size of the hidden layer, and v_{ih} synaptic weights of connections between the input layer (p size) and the hidden layer $\{v_{ih}, i = 0, 1, 2, ..., p, h = 1, 2, ..., H\}$, thus, with a vector of inputs $(x_1, ..., x_p)$, the output of the neural network could be represented by the following function (1):

$$o = w_0 + \sum_{h=1}^{H} w_h g(v_{0h} + \sum_{i=1}^{p} v_{ih} x_i) \tag{1}$$

We have used the R library nnet [56], where multilayer perceptrons with one hidden layer are implemented. The nnet function needs, as parameters, the decay parameter (λ) to prevent overfitting in the optimization problem, and the size of the hidden layer (H). Therefore, providing the vector of all M coefficients of the neural net $W = (W_1, \ldots, W_M)$, and specified n targets $y_1, \ldots, y_n$, the following optimization problem (Equation (2)) is (L2 regularization):

$$\underset{W}{Min} \sum_{i=i}^{n} \|y_i - \hat{y}_i\|^2 + \lambda \left(\sum_{i=i}^{M} W_i^2 \right) \qquad (2)$$

A quasi-Newton method, namely the BFGS (Broyden-Fletcher-Goldfarb-Shanno) training algorithm [44], is employed by nnet, in R with e1071 library using the tune function [57], determining the decay parameter (λ) as $\{1, 2, \ldots, 15\} \times \{0, 0.05, 0.1\}$ by a ten-fold cross-validation search.

The λ parameter obtained for the two transformations presented below has been zero in all the models built, the logical value considering the sample size and the reduced number of predictor variables, which carries little risk of overfitting.

Through prior normalization of the input variables, the performance could be enhanced in the model. For that, we have considered two normalization procedures, a first transformation that subtracts each variable predictor X from its mean, and the centred variable is divided by the standard deviation of X. In this way we manage to normalize with a 0 mean and a standard deviation equal to 1. The second lineal normalization transforms the range of X values into the range (0, 1). We design, respectively, the values of the standards Z_1 and Z_2, which are calculated as follow:

$$Z_1 = \frac{X - x}{s_x} \quad Z_2 = \frac{X - min_x}{max_x - min_x} \qquad (3)$$

These transformations have used the mean, standard deviation, maximums and minimums calculated in the network training dataset, and these same values have been used for the test set, thus avoiding the intervention of the test set in the training of the neural network.

Since the range of values provided by the logistic function is in the range (0, 1) and the dependent variable Y takes values in the range (0, 99). We transform this with the $Y/100$ calculation. However, after obtaining the predictions, the output values obtained in the original range were transformed back to the original range of values by multiplying by 100 to bring it back to the interval (0, 99).

5.2. ANN Models: Deep Learning

We have used the R package h2o [58] to prevent overfitting with several regularization terms, building a neural network with four layers, and with two hidden layers formed by 200 nodes each.

First, L1 and L2 regression terms are both included in the objective function to be minimized in the parameter estimation process (Equation (4)):

$$\underset{W}{Min} \sum_{i=i}^{n} \|y_i - \hat{y}_i\|^2 + \lambda_1 \left(\sum_{i=i}^{M} |W_i| \right) + \lambda_2 \left(\sum_{i=i}^{M} W_i^2 \right) \qquad (4)$$

Another regularization type to prevent overfitting is dropout, which averages a high number of models as a set with the same global parameters. In this type, during the training, in the forward propagation the activation of each neuron is supressed less than 0.2 in the input layer and up to 0.5 in the hidden layers, and provoking that weights of the network will be scaled towards 0.

The two normalization procedures used with nnet have also been used with h2o.

5.3. Alternative Models (SVM): Support Vector Machines (Non-Linear SVM)

Now, we have used the svm function of the R system library e1071 [57] for the development of the SVM models and, concretely, the ε-classification with the radial basis Gaussian kernel function (5); by n training compound vectors $\{x_i, y_i\}$, $i = 1, 2, \ldots, n$ as the dataset, where x_i incorporates the predictor features and $y_i \in \{-1, 1\}$ are the results of each vector:

$$K(\mathbf{u}, \mathbf{v}) = \exp\left(-\gamma \|\mathbf{u} - \mathbf{v}\|^2\right) \tag{5}$$

Therefore, it is solved by quadratic programming optimization (Equation (6)):

$$\begin{array}{c} \underset{w,b,\xi,\xi^*}{\text{Min}} \ \frac{1}{2} w^t w + C \sum_{i=1}^{n} \xi_i + C \sum_{i=1}^{n} \xi_i^* \\ w^t \varphi(x_i) + b - y_i \leq \varepsilon + \xi_i \\ y_i - w^t \varphi(x_i) + b \leq \varepsilon + \xi_i^* \\ \text{with } \xi_i, \xi_i^* \geq 0, \ i = 1, 2, \ldots, n \end{array} \tag{6}$$

With the parameter $C > 0$ to delimit the tolerated deviations from the desired ε accuracy. The additional slack variables ξ_i, ξ_i^* allows the existence of points outside the ε-tube. The dual problem is given by Equation (7):

$$\begin{array}{c} \underset{\alpha,\alpha^*}{\text{Min}} \ \frac{1}{2}(\alpha - \alpha^*)^t Q (\alpha - \alpha^*) + \varepsilon \sum_{i=1}^{n}\left(\alpha_i + \alpha_i^*\right) + y_i \sum_{i=1}^{n}\left(\alpha_i - \alpha_i^*\right) \\ 0 \leq \alpha_i, \alpha_i^* \leq C, \ i = 1, 2, \ldots, n \\ \sum_{i=1}^{n}\left(\alpha_i - \alpha_i^*\right) = 0 \end{array} \tag{7}$$

with $K(x_i, x_j) = \varphi(x_i)^t \varphi(x_j)$ being the kernel function, a positive semi-definite matrix Q is employed by $Q_{ij} = K(x_i, x_j)$, $i,j = 1, 2, \ldots, n$,. The prediction for a vector x (Equation (8)) is computed by:

$$\sum_{i=1}^{n}\left(-\alpha_i + \alpha_i^*\right) K(x_i, x) + b \tag{8}$$

depending on the margins $m_i = \sum_{i=1}^{n} y_i \alpha_i K(x_i, x) + b, i = 1, 2, \ldots, n$.

A cross-validation grid search for C and γ over the set $\{1, 5, 50, 100, 150, \ldots, 1000\} \times \{0.1, 0.2, 0.3, 0.4\}$ was conducted by the R e1071 tune function, while the parameter ε was maintained at its default value, 0.1.

We have built this SVM model with the original input variables, and with the two normalization procedures previously described in the multilayer perceptron description.

5.4. Alternative Models (SVM): LibLineaR (Linear SVM)

A library for linear support vector machines is LIBLINEAR [59] for the case of large-scale linear prediction. We have used the version used in [60], with fast searching estimation (in comparison with other libraries) through the heuristicC function for C and based on the default values for ε, and employing L2-regularized support vector regression (with L1- and L2-loss).

5.5. Alternative Models (DT): Random Forests

The Random Forests (RF) algorithm [61] combines different predictor trees, each one fitted on a bootstrap sample of the training dataset. Each tree is grown by binary recursive partitioning, where each split is determined by a search procedure aimed to find the variable of a partition rule which provides the maximum reduction in the sum of the squared error. This process is repeated until the terminal nodes are too small to be partitioned. In each terminal node, the average of response variable is the prediction. RF is similar to bagging [39], with an important difference: the search for each split is limited to a random selection of variables, improving the computational cost. We have used the R package Random Forest [62]. By default, p/3 variables (p being the predictor's number) are randomly selected in each split, and 500 trees are grown.

5.6. Alternative Models (DT): Boosting

From the different boosting models depending on the used loss functions, base models, and optimization schemes, we have employed one based on Friedman´s gradient boosting machine of the R gbm package [63] where the target is to boost the performance of a single tree with the following parameters:

- The squared error as a loss function ψ (distribution),
- T (n.trees) as the number of iterations,
- The depth of each tree, K (interaction.depth),
- The learning rate parameter, λ (shrinkage), and
- The subsampling rate, p (bag.fraction).

The function $\hat{f}(x) = \arg\min_\rho \sum_{i=1}^n \psi(y_i, \rho)$ is initialized to be a constant. For t in $1, 2, \ldots, T$ do the following:

1. Compute the negative gradient as the working response:

$$z_i = -\frac{\partial}{\partial f(x_i)} \psi(y_i, f(x_i)) \bigg|_{f(x_i) = \hat{f}(x_i)} \quad (9)$$

2. Randomly select pxn cases from the dataset.
3. Fit a regression tree with K terminal nodes and using only those randomly selected observations.
4. Compute the optimal terminal node predictions $\rho_1, \ldots, \rho_k$, as:

$$\rho_k = \arg\min_\rho \sum_{x_i \in S_k} \psi\big(y_i, \hat{f}(x_i) + \rho\big) \quad (10)$$

where S_k is the set of cases that define terminal node k, using again only the randomly selected observations.

5. Update $\hat{f}(x)$ as:

$$\hat{f}(x) = \hat{f}(x) + \lambda \rho_{k(x)} \quad (11)$$

where $k(x)$ indicates the index of the terminal node into which an observation with features x would fall.

Following the suggestions of Ridgeway in his R package, our work considered the following values: shrinkage = 0.001; bag.fraction = 0.5; interaction.depth = 4; n.trees = 5000, but cv.folds 10 performed a cross-validation search for the effective number of trees.

6. Results

The obtained results for each technique are shown below (Table 5), as well as the different transformations made (different ways to normalize variables and to estimate parameters), shading in each technique the one that gives us the best solution.

Table 5. Results of the different techniques.

Models Analysis	Results		
Multilayer Perceptron	Transformation 1	Coefficient Correlation	RMSE
	Test	0.886	9.64
	Training	0.897	9.15
	Transformation 2	Coefficient Correlation	RMSE
	Test	0.883	9.76
	Training	0.895	9.26
Deep Learning	Transformation 1	Coefficient Correlation	RMSE
	Test	0.839	11.5
	Training	0.855	10.93
	Transformation 2	Coefficient Correlation	RMSE
	Test	0.838	11.72
	Training	0.853	11.19
SVM Nonlinear	Transformation 1, 2 and 3	Coefficient Correlation	RMSE
	Test	0.881	10.01
	Training	0.894	9.46
SVM Linear (Lib Linear)	Transformation 1	Coefficient Correlation	RMSE
	Test	0.836	11.57
	Training	0.848	11.1
	Transformation 2	Coefficient Correlation	RMSE
	Test	0.821	13.54
	Training	0.834	13.07
Random Forest		Coefficient Correlation	RMSE
	Test	0.909	8.63
	Training	0.916	8.3
Boosting		Coefficient Correlation	RMSE
	Test	0.856	10.87
	Training	0.868	10.41

We graphically represent (Figure 5) the best result obtained for each of the techniques in order to visualize the one that gives us the best solution for the behaviour pattern of the production of the photovoltaic installation.

A point cloud chart (Figure 6) of the predicted (test) production is shown for the model that give us the best solution (Random Forest).

This model tells us the importance of variables in the result, which shows that all of them are valid and necessary. The higher the percentage, the higher the importance variable (see Table 6).

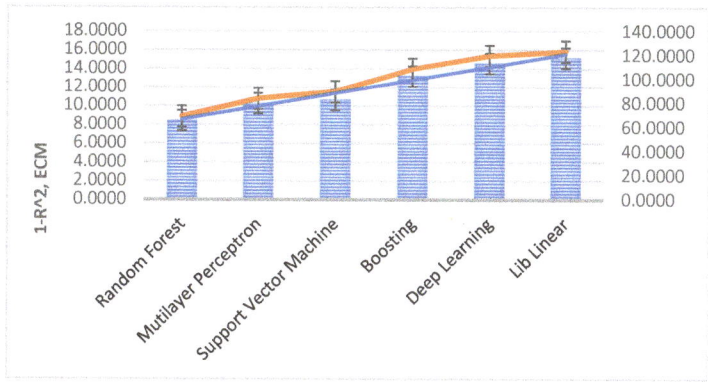

Figure 5. Graphical comparison of the different techniques results.

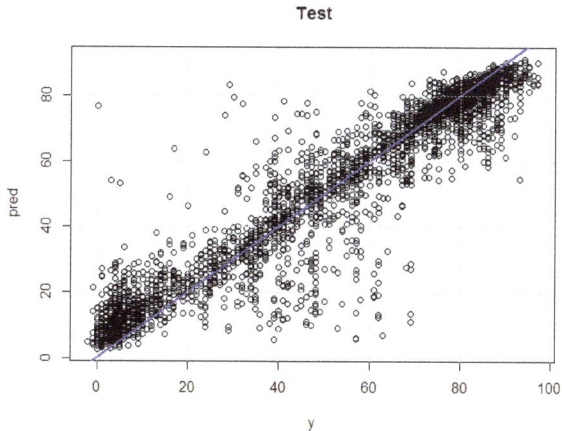

Figure 6. Point cloud (test) Random Forest.

Table 6. Importance of the variables.

VARIABLE	% INC_MSE
TEMP_EXT	49.10
RADIACIÓN	155.63
TEMP_INT	41.60
H. FUNCIONAMIENTO	34.37

The prediction error based on %INC_MSE is estimated by out-of-bag (OOB) for each tree and after permuting each predictor variable, until the difference between them has a standard deviation equal to 0.

7. Conclusions

In this paper a methodology to introduce the use of different data mining techniques for energy forecasting and condition-based maintenance was followed. These techniques compete for the best possible replica of the production behaviour patterns.

A relevant set of DM techniques have been applied (ANN, SVM, DT), and after their introduction to the readers, they were compared when applied to a renewable energy (PV installation) case study.

In this paper a very large sample of data has been considered. This data spans from 1 June 2011 to 30 September 2015.

All of the models for the different techniques offered very encouraging results, with correlation coefficients greater than 0.82. Coincident with other referenced authors' results, Random Forest was the technique providing the best fit, with a linear correlation coefficient of 0.9092 (followed by ANN and SVM). In turn, this technique (RF) gave us as a differential value of the importance of the input variables used in the model, which somehow validates the use of all these variables. In the case study, and by far, the variable resulting with the most affection to production was radiation, followed by the outside temperature, the inverter internal temperature and, finally, the operating hours (which somehow reflects the asset degradation over time).

It is important to mention that these results were obtained using different methods (2) to normalize the variables and to estimate parameters.

Future work could be devoted to the validation of these results by replicating the study at other renewable energy facilities to determine how the improvement in ECM and R^2 values affects early detection of failures by quantifying their economic value.

The implementation of these techniques is feasible today thanks to existing computational capacity, so the effort to use any of them is very similar.

Author Contributions: Conceptualization: J.F.B., J.F.G.F. and A.C.M.; methodology: J.F.B. and J.F.G.F.; software: R.P.; validation, R.P. and J.F.B.; formal analysis: J.F.B. and J.F.G.F.; investigation: J.F.B.; resources, J.F.B.; data curation, J.F.B.; writing—original draft preparation, J.F.B. and A.C.M.; writing—review and editing, A.J.G.L.; supervision, J.F.G.F. and A.C.M.; project administration: A.C.M.; funding acquisition A.C.M.

Funding: This project: Intelligent Assets Management Systems (ES-1794/44/2018) is funded by INGEMAN Association for Maintenance Engineering Development.

Conflicts of Interest: The authors declare no conflict of interest.

Acronyms

ANN	Artificial neural networks
CBM	Condition-based maintenance
DM	Data mining
DP	Deep learning
DT	Decision trees
IDA	Intelligent data analysis
IoT	Internet of Things
MP	Multilayer perceptron
MSE	Mean square error
OOB	Out-of-Bag
PBM	Physics-based model
PdM	Predictive maintenance
PHM	Prognostics and health management
POF	Physics of failure
PV	Photovoltaic
RMSE	Root mean square error
RF	Random Forest
ROI	Return on investment
RSVMG	Recurrent support vector model
RUL	Remaining useful life forecast
SCADA	Supervisory control and data acquisition
SVM	Support vector machine
SVR	Support vector regression

References

1. Shin, Y.C.; Xu, C. *Intelligent Systems: Modeling, Optimization, and Control*; CRC Press: Boca Raton, FL, USA, 2017.
2. IIC-Industrial Internet Consortium. The Industrial Internet of Things, Volume B01: Business Strategy and Innovation Framework (IIC: PUB: B01: V1. 0: PB: 20161115). Available online: http://www.iiconsortiumorg/pdf/Business_Strategy_and_Innovation_Framework_Nov_2016pdf (accessed on 8 November 2016).
3. Barton, D.; Court, D. Making advanced analytics work for you. *Harv. Bus. Rev.* **2012**, *90*, 78–83.
4. Chau, K.W. Kwok-wing Chau Integration of Advanced Soft Computing Techniques in Hydrological Predictions. *Atmosphere* **2019**, *10*, 101. [CrossRef]
5. Fayyad, U.M.; Piatetsky-Shapiro, G.; Smyth, P. Knowledge Discovery and Data Mining: Towards a Unifying Framework. *KDD* **1996**, *96*, 82–88.
6. Clarke, R. Big data, big risks. *Inf. Syst. J.* **2016**, *26*, 77–90. [CrossRef]
7. Polo, F.A.O.; Bermejo, J.F.; Fernández, J.F.G.; Márquez, A.C. Failure mode prediction and energy forecasting of PV plants to assist dynamic maintenance tasks by ANN based models. *Renew. Energy* **2015**, *81*, 227–238. [CrossRef]
8. Mellit, A.; Benghanem, M.; Kalogirou, S.A. Modeling and simulation of a stand-alone photovoltaic system using an adaptive artificial neural network: Proposition for a new sizing procedure. *Renew. Energy* **2007**, *32*, 285–313. [CrossRef]
9. Piatetsky-Shapiro, G. *Advances in Knowledge Discovery and Data Mining*; Fayyad, U.M., Smyth, P., Uthurusamy, R., Eds.; AAAI Press: Menlo Park, CA, USA, 1996; Volume 21.
10. Berthold, M.R.; Hand, D.J. (Eds.) *Intelligent Data Analysis: An Introduction*; Springer: Berlin, Germany, 2007.
11. Guillén, A.J.; Crespo, A.; Gómez, J.F.; Sanz, M.D. A framework for effective management of condition based maintenance programs in the context of industrial development of E-Maintenance strategies. *Comput. Ind.* **2016**, *82*, 170–185. [CrossRef]
12. Banos, R.; Manzano-Agugliaro, F.; Montoya, F.G.; Gil, C.; Alcayde, A.; Gómez, J. Optimization methods applied to renewable and sustainable energy: A review. *Renew. Sustain. Energy Rev.* **2011**, *15*, 1753–1766. [CrossRef]
13. Kusiak, A.; Verma, A. A data-mining approach to monitoring wind turbines. *IEEE Trans. Sustain. Energy* **2012**, *3*, 150–157. [CrossRef]
14. Antonanzas, J.; Osorio, N.; Escobar, R.; Urraca, R.; Martinez-de-Pison, F.J.; Antonanzas-Torres, F. Review of photovoltaic power forecasting. *Sol. Energy* **2016**, *136*, 78–111. [CrossRef]
15. Mellit, A.; Pavan, A.M. A 24-h forecast of solar irradiance using artificial neural network: Application for performance prediction of a grid-connected PV plant at Trieste, Italy. *Sol. Energy* **2010**, *84*, 807–821. [CrossRef]
16. Rehman, S.; Mohandes, M. Artificial neural network estimation of global solar radiation using air temperature and relative humidity. *Energy Policy* **2008**, *36*, 571–576. [CrossRef]
17. Mabel, M.C.; Fernandez, E. Analysis of wind power generation and prediction using ANN: A case study. *Renew. Energy* **2008**, *33*, 986–992. [CrossRef]
18. Kusiak, A.; Zhang, Z.; Verma, A. Prediction, operations, and condition monitoring in wind energy. *Energy* **2013**, *60*, 1–12. [CrossRef]
19. Coulibaly, P.; Anctil, F.; Bobee, B. Daily reservoir inflow forecasting using artificial neural networks with stopped training approach. *J. Hydrol.* **2000**, *230*, 244–257. [CrossRef]
20. Dawson, C.W.; Wilby, R. An artificial neural network approach to rainfall-runoff modelling. *Hydrol. Sci. J.* **1998**, *43*, 47–66. [CrossRef]
21. Voyant, C.; Notton, G.; Kalogirou, S.; Nivet, M.L.; Paoli, C.; Motte, F.; Fouilloy, A. Machine learning methods for solar radiation forecasting: A review. *Renew. Energy* **2017**, *105*, 569–582. [CrossRef]
22. Li, Z.; Rahman, S.M.; Vega, R.; Dong, B. A hierarchical approach using machine learning methods in solar photovoltaic energy production forecasting. *Energies* **2016**, *9*, 55. [CrossRef]
23. Hooman, A.; Marthandan, G.; Yusoff, W.F.W.; Omid, M.; Karamizadeh, S. Statistical and data mining methods in credit scoring. *J. Dev. Areas* **2016**, *50*, 371–381. [CrossRef]
24. Moreno-Sáez, R.; Mora-López, L. Modelling the distribution of solar spectral irradiance using data mining techniques. *Environ. Model. Softw.* **2014**, *53*, 163–172. [CrossRef]

25. Minemoto, T.; Nakada, Y.; Takahashi, H.; Takakura, H. Uniqueness verification of solar spectrum index of average photon energy for evaluating outdoor performance of photovoltaic modules. *Sol. Energy* **2009**, *83*, 1294–1299. [CrossRef]
26. Mellit, A.; Kalogirou, S.A. Artificial intelligence techniques for photovoltaic applications: A review. *Prog. Energy Combust. Sci.* **2008**, *34*, 574–632. [CrossRef]
27. Kalogirou, S.A. Artificial neural networks in renewable energy systems applications: A review. *Renew. Sustain. Energy Rev.* **2011**, *5*, 373–401. [CrossRef]
28. Kalogirou, S.A.; Bojic, M. Artificial neural networks for the prediction of the energy consumption of a passive solar building. *Energy* **2000**, *25*, 479–491. [CrossRef]
29. Renno, C.; Petito, F.; Gatto, A. Artificial neural network models for predicting the solar radiation as input of a concentrating photovoltaic system. *Energy Convers. Manag.* **2016**, *106*, 999–1012. [CrossRef]
30. Polson, N.G.; Sokolov, V.O. Deep learning for short-term traffic flow prediction. *Transp. Res. Part C Emerg. Technol.* **2017**, *79*, 1–17. [CrossRef]
31. Wang, H.Z.; Li, G.Q.; Wang, G.B.; Peng, J.C.; Jiang, H.; Liu, Y.T. Deep learning based ensemble approach for probabilistic wind power forecasting. *Appl. Energy* **2017**, *188*, 56–70. [CrossRef]
32. Li, C.; Bai, Y.; Zeng, B. Deep Feature Learning Architectures for Daily Reservoir Inflow Forecasting. *Water Resour. Manag.* **2016**, *30*, 5145–5161. [CrossRef]
33. Li, Q.; Meng, Q.; Cai, J.; Yoshino, H.; Mochida, A. Predicting hourly cooling load in the building: A comparison of support vector machine and different artificial neural networks. *Energy Convers. Manag.* **2009**, *50*, 90–96. [CrossRef]
34. Chen, J.L.; Liu, H.B.; Wu, W.; Xie, D.T. Estimation of monthly solar radiation from measured temperatures using support vector machines—A case study. *Renew. Energy* **2011**, *36*, 413–420. [CrossRef]
35. Zhang, H.; Chen, L.; Qu, Y.; Zhao, G.; Guo, Z. Support vector regression based on grid-search method for short-term wind power forecasting. *J. Appl. Math.* **2014**, *2014*, 1–11. [CrossRef]
36. Shi, J.; Lee, W.J.; Liu, Y.; Yang, Y.; Wang, P. Forecasting power output of photovoltaic systems based on weather classification and support vector machines. *IEEE Trans. Ind. Appl.* **2012**, *48*, 1064–1069. [CrossRef]
37. Pai, P.F.; Hong, W.C. A recurrent support vector regression model in rainfall forecasting. *Hydrol. Process.* **2007**, *21*, 819–827. [CrossRef]
38. Benedetti, M.; Cesarotti, V.; Introna, V.; Serranti, J. Energy consumption control automation using Artificial Neural Networks and adaptive algorithms: Proposal of a new methodology and case study. *Appl. Energy* **2016**, *165*, 60–71. [CrossRef]
39. Elyan, E.; Gaber, M.M. A genetic algorithm approach to optimising random forests applied to class engineered data. *Inf. Sci.* **2017**, *384*, 220–234. [CrossRef]
40. Lin, Y.; Kruger, U.; Zhang, J.; Wang, Q.; Lamont, L.; El Chaar, L. Seasonal analysis and prediction of wind energy using random forests and ARX model structures. *IEEE Trans. Control Syst. Technol.* **2015**, *23*, 1994–2002. [CrossRef]
41. Moutis, P.; Skarvelis-Kazakos, S.; Brucoli, M. Decision tree aided planning and energy balancing of planned community microgrids. *Appl. Energy* **2016**, *161*, 197–205. [CrossRef]
42. Ren, L.; Hartnett, M. Prediction of Surface Currents Using High Frequency CODAR Data and Decision Tree at a Marine Renewable Energy Test Site. *Energy Procedia* **2017**, *107*, 345–350. [CrossRef]
43. Brillante, L.; Gaiotti, F.; Lovat, L.; Vincenzi, S.; Giacosa, S.; Torchio, F.; Tomasi, D. Investigating the use of gradient boosting machine, random forest and their ensemble to predict skin flavonoid content from berry physical-mechanical characteristics in wine grapes. *Comput. Electron. Agric.* **2015**, *117*, 186–193. [CrossRef]
44. Bishop, C.M. *Neural Networks for Pattern Recognition*; Oxford University Press: Oxford, UK, 1995.
45. Boser, B.E.; Guyon, I.M.; Vapnik, V.N. A training algorithm for optimal margin classifiers. In Proceedings of the Fifth Annual Workshop on Computational Learning Theory, Pittsburgh, PA, USA, 27–29 July 1992; pp. 144–152.
46. Jardine, A.K.; Lin, D.; Banjevic, D. A review on machinery diagnostics and prognostics implementing condition-based maintenance. *Mech. Syst. Signal Process.* **2006**, *20*, 1483–1510. [CrossRef]
47. Xiao, D.; Chang, M.C.; Niu, Q. Berry phase effects on electronic properties. *Rev. Mod. Phys.* **2010**, *82*, 1959. [CrossRef]

48. González-Prida Díaz, V.; Barberá Martínez, L.; Gómez Fernández, J.F.; Crespo Márquez, A. Contractual and quality aspects on warranty: Best practices for the warranty management and its maturity assessment. *Int. J. Qual. Reliab. Manag.* **2012**, *29*, 320–348. [CrossRef]
49. Vachtsevanos, G.J.; Lewis, F.; Hess, A.; Wu, B. *Intelligent Fault Diagnosis and Prognosis for Engineering Systems*; Wiley: Hoboken, NJ, USA, 2006; Volume 456.
50. Lee, J.; Ghaffari, M.; Elmeligy, S. Self-maintenance and engineering immune systems: Towards smarter machines and manufacturing systems. *Ann. Rev. Control* **2011**, *35*, 111–122. [CrossRef]
51. Zio, E. Some challenges and opportunities in reliability engineering. *IEEE Trans. Reliab.* **2016**, *65*, 1769–1782. [CrossRef]
52. Zio, E. Reliability engineering: Old problems and new challenges. *Reliab. Eng. Syst. Saf.* **2009**, *94*, 125–141. [CrossRef]
53. Jaw, L.C.; Merrill, W. CBM+ research environment-facilitating technology development, experimentation, and maturation. In Proceedings of the 2008 IEEE Aerospace Conference, Big Sky, MT, USA, 1–8 March 2008; IEEE: Piscataway, NJ, USA, 2008; pp. 1–6.
54. Seuring, S.; Müller, M. From a literature review to a conceptual framework for sustainable supply chain management. *J. Clean. Prod.* **2008**, *16*, 1699–1710. [CrossRef]
55. Lee, J.; Bagheri, B.; Kao, H.A. A cyber-physical systems architecture for industry 4.0-based manufacturing systems. *Manuf. Lett.* **2015**, *3*, 18–23. [CrossRef]
56. Venables, W.N.; Ripley, B.D. Random and mixed effects. In *Modern Applied Statistics with S.*; Springer: New York, NY, USA, 2002; pp. 271–300.
57. Meyer, D.; Dimitriadou, E.; Hornik, K.; Weingessel, A.; Leisch, F. *e1071: Misc Functions of the Department of Statistics, Probability Theory Group (Formerly: E1071)*; R Package Version 1.6–7; TU Wien: Wien, Austria, 2017.
58. Landry, M.; Angela, B. *Machine Learning with R and H2O*; H2O.ai: Mountain View, CA, USA, 2016.
59. Fran, R.E.; Chang, D.K.; Hsieh, C.J.; Wang, X.R.; Lin, Y.C.J. LIBLINEAR: Una biblioteca para la Clasificación grande lineal. *J. Mach. Learn. Investig.* **2008**, *9*, 1871–1874.
60. Helleputte, T.; Gramme, P. LiblineaR: Linear Predictive Models Based on the LIBLINEAR C/C++ Library. R Package Version, 2–10. 2017. Available online: https://rdrr.io/cran/LiblineaR/ (accessed on 29 October 2019).
61. Breiman, L. Random forests. *Mach. Learn.* **2001**, *45*, 5–32. [CrossRef]
62. Liaw, A.; Wiener, M. Classification and regression by random Forest. *R News* **2002**, *2*, 18–22.
63. Ridgeway, G. The gbm Package. Generalized Boosted Regression Models (Documentation on the R Package 'Gbm', Version 1.6–3). 2015. Available online: https://rdrr.io/cran/gbm/man/gbm.html (accessed on 29 October 2019).

© 2019 by the authors. Licensee MDPI, Basel, Switzerland. This article is an open access article distributed under the terms and conditions of the Creative Commons Attribution (CC BY) license (http://creativecommons.org/licenses/by/4.0/).

Article

Ensemble of Regression-Type and Interpolation-Type Metamodels

Cheng Yan [1], Jianfeng Zhu [1,*], Xiuli Shen [2,*], Jun Fan [3], Dong Mi [4] and Zhengming Qian [4]

1 School of Aerospace Engineering, Xiamen University, Xiamen 361005, China; yanchengmail@xmu.edu.cn
2 School of Energy and Power Engineering, Beihang University, Beijing 100191, China
3 Army Aviation Institute, Beijing 100000, China; fanjun93404@126.com
4 AECC Hunan Aviation Powerplant Research Institute, Zhuzhou 412002, China; mldcapl@126.com (D.M.); qianzhengming87@163.com (Z.Q.)
* Correspondence: zhjf@xmu.edu.cn (J.Z.); shxl606@buaa.edu.cn (X.S.)

Received: 21 December 2019; Accepted: 21 January 2020; Published: 4 February 2020

Abstract: Metamodels have become increasingly popular in the field of energy sources because of their significant advantages in reducing the computational cost of time-consuming tasks. Lacking the prior knowledge of actual physical systems, it may be difficult to find an appropriate metamodel in advance for a new task. A favorite way of overcoming this difficulty is to construct an ensemble metamodel by assembling two or more individual metamodels. Motivated by the existing works, a novel metamodeling approach for building the ensemble metamodels is proposed in this paper. By thoroughly exploring the characteristics of regression-type and interpolation-type metamodels, some useful information is extracted from the feedback of the regression-type metamodels to further improve the functional fitting capability of the ensemble metamodels. Four types of ensemble metamodels were constructed by choosing four individual metamodels. Common benchmark problems are chosen to compare the performance of the individual and ensemble metamodels. The results show that the proposed metamodeling approach reduces the risk of selecting the worst individual metamodel and improves the accuracy of the used individual metamodels.

Keywords: metamodel; ensemble; individual; regression; interpolation

---

1. Introduction

Metamodels, which are also referred to as surrogate models, are essentially approximate mathematical models of real physical systems. In the past decade, metamodels have become increasingly popular in the field of energy sources because of their significant advantages in reducing the computational cost of time-consuming tasks [1,2]. Melo et al. [3] pointed out that researchers in many countries are developing metamodels to estimate the energy performance of the building stock. Bornatico et al. [4] used a kind of metamodel to optimize energy systems, and found that the metamodel converged to the same solution at 150 times the speed of the fine model. Westermann and Evins [5] summarized and discussed recent studies on the application of metamodels in sustainable building design. Ferrero Bermejo et al. [6] reviewed and compared two typical metamodels, namely the artificial neural networks and the support vector machine, for energy forecasting and condition-based maintenance in PV plants.

Actually, a good metamodel mainly depends on its accuracy and generality for different design tasks. To enhance the performance of metamodels, researchers have carried out a lot of studies over the past few decades [7–11]. As a result, a large number of metamodels have been proposed, of which several types have gained wide acceptance in various applications. They are polynomial response surface (PRS) [12–14], support vector regression (SVR) [15–17], radial basis functions (RBF) [18,19], extended radial basis functions (E-RBF) [20], moving least squares (MLS) [21], artificial neural networks

(ANN) [22,23], multivariate adaptive regressive splines (MARS) [24] and Kriging (KRG) [25,26]. These different metamodels give us more options for different tasks. However, lacking the prior knowledge of the actual physical systems, it is challenging to find a suitable metamodel in advance for a new task. In particular, the worst metamodel may be chosen for the task.

A simple way to overcome the difficulty is to build a series of metamodels based on a given training dataset at first, and then select the best one on the basis of some statistical techniques like the cross-validation method. Another favorite way is to construct an ensemble metamodel, which assembles two or more individual metamodels by introducing weight factors. The basic idea of such an ensemble metamodel can be traced back to 1990s [27,28], and currently it has become a research hotspot [8,29]. According to the characteristics of the weight factors, the techniques for building the ensemble metamodels can be mainly categorized into methods based on local errors, methods based on global errors, and methods based on regression.

In the first category, the weight factors ($\omega_i = \omega_i(\mathbf{x})$) are functions of design space, which are determined by the local errors of individual metamodels at the point of interest. Zerpa et al. [30] introduced a local weighted average model for the optimization of alkaline-surfactant-polymer flooding processes by using the prediction variances of three individual metamodels (PRS, KRG, and RBF). Sanchez, Pintos, and Queipo [31] proposed a general approach toward the ensemble of kernel-based models based on the local prediction variances. Acar [32] investigated the efficiency of methods based on the local errors, and developed a new approach to determine the weight factors by using the pointwise cross-validation errors instead of the prediction variances. Zhang, Chowdhury, and Messac [33] proposed a new metamodeling technique called adaptively hybrid functions, whose weight factors are determined based on the local measure of accuracy in the pertinent trust region. Lee and Choi [34] presented a new pointwise ensemble of metamodels, of which the weight factors are calculated by using the v nearest points cross-validation errors.

In the second category, the weight factors ($\omega_i = C_i, \forall \mathbf{x}$) are constant values in the entire design space, which are determined by the global errors of individual metamodels. Goel et al. [35] studied a global weight factor selection approach based on the generalized mean square cross-validation errors (GMSE). Acar and Rais-Rohani [36] developed an accurate ensemble of metamodels by solving an optimization problem that minimizes GMSE or root mean square errors (RMSE). Viana, Haftka, and Steffen [37] obtained the optimal weight factors of the optimization problem by using the Lagrange multipliers. This method was also employed by Toal and Keane [38] to construct an ensemble of ordinary, universal, non-stationary and limit KRG models. Additionally, Acar [39] performed the simultaneous optimization of the weight factors and the shape parameters in the ensemble of RBFs.

It should be noted that in the first two categories the weight factors of individual metamodels are restricted to a positive range ($\omega_i > 0$) and the sum of these factors is equal to 1 $\left(\sum_{i=1}^{M} \omega_i = 1\right)$. Since they are different from the first two categories, the techniques in the third category mainly use the regression methods (like least squares) to determine the weight factors. Accordingly, there is no longer any restriction on the weight factors, which may even have negative values. Polynkin and Toropov [40] introduced a novel mid-range metamodel assembly for the large-scale optimization problems, which is constructed based on the linear regression method. Ferreira and Serpa [41] developed an augmented least-square approach for creating the ensemble of metamodels, which can be extended to the efficient global optimization. Zhou and Jiang [42] constructed an ensemble of four individual metamodels (PRS, KRG, SVR, and RBF) from the view of the polynomial regression, and proposed a metamodel selection method on the basis of the stepwise regression to eliminate the redundant ones from the set of the candidate metamodels.

Motivated by these existing works, this paper proposes a different method for constructing the ensemble metamodels, which combines the advantages of regression-type and interpolation-type metamodels. The regression-type metamodels have better global trend fitting capacity than the interpolation-type metamodels, while the interpolation-type metamodels perform better than the regression-type metamodels in the vicinity of the sampling locations. By thoroughly exploring the characteristics of regression-type and interpolation-type metamodels, the proposed method could extract some useful information from the feedback of the regression-type metamodels to further improve the functional fitting capability of the ensemble metamodels.

2. Proposed Ensemble of Metamodels

2.1. Motivation and Basic Characteristics

The existing individual metamodels can be classified into regression-type and interpolation-type metamodels. The regression-type metamodels aim to fit the global trend of the underlying functions of the real physical systems in the entire design space, while the interpolation-type metamodels aim to achieve the local accuracy in the vicinity of the sampling locations. Accordingly, the regression-type metamodels can build smooth surfaces that pass across all the training points, while the interpolation-type metamodels can construct models that go through each training point. That is to say, for the regression-type metamodels there may be obvious deviations between the actual responses and the approximate responses at the sampling locations, while for the interpolation-type metamodels there is no deviation. These different characteristics make the two types of metamodels possess different advantages and limitations. For example: (i) the regression-type metamodels have better global trend fitting capacity than the interpolation-type metamodels, while (ii) the interpolation-type metamodels perform better than the regression-type metamodels in the vicinity of the sampling locations.

It should be noted that obtaining the training dataset required for constructing the metamodels may be time-consuming. Therefore, as much information as possible should be extracted from these data. However, for the regression-type metamodels, there are apparent deviations between the actual responses and the approximate responses at the sampling locations, from where some useful information may be still extracted to further improve the performance of these metamodels. Exploring the underlying knowledge of the training dataset and combining the characteristics of regression-type and interpolation-type metamodels, this paper proposes a novel metamodeling approach for the ensemble metamodels. The flowchart of the proposed metamodeling technique is shown in Figure 1, which involves four main steps as follows.

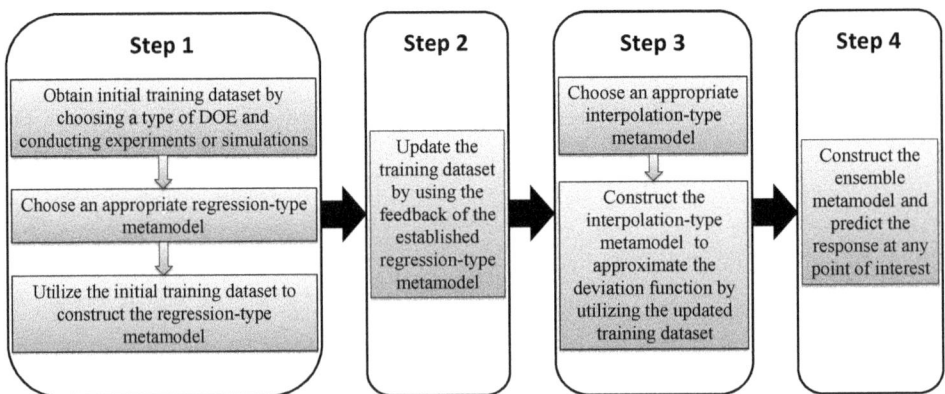

Figure 1. Flowchart of the proposed approach for building ensembles of regression-type and interpolation-type metamodels.

Step 1: An appropriate design of experiment (DOE) should be first chosen to generate n sampling locations $(\mathbf{x}^1, \mathbf{x}^2, \ldots, \mathbf{x}^n)$, at where the actual responses $(y^1, y^2, \ldots, y^n)$ are obtained by conducting experiments or simulations. By using the initial training dataset $(\mathbf{x}^i, y^i)$ ($i =$

$1, \ldots, n$), a regression-type metamodel $\hat{y}_1(\mathbf{x})$ in Equation (1) is subsequently constructed to approximate the actual model $y(\mathbf{x})$.

$$\hat{y}_1(\mathbf{x}) \approx y(\mathbf{x}), \quad \mathbf{x} = (x_1, x_2, \ldots, x_k)^T \tag{1}$$

where $\mathbf{x}$ denotes any point of interest.

Step 2: We suppose that there is a deviation function $y_d(\mathbf{x})$. It is obtained by subtracting the approximate model $\hat{y}_1(\mathbf{x})$ from the actual model $y(\mathbf{x})$.

$$y_d(\mathbf{x}) = y(\mathbf{x}) - \hat{y}_1(\mathbf{x}) \tag{2}$$

Some useful information may be still extracted from the deviation function $y_d(\mathbf{x})$. To approximate the deviation function, the training dataset should be updated. In detail, this paper first uses the established regression-type metamodel in Equation (1) to predict the approximate responses $(\hat{y}_1^1, \hat{y}_1^2, \ldots, \hat{y}_1^n)$ at the initial sampling locations. Subsequently, the deviations $(y_d^1, y_d^2, \ldots, y_d^n)$ between the actual responses and approximate responses at these locations are calculated as the updated training dataset.

$$\begin{aligned} &\left\{ (\mathbf{x}^1, y_d^1), (\mathbf{x}^2, y_d^2), \ldots, (\mathbf{x}^n, y_d^n) \right\} = \\ &\left\{ (\mathbf{x}^1, y^1 - \hat{y}_1^1), (\mathbf{x}^2, y^2 - \hat{y}_1^2), \ldots, (\mathbf{x}^n, y^n - \hat{y}_1^n) \right\} \end{aligned} \tag{3}$$

Step 3: By using the updated training dataset in Equation (3), an interpolation-type metamodel $\hat{y}_2(\mathbf{x})$ in Equation (4) is constructed to approximate the deviation function $y_d(\mathbf{x})$.

$$\hat{y}_2(\mathbf{x}) \approx y_d(\mathbf{x}) \tag{4}$$

Step 4: Finally, the ensemble metamodel $\hat{y}_{ens}(\mathbf{x})$ in Equation (5) is constructed by adding the established regression-type metamodel $\hat{y}_1(\mathbf{x})$ and interpolation-type metamodel $\hat{y}_2(\mathbf{x})$ together. By using Equations (1), (4) and (5), the established ensemble metamodel $\hat{y}_{ens}(\mathbf{x})$ can be used to predict the response at any point of interest in the entire design space.

$$\hat{y}_{ens}(\mathbf{x}) = \hat{y}_1(\mathbf{x}) + \hat{y}_2(\mathbf{x}) \approx \hat{y}_1(\mathbf{x}) + y_d(\mathbf{x}) \approx y(\mathbf{x}) \tag{5}$$

2.2. Detailed Modeling Process

To clearly illustrate the proposed metamodeling technique, this paper selects two common regression-type metamodels (PRS and SVR) and two popular interpolation-type metamodels, namely RBFM (RBF with multiquadric-form basis function) and RBFI (RBF with inverse multiquadric-form basis function). Accordingly, four types of ensemble metamodels can be obtained, which are PrsRbfm (Ensemble Scheme 1, ensemble of PRS and RBFM), PrsRbfi (Ensemble Scheme 2, ensemble of PRS and RBFI), SvrRbfm (Ensemble Scheme 3, ensemble of SVR and RBFM) and SvrRbfi (Ensemble Scheme 4, ensemble of SVR and RBFI). The detailed modeling processes of these involved metamodels are introduced as follows.

2.2.1. Step 1: Construction of Regression-Type Metamodels

PRS is a general designation of a series of polynomial regression functions, of which the most popular one is the second-order polynomial model. This paper adopts the second-order polynomial model $\hat{y}_{1,prs}(\mathbf{x})$, which can be written as

$$\hat{y}_{1,prs}(\mathbf{x}) = \mathbf{z}^T \boldsymbol{\beta} = \beta_0 + \sum_{i=1}^{k} \beta_i x_i + \sum_{i=1}^{k} \sum_{j=i}^{k} \beta_{2j+i(2k-i+1)/2} x_i x_j \tag{6}$$

where $\boldsymbol{\beta} = (\beta_0, \beta_1, \ldots, \beta_{\frac{k^2+3k}{2}})^T$ denotes a coefficient vector, $\mathbf{z} = (1, x_1, x_2, \ldots, x_{k-1}x_k, x_k x_k)^T$ denotes a polynomial basis-function vector.

To estimate $\boldsymbol{\beta}$, the regression problem in Equation (6) can be transformed as follows by using the initial training dataset.

$$\begin{bmatrix} y^1 \\ y^2 \\ \vdots \\ y^n \end{bmatrix} = \begin{bmatrix} y^1_{d,prs} \\ y^2_{d,prs} \\ \vdots \\ y^n_{d,prs} \end{bmatrix} + \begin{bmatrix} 1 & x^1_1 & \cdots & x^1_k & \cdots & x^1_1 x^1_1 & \cdots & x^1_{k-1} x^1_k & x^1_k x^1_k \\ 1 & x^2_1 & \cdots & x^2_k & \cdots & x^2_1 x^2_1 & \cdots & x^2_{k-1} x^2_k & x^2_k x^2_k \\ \vdots & \vdots & \vdots & \vdots & \ddots & \vdots & \ddots & \vdots & \vdots \\ 1 & x^n_1 & \cdots & x^n_k & \cdots & x^n_1 x^n_1 & \cdots & x^n_{k-1} x^n_k & x^n_k x^n_k \end{bmatrix} \begin{bmatrix} \beta_0 \\ \beta_1 \\ \vdots \\ \beta_{\frac{k^2+3k}{2}} \end{bmatrix} \tag{7}$$

where $\mathbf{y}_{d,prs} = (y^1_{d,prs}, y^2_{d,prs}, \ldots, y^n_{d,prs})^T$ denotes the deviation vector.

Equation (7) can be also expressed as

$$\mathbf{y} = \mathbf{X}\boldsymbol{\beta} + \mathbf{y}_{d,prs} \tag{8}$$

According to the least squares method, $\boldsymbol{\beta}$ can be calculated as follows.

$$\boldsymbol{\beta} = (\mathbf{X}^T \mathbf{X})^{-1} \mathbf{X}^T \mathbf{y} \tag{9}$$

SVR is a regression function $\hat{y}_{1,svr}(\mathbf{x})$ in the high-dimensional space, as shown in Equation (10).

$$\hat{y}_{1,svr}(\mathbf{x}) = \boldsymbol{\omega}^T \boldsymbol{\psi}(\mathbf{x}) + b \tag{10}$$

where $\boldsymbol{\omega}$ denotes the weight vector, $\boldsymbol{\psi}(\mathbf{x})$ denotes the mapping function, and b denotes the bias.

To estimate $\boldsymbol{\omega}$ and b, the regression problem in Equation (10) can be transformed as an optimization problem in Equation (11) by introducing ϵ-insensitive loss function.

$$\begin{aligned} \min \quad & \frac{1}{2}||\boldsymbol{\omega}||^2 \\ \text{subject to} \quad & \begin{cases} \boldsymbol{\omega}^T \boldsymbol{\psi}(\mathbf{x}^i) + b - y^i \leq \epsilon \\ y^i - \boldsymbol{\omega}^T \boldsymbol{\psi}(\mathbf{x}^i) - b \leq \epsilon \\ i = 1, \ldots, n \end{cases} \end{aligned} \tag{11}$$

To solve Equation (11), the regularization parameter, C (> 0), and the slack variables, $\xi^{+(i)}$ and $\xi^{-(i)}$, are introduced. In addition, Equation (12) can be obtained

$$\min \quad \frac{1}{2}||\boldsymbol{\omega}||^2 + C\sum_{i=1}^{n}(\xi^{+(i)} + \xi^{-(i)})$$

$$\text{subject to} \quad \begin{cases} \boldsymbol{\omega}^T\boldsymbol{\psi}(\mathbf{x}^i) + b - y^i \leq \epsilon + \xi^{+(i)} \\ y^i - \boldsymbol{\omega}^T\boldsymbol{\psi}(\mathbf{x}^i) - b \leq \epsilon + \xi^{-(i)} \\ \xi^{+(i)}, \xi^{-(i)} \geq 0 \\ i = 1, \ldots, n \end{cases} \quad (12)$$

The Lagrange dual model of Equation (12) can be expressed as

$$\max \quad \begin{cases} -\frac{1}{2}\sum_{i,j=1}^{n}(\alpha^{+(i)} - \alpha^{-(i)})(\alpha^{+(j)} - \alpha^{-(j)}) \\ k\langle \mathbf{x}^i, \mathbf{x}^j \rangle + \sum_{i=1}^{n}(\alpha^{+(i)} - \alpha^{-(i)})y^i \\ -\sum_{i=1}^{n}(\alpha^{+(i)} + \alpha^{-(i)})\epsilon \end{cases}$$

$$\text{subject to} \quad \begin{cases} \sum_{i=1}^{n}(\alpha^{+(i)} - \alpha^{-(i)}) = 0 \\ 0 \leq \alpha^{+(i)}, \alpha^{-(i)} \leq C \\ i = 1, \ldots, n \end{cases} \quad (13)$$

where $\alpha^{+(i)}$ and $\alpha^{-(i)}$ denote the Lagrange multipliers, $k\langle \mathbf{x}^i, \mathbf{x}^j \rangle = \boldsymbol{\psi}(\mathbf{x}^i)^T\boldsymbol{\psi}(\mathbf{x}^j)$ denotes a kernel function, which has several different forms. This paper chooses the Gaussian kernel function, which can be expressed as

$$k\langle \mathbf{x}, \mathbf{x}^i \rangle = \exp(-\gamma||\mathbf{x} - \mathbf{x}^i||^2) \quad (14)$$

According to Equation (13), $\alpha^{+(i)}$ and $\alpha^{-(i)}$ can be first obtained. According to KKT conditions [43], $\boldsymbol{\omega}$ and b can be then calculated.

2.2.2. Step 2: Update of Training Dataset

First, β calculated by Equation (9) can be used to substitute the one in Equation (6). Second, the approximate responses of established PRS $(\hat{y}^1_{1,prs}, \hat{y}^2_{1,prs}, \ldots, \hat{y}^n_{1,prs})$ at the initial sampling locations $(\mathbf{x}^1, \mathbf{x}^2, \ldots, \mathbf{x}^n)$ can be calculated according to Equation (6). Then, the updated training dataset of PRS can be expressed as

$$\begin{aligned} &\left\{ (\mathbf{x}^1, y^1_{d,prs}), (\mathbf{x}^2, y^2_{d,prs}), \ldots, (\mathbf{x}^n, y^n_{d,prs}) \right\} = \\ &\left\{ (\mathbf{x}^1, y^1 - \hat{y}^1_{1,prs}), (\mathbf{x}^2, y^2 - \hat{y}^2_{1,prs}), \ldots, (\mathbf{x}^n, y^n - \hat{y}^n_{1,prs}) \right\} \end{aligned} \quad (15)$$

Similarly, according to Equation (10), the updated training dataset of SVR can be obtained and expressed as

$$\begin{aligned} &\left\{ (\mathbf{x}^1, y^1_{d,svr}), (\mathbf{x}^2, y^2_{d,svr}), \ldots, (\mathbf{x}^n, y^n_{d,svr}) \right\} = \\ &\left\{ (\mathbf{x}^1, y^1 - \hat{y}^1_{1,svr}), (\mathbf{x}^2, y^2 - \hat{y}^2_{1,svr}), \ldots, (\mathbf{x}^n, y^n - \hat{y}^n_{1,svr}) \right\} \end{aligned} \quad (16)$$

2.2.3. Step 3: Construction of Interpolation-Type Metamodels

The general form of RBF can be expressed as

$$\hat{y}_{rbf}(\mathbf{x}) = \sum_{i=1}^{n} \lambda_i \phi\left(||\mathbf{x} - \mathbf{x}^i||\right) \tag{17}$$

where λ_i denotes an interpolation coefficient, $r = ||\mathbf{x} - \mathbf{x}^i|| = \sqrt{(\mathbf{x} - \mathbf{x}^i)^T(\mathbf{x} - \mathbf{x}^i)}$ denotes the distance between points $\mathbf{x}$ and $\mathbf{x}^i$. $\phi(r)$ denotes a radially symmetric basis function, which has several different forms, such as:

- Gaussian $\phi(r) = e^{(-r^2/c^2)}$
- Multiquadric $\phi(r) = (r^2 + c^2)^{\frac{1}{2}}$
- Inverse multiquadric $\phi(r) = (r^2 + c^2)^{-\frac{1}{2}}$
- Thin plate spline $\phi(r) = (r^2)\log(r)$

The interpolation coefficient λ_i can be calculated by using the given training dataset $(\mathbf{x}^i, y^i)$ ($i = 1, \ldots, n$).

$$\boldsymbol{\lambda} = \mathbf{A}^{-1}\mathbf{y} \tag{18}$$

where

$$\boldsymbol{\lambda} = \begin{bmatrix} \lambda_1, \lambda_2, \ldots, \lambda_n \end{bmatrix}^T$$

$$\mathbf{A} = \begin{bmatrix} \phi(||\mathbf{x}^1 - \mathbf{x}^1||), & \phi(||\mathbf{x}^1 - \mathbf{x}^2||), & \cdots & \phi(||\mathbf{x}^1 - \mathbf{x}^n||) \\ \phi(||\mathbf{x}^2 - \mathbf{x}^1||), & \phi(||\mathbf{x}^2 - \mathbf{x}^2||), & \cdots & \phi(||\mathbf{x}^2 - \mathbf{x}^n||) \\ \vdots & \vdots & \ddots & \vdots \\ \phi(||\mathbf{x}^n - \mathbf{x}^1||), & \phi(||\mathbf{x}^n - \mathbf{x}^2||), & \cdots & \phi(||\mathbf{x}^n - \mathbf{x}^n||) \end{bmatrix}$$

After choosing the multiquadric-form basis function, **RBFM** ($\hat{y}_{rbfm}(\mathbf{x})$) can be constructed to approximate the actual model $y(\mathbf{x})$ by replacing $\hat{y}_{rbf}(\mathbf{x})$ and λ_i in Equation (17) with $\hat{y}_{rbfm}(\mathbf{x})$ and $\lambda_{i,rbfm}$. The coefficient $\lambda_{i,rbfm}$ can be calculated based on Equation (18). Similarly, after choosing the inverse multiquadric-form basis function, **RBFI** ($\hat{y}_{rbfi}(\mathbf{x})$) can be constructed to approximate the actual model $y(\mathbf{x})$. The coefficient $\lambda_{i,rbfi}$ of $\hat{y}_{rbfi}(\mathbf{x})$ can be calculated based on Equation (18).

Additionally, by choosing the multiquadric-form basis function, a model $\hat{y}_{2,rbfm1}(\mathbf{x})$ can be constructed to approximate the deviation function of PRS $\mathbf{y}_{d,prs}$. By replacing the initial training dataset $(\mathbf{x}^i, y^i)$ ($i = 1, \ldots, n$) with the updated training dataset of PRS $(\mathbf{x}^i, y^i_{d,prs})$ ($i = 1, \ldots, n$), the coefficient $\lambda_{i,2rbfm1}$ of $\hat{y}_{2,rbfm1}(\mathbf{x})$ can be calculated on the basis of Equation (18). Similarly, by choosing the inverse multiquadric-form basis function, a model $\hat{y}_{2,rbfi1}(\mathbf{x})$ can be constructed to approximate the deviation function of PRS $\mathbf{y}_{d,prs}$.

Finally, by choosing the multiquadric-form basis function, a model $\hat{y}_{2,rbfm2}(\mathbf{x})$ can be constructed to approximate the deviation function of SVR $\mathbf{y}_{d,svr}$. By choosing the interpolation-type metamodel, a model $\hat{y}_{2,rbfi2}(\mathbf{x})$ can be constructed to approximate the deviation function of SVR $\mathbf{y}_{d,svr}$.

2.2.4. Step 4: Construction of Ensemble Metamodels

By adding the established $\hat{y}_{1,prs}(\mathbf{x})$ and $\hat{y}_{2,rbfm1}(\mathbf{x})$ together, **PrsRbfm** ($\hat{y}_{prsrbfm}(\mathbf{x})$) can be subsequently constructed as follows.

$$\hat{y}_{prsrbfm}(\mathbf{x}) = \hat{y}_{1,prs}(\mathbf{x}) + \hat{y}_{2,rbfm1}(\mathbf{x}) \tag{19}$$

Being similar to PrsRbfm, **PrsRbfi** ($\hat{y}_{prsrbfi}(\mathbf{x})$) can be constructed as follows.

$$\hat{y}_{prsrbfi}(\mathbf{x}) = \hat{y}_{1,prs}(\mathbf{x}) + \hat{y}_{2,rbfi1}(\mathbf{x}) \tag{20}$$

SvrRbfm ($\hat{y}_{svrrbfm}(\mathbf{x})$) can be constructed as follows.

$$\hat{y}_{svrrbfm}(\mathbf{x}) = \hat{y}_{1,svr}(\mathbf{x}) + \hat{y}_{2,rbfm2}(\mathbf{x}) \tag{21}$$

SvrRbfi ($\hat{y}_{svrrbfi}(\mathbf{x})$) can be constructed as follows.

$$\hat{y}_{svrrbfi}(\mathbf{x}) = \hat{y}_{1,svr}(\mathbf{x}) + \hat{y}_{2,rbfi2}(\mathbf{x}) \tag{22}$$

The established ensemble metamodels, namely PrsRbfm, PrsRbfi, SvrRbfm, and SvrRbfi, can be used to predict the response at any point of interest in the entire design space by using Equations (19)–(22).

3. Numerical Experiments

3.1. Benchmark Problems

Referred to the website (http://www.sfu.ca/~ssurjano/index.html) and relevant literature [32], six common benchmark problems (BPs) are selected to compare the performance of the individual metamodels (PRS, SVR, RBFM, and RBFI) and the ensemble metamodels (PrsRbfm, PrsRbfi, SvrRbfm, and SvrRbfi).

BP1: Goldstein Price Function

$$f(\mathbf{x}) = \left[1 + (x_1 + x_2 + 1)^2 \times (19 - 14x_1 + 3x_1^2 - 14x_2 + 6x_1x_2 + 3x_2^2)\right] \times \\ \left[30 + (2x_1 - 3x_2)^2 \times (18 - 32x_1 + 12x_1^2 + 48x_2 - 36x_1x_2 + 27x_2^2)\right] \tag{23}$$

where $x_i \in [-2, 2]$, for $i = 1, 2$.

BP2: Friedman Function

$$f(\mathbf{x}) = 10 \sin(\pi x_1 x_2) + 20 (x_3 - 0.5)^2 + 10x_4 + 5x_5 \tag{24}$$

where $x_i \in [0, 1]$, for all $i = 1, \ldots, 5$.

BP3: Power Sum Function

$$f(\mathbf{x}) = \sum_{j=1}^{6} \left[\left(-\sum_{i=1}^{6} x_i^j\right) - 36\right]^2 \tag{25}$$

where $x_i \in [0, 6]$, for all $i = 1, \ldots, 6$.

BP4: Rosenbrock Function

$$f(\mathbf{x}) = \sum_{i=1}^{6} \left[100 \left(x_{i+1} - x_i^2\right)^2 + (x_i - 1)^2\right] \tag{26}$$

where $x_i \in [-5, 10]$, for all $i = 1, \ldots, 7$.

BP5: Zakharov Function

$$f(\mathbf{x}) = \sum_{i=1}^{9} x_i^2 + \left(\sum_{i=1}^{9} 0.5 i x_i\right)^2 + \left(\sum_{i=1}^{9} 0.5 i x_i\right)^4 \tag{27}$$

where $x_i \in [-5, 10]$, for all $i = 1, \ldots, 9$.

BP6: Powell Function

$$f(\mathbf{x}) = \sum_{i=1}^{2} \left[(x_{4i-3} + 10x_{4i-2})^2 + 5(x_{4i-1} - x_{4i})^2 + (x_{4i-2} - 2x_{4i-1})^4 + 10(x_{4i-3} - x_{4i})^4\right] \tag{28}$$

where $x_i \in [-4, 5]$, for all $i = 1, \ldots, 10$.

3.2. Numerical Setting

For all the benchmark problems, the MATLAB routine "lhsdesign" is used to generate training points and test points. Referred to Jin, Chen, and Simpson [44], $n = \frac{3(k+1)(k+2)}{2}$ training points are selected for a k-dimension problem. Moreover, as many test points as possible should be used in practice, since insufficient test points may increase the uncertainty of the results. This paper selects $n_{tst} = 20{,}000$ test points for each benchmark problem. Since the DOE sampling scheme may have an obvious influence on the performance of the metamodels, 100 different training and test sets are selected for each problem. The detailed numerical settings for all the benchmark problems are listed in Table 1. The shape parameters (c) of RBFM and RBFI are both selected as 1 by referring to relevant literature [34,45,46]. The parameters (ϵ, C, and γ) of SVR are selected by using the cross-validation method, which was introduced in detail in the published paper of the authors [47].

Table 1. Detailed numerical settings for the benchmark problems.

Benchmark Problem	NO. of Variables	NO. of Training Points	NO. of Test Points	NO. of Training and Test Sets
BP1	2	18	20,000	100
BP2	5	63	20,000	100
BP3	6	84	20,000	100
BP4	7	108	20,000	100
BP5	9	165	20,000	100
BP6	10	198	20,000	100

3.3. Performance Criteria

The root mean square error (RMSE) and the max absolute error (MAE) are selected as the performance criteria.

RMSE can be expressed as

$$RMSE = \sqrt{\frac{\sum_{i=1}^{n_{tst}} (y^i - \hat{y}^i)^2}{n_{tst}}} \qquad (29)$$

where n_{tst} denotes the number of test points.

MAE can be expressed as

$$MAE = \max |y_i - \hat{y}_i|, \quad i = 1, 2, \ldots, n_{tst} \qquad (30)$$

4. Results and Discussion

4.1. RMSE

Figure 2 shows the boxplots of RMSE of the metamodels over 100 test sets for each benchmark problem with $\frac{3(k+1)(k+2)}{2}$ training points. It can be seen that: (1) for all the benchmark problems, the most accurate ensemble metamodels outperform the most accurate individual metamodels; (2) without exception, the least accurate individual metamodels perform worse than the least accurate ensemble metamodels; (3) for each benchmark problem, the performance differences among the four individual metamodels are greater than that among the four ensemble metamodels.

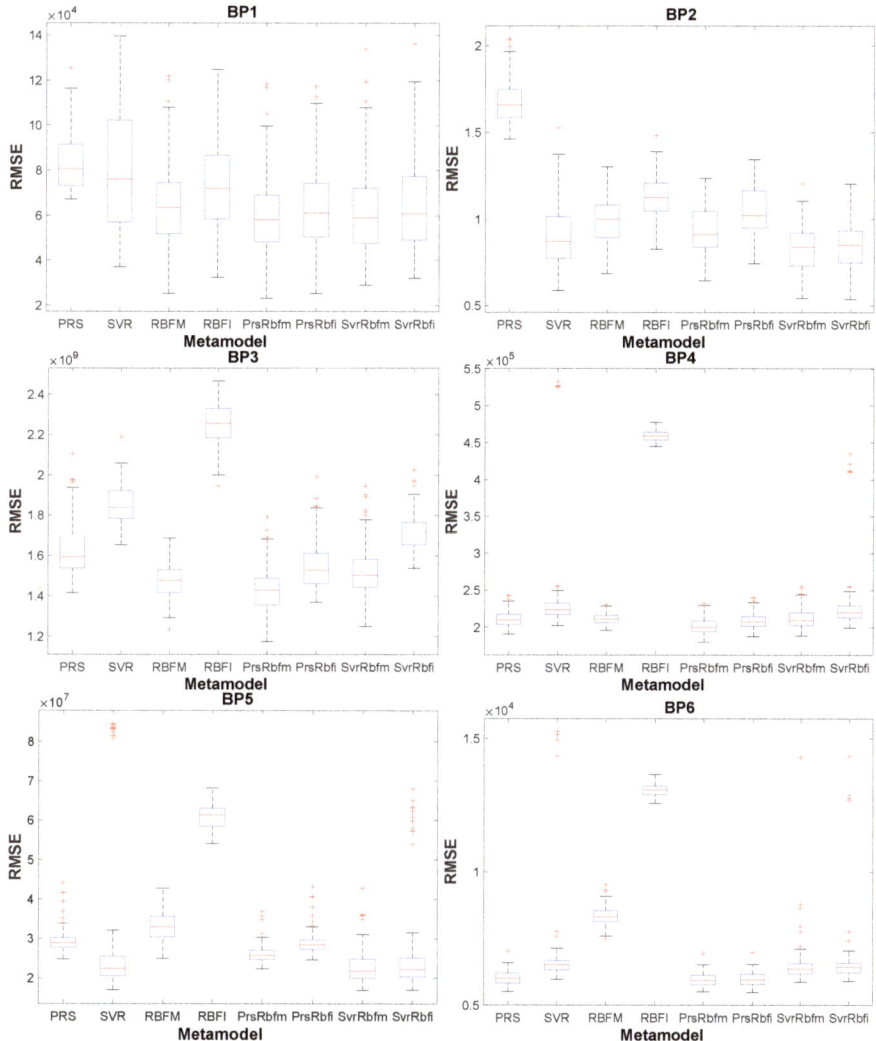

Figure 2. Boxplots of RMSE of the metamodels over 100 test sets for each benchmark problem with $\frac{3(k+1)(k+2)}{2}$ training points.

To provide a better comparison for these metamodels, the error values are normalized with respect to the most accurate individual metamodel for each benchmark problem. Table 2 shows the normalized means of RMSE of the metamodels for each benchmark problem with $\frac{3(k+1)(k+2)}{2}$ training points. The bold values in Table 2 are the most accurate individual/ensemble metamodels, the italic values are the least accurate individual/ensemble metamodels, the underlined values are the ensemble metamodels that perform better than all the individual metamodels, the "Best & Best" values denote the differences between the most accurate ensemble metamodels and individual metamodels, and the "Worst & Worst" values denote the differences between the least accurate ensemble metamodels and individual metamodels. From Table 2, it can be seen that: (1) compared with the most accurate individual metamodels, the means of RMSE of the most accurate ensemble metamodels are reduced, ranging from 1.1% to 22.2%; (2) compared with the least accurate individual metamodels, the means of RMSE of the least accurate ensemble metamodels are reduced, ranging from 21.1% to 52.5%; (3) except for BP3, more than two ensemble metamodels perform better than the most accurate individual metamodels; (4) for BP5, all the four ensemble metamodels perform better than the most accurate individual metamodel.

Table 2. Normalized means of RMSE of the metamodels for each benchmark problem with $\frac{3(k+1)(k+2)}{2}$ training points.

BPs	BP1	BP2	BP3	BP4	BP5	BP6
PRS	1.280	1.866	1.113	**1.000**	**1.000**	**1.000**
SVR	1.224	**1.000**	1.262	1.149	1.006	1.133
RBFM	**1.000**	1.108	**1.000**	1.001	1.123	1.385
RBFI	1.133	1.261	1.536	2.175	2.073	2.166
PrsRbfm	0.929	1.043	0.981	0.957	0.889	0.989
PrsRbfi	0.977	1.173	1.062	0.990	0.985	0.994
SvrRbfm	0.968	0.922	1.039	1.006	0.778	1.080
SvrRbfi	1.010	0.937	1.176	1.102	0.910	1.109
Best & Best	−7.1%	−7.8%	−1.9%	−4.3%	−22.2%	−1.1%
Worst & Worst	−21.1%	−37.1%	−23.5%	−49.3%	−52.5%	−48.8%

Table 3 shows the frequency of the accuracy ranking (using RMSE) of the metamodels for the six benchmark problems with $\frac{3(k+1)(k+2)}{2}$ training points. It can be seen that: (1) the frequency of the ensemble metamodels that rank 1st or 2nd is 11, yet the frequency of the individual metamodels is only one; (2) the frequency of the individual metamodels that rank 7th or 8th is 12, yet the frequency of the ensemble metamodels is zero; (3) considered the frequency of the metamodels that rank the top/bottom two, all the ensemble metamodels have better performance than the individual metamodels; (4) PrsRbfm performs best among the four ensemble metamodels, followed by SvrRbfm, PrsRbfi, and SvrRbfi.

Table 3. Frequency of the accuracy ranking (using RMSE) of the metamodels for the six benchmark problems with $\frac{3(k+1)(k+2)}{2}$ training points.

Ranking	1st	2nd	3rd	4th	5th	6th	7th	8th
PRS	0	0	2	0	2	0	0	2
SVR	0	0	1	0	0	2	3	0
RBFM	0	1	0	2	1	0	2	0
RBFI	0	0	0	0	0	1	1	4
Total	0	1	3	2	3	3	6	6
PrsRbfm	4	1	0	1	0	0	0	0
PrsRbfi	0	2	1	2	0	1	0	0
SvrRbfm	2	1	1	1	1	0	0	0
SvrRbfi	0	1	1	0	2	2	0	0
Total	6	5	3	4	3	3	0	0

To clearly compare the accuracy of each ensemble metamodel with their corresponding individual metamodels, Figure 3 shows the normalized means of RMSE of each ensemble scheme for the six benchmark problems with $\frac{3(k+1)(k+2)}{2}$ training points. It can be seen that: (1) in Scheme 1, PrsRbfm ranks 1st among PRS, RBFM, and PrsRbfm for all the benchmark problems; (2) in Scheme 2, PrsRbfi ranks 1st for all the benchmark problems; (3) in Scheme 3, SvrRbfm ranks 1st for four benchmark problems and 2nd for two benchmark problems; although RBFM ranks 1st for two benchmark problems, it is the worst performer for three benchmark problems; (4) in Scheme 4, without exception, the accuracy of SvrRbfi outperforms that of SVR and RBFI.

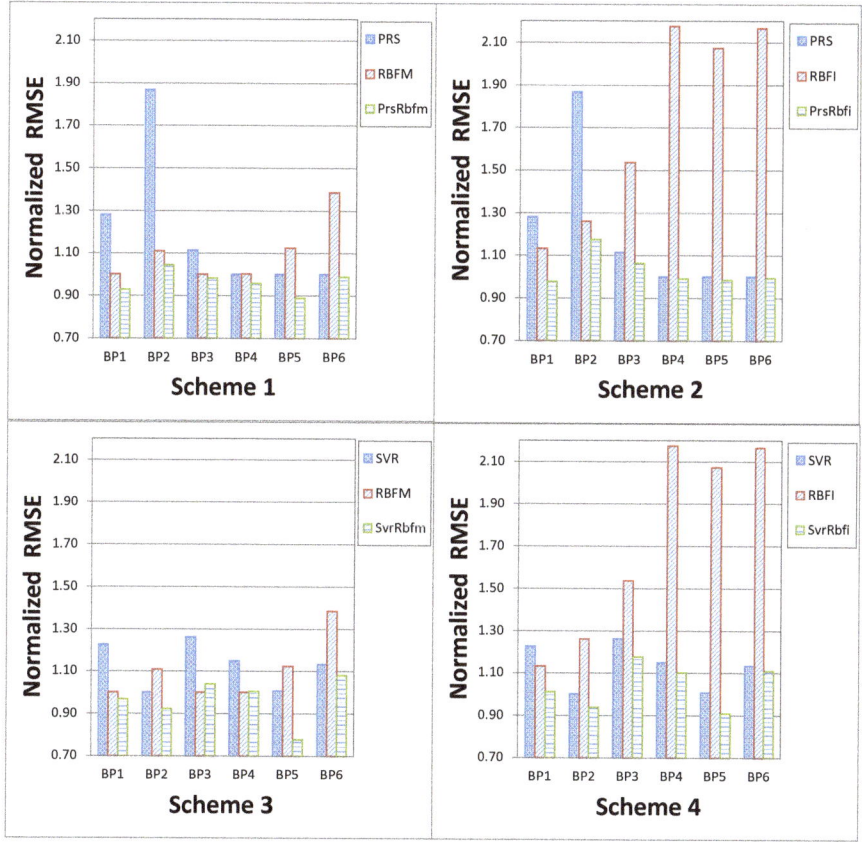

Figure 3. Normalized means of RMSE of each ensemble scheme for the six benchmark problems with $\frac{3(k+1)(k+2)}{2}$ training points.

Table 4 shows the normalized standard deviations of RMSE of the metamodels for each benchmark problem with $\frac{3(k+1)(k+2)}{2}$ training points. It can be seen that: (1) compared with the most accurate individual metamodels, the standard deviations of RMSE of the most accurate ensemble metamodels are reduced for BP5 and BP6, yet the standard deviations are increased for the other four benchmark problems; (2) compared with the least accurate individual metamodels, the standard deviations of RMSE of the least accurate ensemble metamodels are reduced, ranging from 8.4% to 35.5%.

According to the above experimental results, we think the proposed metamodeling approach could reduce the risk of selecting the worst individual metamodel, and the constructed ensemble metamodels perform better than the used individual metamodels in terms of accuracy. In particular, PrsRbfm performs best among the four ensemble metamodels, followed by SvrRbfm, PrsRbfi, and SvrRbfi.

To provide an explicit explanation for the better performance of the proposed approach, a low-dimensional problem (BP1) and an ensemble scheme (ensemble of SVR and RBFM) are selected as examples. Figure 4 shows the contour plot of the actual function and the approximate functions of SVR, RBFM, and SvrRbfm. It can be seen that: (1) SVR has better global trend fitting capacity than RBFM, such as in the red box area; (2) RBFM performs better in the vicinity of the sampling locations, such as in the red ellipse region; (3) SvrRbfm combines the global trend of SVR and the local accuracy of RBFM, such as in the red box area and the red ellipse region.

Table 4. Normalized standard deviations of RMSE of the metamodels for each benchmark problem with $\frac{3(k+1)(k+2)}{2}$ training points.

BPs	BP1	BP2	BP3	BP4	BP5	BP6
PRS	**1.000**	**1.000**	1.646	1.566	1.001	1.072
SVR	2.067	1.542	1.121	10.663	6.188	6.844
RBFM	1.462	1.167	**1.000**	**1.000**	1.204	1.488
RBFI	1.660	1.100	1.235	1.117	**1.000**	**1.000**
PrsRbfm	*1.397*	1.185	1.304	1.592	**0.744**	**0.995**
PrsRbfi	1.423	1.193	1.493	**1.577**	0.953	1.055
SvrRbfm	1.581	**1.143**	*1.509*	2.021	1.427	3.714
SvrRbfi	*1.696*	*1.199*	**1.123**	*7.041*	*3.991*	*5.542*
Best & Best	39.7%	14.3%	12.3%	57.7%	−25.6%	−0.5%
Worst & Worst	−17.9%	−22.2%	−8.4%	−34.0%	−35.5%	−19.0%

Therefore, the reason for the better performance of the ensemble metamodels may be that the proposed metamodeling approach combines the advantages of the regression-type and interpolation-type metamodels. The actual model is regarded as the sum of a regression-type model and a deviation function. Some useful information is first extracted by the regression-type metamodel to capture the global trend of the actual model in the entire design space. Then, some other information is extracted from the deviations at the sampling locations by using the interpolation-type metamodel to achieve the local accuracy in the vicinity of sampling locations.

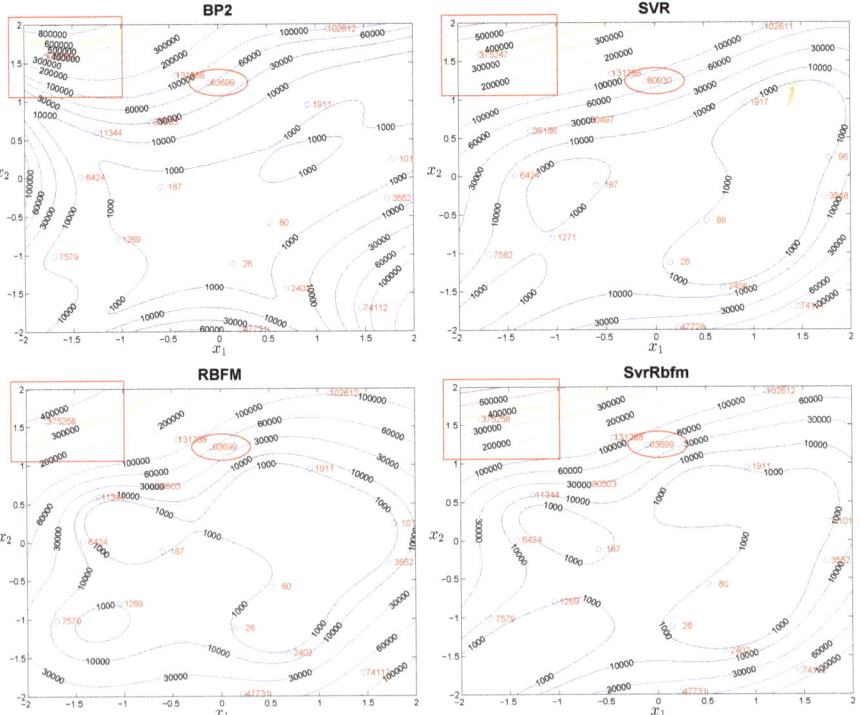

Figure 4. Contour plot of the actual function and the approximate functions of SVR, RBFM, and SvrRbfm.

4.2. Effect of Performance Criteria

The choice of different performance criteria may influence the results of the metamodels. To reduce the source of uncertainty in the results as much as possible, the max absolute error (MAE) is selected as another performance criterion.

Figure 5 shows the boxplots of MAE of the metamodels over 100 test sets for each benchmark problem with $\frac{3(k+1)(k+2)}{2}$ training points. Table 5 shows the normalized means of MAE of the metamodels for each benchmark problem with $\frac{3(k+1)(k+2)}{2}$ training points. From Figure 5 and Table 5, it can be seen that: (1) for each benchmark problem, the performance differences among the four ensemble metamodels are less than that among the four individual metamodels; (2) except for BP6, more than two ensemble metamodels perform better than the most accurate individual metamodels; (3) compared with the most accurate individual metamodels, the means of MAE of the most accurate ensemble metamodels are reduced for five benchmark problems; (4) compared with the least accurate individual metamodels, the means of MAE of the least accurate ensemble metamodels are reduced, ranging from 14.2% to 48.9%.

Table 5. Normalized means of MAE of the metamodels for each benchmark problem with $\frac{3(k+1)(k+2)}{2}$ training points.

BPs	BP1	BP2	BP3	BP4	BP5	BP6
PRS	1.055	1.583	1.000	1.000	1.000	1.000
SVR	1.149	1.000	1.405	1.312	1.080	1.325
RBFM	1.000	1.148	1.165	1.174	1.385	1.708
RBFI	1.189	1.200	1.626	2.515	1.939	2.353
PrsRbfm	0.910	1.111	0.952	0.980	0.944	1.015
PrsRbfi	0.965	1.278	0.999	0.999	0.996	1.002
SvrRbfm	0.950	0.933	1.164	1.168	0.957	1.244
SvrRbfi	1.021	0.956	1.338	1.285	1.052	1.302
Best & Best	−9.0%	−6.7%	−4.8%	−2.0%	−5.6%	0.2%
Worst & Worst	−14.2%	−19.3%	−17.7%	−48.9%	−45.7%	−44.7%

Table 6 shows the frequency of the accuracy ranking (using MAE) of the metamodels for the six benchmark problems with $\frac{3(k+1)(k+2)}{2}$ training points. It can be seen that: (1) considered the frequency of the metamodels that rank the top/bottom two, PrsRbfm, PrsRbfi, and SvrRbfm outperform all the individual metamodels; (2) although SvrRbfi is a little worse than PRS, it still performs better than its corresponding individual metamodels (SVR and RBFI); (3) PrsRbfm is the best performer of the four ensemble metamodels, followed by SvrRbfm, PrsRbfi, and SvrRbfi.

Table 6. Frequency of the accuracy ranking (using MAE) of the metamodels for the six benchmark problems with $\frac{3(k+1)(k+2)}{2}$ training points.

Ranking	1st	2nd	3rd	4th	5th	6th	7th	8th
PRS	1	0	2	1	0	1	0	1
SVR	0	0	1	0	0	2	3	0
RBFM	0	0	0	1	3	0	2	0
RBFI	0	0	0	0	0	1	0	5
Total	1	0	3	2	3	4	5	6
PrsRbfm	4	0	1	1	0	0	0	0
PrsRbfi	0	3	2	0	0	0	1	0
SvrRbfm	1	2	0	3	0	0	0	0
SvrRbfi	0	1	0	0	3	2	0	0
Total	5	6	3	4	3	2	1	0

In summary, the choice of the performance criteria influence the results slightly, but the conclusions obtained by the two criteria remain unchanged.

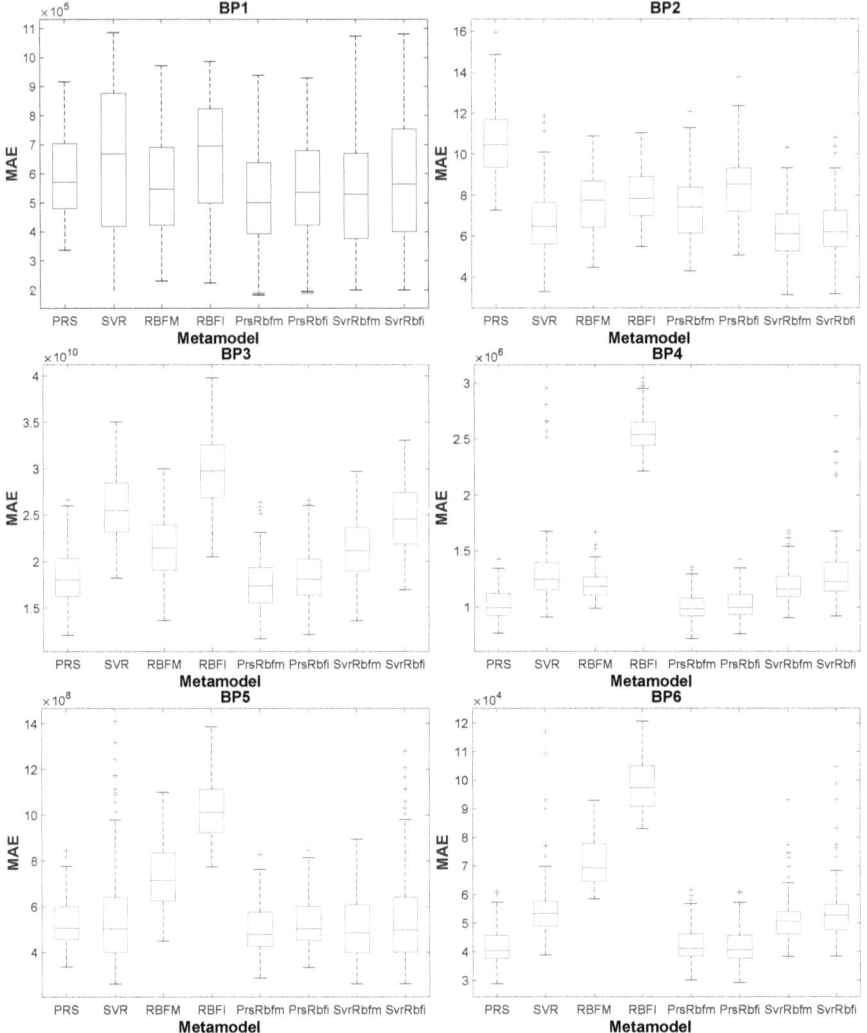

Figure 5. Boxplots of MAE of the metamodels over 100 test sets for each benchmark problem with $\frac{3(k+1)(k+2)}{2}$ training points.

4.3. Effect of Sampling Densities

The choice of different sampling densities may also influence the results of the metamodels. To investigate the effect of the sampling densities, this paper selects another two schemes with different sampling densities, which are $n = \frac{5(k+1)(k+2)}{4}$ and $n = \frac{7(k+1)(k+2)}{4}$.

Table 7 shows the normalized means of RMSE of the metamodels for each benchmark problem with $\frac{7(k+1)(k+2)}{4}$ training points. It can be seen that: (1) compared with the most accurate individual metamodels, the means of RMSE of the most accurate ensemble metamodels are reduced, ranging from 0.9% to 8.1%; (2) compared with the least accurate individual metamodels, the means of RMSE of the least accurate ensemble metamodels are reduced, ranging from 23.4% to 53.8%; (3) except for BP3, more than two ensemble metamodels perform better than the most accurate individual metamodels;

(4) all the ensemble metamodels perform better than the four individual metamodels; (5) PrsRbfm is the best performer among the four metamodels, while SvrRbfi is the worst performer.

Table 7. Normalized means of RMSE of the metamodels for each benchmark problem with $\frac{7(k+1)(k+2)}{4}$ training points.

BPs	BP1	BP2	BP3	BP4	BP5	BP6
PRS	1.400	2.282	1.104	**1.000**	1.342	**1.000**
SVR	1.209	**1.000**	1.283	1.154	**1.000**	1.130
RBFM	**1.000**	1.186	**1.000**	1.012	1.496	1.371
RBFI	1.174	1.383	1.555	2.188	2.847	2.195
PrsRbfm	**0.921**	1.102	**0.952**	0.946	1.158	**0.991**
PrsRbfi	0.985	1.271	1.044	0.987	1.316	0.992
SvrRbfm	0.958	**0.937**	1.040	**1.000**	**0.919**	1.076
SvrRbfi	1.014	0.949	1.191	1.102	0.972	1.105
Best & Best	−7.9%	−6.3%	−4.8%	−5.4%	−8.1%	−0.9%
Worst & Worst	−27.6%	−44.3%	−23.4%	−49.6%	−53.8%	−49.7%

Table 8 shows the normalized means of RMSE of the metamodels for each benchmark problem with $\frac{5(k+1)(k+2)}{4}$ training points. It can be seen that: (1) compared with the most accurate individual metamodels, the means of RMSE of the most accurate ensemble metamodels are reduced for five benchmark problems, ranging from 0.9% to 16.9%; (2) compared with the least accurate individual metamodels, the means of RMSE of the least accurate ensemble metamodels are reduced, ranging from 20.9% to 51.3%; (3) all the ensemble metamodels have better performance than the four individual metamodels.

Table 8. Normalized means of RMSE of the metamodels for each benchmark problem with $\frac{5(k+1)(k+2)}{4}$ training points.

BPs	BP1	BP2	BP3	BP4	BP5	BP6
PRS	1.268	1.577	1.115	1.022	**1.000**	**1.000**
SVR	1.248	**1.000**	1.242	1.206	1.027	1.174
RBFM	**1.000**	1.020	**1.000**	**1.000**	1.134	1.379
RBFI	1.100	1.126	1.517	2.151	2.030	2.093
PrsRbfm	**0.937**	1.008	**1.015**	**0.991**	0.918	**0.991**
PrsRbfi	0.980	1.098	1.079	1.014	0.989	0.995
SvrRbfm	0.965	**0.924**	1.053	1.035	**0.831**	1.073
SvrRbfi	1.002	0.938	1.167	1.152	0.951	1.139
Best & Best	−6.3%	−7.6%	1.5%	−0.9%	−16.9%	−0.9%
Worst & Worst	−20.9%	−30.4%	−23.1%	−46.4%	−51.3%	−45.6%

In summary, the choice of different sampling densities influences the results slightly, but the conclusions obtained by the three schemes with different sampling densities remain unchanged.

4.4. Significance of Results

The results above have proven the effectiveness of the proposed method to some extent. To further demonstrate the advantages, the proposed method is compared with some other popular ensemble metamodels, which are BPS (Best PRESS surrogate), PWS (PRESS weighted average surrogate), and OWSD (Optimal weighted surrogate using the diagonal elements). The detailed descriptions of these ensemble metamodels can be found in relevant literature [35,37]. Additionally, Kriging with first order polynomial regression function (KRG1) and Kriging with second-order polynomial regression function (KRG2) are also included in the performance comparison. To be noted, the principle and modeling process of Kriging are different from that of the proposed metamodeling approach in this paper.

Figure 6 compares the performance of PrsRbfm, SvrRbfm, KRG1, KRG2, BPS, PWS, and OWSD. It can be seen that: (1) for BP1, PrsRbfm and SvrRbfm perform better than the other five metamodels; (2) for BP2, SvrRbfm and BPS are the best two performers; (3) for BP3, the accuracy of PrsRbfm and BPS are better than that of the other metamodels; (4) for BP4, PrsRbfm and KRG2 are the best two performers; (5) for BP5, SvrRbfm and BPS are more accurate than other metamodels; (6) for BP6, PrsRbfm and KRG2 perform better the other metamodels.

In summary, the proposed metamodeling approach possesses some advantages when compared with KRG1, KRG2, BPS, PWS, and OWSD.

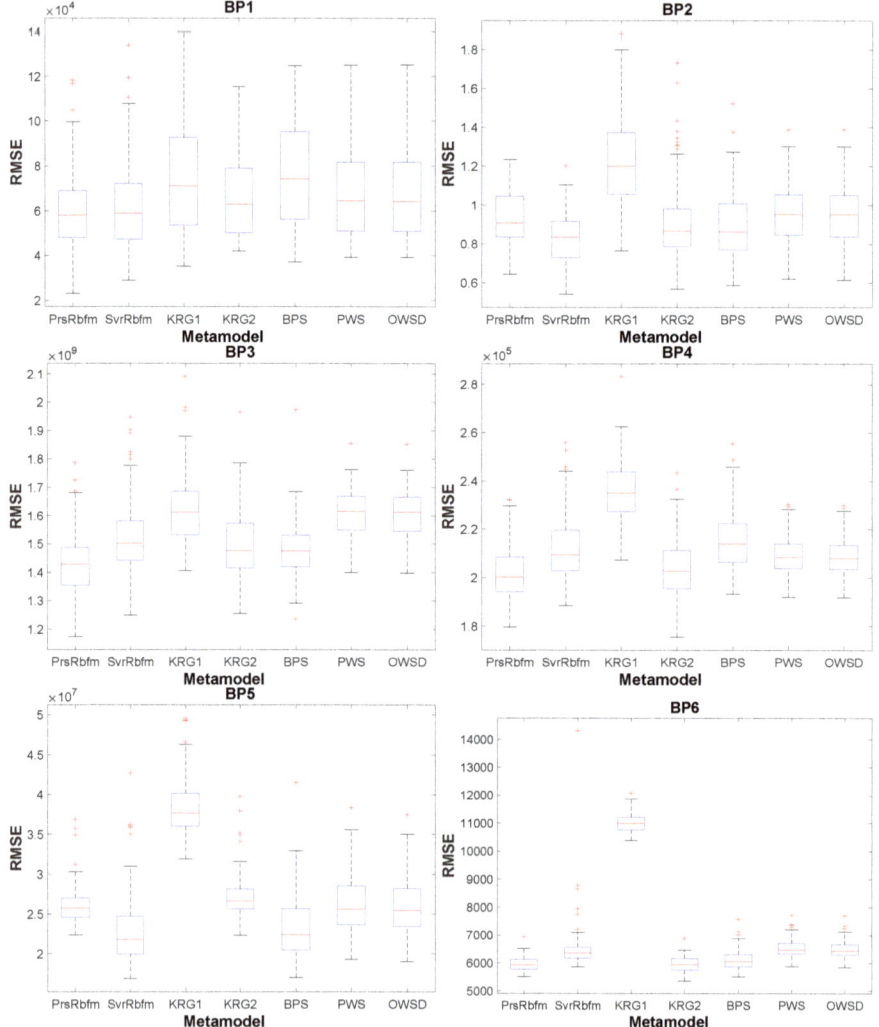

Figure 6. Boxplots of RMSE of PrsRbfm, SvrRbfm, KRG1, KRG2, BPS, PWS, and OWSD for the benchmark problems.

5. Conclusions

This paper proposed a novel metamodeling approach for building ensemble metamodels. Four types of ensemble metamodels, namely PrsRbfm, PrsRbfi, SvrRbfm, and SvrRbfi, were constructed by choosing four individual metamodels, namely PRS, SVR, RBFM, and RBFI. The performance of these metamodels was investigated through six popular benchmark problems. The effects of the performance criteria and sampling densities on the performance of the metamodels were studied. Additionally, the significance of the results was discussed by comparing the proposed method with some other popular ensemble metamodels. According to the results, some findings of this work could be concluded as follows:

(1) According to the experimental results, the proposed metamodeling approach could reduce the risk of choosing the worst individual metamodel, and the constructed ensemble metamodels perform better than the selected individual metamodels in terms of accuracy.
(2) The reason for the better performance of the ensemble metamodels may be that the proposed metamodeling approach combines the advantages of the regression-type and interpolation-type metamodels. The ensemble metamodels not only capture the global trend of the actual model in the entire design space, but also achieve the local accuracy in the vicinity of sampling locations.
(3) The choices of different performance criteria and sampling densities influence the results slightly, but the obtained conclusions remain unchanged.
(4) The proposed metamodeling approach possesses some advantages when compared with some other popular ensemble metamodels.

Author Contributions: Conceptualization, C.Y. and J.Z.; Formal analysis, C.Y. and J.F.; Methodology, C.Y. and J.Z.; Software, Z.Q. and J.F.; Validation, C.Y. and Z.Q.; Investigation, C.Y. and Z.Q.; Resources, X.S. and D.M.; Data curation, J.Z., Z.Q. and J.F.; Writing—original draft, C.Y.; Writing—review and editing, C.Y., J.F. and J.Z.; Visualization, J.Z. and D.M.; Supervision, X.S. and D.M.; Project administration, X.S. and D.M.; Funding acquisition, X.S. and D.M. All authors have read and agreed to the published version of the manuscript.

Funding: This research received no external funding.

Conflicts of Interest: The authors declare no conflict of interest.

References

1. An, X.; Song, B.; Mao, Z.; Ma, C. Layout Optimization Design of Two Vortex Induced Piezoelectric Energy Converters (VIPECs) Using the Combined Kriging Surrogate Model and Particle Swarm Optimization Method. *Energies* **2018**, *11*, 2069. [CrossRef]
2. Wang, D.; Hu, Q.; Tang, J.; Jia, H.; Li, Y.; Gao, S.; Fan, M. A kriging model based optimization of active distribution networks considering loss reduction and voltage profile improvement. *Energies* **2017**, *10*, 2162. [CrossRef]
3. Melo, A.; Versage, R.; Sawaya, G.; Lamberts, R. A novel surrogate model to support building energy labelling system: A new approach to assess cooling energy demand in commercial buildings. *Energy Build.* **2016**, *131*, 233–247. [CrossRef]
4. Bornatico, R.; Hüssy, J.; Witzig, A.; Guzzella, L. Surrogate modeling for the fast optimization of energy systems. *Energy* **2013**, *57*, 653–662. [CrossRef]
5. Westermann, P.; Evins, R. Surrogate modelling for sustainable building design—A review. *Energy Build.* **2019**, *198*, 170–186. [CrossRef]
6. Ferrero Bermejo, J.; Gómez Fernández, J.F.; Pino, R.; Crespo Márquez, A.; Guillén López, A.J. Review and Comparison of Intelligent Optimization Modelling Techniques for Energy Forecasting and Condition-Based Maintenance in PV Plants. *Energies* **2019**, *12*, 4163. [CrossRef]
7. Asher, M.J.; Croke, B.F.W.; Jakeman, A.J.; Peeters, L.J.M. A review of surrogate models and their application to groundwater modeling. *Water Resour. Res.* **2015**, *51*, 5957–5973. [CrossRef]
8. Viana, F.A.C.; Simpson, T.W.; Balabanov, V.; Toropov, V. Special section on multidisciplinary design optimization: metamodeling in multidisciplinary design optimization: How far have we really come? *AIAA J.* **2014**, *52*, 670–690. [CrossRef]
9. Razavi, S.; Tolson, B.A.; Burn, D.H. Review of surrogate modeling in water resources. *Water Resour. Res.* **2012**, *48*, 54–62. [CrossRef]

10. Forrester, A.I.J.; Keane, A.J. Recent advances in surrogate-based optimization. *Prog. Aerosp. Sci.* **2009**, *45*, 50–79. [CrossRef]
11. Wang, G.G.; Shan, S. Review of metamodeling techniques in support of engineering design optimization. *J. Mech. Des.* **2007**, *129*, 370–380. [CrossRef]
12. González-Fernández, C.; Molinuevo-Salces, B.; García-González, M.C. Evaluation of anaerobic codigestion of microalgal biomass and swine manure via response surface methodology. *Appl. Energy* **2011**, *88*, 3448–3453. [CrossRef]
13. Yan, C.; Shen, X.; Guo, F. Novel two-stage method for low-order polynomial model. *Math. Probl. Eng.* **2018**, *2018*, 8156390. [CrossRef]
14. Yan, C.; Yin, Z.; Shen, X.; Guo, F.; Wu, Y. Axisymmetric hub-endwall profile optimization for a transonic fan to improve aerodynamic performance based on an integrated design optimization method. *Struct. Multidiscip. Optim.* **2019**, *60*, 1267–1282. [CrossRef]
15. Yan, C.; Shen, X.; Guo, F.; Zhao, S.; Zhang, L. A novel model modification method for support vector regression based on radial basis functions. *Struct. Multidiscip. Optim.* **2019**, *60*, 983–997. [CrossRef]
16. Lee, C.W.; Lin, B.Y. Applications of the chaotic quantum genetic algorithm with support vector regression in load forecasting. *Energies* **2017**, *10*, 1832. [CrossRef]
17. Hong, W.C.; Fan, G.F. Hybrid Empirical Mode Decomposition with Support Vector Regression Model for Short Term Load Forecasting. *Energies* **2019**, *12*, 1093. [CrossRef]
18. Fang, H.; Horstemeyer, M.F. Global response approximation with radial basis functions. *Eng. Optim.* **2006**, *38*, 407–424. [CrossRef]
19. Zhou, Q.; Cao, L.; Zhou, H.; Huang, X. Prediction of angular distortion in the fiber laser keyhole welding process based on a variable-fidelity approximation modeling approach. *J. Intell. Manuf.* **2018**, *29*, 719–736. [CrossRef]
20. Mullur, A.; Messac, A. Metamodeling using extended radial basis functions: A comparative approach. *Eng. Comput.* **2006**, *21*, 203–217. [CrossRef]
21. Kim, C.; Wang, S.; Choi, K.K. Efficient response surface modeling by using moving least-squares method and sensitivity. *AIAA J.* **2005**, *43*, 2404–2411. [CrossRef]
22. Runge, J.; Zmeureanu, R. Forecasting Energy Use in Buildings Using Artificial Neural Networks: A Review. *Energies* **2019**, *12*, 3254. [CrossRef]
23. Silitonga, A.S.; Mahlia, T.M.I.; Shamsuddin, A.H.; Ong, H.C.; Milano, J.; Kusumo, F.; Sebayang, A.H.; Dharma, S.; Ibrahim, H.; Husin, H.; et al. Optimization of Cerbera manghas Biodiesel Production Using Artificial Neural Networks Integrated with Ant Colony Optimization. *Energies* **2019**, *12*, 3811. [CrossRef]
24. Crino, S.; Brown, D.E. Global optimization with multivariate adaptive regression splines. *IEEE Trans. Syst. Man Cybern. Part B Cybern.* **2007**, *37*, 333–40. [CrossRef]
25. Nam, S.; Hur, J. Probabilistic Forecasting Model of Solar Power Outputs Based on the Naïve Bayes Classifier and Kriging Models. *Energies* **2018**, *11*, 2982. [CrossRef]
26. Venturelli, G.; Benini, E.; L, L.W. A Kriging-assisted multiobjective evolutionary algorithm. *Appl. Soft Comput.* **2017**, *58*, 155–175. [CrossRef]
27. Perrone, M.P.; Cooper, L.N. When networks disagree: Ensemble methods for hybrid neural networks. In *Artificial Neural Networks for Speech and Vision*; Mammone, R.J., Ed.; Chapman and Hall: London, UK, 1993; pp. 126–142.
28. Bishop, C.M. *Neural Networks for Pattern Recognition*; Oxford University Press: New York, NY, USA, 1995; pp. 364–371.
29. Zhou, Q.; Rong, Y.; Shao, X.; Jiang, P. Optimization of laser brazing onto galvanized steel based on ensemble of metamodels. *J. Intell. Manuf.* **2018**, *29*, 1417–1431. [CrossRef]
30. Zerpa, L.E.; Queipo, N.V.; Pintos, S.; Salager, J.L. An optimization methodology of alkaline-surfactant-polymer flooding processes using field scale numerical simulation and multiple surrogates. *J. Pet. Sci. Eng.* **2005**, *47*, 197–208. [CrossRef]
31. Sanchez, E.; Pintos, S.; Queipo, N.V. Toward an optimal ensemble of kernel-based approximations with engineering applications. *Struct. Multidiscip. Optim.* **2008**, *36*, 247–261. [CrossRef]
32. Acar, E. Various approaches for constructing an ensemble of metamodels using local measures. *Struct. Multidiscip. Optim.* **2010**, *42*, 879–896. [CrossRef]

33. Zhang, J.; Chowdhury, S.; Messac, A. An adaptive hybrid surrogate model. *Struct. Multidiscip. Optim.* **2012**, *46*, 223–238. [CrossRef]
34. Lee, Y.; Choi, D.H. Pointwise ensemble of meta-models using v nearest points cross-validation. *Struct. Multidiscip. Optim.* **2014**, *50*, 383–394. [CrossRef]
35. Goel, T.; Haftka, R.T.; Shyy, W.; Queipo, N.V. Ensemble of surrogates. *Struct. Multidiscip. Optim.* **2007**, *33*, 199–216. [CrossRef]
36. Acar, E.; Rais-Rohani, M. Ensemble of metamodels with optimized weight factors. *Struct. Multidiscip. Optim.* **2009**, *37*, 279–294. [CrossRef]
37. Viana, F.A.C.; Haftka, R.T.; Steffen, V. Multiple surrogates: How cross-validation errors can help us to obtain the best predictor. *Struct. Multidiscip. Optim.* **2009**, *39*, 439–457. [CrossRef]
38. Toal, D.J.; Keane, A.J. Performance of an ensemble of ordinary, universal, non-stationary and limit Kriging predictors. *Struct. Multidiscip. Optim.* **2013**, *47*, 893–903. [CrossRef]
39. Acar, E. Simultaneous optimization of shape parameters and weight factors in ensemble of radial basis functions. *Struct. Multidiscip. Optim.* **2014**, *49*, 969–978. [CrossRef]
40. Polynkin, A.; Toropov, V.V. Mid-range metamodel assembly building based on linear regression for large scale optimization problems. *Struct. Multidiscip. Optim.* **2012**, *45*, 515–527. [CrossRef]
41. Ferreira, W.G.; Serpa, A.L. Ensemble of metamodels: The augmented least squares approach. *Struct. Multidiscip. Optim.* **2016**, *53*, 1019–1046. [CrossRef]
42. Zhou, X.; Jiang, T. Metamodel selection based on stepwise regression. *Struct. Multidiscip. Optim.* **2016**. [CrossRef]
43. Fletcher, R. *Practical Methods of Optimization*; Wiley: New York, NY, USA, 2013.
44. Jin, R.; Chen, W.; Simpson, T.W. Comparative Studies Of Metamodeling Techniques Under Multiple Modeling Criteria. *Struct. Multidiscip. Optim.* **2001**, *23*, 1–13. [CrossRef]
45. Forrester, A.; Sobester, A.; Keane, A. *Engineering Design via Surrogate Modelling: A Practical Guide*; Wiley: New York, NY, USA, 2008. [CrossRef]
46. Chen, R.; Liang, C.Y.; Hong, W.C.; Gu, D.X. Forecasting holiday daily tourist flow based on seasonal support vector regression with adaptive genetic algorithm. *Appl. Soft Comput.* **2015**, *26*, 435–443. [CrossRef]
47. Yan, C.; Shen, X.; Guo, F. An improved support vector regression using least squares method. *Struct. Multidiscip. Optim.* **2017**, *57*, 2431–2445. [CrossRef]

© 2020 by the authors. Licensee MDPI, Basel, Switzerland. This article is an open access article distributed under the terms and conditions of the Creative Commons Attribution (CC BY) license (http://creativecommons.org/licenses/by/4.0/).

MDPI
St. Alban-Anlage 66
4052 Basel
Switzerland
Tel. +41 61 683 77 34
Fax +41 61 302 89 18
www.mdpi.com

Energies Editorial Office
E-mail: energies@mdpi.com
www.mdpi.com/journal/energies

www.ingramcontent.com/pod-product-compliance
Lightning Source LLC
LaVergne TN
LVHW071941080526
838202LV00064B/6648